Dedicated to all our Children
Past... Present... and Future

Elon Musk

The Unauthorized Autobiography

J.T. Owens

Copyright 2018 J.T. Owens

Chapters

1. The Early Years 9

2. The Meaning of Life 15

3. First Principles 17

4. Coming to Canada 23

5. Down in the Valley 29

6. The Internet 35

7. Zip2 38

8. PayPal 45

9. Mars Oasis 58

10. Why Space? 71

11. SpaceX 80

12. Climate Roulette 84

13. Tesla 98

14. The Plan 107

15. SolarCity 115

16. All Systems are Go! 122

17. Roadster 130

18. Hard Times 137

19. For Starters 149

20. NeXt 158

21. Electrifying 171

22. In the Loop 187

23. Getting Personal 202

24. Falcons and Dragons 218

25. Dawn of a New Era 232

26. Innovation 247

27. Summoning the Demon 258

28. SkyNet 280

29. Life on Mars 290

30. The Trip 307

31. Autopilot 326

32. Charged 344

33. Goin Giga 349

34. The Machine 359

35. Production 366

36. Synergy 378

37. Good Company 395

38. Government 406

39. The Market 420

40. Das Model 432

41. Civilization 442

42. Things to Come.. 448

1. The Early Years

Hi, I'm Elon Musk, I currently run Tesla, SpaceX, Neuralink, The Boring Company, and I'm co-chairman of OpenAI. I was trying to think what the most useful thing is that I can say to be useful to you in the future. I'm surprised by the whole thing honestly. I certainly didn't expect any of these things to happen, and I often find myself wondering, how did this happen? I guess I'll just tell you the story of how I came to be here, the various things that I did, and maybe why I did them. Maybe there are lessons there, and hopefully, that's a bit helpful.

I was born in '71, in Pretoria, South Africa, and lived in Johannesburg and Durban as well. My father was an engineer, an electromechanical engineer, so I grew up in sort of an engineering household. My mother is a model and nutritionist and was born in Canada.

I do have some American background, my grandfather was an American from Minnesota. A lot of people think my name must be from some exotic location, but I was named after my great grandfather John Elon Haldeman who was from Minneapolis, actually St. Paul I should say. He was like a school superintendent and a part-time sheriff in 1900. So I'm actually from Africa and named after my American ancestor.

My grandfather moved with all his kids and my mom and everyone to South Africa because he wanted to use it as a base of exploration. He was sort of an amateur archaeologist and he liked to explore things. He had this little plane that he liked to fly all over the place, and he flew it all through Africa and Asia. He was the first person to fly from South Africa to Australia. He did this in a plane with no electronic instruments, and in some places they had diesel and some places they had gasoline, so he had to rebuild the engine to whatever fuel they had. Luckily, he survived on that one.

I was able to travel to a few countries growing up, within Africa and around the world. On the first trip that I went out of South Africa, Paris, that was where I went when I was a little kid. My parents brought me there when I was like 6 years old, I've loved Paris ever since.

I was very driven as a kid and very willful. One of the things that I remember from my childhood, I was I think six, or something maybe around that age, so the memory is a little fuzzy at this point. I was just learning to read basically. As I recall I was grounded one afternoon for some reason, I don't know why and prevented from going to play with my cousins who lived on the other side of town. I felt it was unjust, and I really wanted to go to my cousin's party, who was five - so it was a kid's party. At first, I was going to take my bike, and I told my mum this, which was a mistake. She told me some story about how you needed a license for a bike, and the police would stop me. I wasn't 100% sure if that was true or not, but I thought I better walk, just in case. I escaped from my nanny and just started walking to my cousin's house. I didn't really know the way, I kind of knew the way, and I could barely read the roadsigns. It was 10 or 12 miles away clear across town, it's quite far. Further than I realized actually. I think it took me about four hours. I was getting to my cousin's house just as my mum was leaving that party with my brother and sister. She saw me walking along the sidewalk and she freaked out because she didn't know how I got there. I saw she saw me, so I then sprinted to my cousin's house and I was just about two blocks away and I climbed a tree and refused to come down until they promised that they wouldn't punish me, and I could play with my cousins. I didn't get punished actually, but they didn't let me play with my cousins either.

In retrospect it was obviously a very foolish thing to do because something terrible could've happened, I could've been kidnapped, or run over, or something like that, but I was so determined to go play with my cousins that I walked clear across the capital city.

I got bored easily unless I was doing something like reading or playing a video game or watching TV. We had like very lame TV. I mean South Africa had terrible TV, like really bad. I liked watching but there was just not so much of it. We literally in the early days had one channel and it was only on for half a day. Boredom led to a lot of reading.

I read all the comics I could buy or they let me read at the bookstore before chasing me away. I liked Batman, Superman, and stuff, Green Lantern, Iron Man. Better not say Iron Man first, because then people will think... but I did think that was a pretty cool one. Doctor Strange.. if there was a comic on the rack, I read it. I would read everything that I could get my hands on, from when I woke up to when I went to sleep.

I read the encyclopedia about age 9 or 10. Not that I wanted to read the encyclopedia, but I ran out of things to read so in desperation I read the encyclopedia. You can learn things very quickly by just reading books, the information is all there. If your data rate of reading books is much faster, you can read information much faster than you can hear it.

I would just be questioning things, maybe it's sort of built in to question things. When I was a little kid I was really scared of the dark, but then I sort of came to understand that dark means the absence of photons in the visible wavelength, 400 to 700 nanometer. Then I thought it's really silly to be afraid of a lack of photons. I wasn't afraid of the dark anymore after that. I would always think about something, and whether that thing was really true or not and could something else be true, or is there a better conclusion that one could draw that's more probable. I was doing that when I was in elementary school. It would infuriate my parents by the way, that I just wouldn't believe them when they said something, because I would ask them why then I would consider if that response makes sense given everything else I know.

I hated going to school when I was a kid, it was torture. I was actually for quite a while the youngest and smallest in the class, and my parents moved a lot so I went to six different schools. You'd make friends the one year then you'd be in the new school the next. I got beaten up a lot at school. Yeah, it sucked. For no good reason, I think. Mostly I ran, or hide in classrooms during recess. Run or hide, are the two options really, so I just read a lot of books and try to stay out of people's way during school. Part of it was probably because I was a bit of a smart ass sometimes. Up until tenth grade, I was pretty much the smallest kid in my class, and then I kind of grew after that. Being sort of little book wormy kid smart ass was a recipe for disaster.

The best teacher I ever had was my elementary school principal. Our math teacher quit for some reason, and so he decided to sub in himself for math and accelerate the syllabus by a year. We had to work like the house was on fire for the first half of the lesson and do extra homework, but then we got to hear stories of when he was a soldier in WWII. If you didn't do the work, you didn't get to hear the stories. Everybody did the work.

When I was young we did sort of a variety of things. We went selling chocolate door-to-door, we created a little business plan to create a video arcade. We had this brilliant idea to start a video arcade because we knew what games were popular. That got shut down by our parents. I think we would've made money by the way, because we really understood what games were good.

I loved playing video games. I had one of the first video game consoles, that didn't even have cartridges. You had like four games that you could play, and you had to pick one of the four, that was it. I went from there to the original Atari when I was maybe 6 or 7, and then Intellivision and other game consoles. My father brought me on a trip to the United States when I was about 10. I remember it was a really awesome experience because the hotels all had arcades. My number one thing when we went to a new hotel or motel or whatever it was, was going to the arcades.

I must've been like 9 or 10 or something when I walked into a computer store in South Africa and saw a Commodore VIC-20. That was super exciting, I thought it was the most awesome thing I had ever seen. An actual computer you could program and write your own video games with. I was like holy crow you can actually have a computer and make your own games. I just thought this was one of the most incredible things possible. I took all of my saved allowances and hounded my father until we got the Commodore VIC-20.

I think on Wikipedia it says that I was inspired by my father in terms of technology. This is not true and I think it needs to be corrected. He is somewhat of a Luddite actually in many respects, particularly computers. He didn't want to buy a computer and refused to use computers because he said they would never amount to anything. He did contribute after I saved up my allowance, but he initially refused to buy a computer for me. I was exposed to technical subjects when I was growing up, it was just that he wasn't much of a technologist.

But that was my first computer, that Commodore VIC-20. I think it had like 8k of memory. It came with this manual on how to program in BASIC. So I spent all night and a couple of days just sort of absorbing that. I kind of went OCD on the thing, maybe not technically OCD, but I certainly got obsessive, so certainly the O part.

I got some books on how to teach yourself programming and taught myself how to write software. I just started writing software, I really liked computers and programming was fun. I could make my own games, and I also wanted to see how the games worked. Like, how did you create a video game? It was kind of amazing that computers do all those things. You construct a little universe. When you first do it you go like wow this is incredible, you can actually make things happen. You can type these commands and something happens on the screen, that's pretty amazing.

I tried taking some computer classes but I was way ahead of the teacher, so it didn't help.

I read a lot of computer magazines, and there was a computer magazine that you could sell software to, and they would publish your software and then send you a check. I needed more money to buy a better computer and more video games, so I started programming a space game called 'Blastar' it was just a primitive sort of a space war game. I was maybe about 12 or so. I didn't think they would actually buy the software, but if you don't try then you have 0% chance. I just mailed it in and they bought it for several hundred dollars. Made a lot of money for a little kid. I don't think they knew I was 12 years old actually. That was cool because I thought, 'Wow, I got paid money to make a game, that's great.' I started programming games and then selling games to actually buy more games - a bit of a circular thing - more games and better computers and that kind of thing. I would spend money on better computers and Dungeons & Dragons modules and things like that. Nerdmaster 3000 basically.

2. The Meaning of Life

I wasn't that much of a loner, at least not willingly. I certainly was quite - I was very bookish, I was reading all the time. Generally, sort of the fantasy and sci-fi genre I found most interesting. I read thousands and thousands of books sort of like The Lord of the Rings and The Hobbit and that kind of thing. A lot of nonfiction as well, in fact, I remember when I was just in elementary school I was reading about ion engines and I thought they were super cool, and now we're launching satellites with ion engines.

I had sort of a dark childhood, it wasn't good. I always had sort of a slight existential crisis, trying to figure out 'what does it all mean?' like, what's the purpose of things?

I was reading various books, like most of the philosophers, and religious texts, and those kinds of things trying to figure like what's the meaning of life, cause it all seemed quite meaningless. I got quite sad about it when I was a teenager. Puberty I guess - 13 through 15, probably the most traumatic years. Probably partially brought on by reading some of the philosophers and some of the really boring, boring awful books if you ask me, like Dostoevsky ahh.. brutal. We also happened to have some books by Nietzsche and Schopenhauer, and that sort of thing in the house, which you should not read at age 14, it's bad, it's really negative. Most of the philosophers are awful.. - particularly the Germans. They're depressing, some of the things they say are good ideas but it's interspersed with so much rubbish.

Anyway, I was in my early teen years trying to figure out the meaning of the universe, and all that, and it was very difficult to come up with something that wasn't some piece of arbitrary claptrap. I eventually came to the conclusion that nobody has any idea what the meaning of the universe is. Then I read Douglas Adams 'The Hitchhikers Guide to the Galaxy' Douglas Adams is awesome, one of the greatest philosophers of all time, not recognized as such, but he is. I think the most interesting thing he said was: "The question is harder than the answer." In 'The Hitchhikers Guide to the Galaxy' the Earth turns out to be a giant computer used to answer the question "What is the meaning of life?" and he comes up with the answer I think '42' then it's like "What the hell is 42?" It turns out that it's the question that's the hard part, and it takes a bigger computer than Earth to figure it out. It sort of highlighted the point that often the issue is understanding what questions to ask. If you properly frame the question, the answer is the easy part. I think there's some truth to that, when we ask questions they come along with all of our biases, there are so many things implied in the question that you should ask "Is that the right question?"

I thought things that expand the scope and scale of consciousness, and human knowledge, and allows us to achieve greater enlightenment those are good things. What can we do that's going to most likely lead to that outcome?

I didn't expect to be involved in creating companies when I was in Pretoria Boys' High School or middle school. I was going to pursue sort of physics, and a career in physics and science in general, from the standpoint of trying to understand the nature of reality. What is it all about? That was my main motivation. Sort of gain greater enlightenment over time that seemed like a good goal. If we can improve our understanding of the universe then eventually we can figure out what right questions to ask.

That's not the meaning of life, but it's something.

3. First Principles

It's kind of funny if you think "what is education?" You're basically downloading data and algorithms into your brain, and it's amazingly bad in conventional education. I think just in general conventional education should be massively overhauled because it shouldn't be like this huge chore. Everyone normally goes through English, math, science, and so forth from fifth grade, the sixth grade, seventh grade, and on like it's an assembly line. It shouldn't be that you got like these grades where we have people walking in lockstep. People are not objects on an assembly line, that's a ridiculous notion. People learn and are interested in different things at different paces. You want to disconnect the whole grade level from the subjects, and allow people to progress at the fastest pace they can or are interested in, in each subject. It seems like a really obvious thing.

A lot of kids are probably just in school puzzled as to why they're there. They don't know why they're there, like why are we learning this stuff? We don't even know why. You're asked to memorize formulas, but you don't know why this is the case. You have this cognitive dissonance of it seems irrelevant, but I've been told to remember it, I'll be punished if I don't remember it.

I think a lot of the things that people learn, probably there's no point in learning them because they never use them in the future. People, I think don't stand back and say, well, why are we teaching people these things? and we should tell them, probably why we're teaching these things. I think if you can explain the why of things, then that makes a huge difference to people's motivation. Then they understand the purpose. I think that's pretty important.

The more you can game-ify the process of learning, the better. Generally, you want your education to be as close to a video game as possible, like a good video game. Just make it entertaining. You don't need to tell your kid to play video games. For my kids, I do not have to encourage them to play video games. I have to like pry them from their hands like crack, it's like "drop that crack needle!" they will play video games on autopilot all day. To the degree that you can make somehow learning like a game, make it interactive and engaging, then you can make education far more compelling and far easier to do. I think that's how it should be.

It's also very important to teach to the problems and not to the tools. You can imagine like if you say, we want to understand how an internal combustion engine works. The best way to do that is to say let's take apart the engine and put it back together again. Now, what tools do we need for this? We need a screwdriver, we need a wrench, maybe a winch, and as you take the engine apart you understand the reason for these tools. If on the other hand, you have a course on screwdrivers and a course on wrenches, that would be a terrible way to do it, it's difficult to remember. The way that our mind has evolved is to remember things that are relevant, and to discard information that it thinks has irrelevance, so we must establish relevancy. Tying it to a problem is very powerful for establishing relevance, and getting kids excited about what they're working on, and having the knowledge stick. In the course of solving a problem, taking the engine apart, and putting it back together, you learn about the relevance. It's very painful and difficult to remember things if they seem abstract and unimportant. You have to establish the relevancy and importance and establish the why of things in order for the knowledge to naturally stay in your brain.

It is important to view knowledge as sort of a semantic tree -- make sure you understand the fundamental principles, i.e. the trunk and big branches, before you get into the leaves and details, or there is nothing for them to hang on to.

Frankly, I think most people can learn a lot more than they think they can. They sell themselves short without trying. I think generally people's thinking processes are too bound by convention or analogy to prior experiences. They'll say we will do that because it was always done that way, or they will not do it because nobody has ever done that before, so it must not be good. That is just a ridiculous way to think. Analogies are very seductive they can sound very compelling, but analogy is just a story. The way we get through daily life is mostly by analogy or sort of copying things with minor variations. The amount of thinking you need for it is not much because it is a computational shortcut, which is fine for everyday life.

If you want to do something that is fundamentally new or is particularly counterintuitive, then analogies don't work very well. You won't know what's true, or what's really possible if you reason by analogy. You have to do a first-principles analysis, rather than reasoning by analogy, you boil things down to the most fundamental truths you can imagine, and then you reason up from there. You have to build up the reasoning from the ground up. This is a good way to figure out if something really makes sense, or if it's just what everybody else is doing. It's hard to think that way, you can't think that way about everything. It takes a lot of effort, it requires a lot of thinking. It's rare that people try to think of something on a first-principles basis.

First-principles is a phrase that is used in physics. Physics has this problem where they are trying to figure out things that are counterintuitive, like quantum mechanics. They had to get a framework for getting there. My main training and mindset are that of a physicist, so I tend to think in a very sort of physics brainwork. I think it is the best brain work for thinking, and for evaluating technologies at a fundamental level. You look at the fundamentals and construct your reasoning from that, and then see if you have a conclusion that works or doesn't work. It means that you go to the very basic laws of physics, the things which we believe to be extremely well demonstrated. In other words, the reason they call it a law is that no one has demonstrated an exception to that ever. That's how it qualifies as being a law, but even then laws can be broken, where you find that one case in the very unusual circumstance that will break it. That is the transition from Newtonian to Einsteinian mechanics. Newtonian mechanics are extremely predictive of reality, except when you approach the speed of light. Since back in the day, with their primitive instruments, they couldn't detect these tiny little differences, Newtonian mechanics seemed to predict everything perfectly. You take these very fundamental laws and say now let's use those as the ingredients from which we will construct a theory, a conclusion because we know that base is sound. If we, therefore, are able to combine those elements in a way that's cogent, that conclusion will be sound, and it may or may not be different from what people have done in the past. That's what I mean with reasoning from first principles, and I think that general approach can be taken in many fields.

I think that physics is usually not taught the right way. The way physics is usually taught is with a series of raw formulas. The wonder and awe of physics are not conveyed in classrooms, the fundamental meaning is not conveyed. Like what do these formulas represent in reality? It's incredible that a formula can actually describe reality, that's amazing.

The very framework of how to think about physics is by far the most helpful. To sort of understand how the first scientists learned anything, how they changed the way they learned things. How they build the framework of analysis over time, as they learned that one mode was better than another. This is extremely helpful to learn. If people really pay attention to physics 101 that is the most valuable. Physics is true everything else is debatable, and even physics is questionable. Quantum mechanics is really interesting too. It's amazing that quantum mechanics is true, it's still hard to believe.

I do think more people should study engineering and science. Software engineering is probably the single biggest area that people should learn, and I'm always sort of a fan of general economics and critical thinking. We should teach critical thinking a lot more. That may seem like a simple thing. You just need to tell people this is how you know whether you should believe something or not. Just teaching people these are general types of fallacies, and this is how people generally trick you, and how to avoid being tricked, that would be really great.

A University education is often unnecessary, That's not to say that it is unnecessary for all people. It depends on what somebody's goal is. I think you learn the vast majority in the first two years, and most of it is from your classmates. You can always buy the textbooks and read them.

Unfortunately, I think a lot of teaching today is a lot like vaudeville, and as a result of that not that compelling. You've got someone standing up there kind of lecturing at people. They've done the same lecture 20 years in a row, so they're not necessarily all that engaged doing it, and they're not very excited about it. That lack of enthusiasm is conveyed to the students, so they're not very excited about it. Compare that to let's say "Batman: The Dark Knight" the Chris Nolan movie, it's pretty freaking awesome. You got incredible special effects, amazing actors, great script, multiple cuts, and great sound. That's amazing, and it's very engaging. Now, imagine if instead, you had the same script, so at least it's the same script, and you said instead of having movies, we're going to have that script performed by the local town troupe. In every small town in America, if movies didn't exist, they'd have to recreate "The Dark Knight" with like home-sewn costumes, and like jumping across the stage, and not really getting their lines quite right, and not looking like the people in the movie, and no special effects. That would not be compelling, I mean that would suck, it would be terrible. That's education.

4. Coming to Canada

Growing up I was very technology-oriented, but I didn't really know what I was going to do when I got older. People kept asking me, so eventually, I thought the idea of inventing stuff or creating things would be a cool thing to do. The reason I thought that was because I read a quote from Arthur C. Clark which said: "A sufficiently advanced technology is indistinguishable from magic" and that's really true. I'd say particularly engineering is the closest thing to magic that exists in the real world. Engineering is creating some new device that never existed before, that can do things today that would be considered magic hundreds of years ago. I think it actually goes beyond that, there are many things we take for granted today that weren't even imagined in times past, they weren't even in the realm of magic, so it goes beyond that. If you go back say 300 years, the things that we take for granted today, you'd be burned at the stake for. Being able to fly that's crazy, being able to see over long distances, being able to communicate, having effectively with the internet a group mind of sorts, having access to all the world's information instantly from almost anywhere on Earth. It's pretty amazing what we can do, we can create images, we can do holograms and things like that. This is the stuff that really would be considered magic in times past, and all of these things would've gotten you burned at the stake 300 years ago.

I thought, If I can do some of those things -- if I can advance technology that is like magic, that would be really cool. I wasn't sure if that meant starting a company, or whether that meant working for a company that made cool stuff.

Whenever I would read about cool technology and great innovation it just seemed like interesting things happened in America almost all the time. Of course within the United States, Silicon Valley is where the heart of things is, although, at the time, I didn't know where Silicon Valley was. When I was growing up, Silicon Valley seemed like some mythical place, like Mount Olympus or something. That's where I wanted to be, I just wanted to be where technology was being created. I just wanted to be involved with things that were on the cutting edge. That's what got me excited and I knew I wanted to come to America. I remember thinking and saying that America is where great things are possible, more than any other country in the world. It is true, America is the land of opportunity.

I was trying to figure out how to get to the US, and I tried to convince my parents to move there. My parents were divorced, so if at least one of them could move there I could move there with them, but I wasn't successful in convincing them. At one point I convinced my father but then he reneged, unfortunately. He did say yes, and then he changed his mind. I guess he was fairly established, he was an engineer established in South Africa and didn't want to have to go through that again in another country.

Then I found out my mother was born in Canada. Her father was American, but my mother hadn't gotten her US citizenship before he died, and before certain age restrictions, so that broke the link and I couldn't get my American citizenship unfortunately directly. I walked her through the process of getting her Canadian citizenship which allowed me to get my Canadian citizenship. I applied for her Canadian passport and mine at the same time. I actually filled out the forms for her and got her Canadian passport and me too, and within three weeks of getting my Canadian passport, I was in Canada. I couldn't convince my parents to move, so I had to move myself. They tried to convince me not to leave, but being conscripted in the South African army didn't seem like a great way to spend time. So I left by myself against my parents' wishes, with almost no financial support. I wouldn't say they were unsupportive, but I can't say they were particularly supportive.

I arrived in North America when I was about 17. I had a relative in Canada and I send letters that I was coming. I didn't get any letter back, but I went anyway. I had a great uncle in Montreal, and when I got to Montreal my mom finally got a letter back that he was in Minnesota for the summer. I just stayed at a student hospital and bought a bus ticket across Canada. I bought a bus ticket from Montreal to Vancouver, and that allowed me to see Canada at least from the highway. Canada is a great country.

I wasn't quite sure how easy it would be to get a job or anything like that. I didn't have a real job as I was only 17 and only did paper routes and stuff like that. I thought well just in case it takes me a long time to get a job I better make sure that tiny stash of money lasts a long time. I only had a few thousand dollars, so I thought let me see what it takes to live. See if I can live for under a dollar a day, which I was able to do. You can do it, just sort of buy food in bulk at the supermarket. You just buy hotdogs in bulk and oranges in bulk. Scurvy is bad so you got to have an orange in there, an orange every couple of days will keep scurvy away. You get really tired of hotdogs and oranges after a while. Of course stuff like pasta and green pepper and a big thing of pasta sauce, that can go pretty far too. Just buy stuff in bulk and most of the time you can get under a buck a day. It does get a little monotonous after a while. I was like you know I can live for a dollar a day, at least from a food cost standpoint it's pretty easy to earn like $30 a month, so I'll probably be OK. I supported myself through various odd jobs for several months in various computer-related roles, mostly in Toronto.

I wasn't sure if I wanted to go to college before I came. My college education wasn't super well planned out. I wasn't sure whether I should go or not. Then I decided that I wanted to go to college because otherwise it was a hard time getting girls because everybody was much older than I was at the companies that I was working at. It seemed like that I would be missing out on an important social experience, so that was really the deciding factor. I managed to get a student loan and go to college. In Canada colleges are less expensive, it's kind of like maybe a state school or kind of like the University of California or CalState. The tuition is much less than it is in other places.

I was considering two possibilities, one was to study computer engineering at the University of Waterloo, and the other one was to go to Queen's University. I went to Waterloo and I saw there were not many girls there, so I thought like OK that doesn't seem so much fun, so then I went to Queen's. The big thrill of the university was to date girls of my own age. I actually met my first wife there so that worked out.

I had kind of a broad range of subjects in commerce, engineering, and math. I rarely went to class, I just read the textbook and show up for the exams.

The first really important person I met was this guy by the name of Peter Nicholson when I had a summer job. I read this article in the newspaper about this guy and he seemed really smart. I couldn't get to him directly, but then I called the newspaper to talk to the writer, and then the writer connected me with Peter Nicholson. He was the head of strategy for the

Bank of Scotia, which is the largest bank in Canada. He later became the chief economic adviser to the prime minister, so he was a really smart guy. I talked to him and I said: if there's any chance of a summer internship that would be great, and he ended up giving me a job that summer.

Some students I met at Queen's got transferred to Wharton at the University of Pennsylvania, and they gave a very good report. I thought well I'll try to go there. I didn't have any money so in order to go there, I needed a scholarship. One of the downsides of coming to a university in North America was that my parents said they would not pay for college - or, my father said he would not pay for college unless it was in South Africa. I could have free college in South Africa or find some way to pay it here. After my second year at Queen's, I applied to UPenn, and fortunately, I got a scholarship.

I came down to the US to go to college at the University of Pennsylvania and did a dual undergraduate in business and physics there in the third year.

Actually, the only reason I studied business at all was if I graduated, and I have to work for someone who has a business degree, if they knew special things that I didn't know then I would have a disadvantage. I was mostly afraid of having a boss that I didn't like. I figured if I don't learn the business stuff then somebody else is going to make me do things that I don't want to do, so I better learn the secrets of business.

I finished my business courses in a year. Then I said well I like physics, I'll study physics for the second year. Then I went into science and engineering. I'm more an engineer than anything else. Engineering and design is my interest, but you also need to be able to bring a lot of people together to create something. It's very difficult to create something as an individual if it's a significant technology. I figured in order to do a lot of these things you need to know how the universe works, and you need to know how the economy works, that's why I did the physics degree as well as the Wharton finance degree. The finance that was easy by the way. All my business courses in the final year were not as hard as quantum mechanics.

Graduating from undergrad I had to make a decision. One path would have sort of led to Wall Street and I guess quite a big salary, and the other was to do grad studies and try to figure out a technical problem and I didn't much like the first one.

5. Down in the Valley

When you're starting out in college, during sort of freshman and sophomore year, you have these sort of philosophical wonderings. At Queens and then also at UPenn, I was trying to think of what were the most important areas that could have a significant positive effect on the future of humanity. What are the problems we have to solve? You have these philosophical discussions on a sophomoric level I suppose. I talked a lot to friends and my housemates, and dates - which was probably not the best thing. The three areas that I came up with were, the Internet, sustainable energy, both in production and consumption and space exploration, particularly if humanity becomes a multi-planet species. I thought about these things kind of in the abstract, not from the expectation that I would actually have careers in those arenas. Those were just the areas that I thought would most affect the future, and as it turned out I was fortunate enough to be involved in those areas. That's the thread that connects them - it's kinda my best guess at what would most likely affect the future in the biggest way, and I wanted to be involved in at least one of them.

At first, I thought the best bet was going to be helping with the electrification of cars, that's how I would start out. Purely from the standpoint of us eventually running out of hydrocarbons to mine and burn. There is obviously a limited supply of oil in the ground, so eventually, we would have to transition to something sustainable. When we are drawing oil from the ground, we are essentially taking the accumulated solar energy that was bound up in plants and animals that over hundreds of millions of years was turned into oil. That is obviously finite, and if we run out of that and we don't have a good solution then there would be economic collapse, independent of any environmental concern. That's actually what initiated my interest in electric vehicles before global warming became an issue.

At Penn, there was a professor who was chairman of a company in Silicon Valley that was working on advanced capacitors, potentially for use in electric cars. I asked if I could get a summer job because it was in Silicon Valley and working on technology for electric cars. I thought this is really awesome, I'll come out to California to do energy physics at Stanford, that's pretty much as good as it gets. I just want to go to where the exciting breakthroughs were occurring. Stanford is in Silicon Valley, it's sort of the epicenter, so that's where I wanted to come, near Stanford or Berkeley and Stanford is sort of sunnier, so I liked it.

I got a summer job in Los Gatos actually, doing electrolytic ultra-capacitors. Capacitors are a very common component in circuit boards and are occasionally used to store limited amounts of energy. The problem is that their energy density does not compare to that of the battery. They have a very high power density, but a low energy density, and there's the potential to do some very interesting things if you can drive the energy density of a capacitor up high enough. If you could make a capacitor that had anywhere near the energy density of a battery with this incredibly high power density and this quasi-infinite cycle and calendar life, and extremely high charge/discharge rate, really you'd be able to charge your car faster than you can fill it with gasoline. Charging could be done in minutes or seconds technically. You'd have an awesome solution for energy storage in mobile applications. It's the ideal solution for electric vehicles.

I met a woman I dated briefly in college, who works at Scientific American as a writer, and she related the anecdote that when we went on a date, all I was talking about was electric cars. That was not a winning conversation, she said the first question I asked her was: "do you ever think about electric cars?" she said no, she never did. That wasn't great, but recently it's been more effective.

I was working I think two jobs, one was a video company that was ironically called rocket science and then working on electrolytic ultracapacitors during the day as an intern at a company called Pinnacle Research. They were pretty good, they had a pretty high energy density, roughly equivalent to a lead-acid battery, which for a capacitor is huge. As it turns out they're way too expensive. The problem was that they used ruthenium tantalum oxide. There was I think at the time maybe like one or two tons of ruthenium mined per year in the world, so not a very scalable solution, you know, they'd sell it to you by the sort of milligram, that's a problem.

I thought there could be some solid-state solution, like just using chip-making equipment. That was going to be the basic idea when I came out to get a Ph.D. at Stanford. The area I was going to be researching and was going to be doing my grad studies on was the material science and physics of high energy density capacitors. Very applied, almost really engineering, sort of the intersection between applied physics and material science. I was going to try to work on that and try to leverage the equipment that was developed for advanced chip-making and photonics to create ultra-precise capacitors at sort of the molecular level. I think there's potential for a significant breakthrough in that area and to have an energy storage mechanism that's better than batteries.

I didn't care about the degree actually. I just really needed their labs. I knew I could get sort of free labs if I was a student, so that was why I did the grad program.

Just towards the end of my undergrad, I was thinking that the Internet would be a pretty huge thing. Once it became clear that the Internet was going to become widespread, that everyone would have access to it, that's when it occurred to me that this was going to fundamentally change the nature of humanity, which became clear around the "94 timeframe. I had been on the Internet a few years before that since I had been in the physics arena. In the sciences, people were using the Internet as early as the 70s. It was difficult to use, it was text-based, and it was very difficult to get access to it. You had to be either in the government or in some academic institution.

I just couldn't figure out how to make enough money to feed myself. If I couldn't make money then I'd run out of food and die. That was not good. If I was a student, then I could be a teaching assistant and do various things and do research on electric vehicle technologies - that was my default plan.

I wasn't entirely certain that the technology I'd be working on would succeed. And generally, if you want to embark on something-- it's desirable to figure out if success is at least one of the possibilities. For sure failure is one of the possibilities, but, ideally, you want to try to bracket it and say success is in the envelope of outcomes. I wasn't sure what I was working on would be useful. I mean it could be academically useful but not practically useful. Like it could result in a Ph.D., and adding some leaf to the tree of knowledge, but then discovering that it's not gonna matter. Is it going to be a good enough thing that is actually going to be used in an electric vehicle? you can get a doctorate on many things that ultimately do not have a practical bearing on the world. I think success on an academic level would have been quite likely because you can publish some useless paper-- and most papers are pretty useless-- I mean, how many Ph.D. papers are used by someone ever? percentage-wise it's not good, and so it could have been one of those outcomes where you add some leaves to the tree of knowledge, and that leaf is, nope, it's not possible.

That was one path, and I was prepared to do that, but then things like the superconducting supercollider got canceled. I thought well what if I am stuck in some situation like that, and then some act of government basically stops things, then all of it would be a waste. I could not bracket the uncertainty on that.

I also thought that if I did a Ph.D. then I would spend several years watching the Internet go through this incredibly rapid growth phase, and that would be really difficult to handle because there does seem to be a time for particular technologies when they're at a steep point in the inflection curve.

It was a tough decision actually, this was before Netscape even went public. I was like, OK, the Internet, I'm pretty sure success is one of the outcomes, and it seemed like I could either spend five years in a graduate program and discover that the answer is that there is no way to make a capacitor work and watch the Internet happen, or I can work on building elements of the Internet, participate and help build it in some fashion. This was in 1995, so nobody had actually made any money on the Internet.

It got to the start of the quarter for Stanford and I had to make a decision. I was just working on some Internet software that summer. In that summer it became clear that the Internet was going to become something very significant. It was one of those things that came along once in a very long while, and I wanted to be a part of it. I just couldn't stand the idea of watching it happen, so I decided to drop out.

I thought I'm going to be involved in the internet, I can help build a few things there and than get back to electric cars later' which is what happened. I decided to go on deferment. I figured if it doesn't work then I can always go back to grad school. Since I already had my undergraduate I could then get the H1B visa, the H1B visa requires a degree. If your goal is to start a company there's no point in finishing college. In my case, I had to otherwise I would get kicked out of the country.

I didn't even go to class I called the chairman of the department and said: "I would like to start this Internet company, it probably won't succeed and so when it fails I want to make sure I still can come back." He let me go on deferment and I said I'd probably be back in 6 months, I thought I'd give it a couple of quarters. If it didn't work out, which I thought it probably wouldn't, then I'd come back to this school. I talked to my professor and I told him this and he said, well, I don't think you'll be coming back, and that was the last conversation I had with him.

6. The Internet

The Internet is like the world acquiring a nervous system. Before the Internet, and particularly before the telegraph, telephone, and advanced telecommunications, communication was incredibly slow. It would have to go from one person literally to another. Maybe at best that person could carry a note from another person, but it's still literally person to person. Unless one person bumps into another person they are pretty much not going to communicate. You had to basically physically connect with somebody to communicate, like a letter, like you would send letters... on paper.

People were sort of like isolated cells if you will, they would communicate information almost by osmosis relative to how the Internet works. With the Internet suddenly all the world's information, all of humanity's knowledge is instantly available to any person. That is just like one cell in your body having access to all the information about the rest of your body. In the same way that when we just had multicellular creatures without nervous systems, they would just communicate via osmosis. Imagine a simple multi-cellular creature that would communicate via quite slow chemical signals, there was no way that one cell had access to the collective consciousness. Now if you have a nervous system any part of the human collective can know about any other part instantly. I think it has literally gone from a situation where people would communicate almost like via osmosis, to any part of humanity knows what every other part of humanity is immediately, it's pretty incredible.

Humanity is effectively becoming a superorganism and qualitatively different than what it had been before. I think we have effectively created a kind of superorganism. It is evolution on a new plane. It's really quite a remarkable transformation. In the past, if you wanted access to a lot of information you had to go to libraries here and there, and you would have to talk to people, you had to be near to a big library or something - like the great Bodleian library - but that would be the only way to gain access to information. Unless you were physically where the books were, you didn't have access to the information. Now with the Internet, with everything online, you can be somewhere in the jungles of South America and if you've got access to an Internet connection, you've got access to essentially all the world's information, with a tremendous amount of analytical power behind that. It's some sort of 'human-machine collective intelligence.' With everything digitized you can be anywhere with an Internet connection and have access to the accumulative knowledge of humanity. You have access to more information than the Library of Congress through your iPhone.

Having a supercomputer in your pocket is something that people would not have predicted. You have basically superpowers with your computer, and your phone, and the applications that are there. You have more power than the President of the United States had 20 years ago. You can answer any question, you can video conference anywhere with anyone, you can send a message to millions of people instantly.

I do think that the Internet is a great equalizer of access to information. Access to information is incredible, anyone with a $100 device has access to all the world's information. Which is an incredible thing. This is maybe not talked about as much as it should be but you can learn anything if you have a $100 Internet device. You can just learn anything. Which is amazing compared to the past. You don't need to have access to a library. In principle, you can just learn everything you want for free really. I think that is a pretty great part of the future we are in right now.

7. Zip2

The only way to get involved in the internet in '95, that I could think of, was to start a company. There weren't a lot of companies to go and work for, apart from Netscape maybe one or two others, and I couldn't get a job at any of them.

What I first started to do was I tried to get a job at Netscape at the time, but they didn't respond to me, I didn't get any reply. I guess because I didn't have a computer science degree or several years working at a software company. I mean I had a physics and economics degree, or physics and a business degree from Wharton, and I was doing grad studies applied physics and materials science. For whatever reason, I didn't get a reply from Netscape. I tried hanging out in the lobby, but I was too shy to talk to anyone, so I'm just like standing in the lobby, it was pretty embarrassing. I was just sort of standing there trying to see if there was someone I can talk to but I just couldn't, I was too scared to talk to anyone, so then I left.

I was writing software during that summer and trying to make useful things happen on the internet. I wanted to be part of putting a small brick in the construction of that edifice. It wasn't really with the thought of being wealthy. I got nothing against being wealthy, but it was from a standpoint of wanting to be a part of the Internet.

It seemed like things were going to take off, although nobody had made any money on the Internet at the time. Really no-one was making any money on the Internet. It wasn't at all clear that the Internet was going to be a big commercial thing.

I thought I guess I'm going to start a company because I can't get a job anywhere.

I figured if we could make enough money to just get by that would be OK. Initially, it was just about making money to pay the rent. My perspective was hopefully I can make enough money to pay the rent and buy food otherwise I would have to do my graduate program at Stanford. In America, it is pretty easy to keep yourself alive, and my threshold for existing is pretty low, I figured I could be in some dingy apartment with my computer and be OK and not starve.

My brother was in Canada at the time and I said: "look I think we should try to create an Internet company" I always wanted to do something with my brother, and he always wanted to do something with me. I think Kimball is one of the nicest people I know in the world I've never in all my life see Kimball intentionally do a mean thing, so I admire him a great deal. I convinced my brother to come down from Canada, so he came down and joined me.

The Internet was also helpful because anything that has to do with software is a low-capital endeavor. Software you can just write yourself. You don't need a lot of tools and equipment, so it's not capital intensive. The ability to build a company that's software-related it's much much easier. I didn't have any money. I just had a bunch of student debt. I had about $3000 and a computer, and then my brother came and joined and he had about I think $5000, and then Greg Kouri, a friend of my Mom's, came and he had $6000.

The three of us created Zip2 in the summer of 95 before Netscape had gone public.

Funny name, we thought, we don't know anything about names, so we'll get some ad agencies to suggest a bunch of options, and then Zip2 seemed kind of speedy. I don't know why the hell we chose that stupid name, and it has a digit in it. Why would you chose - it could be ZipTo, it could be ZipTwo, it could be ZipToo, so people literally spelled the name every variation - which is bad if you've got a URL and you don't have the other ones. We were just incredibly stupid at the time, I think. That's the main reason for that name.

Things were pretty tough in the early going. I didn't have any money in fact, I had negative money. I had huge student debts. I thought we got to make something that's going to return money very, very quickly. There was no advertising revenue on the Internet at the time. The initial idea was to create software that could help bring the media companies online, we thought that the media industry would need help converting its content from print media to electronic. They clearly have money, so if we could find a way to help them move their media to the internet that would be an obvious way of generating revenue. That was the basis of Zip2.

I still had my core programming skills, so I was able to write the software needed.

In the beginning, we didn't have enough money to rent an apartment and an office. The office was cheaper, and we thought it was probably more impressive to have an office instead of letting people come to an apartment. We just got a small office in Palo Alto back when rent was not insane, it cost us like $450 a month. We slept in the office, my brother and I just got 2 futons that turned into couches during the day, with a little table, and we would have our meetings there. It would be unbeknown to the people that we slept on those. I sort of briefly had a girlfriend in that period and in order to be with me, she had to also sleep in the office. At night we would just sleep on the futon in the office and then we would walk over to the YMCA on Page Mill and El Camino to shower. You could work out as well, so I was in the best shape I've ever been. Just shower and work out and you're good to go. It's really difficult to get food in Palo Alto after 10 p.m. There was Jack in the

Box and a few other options so we rotated through the Jack in the Box menu.

At the very beginning, we were so hard up that we had just one computer. It would be our Web server during the day, and I would code at night. The website only worked during the day, because at night I was programming software. Seven days a week, all the time. There was an ISP on the floor below us, just like a little tiny ISP, and we drilled a hole through the floor and connected to the main cable. That gave us our internet connectivity for like a hundred bucks a month.

There were, basically, only six of us. There were me, my brother, and Greg, and then three salespeople we hired on contingency by putting an ad in a newspaper. Zip2 started as, basically, like I said, trying to figure out how to make enough money to exist as a company since there wasn't any advertising money being made. In fact, the idea of advertising on the internet seemed like a ridiculous idea to people. Obviously, not so ridiculous anymore, but, at the time, it seemed like a very unlikely proposition.

We thought we could help existing companies bring their stuff online. I wrote something that allowed you to keep maps and directions on the Internet and something that allowed you to do online manipulation of content; kind of a really advanced blogging system. We started talking to small newspapers and media companies and so forth, and we started getting some interest. I mean, half of the time it'd be like: "What's the internet?" even in Silicon Valley. In fact, most of the venture capitalists that I talked to hadn't even heard of the internet, which sounds bizarre, on Sand Hill Road. Amazingly, when we tried to get funding for a company in, I think it was, October/November of '95, more than half of the venture capitalists did not know what the Internet was and had not used it. Yeah, they'd literally ask, isn't that something that the government and universities use? and I'd be like, uhh, for now. Most people thought that the Internet was going to be a fad. Since there weren't that many people on the Internet it wasn't very clear that there was a business, and even if the Internet became widespread nobody could make any money on it.

Occasionally, somebody would buy it and we would get a little bit of money from them. A lot of the media companies weren't even sure that they should be online, like, what's the point of that? a lot of them just didn't know what the Internet was, and even the ones that were aware of the Internet didn't have a software team, so they weren't very good at developing functionality.

Then Netscape went public in late 1995, I think it was, that changed people's mindset a little bit. After that, even a lot of venture capitalists still didn't understand it, and still hadn't used it, but somebody had made money on it, so the second time we went to get funding, everyone was interested. Even if just from the standpoint of the greater fools theory, even if those Internet companies can't make any money at least some fool is willing to pay a lot if they go public, so that got things more interested. Whether or not they knew what the Internet was they knew you could make money on the Internet somehow. When we went and talked to venture capitalists in early '96 there was a much greater interest in what we were doing. In fact the round closed in maybe about a week or so. We had just an absurdly tiny burn rate, and we also had a tiny revenue stream, but we had more revenue than we had expenses. When we went and talked to VC's we could actually say we had positive cash flow. That helps, I think.

I reluctantly started off being the CEO, not my preference actually. I think of myself more like an engineer who in order to invent the things that I want to invent and create I have to do the company as well. I was CEO for probably the first year and then after we got VC funding, the venture capitalists wanted to hire a professional CEO. At the time I thought it was a good idea because I didn't know what I was doing, and I figured they would hire someone who is really good and that person would increase the chances of the success of the company. That seemed like a good thing and then I could work on software and kinda product direction and that's what I like doing, so that seemed like a great thing. In retrospect, I think that wasn't the best thing. The person that was hired, in my opinion, was not that great. I think, quite frankly, the company succeeded in spite of that person, not because of him.

Essentially Zip2 helped bring the media companies online in the early days.

We had as investors and customers: The New York Times Company, Knight Ridder, Hearst Corporation, and most of the major US print publishers. We helped, in a small way to bring those companies online. They weren't always online, people don't realize that. We ended up building quite a bit of software for the media industry; primarily, the print media industry. We were able to get them to pay us to develop software for them to bring them online, publishing stuff. It did a bunch of things it was Internet publishing, mapping, Yellow Pages, White Pages, calendar, and various other things. We developed quite sophisticated technology actually, but it wasn't being employed super well by the media companies. We would suggest ways to use it and then it would not be used as effectively as it could be. It was very frustrating.

We build that up and then we had the opportunity to sell to Compaq in early '99. The deal was struck sort of late '98 and concluded it early '99.

Compaq had Altavista, so their thought was to combine Altavista and a bunch of other technology companies and see if that would work, which it did not. Nonetheless, they were pretty nice guys and bought the company.

Zip2 was acquired by Compaq for a little over 300 million dollars in cash. That's the currency I highly recommend. I thought that was crazy why would somebody pay such a huge amount of money for this little company that we have. It turned out really well for them so they knew a lot more about it than I did. I made about $20-$22 million as a result of that, which was a phenomenal amount of money for me.

In fact, they mailed the check, they send a check in the mail, that was kind of crazy.

8. PayPal

I certainly had a choice at that point of retiring and go buy one of the islands in the Bahamas somewhere, sipping mai-tais, and turn it into my personal fiefdom, but that was not of interest to me at all. I mean, I like going to the beach for a short period of time, but not much longer than a few days or something like that. The idea of lying on a beach as my main thing just sounds like the worst - it sounds horrible to me. I would go bonkers. I would have to be on serious drugs, I'd be super-duper bored. I like high intensity.

When I was in college I was reading about the fastest car in the world, the McLaren F1. It's an interesting work of art, it's really done right. I thought if I ever made enough money, I would buy the McLaren. I was living in an apartment in Palo Alto that cost significantly less than the $1 million car. It was either upgrade to a house or buy the car, and I bought the car. I was pretty excited about getting it. There were 62 McLaren F1s in the world, and I owned one of them. It probably wasn't the best idea.

I had it for several years and I put 11.000 miles on it, and I drove it from LA to San Francisco. I had it as my daily driver, which is a crazy car to have as a daily driver, particularly on the 405. In fact, it was kind of funny there was this show, if there ever was a show on hubris it would probably be it, called 'Silicon Valley Gold Rush' and it was filmed in 1999. They filmed me getting the McLaren and a number of other people as well. Just four years earlier showering at the Y and sleeping on the office floor to quite a few creature comforts. Fortunately,

PayPal worked out otherwise it would've been extremely embarrassing.

The PayPal story is quite complicated, even though it took place in a relatively short time, about roughly three and half years from the creation of the company and it being sold to eBay mid 2002. PayPal was created from the merger of two companies X.com which I founded, and Confinity which was founded by Peter Thiel and Max Levchin.

The goal in doing my second Internet company was creating something that would have a profound effect because I thought we hadn't reached the potential that we could have with Zip2. We had really sophisticated software, our software was at least comparable to what Yahoo or Excite or others had. I thought in some ways it was better, but because it was all filtered through these partners it wasn't getting properly used. I thought I want to do something that can be a more significant contribution to the Internet, so immediately post the sale, I didn't take any time off, I tried to get where the opportunities remained on the internet. The initial thought was financial services because money is digital, it's low bandwidth, at the time most people were on slow modems because this was late '98, early '99. It seemed to me that the financial sector had not seen a lot of innovation on the Internet. At the time transactions were very slow. If you bought something, people had to mail checks to each other. It would take weeks to conduct the transfer. It could take weeks just to complete a single transaction. When you think about it, money is just an entry in a database, so it's low bandwidth. Essentially prices are just information, the primary information to allow for labor allocation. You don't need some sort of big infrastructure improvement to do things with it. The paper form of money is only a small percentage of all the money that's out there. It should lend itself to innovation on the internet.

We thought of a couple of different things we could do. One of the things was to combine all of somebody's financial services needs into one website, so you could have banking, brokerage, insurance, and all sorts of things in one place.

In the early going our company was called X.com. X started as a financial services company, to aggregate all of your financial services seamlessly in one place, and make it really easy to use, so you don't have to go to multiple financial institutions to take care of your mortgage, your credit card, your banking relationship, insurance, mutual funds. You could just go to one location.

I sunk the great majority of my net worth into X.com. I had essentially no background in financial services except for an internship at a bank. It was all like a series of poker games, now I'd gone on to a higher stakes poker game. Raising $50 million was a matter of making a series of phone calls and the money was there.

So the thought with X was to create one place and do any financial anything.

Then we had a little feature, which took us about a day, that was the ability to email money from one customer to another. You could type in an email address or, actually, any unique identifier - so, like, an email address or a phone number or something like that - and transfer funds, or conceivably stocks or mutual funds or whatever, from one account holder to another. We had that as a feature and whenever we'd demo and show the system off to someone, they wouldn't get excited about the hard stuff, the conglomeration of financial services, which was quite difficult to put together. We'd say: "This took us a lot of effort to do and look how you can see your bank statement and your mutual funds and insurance and all that. It's all in one page and look how convenient that is." and people would go, ho hummm, and we would say, and by the way, we have this feature where you can enter somebody's email address and transfer his funds, and they go, "Wow! All right, OK." They would really be wowed by the fact that you could email the money to somebody, so we started focusing more and more on the email payments part of it.

It's important to take feedback from your environment. You want to be as closed-loop as possible. If we hadn't responded to what people said, we probably would not have been successful. It's important to look for things like that, and focus on when you see them and correct your prior assumptions.

There was another company called Confinity, which started out from a different angle. They started as a PalmPilot cryptography company and developed an application with that cryptography that was able to beam money tokens via the infrared port of the PalmPilot. Yeah, if people remember that one, that was big at one point. If you remember back in the day PalmPilots did not have any connectivity really, but they had infrared ports. You could beam token payments from one Palm Pilot to another via the infrared port. Then they had a website which was called Paypal, sort of parallel to that because once you'd beamed the infrared tokens you had to still then synchronize your Palm Pilot and do the transfer via the website. What they found was that people weren't that interested in the PalmPilot stuff, but they were interested in the website, so they started leaning their business in that direction. We kind of converged to the same point, and were quite close together so we decided to merge the companies, and in I think January or so of 2000, X.com acquired Confinity, and then about a year later we ended up changing the company name to PayPal. We combined our resources when both companies were only about a-year-old at the time. Yeah, it worked out better than we expected. Initially, Confinity and X.com started out from slightly different directions and converged to the same point, and by pulling our resources we were able to compete effectively against eBay's build-in system and survive the dotcom implosion of late 2000. It was a very turbulent period.

I was once driving on Sandhill Road with Peter Thiel, one of the cofounders of PayPal, and we were just going to visit Mike Moritz at Sequoia Capital. This is in 2000. I didn't really know how to drive the McLaren, and Peter says: "so what can this do?" I'm probably number one on the list of famous last words, I said: "Watch this." I floored it and did a lane change. The McLaren doesn't have traction control or anything, it's just massive power to the wheels 640 brake horsepower, and it only weighs a ton, so it has massive power to weight. It can break the wheels free at 80 miles an hour. It broke the rear end free and it started spinning, I was going straight, and I can remember seeing the cars coming towards me while I was going backward. We hit an embankment, sort of a 45-degree embankment which knocked the car into the air, which continued spinning like a discus, like 3 feet in the air according to witnesses, and then Bam!! Slammed down on the ground going the original direction. It was like in a movie, I drove to the side of the road and I was like "Holy cow."

Peter hitched a ride to Mike. I waited till the fire truck and ambulance arrived. Once the car was taken care of I hitched a ride to, so we continued the meeting. Lucky to be alive really. I blew out the suspension and didn't actually wreck the car, the core chassis and the engine were OK, but all the glass and the wheels were shredded. There was massive body damage to the front and rear. That was crazy. After that, I took driving lessons on the McLaren, because it's a difficult car to drive.

As far as PayPal, we focused on e-mail payments and tried to make that work. That's what really got things to take off. It was very easy to implement in the beginning, it gets harder as you try to minimize the fraud in the system, but the initial implementation of email payment is trivial. Although it's easy in principle, what gets hard is adding security while still keeping it easy to use. It's like the Willy Loman quote, why do you rob banks? because that's where the money is. Why do people rob PayPal? same reason. You can dial up the security to a high level, but then you're going to make it very hard to use. That was one of the toughest things we wrestled with, and that was quite a difficult problem to solve, but we solved most of the issues associated with that.

There were a lot of back-office relationships that we needed to establish and to attach to various heterogeneous data sources. We needed to attach to the credit card system for processing credit cards, we needed to attach to the Federal Reserve System for doing electronic funds transfers, we needed to attach to various fraud databases to run fraud checks. There was a lot that we had to interface with. That took a while. It all came together I think roughly simultaneously. I mean developing the software and having it ready for the general public reasonably coincided with us being able to conclude those deals, and interface with the outside vendors, and all that took about a year.

We figured out how to make it really fast and easy to transfer funds from one person to another. The key was figuring out how to make the friction of signing up for an account very very low and make it easy for one person to refer another. We did a bunch of things to decrease the friction. If you tried to transfer money to somebody who didn't have an account in the system, it would then forward an email to them saying, hey, why don't you sign up and open an account? We started first by offering people $20 if they opened an account, and $20 if they referred anyone. Then we dropped it to $10, and then we dropped it to $5. That cost a fair amount. I think it was probably $60 or $70 million. As the network got bigger and bigger, the value of the network itself exceeded any sort of carrot that we could offer.

The growth of the company was pretty crazy. I didn't expect PayPal's growth rate to be what it was. It grew super fast, it grew virally. At the end of the first 4 or 5 weeks of the website being active, we had 100,000 customers. Yeah, it was nutty. PayPal is a perfect case example of viral marketing like Hotmail was. Where one customer would essentially act as a salesperson for you by bringing in other customers. They would send money to a friend and, essentially, recruit that friend into the network, so you had this exponential growth. The more customers you had the faster it grew. It was like bacteria in a Petri dish, it just goes like this S-curve. What you want to do is try to have one customer generate like two customers, or something like that, maybe three customers, ideally, and then you want that to happen really fast. You could probably model it just like bacteria growth in a Petri dish, and then it'll just expand very quickly until it hits the sides of the Petri dish, and then it slows down.

That created major problems. It wasn't all good because we had some bugs in the software and, you know, even if the bug only occurs 1 in 1000 times, it's still 100 very angry customers like "where's my money?" that would be a reasonable concern that people would have. We had customer service on University Avenue in Palo Alto where we started PayPal. There were five people, so when something went wrong, customer service phones would basically explode.

About a year after we opened the website we had about 1 million customers and we really didn't expect 1 million customers. It was something like expecting The Spanish Inquisition, it's not something you expect. It gives you a sense of how fast things grow in that scenario. We didn't have a sales force, we didn't have a VP of Sales, we didn't have a VP of Marketing, and we didn't spend any money on advertising.

PayPal was not the first to do email payments. There was a company that was acquired by Amazon, it was also an email payments company, I forget what it's called. eBay had initially acquired Billpoint, and then there was eBay Payments. It was a pretty tough long-running battle of PayPal versus eBay's payment system. It was certainly very challenging. I think there were times when it felt like we were trying to win a land war in Asia and they kind of set the ground rules, or trying to beat Microsoft in their own operating system. It's really pretty hard. That took a lot of our effort to beat eBay on their own system.

NASDAQ kind of peaked in March 2000 and that was when we did the evaluation of PayPal for $500 million. We had many challenges and then the various financial regulatory agencies were trying to shut us down. Visa and Mastercard were trying to shut us down, eBay was trying to shut us down, FTC was trying to shut us down. There were a lot of battles there. It was a close call. We definitely came very close to dying there in 2000 and 2001. The challenge was really to keep the company alive till we sold the company 2 years later to eBay.

I ran PayPal for about the first two years of its existence. I think it's not a good idea to leave the office when there's a lot of major things underway which are causing people a great deal of stress. It was a combination of needing to raise money, and I had gotten married earlier that year and had not had a vacation or honeymoon or anything. I had this kind of financing trip/honeymoon, I went away for two weeks and there was a just lot of worry, and that caused the management team to decide I wasn't the right guy to run the company. I could have fought it hard at the time, but I said rather than fight it at this critical time it's best to sort of concede. I didn't agree with their conclusion, but I understood why they did what they did.

Since PayPal was not the first to do email payments, you have to say why did it succeed where others did not. How is it that PayPal was able to beat all of them, in particular, how is it possible to beat Billpoint, when Billpoint was eBay's in-house service? very few people understand why. There's a couple of things, first of all, if you look at the underlying economics of the system, we figured out a way to authenticate bank accounts. It's really hard from the standpoint of pulling money from somebody's bank account because you can give us a bank account number, but how do we know it's you? The Federal Reserve has no authentication system that works for pulling money from people's accounts. We came up with an idea for authenticating it by making two small deposits in somebody's bank account which effectively made it a four-digit pin. Only the person that had the bank account could tell what the four-digit pin was because of those two tiny deposits. We figured out how to authenticate a bank account without even seeing you. That was one of the fundamental breakthroughs, there were many, but that's a very big one.

Another big reason is when you send money from one person to another using a credit card, you have a very high fee associated with that, but if you send it using an electronic check it only costs a few cents. Plus the electronic check is very unlikely to be fraudulent, whereas with the credit card there is a huge amount of fraud associated with credit cards. With the credit card system, your effective costs including fraud are probably about 3.5% of the transaction, and the effective cost of the electronic check is maybe a quarter of a percent.

We initially took PayPal public in February 2002. Which was quite a dark time for Internet companies. I think we were the only internet company to go public in the first part of that year. It went off reasonably well, although I think we had more SEC rewrites than any company I can imagine. I think we set a record on SEC rewrites. This was right around the Enron time when there were all sorts of corporate scandals, so they put us through the wringer.

Shortly thereafter, about June, July, we struck a deal with eBay, to sell the company to eBay for about 1,5 billion dollars. One of the long-term risks certainly for the company was that eBay would one day prevail, and one way to retire that risk was to sell to eBay.

We had several offers actually from a number of different entities for PayPal, and in fact the closer we got to IPO, the more offers we got. We always felt that those undervalued the company, and subsequently when we went public, I think the public markets kind of indicated the value of the company. That's one of the good things about public markets, it's that they're an objective valuer of companies. When you're a private company it's very hard to say how much you're worth, because you have to think of some metric. Are you going to go for a multiple of future earnings? Are you going to go off something of revenue? What are your comparables going to be? There are all sorts of questions. It's really up for debate what sort of value your company is. When you're public, it's what the market says you're worth, that's what you're worth. eBay made a number of offers prior to going public that were substantially below the value. Once we went post public that kind of cleared up the disagreement and then we sold to them. I actually was against the sale. I wasn't in favor of the sale. I was the largest owner of PayPal at the time, but I only had like 12%. Everybody else really wanted to sell so we went forward with that, but I think we probably should not have.

As far as common themes between Zip2 and PayPal. I guess both of them involved software and internet-related stuff as the heart of the technology. Certainly, that's a huge commonality. They were both in Palo Alto, where I lived. I think we took a similar approach to build both companies, which was to have a small group of very talented people and keep it small. I think PayPal had, at its height, probably 30 engineers for a system that, I would say, is more sophisticated than the Federal Reserve clearing system. I'm pretty sure it is actually because the Federal Reserve clearing system sucks. What else is there? Generally, I think the way both Zip2 and PayPal operated was, it was really your canonical Silicon Valley start-up. You know, pretty flat hierarchy, everybody had a roughly similar cube, and anyone could talk to anyone. We had a philosophy of 'best idea wins' as opposed to a person proposing the idea winning because they are who they are. Even though there are times when I thought that should have been the way. Obviously, everyone was an equity stake holder. If there were two paths that, let's say, we had to choose one thing or the other, and one wasn't obviously better than the other. Then rather than spend a lot of time trying to figure out which one was slightly better, we would just pick one and do it. Sometimes we'd be wrong, and we'd pick ourselves up from our path. Often it's better to pick a path and do it than to just vacillate endlessly on a choice. We didn't worry too much about intellectual property, paperwork, or legal stuff. We were very focused on building the best product that we possibly could. Both Zip2 and PayPal were very product-focused companies. We were incredibly obsessive about how do we build something that is going to be the best possible customer experience. That was a far more effective selling tool than having a giant sales force or thinking of marketing gimmicks or twelve-step processes or whatever.

PayPal definitely hasn't moved much since it was bought by eBay. The long-term vision that I had for PayPal in finance was to, it sounds a bit strange, convert the financial system from a series of heterogeneous insecure databases into one secure database. Well, maybe not one database there would be a few more. Money is just a number in a database, that's what it is. It's primarily an information mechanism for labor allocation, and the current databases are not very efficient. There are these old legacy mainframes that don't talk to each other very well, have poor security, and only do their batch processing once a day. I think I would convert more into a full-service financial institution, so you just want to do all the things. You want to have all the financial services that somebody needs in one place, seamlessly integrated and easy to use, and I think really care about the consumer, I think a lot of banks don't seem to care that much about the customer. I think there is an opportunity to be like a really good bank, but much more than what people think of as a bank. I think payment systems are pretty easy, particularly if you don't have to integrate with a lot of legacy stuff, then payment systems are super easy. That's just like World of Warcraft, you know, credits, how many credits do you have in your database? You don't have exchange rates and have to, like, interface with bills and coins, and have credit cards, and have a Federal Reserve and all these things, they complicate things. What PayPal did was de-complicate things, but PayPal would be, like, super-trivial in a new environment.

I think Bitcoin is probably a good thing. I think it's primarily going to be a means of doing illegal transactions. That is not necessarily entirely bad. You know somethings maybe shouldn't be illegal. It will be used for legal and illegal transactions otherwise it would have no value as use for illegal transactions. Because you have to have a legal/illegal bridge. I don't own any Bitcoin by the way.

I think we had a really talented group of people at PayPal and a lot of those people have gone on to start many other companies - YouTube, Linked-In, Yelp, Yammer, it's quite a long list.

Anyway, that's just an approximate evolution of the company. That's summarizing a crazy amount of stuff that happened over that period.

I did take a bit of time off after PayPal. I did reasonably well from PayPal. I was the largest shareholder in the company, and we were acquired for about a billion and a half in stock and then the stock doubled. Ultimately after taxes, I had about $180 million, and I ended up investing all of that. I could've bought probably a chain of islands, but again that was obviously not of interest to me.

9. Mars Oasis

Maybe I should give some preface of what happened before I started SpaceX. I'll give you a little bit of background of my genesis of how I got into space, and walk you through the basic logic.

The space stuff came from a conversation I had with Andeo, a good friend of mine from college, my college housemate actually. I think it was around 2001 or so and we were coming back from Andeo's parents' place in Long Island, and he asked me what I was going to do after PayPal. When I was very young space just seemed really cool. I said well, I've always been pretty interested in space, but of course, there's nothing that I as an individual could do about that because it's the province of government, and usually a large government. I grew up in South Africa, you know, not much space stuff happening there. I told him there was maybe something philanthropic that could be done in space. To get the public more excited about space travel, and in particular, sending people to Mars, but I said I'm sure that NASA has got that covered.

The question got me curious as to sort-of find out when we were going to send someone to Mars. After I got back to my hotel room, I went to the NASA website to look up the schedule, and try to figure out where is the place that tells you that. I couldn't find it, and I thought the problem was me. I was like, either I'm bad at looking at the website, or they have a terrible website because surely there must be a date. This should be on the front page. Of course, it must be here somewhere on this website, but just well hidden. It turned out it wasn't on the website at all.

This was really disappointing, and I just couldn't understand why there was nothing about people going to Mars, because if you look at the literature in the 70s, it was all about how we went to the Moon, and now we're going to go to Mars. Then I discovered actually that NASA had no plans to send people to Mars, or even really back to the Moon. Which was shocking. I mean think of how incredible the Apollo program was. It was not something I was able to witness in real-time, because I was -2 when they landed, but if you ask anyone to name some of humanity's greatest achievements of the twentieth century, the Apollo program - landing on the moon - would be in many, if not most places number One. If in 1969 you would have asked the public to imagine what 2009 would look like, they would have said, there will be a base on the Moon, we would have at least sent some people to Mars, and maybe there'd even be a base on Mars, there'd be like orbiting space hotels all over the Solar System. There'd be all this awesome stuff in space, that's what people expected. That sort of seemed like the natural progression of things.

I sure kept expecting that the things that were projected in science fiction movies and books would come true, but they, unfortunately, did not. ..and then amazingly it didn't happen. I kept thinking, well, it's about to happen. ..and again, it just didn't happen. There's a Monty Python skit about this. Suddenly, nothing happened! Before you know it, nothing happened.

What happened was that we sent a few people to the Moon, and then we didn't send anyone after that to the Moon, or Mars, or anything.

I was quite bothered by it. It just seemed as though that if I thought about the future, one where we were a true spacefaring civilization out there exploring the stars, and making the things real that we read in science fiction books and movies, that seems like a really exciting future. That made me feel good about the future, and one where we are forever confined to Earth made me feel a bit sad. I thought it was quite sad that the Apollo program represented the high watermark of human space exploration. There was this incredible dream of exploration that was ignited with Apollo and it seemed - it just felt as though the dream had died. I thought that we had lost the will to explore, that we have lost the will to push the boundaries. This turned out to be a false premise. In retrospect that was a very foolish error, but that was my initial thought.

I just thought that it was important that humanity expands beyond Earth, so maybe there was something I could do to spur that on. I thought maybe this is a question of national will. Like how do we get people excited about space again? The roundabout way I thought that might be accomplished was, I thought, well, if NASA's budget was larger then we could do more in space exploration. Particularly, if we could get the public excited about sending people to Mars. That's why I got into space, to make that a reality and not just be forever fiction.

I thought, well, perhaps that funding can be garnered by really marshaling public support - to reignite the passion for space exploration such that we could go beyond what we did with the Apollo program. One way to get the public excited about space would be to do, maybe, a philanthropic privately funded robotic space mission to Mars. If that could get the public excited about sending people to Mars, then that would translate into congressional support for a bigger NASA budget, and then we could do exciting things and get the ball rolling again. That was the goal.

I started getting into this, researching the area, becoming more familiar with space, reading lots of books. That's about the time I started talking to Robert Zubrin and a few other people.

I came up with this idea called Mars Oasis. I thought what would make a difference is to land a small robotic land rover with a small greenhouse on the surface of Mars, with seeds in a dehydrated nutrient gel. You'd hydrate the gel upon landing, and you'd have this great shot of this little miniature greenhouse with little green plants on a red background. You'd have plants growing in Martian radiation and gravity conditions. You'd also be maintaining, essentially, life support systems on the surface of Mars. I thought that would get people really excited about sending life to Mars. This should be interesting to the public because people tend to get interested and excited about precedents and superlatives. This would be the first life on another planet, It would be the first life on Mars, as far as we know, the furthermost that life has ever traveled, so pretty significant. You would have this great shot of these green plants with a red background, and that would be the money shot essentially. Money shot.. I'm never quite sure if that's the sort of word that you can use or not. I didn't know its origins until someone pointed it out to me. Anyway, that was the basic idea, trying to get us back on track of extending life beyond Earth and resume the dream of Apollo.

We would certainly be able to figure out a lot of engineering insights and data into what it took to maintain planet life on the surface of Mars, and you'd get some engineering data about what does it take to maintain a little habitat on Mars type of thing.

I spent several months on this trying to figure out, OK, well can I afford to build a spacecraft? I had some money as a result of PayPal, but it had to fit within that budget. Coming out of PayPal I was fortunate enough to have about $180 million. I thought wow that is a lot of money, if I assign half of this I still have the other half and I will be fine. My expectation from that project would be 100% loss. Maybe you could make a little bit back on advertising or sponsorship or something, but it would be essentially a complete loss. I figured I was willing to spend half the money with no expectation of return because I thought this was just something that was pretty important, and worth doing. If that resulted in us going to Mars, that would be a pretty good outcome.

It would have been a small greenhouse, like a meter across, or something like that. Yeah, I hope we've got that somewhere, I mean, I'm sure it looks pretty goofy in retrospect, but that's the idea that we had. I spent several hundred thousand dollars getting the design worked out and engaging some companies to come up with the design specifications for the subsystems. I figured out how to compress the cost of the spacecraft, and the communications systems, and the payload, and so forth. I started investigating what that would take, and I was able to figure out how to get the cost down to a reasonable number - reasonable meaning several million dollars.

I figured we had to do two identical missions, two parallel missions, in case there was an equipment failure because then it could be counterproductive. It might have the opposite effect - like, look at that fool, he did that Mars mission and it didn't work, now we definitely shouldn't do Mars. Look how dumb it is to try to send something to Mars. What an idiot.

I was able to get the cost of the spacecraft down to low single-digit millions, and the cost of communications down, and I was able to get everything compressed down to a relatively manageable number, except for the cost of the rocket. The thing that I got hung up on was the rocket. Getting there in the first place.

At first, I tried to buy just a normal launch vehicle that they use to launch satellites, but the US options from Boeing and Lockheed were simply too expensive, I couldn't afford them. The lowest cost rocket in the US at the time was the Boeing Delta II, and that would have been about $50 million, and you'd still need to have an upper stage for Mars, so probably like $65 million all-in. I wanted to do two of these missions, so two would have been $130 million. I was like, woah that's a bit steep for what we were trying to do, OK, that breaks my budget right there. I tried to negotiate with them, and that was not-- I did not make progress.

I went to Russia in late 2001, early 2002 to try to buy refurbished ICBMs, and that is as crazy as it sounds, but desperate times call for desperate measures. On the range of interesting experiences, going to the Russian military and saying: "I want to buy two of your biggest rockets, but minus the nuke" is pretty far out there. It turns out Russia is quite a capitalist society. I think they thought that I was a bit crazy I guess, this about 30 years old Internet guy arrives in Moscow, wants to buy the biggest ICBM in the Russian rocket fleet. They just thought I was crazy, but that's not good either if you're buying ICBMs. Then they read about PayPal so they thought, okay, he's crazy but he's got money, so more important I could pay them, so, that was okay. Remarkably capitalist, was my impression.

It was a trippy experience. I had some weird meetings at places that I swear looked like sanitariums or something, it was very odd. Seriously, this place had padded walls, I mean like why do you have padded walls? It was weird. Then there was this Russian guy who was missing a front tooth yelling at me, and because he was missing a front tooth there was spit flying at me, in this place with padded walls. It was like really bizarre. Yeah, there were some strange trips that's for sure.

I ended up going to Russia three times to negotiate a purchase of two of the biggest ICBMs in the Russian nuclear fleet and was able to negotiate a deal to buy a couple of Dneprs minus the nukes. I sort of got the feeling that I could have bought the nuke too, I think that would have been a lot more, but I slightly got the feeling that that was on the table. Which was very alarming.. I don't want to go there.

Anyway, I did three visits there and at the end of it, I was able to negotiate a price actually, to buy two of these things - two of the largest ICBMs in the Russian fleet. It's gone up a lot since then, but in 2001, it would've been about $10 million each, so two would have been $20 million. Then I thought I could get the rest of the mission down to also around $10 million per. We figured out a mission that would cost about $15 or $20 million, which isn't a lot of money, but it's about a tenth of what a low-cost NASA mission would be. We'd have a dual mission with like two identical launches, two identical spacecraft for roughly $40 million, and so I thought, OK, I can do that.

I did come to terms with the Russians, but the only reason the rockets were lower cost was because of reduction talks, so they were essentially spare rockets. It's kind of a long story, but on my way back from the third trip to Russia I was really fed up with going to Russia, and I was like OK this is kind of silly, because if we launched this on a refurbished ICBM, there's only so many of those and we would run out, so this wouldn't be a long-term solution. One could use those rockets, but once you ran out of the spare rockets of the reduction talks, then you were back at the high price again. It would not result in a long-term benefit. We actually did get to a deal, but there were so many complications associated with the deal, that I wasn't comfortable with the risks associated with it. At the end of all that I decided not to conclude the deal, so negotiated a price but decided not to take the deal.

After my third trip to Russia was also about the time that I realized that my original premise was wrong. That I was mistaken that there was a lack of will. In fact, there's not such a shortage, but people don't think there's a way. In retrospect, it was quite silly of me to think that people were not interested in such a thing, or had lost the will to do this. I think that there's a tremendous amount of will, particularly in the United States, perhaps the world as a whole, but particularly the United States does not lack the will to explore, not in the least. Which I think is kind of obvious, because the United States is a distillation of the human spirit of exploration. Almost everyone came here from somewhere else. No nation is more a nation of explorers than the United States, but people need to believe that it's possible, and they're not going to have to give up something important. What people don't want to think is that sending people to Mars is going to be so expensive, that they'll have to give up health care or something. They're not going to do that. People had thought that it's not possible for an amount of money that wouldn't materially affect their standard of living. It's got to be that going to Mars is not going to cause some meaningful drop in their standard of living. If people think it's impossible or it's going to break the national budget, they're not going to do it. You know, you're not going to bash your head against a brick wall if you're confident that your head will break before the wall will break. It's just not going to happen. If people thought there was a way or at least something that wouldn't break the federal budget, then people would support it.

I thought, OK, it's not going to maybe matter that much if we succeeded in doing this mission, that wouldn't be enough. I came to the conclusion that if we don't make rockets way better, then it won't matter. We can get a budget increase, but then we'd just send one mission to Mars and then maybe never go there again. The last time we went to the moon was 1973 or '74 I believe. We don't just want to have flags and footprints and then never go to Mars again. If we just have one mission that would also be a super inspiring thing, but it's not going to fundamentally change the future of humanity. That would perhaps add a little bit more to the will to do it, but it wouldn't make it clear to people that there was a way. This is the case of sort of almost the opposite, "If you can show people that there is a way, then there is plenty of will." so then I said, OK, well, I need to work on the way.

After that third trip, I had learned a lot more about rockets at that point, and I held a series of meetings - just sort of brainstorming sessions - with people from the space industry, to try to understand if I was missing something fundamental about the ability to improve rocketry, because year over year, we did not see improvements in rocket technology.

If after we had put people on the moon in 1969 you said: in 2009 which one of the following do you think will be true? There'll be this device that you can fit into your pocket and take anywhere in the world, that's smaller than a deck of cards, has access to all the world's information, can send megabytes of data, and you can talk to anyone on planet Earth. Even if you're like in some remote village somewhere so long as there's something called the Internet-- they wouldn't know what that means of course—then you would be able to communicate to anyone instantly, and have access to all of humanity's knowledge... or humanity will be on Mars? You would have gotten I don't know hundred to one that humanity will be on Mars, and what is that ridiculous thing you're talking about, that little device that can communicate anywhere in the world and can fit in your pocket, that's nonsense. They would have said like, bullshit, there's no way that that's going to be true, and yet we all have that, and space is not happening.

In the '60's we went from basically nothing, not being able to put anyone into space to putting people on the Moon. Developing all the technology from scratch to do that, and yet in the '70s and '80s and the '90s we kind of gone sideways. We were even in a situation where we couldn't even put a person into Lower Earth Orbit. That doesn't gel with all of the other technology sectors out there. The computer that you could have bought in the early '70s would have filled a room and had less computing power than your cell phone.

Just about every sector of technology has improved, why has this not improved? I started looking into that, trying to figure out what was the deal here. Essentially trying to figure out why we had not made more progress. The rocket technology was actually going worse. It was costing more and more to send things to space than in the past, so we had a negative technology curve. This is counterintuitive because we're so used to things in the consumer electronics realm, and in everyday life, improving.

I started reading quite a bit about rockets to try to understand why they are so friggin' expensive. Where does the $60 million go for the Delta II? and now I think a Delta II is $100 million or something even, some crazy number, and Delta II is a relatively small rocket. If you go to one of the bigger rockets it's nearer to about $200 million to $400 million.

I thought, well, why is it the Russians can build these low-cost launch vehicles? I think the US is a pretty competitive place, and we should be able to build a cost-efficient launch vehicle. How hard is it really to make a rocket? it's not like we drive Russian cars, fly Russian planes, or have Russian kitchen appliances. When was the last time we bought something Russian which wasn't vodka?

This is where I think it is helpful to use the analytical approach in physics, to try to boil things down to first principles and reason from there. As opposed to trying to reason by analogy, historically, all rockets have been expensive, so, therefore, in the future, all rockets will be expensive. That's not true if you say, what is a rocket made of, what are the materials that go into a rocket, how much does each material constituent weigh, what's the cost of that raw material, that's going to set some floor as to the cost of the rocket. That turns out to be a relatively small number. Certainly well under 5% of the cost of a rocket and, in some cases closer to 1% or 2%. You can call it may be, the "magic wand number" If you had piles of raw materials on the floor, and say, OK, it's made of aluminum, titanium, some copper, carbon fiber, if you want to go that direction. You can break it down and say, what is the raw material cost of all these components. If you have them stacked on the floor, and could wave a magic wand so that the cost of rearranging the atoms was zero, then what would the cost of the rocket be? I was like, wow, OK, it's really small. It's like 2% of what a rocket costs, so clearly it would be in how the atoms are arranged. You've got to figure out how can we get the atoms in the right shape much more efficiently.

Anyway, I came to the conclusion that there wasn't really a good reason for rockets to be so expensive, and they could be a lot less. Rockets had not evolved since the 60s. The big aerospace companies just had no interest in radical innovation. All they wanted to do was try to make their old technology slightly better every year. In fact, sometimes it would get worse, particularly in rockets, it was pretty bad. It went backward. We got the Space Shuttle, but the Space Shuttle turned out to be a big mistake, it could only barely go to Low Earth Orbit, whereas a Saturn V could go to the Moon. Then the Space Shuttle was to be retired, and that trend line trends to zero. What I was trying to figure out is, how do we reverse that? Like I said, at first it didn't seem like it would be possible to start a space company, because it seemed like the province of governments. I came to the conclusion that if there wasn't some new entrance into the space arena with a strong ideological motivation, then it didn't seem like we were on a trajectory to ever be a space-faring civilization, and be out there among the stars. Then as I learned more and more it became clear that unless there was a fundamental improvement in rocket technology, an exciting future in space was not possible. In order for us to be a space-faring civilization and out there among the stars, we need dramatic improvements in rocket technology and in particular reusable orbital rockets.

I met a bunch of space engineers in the process of trying to figure out the Mars Oasis mission, and we got along pretty well. I gathered the little team that I put together to try to figure out the mission, and I said: "Hey why don't we talk about the feasibility of building a rocket in the US. Is there some fundamental limitation that prevents us from making substantial improvements, like have Boeing and Lockheed approached some asymptotic optimum, or is it possible to do much better?" I put together a feasibility study that consisted of engineers that had been involved with all major launch vehicle developments over the last three decades. I engaged a bunch of consultants and started to just get familiar with the space industry.

We iterated over a number of Saturdays at the beginning of 2002, to figure out what would be the smartest way to approach this problem of not just launch cost, but also launch reliability. We came up with a default design, and that actually was fortunate timing. That feasibility study finished up right around the time that we agreed to sell PayPal to eBay. Coincident with that sale I moved down to LA, where there's the biggest concentration of aerospace industry in the world. It's the biggest industry in southern California and much bigger than entertainment or anything else. I was living in Palo Alto for about nine years before that.

I had those series of meetings on Saturdays with people, some of whom were still working at the big aerospace companies. I think sort of in the course of working with them on the philanthropic mission I guess we had gotten a pretty good rapport. Most of them, not all of them, were willing to join and start a company. They were at big aerospace companies and they were like top guys at those companies, so it was a big risk for them. We went through this exercise together of trying to figure out could a rocket be built? We all came to the conclusion that it could, so success was one of the possible outcomes. I just tried to figure out is there some catch here that I'm not appreciating, and I couldn't figure it out. There doesn't seem to be any catch, so I started SpaceX.

10. Why Space?

I want to explain why I think space is really important, and what about space. If you don't mind me exploring that issue a little bit, you break it down and say: "Why is it important that life becomes multi-planetary?" Why go anywhere, right?

I believe in building things up from a rational framework of logic, and so you start with, sort of, how do you decide that anything is important? I guess you should look at the nature of importance itself. I think the lens of history is a helpful guide. The lens of history is a helpful way to distinguish more from less important in that things that may seem important at the moment, aren't that important in the grand scheme - over time. The further out you zoom the more you can distinguish less important from the more important. If you look at things over a broad span of time, things that are less important kind of fall away. The important milestones remain and the less important ones disappear.

If you look at things from the broadest possible span of time, at the whole 4.5 billion year history of Earth, and say what are the milestones in the evolution of life itself? If you think about the really big milestones, and that means going beyond the colloquial concerns of humanity. Primitive life, I think, started around 3.5 to 3.8 billion years ago. Initially, there was single-celled life, and then there was multicellular life, there was differentiation into plants and animals, then things acquired skeletons, and that allowed the transition from the oceans to land, and then we had the development of mammals and consciousness, those are sort of the big things. There are probably about ten or twelve really big milestones in the

71

history of life itself. I think on that list would fit life going from one planet to multiple planets. I think it's one of the most significant things that will occur in the history of life itself. I think it's at least as important as life going from the oceans to land, and arguably more important, because at least oceans to land can be a gradual affair, if it gets uncomfortable you can hop back into the ocean. Now if there's something important enough to arguably fit on the scale of evolution of life itself, it's fair to say that it should be considered important.

The human consciousness has not been around very long from an evolutionary standpoint. It's worth noting that civilization in terms of having writing has been around for 10,000 years, and that's being generous. History is going to bifurcate along two directions. I think there are really two fundamental paths. One path is we stay on Earth forever, and then there will be some eventual extinction event. We'll be one of perhaps many single planet species that never went anywhere. Eventually, something terrible happened, and that caused the end of that civilization. Or we're going to be the multi-planet species that is out there among the stars. That's the thing that makes all the difference in the world because eventually there will be something that happens on Earth. Either as a result of something humanity does, or as a result of something natural like a giant asteroid hitting us or something, that civilization - life as we know it - could be destroyed. I don't have an immediate doomsday prophecy, but it's just history, eventually, there will be some doomsday event. That's pretty obvious from the fossil record, it's just a question of when. There's clear evidence for life being destroyed, multiple times, in the fossil record. We don't need to guess that this is something that can occur, it already has occurred. The Permian Extinction being a particularly interesting one, as I think that destroyed between 90 to 95% of all species on

Earth, which doesn't tell the full story as most of the remaining species were fungi. So, unless you're a mushroom, you're out of luck.

The Sun is also gradually expanding, and in roughly 500 million years, maybe 1 billion years on the outside, the oceans will boil and there will be no meaningful life on Earth. Maybe some chemo tropes or ultra-high temperature bacteria or something, but nothing that can make a spaceship. If you think about the 500 million years it's only about a 10% increase in the lifespan of the Earth. If humanity had taken an extra 10% longer to get here, we would not have gotten here at all. Civilization has been around for such a very short period of time that these time scales seem very long, but on an evolutionary time scale, they're very short. A million years on an evolutionary time scale is really not much, and Earth's been around for four and a half billion years, so that's a very tiny, tiny amount of time. It's somewhat of a tenuous existence that civilization and consciousness as we know have been on Earth, and we face dangers that the dinosaurs didn't face. We could do ourselves in.

I'm fairly optimistic about the future of Earth. I am more optimistic than Stephen Hawking or Martin Rees the Astronomer Royal. He thinks it's quite likely that civilization will end this century. He's at the Royal Society, so he's a smart guy, I hope he's wrong. I personally am more optimistic about civilization.

I did say multi-planetary, so it's not from the standpoint of let's have one planet but somewhere else. We want to have multiple planets. If you can imagine some, I hesitate to use the word "utopian society" in the future, but say what is the future you want? What is the future that you would say that be a good one? Then I think you want to have a future where we are a space-faring civilization, a multi-planet species, we are out there exploring the stars. I think that would be great.

To the best of our knowledge Life exists only on Earth, so if we don't at some point propagate beyond Earth, then if there's some calamity that befalls life here, that will extinguish it. One can think of it from a standpoint of life insurance. I mean something bad is bound to happen if you give it enough time. For all we know that might be the extinguishment of life itself.

I think it is consciousness which makes this the next step. You really need consciousness to design vehicles that can transport life over hundreds of millions of miles of irradiated space, to an environment that they did not evolve to exist in. It would be very convenient of course if there was another planet just like Earth nearby, but that's unlikely, and as it turns out not the case. There's no way for life to just, by dint of natural selection, just sort of getting over to Mars and survive. I think given the immense difficulty of that, you actually need consciousness to have developed in order to achieve that goal. I can't see any way that life could just evolve in a Darwinian fashion to go across hundreds of millions of miles of irradiated space to an environment that is completely different from Earth, and still live.

You need consciousness in order to design a mechanism of making that journey. It feels to me that this little light appeared suddenly on Earth after 4 1/2 billion years. It's hard to say how often that does happen, maybe it's quite rare. In fact, it would appear to be quite rare, or they are very good at hiding. If it's a very rare thing, then we should take whatever actions we can to ensure its long-term survival. Life is a terrible thing to waste.

So far nobody has found any direct signs of life from other worlds. We have not detected anything. Hopefully, we do, and hopefully, it's not a warship coming towards us. The telescopes are indicating that there is a huge number of planets out there that are similar to Earth, so it seems likely that there is at least primitive life, like single-celled life, bacteria, and that kind of thing. Then there is a much smaller number that would have sophisticated life, like plants or animals. Then a much much tinier number that would have Life that we can talk to, and that number might be zero in our region of the Galaxy. We haven't seen any direct signs of communication from any nearby Solar systems. I think there is quite a high chance of microbial life, then as you get more advanced in life there is less and less likelihood of sophisticated life.

It's not just that there has to be intelligent life that evolved somewhere, but that that life has to last for a long time for us to exist at the same time as that.

There is this great question called the Fermi paradox: where are the aliens? If there are so many planets out there, and the universe is almost 14 billion years old, why aren't the aliens everywhere? This is one of the most perplexing questions because you could basically bicycle to Alpha Centauri in a few hundred thousand years meaning at bicycle speed. In a hundred billion years even at a very slow speed, you could completely blanket the Galaxy, so why not, where are they? If there are super intelligent aliens out there they're probably already observing us, that would seem quite likely, and we just are not smart enough to realize it. Maybe they're among us, I don't know. Some people think I'm an alien. Not true, not true, of course, I'd say that, wouldn't I?

Anyway to the best of our knowledge Life exists only on Earth. There's a good argument that it exists elsewhere but we see no sign of it, and for the first time in the history of Earth the window of possibility has opened for us to extend life to another planet. Personally I think that would really be one of the most important things that we could possibly achieve because a multi-planet version of humanity's future is going to last a lot longer. We'll propagate civilization in the future far longer if we're a multi-planet species than if we're a single planet species. It's like planetary redundancy, backing up the biosphere. We've got all of our eggs in one basket here. We should try to protect that basket and do everything we can. It just seems like the right thing to do

Then the next question is should we do it now, or should we wait for some point in the future? I think the wise move is to do it now, because the window of technology for this is open, and it's the first time that window's been open. Earth's been around for 4.5 billion years and civilization about 10.000 years and it's only now that we have this little - this little window has just cracked open where it's possible for life to extend beyond Earth and so - I think it's sort of sensible to take advantage of that window while it's open. Hopefully, it will be open for a long time, but it could be open for a short time, and so we should take action. I certainly hope that the window will be open forever, but it may also close. I don't know if our technology level will keep going or subside. I think it's easy to take for granted that it is going to stay above that level, and if it does fall below that, would it return who knows? People are mistaken when they think that technology just automatically improves. It does not automatically improve. It only improves if a lot of people work very hard to make it better, and actually, it will I think by itself degrade. If you look at the history of technology in various civilizations - if you look at, say, ancient Egypt where they were able to build these incredible giant pyramids, and then they forgot how to build the pyramids, and then they couldn't read hieroglyphics. You look at say Roman civilization, they were able to build these incredible aqueducts and roads, and then they forgot how to do that. They had indoor plumbing, and they forgot how to do indoor plumbing.

There's clearly been a cycle with technology. Hopefully, that's an upward-sloping sine wave that continues to be great in the future, but maybe it doesn't. Maybe there's some bad thing that happens.

I think it is important for us to take advantage of the window while it is open and to establish life on another planet in the Solar System, just in case something goes wrong and knocks the technology level below where it is possible to travel to another planet. Can you can imagine if human civilization continued at anything remotely like the current pace of technology advancement for a million years? Where would we be? I think we're either extinct or on a lot of planets. Those are the two options.

I don't want to give the wrong impression that I think we're all about to die. I think things will most likely be okay for a long time on Earth. Not for sure, but, most likely. Even if it's 99% likely, a 1% chance is still worth spending a fair bit of effort to back up the biosphere and achieve planetary redundancy. To be clear this is not about everyone moving to Mars. It's about becoming multi-planetary. I think Earth is going to be a good place for a long time, but the probable lifespan of human civilization will be much greater if we are a multi-planetary species.

If one could make a reasonable argument that something is important enough to fit on the scale of evolution, then it's important, and maybe worth a bit of our resources. If we think it's worth buying life insurance on an individual level, then perhaps it's worth spending something on life insurance for life as we know it, and arguably that expenditure should be greater than zero. Then we can just get to the question of what is an appropriate expenditure for life insurance? I'm not talking about a huge portion, but perhaps we can bound it quite easily by saying it's not as important as, say, health care, but it's more important than let's say cosmetics. You want it to be some sort of number that is much less than what we spend on health care, but maybe more than what we spend on lipstick. I like lipstick, it's not like I've got anything against it. I think lipstick's very important, but you know, lipstick or colony on Mars? people may have a different opinion. Maybe .2 or .3 percent of our GDP, something like that is warranted. I think most people would say, okay, that's not so bad.

That's kinda the thing that I think is important that we give a little bit of our mind-space towards. For less than 1% of our resources, we could buy life insurance for life, collectively, and I think that would be a good thing to do.

Now that is the defensive argument, but it's not the reason that gets me most fired up. I just think there have to be reasons that you get up in the morning, and you want to live. Like, why do you want to live? What's the point? What inspires you? What do you love about the future? Life has to be more than just about solving problems, it can't be that all you do every day is just wake up and solve one miserable problem after the other. There have to be inspiring and exciting events that make life worth living in the first place. The thing that gets me the most excited about it is that I just think it's the grandest adventure I could possibly imagine. It's the most exciting thing, I couldn't think of anything more exciting, more fun, more inspiring for the future than to have a base on Mars. I think it'll be really great. It will be incredibly difficult, and probably lots of people will die, and terrible and great things will happen along the way, just as happened in the formation of the United States, but it will be one of those things that are incredibly inspiring, and we must have inspiring things in the world. Things that are exciting and inspiring and make you want the future to happen, I love that. I think that would make for a very exciting future. We could start by establishing on Mars and eventually spread out to the rest of the Solar System and start sending ships to other star systems. Once we've got a large base on Mars, and a lot of travel between the planets, that's a great forcing function for the improvement of space transport technology. I think we'll see rapid improvement and all sorts of inventions that we just can't envision today.

There are bad things that humanity does, and there are good things, and this is one of the good things. There have to be things that inspire you, to be proud to be a member of humanity. The Apollo program is certainly an example of that. Only a handful of people went to the Moon, and yet, actually, we all went to the Moon. We went with them vicariously. We shared in that adventure. I don't think anyone would say that was a bad idea. That was great. You know, we need more of those things, at least we need some of those things. Even if someone is in a completely different industry, and a completely different walk of life, it's still something that's going to make you feel good about the world, and that's the other reason why I think we should try to do these great things.

This is different from Apollo, this is really about minimizing existential risk, and protecting Life in ensuring that the light of consciousness is not extinguished, and having a tremendous sense of adventure. I'm sure it'll make it more awesome to be a human.

11. SpaceX

I only started SpaceX in basically July of 2002. The full company name is Space Exploration Technologies. In 2002 SpaceX basically consisted of carpet and a mariachi band, I really like mariachi bands. That was it. I don't know what the freak I was doing, I was clueless. When I started it wasn't with the perspective of we'll just take over the world with awesome rockets. We didn't even know what rocket we were making in 2002.

I had many people try to convince me not to start the company. Really tried their best. Many of my closest friends definitely thought I was crazy. If there was anything they could have done to stop me from starting a rocket company, they would have done it.

There's some other friends of mine that had been involved in a rocket startup: they said it was a terrible idea. One of my best friends compiled a long video of rockets crashing, and blowing up, and forced me to watch the whole thing. I've seen them all. Let me tell you he wasn't far wrong. I had a lot of friends of mine trying to talk me out of starting a rocket company, because they thought it was crazy, very crazy for sure, and they were not shy of saying that. I agreed with them that it was quite crazy. Real crazy, if the objective was to achieve the best risk-adjusted return, starting a rocket company is insane, but that was not my objective. The thing is that their premise for talking me out of it was, well, we think you're going to lose the money that you invest. I was like, well, that was my expectation anyway, so I don't really mind if I lose, I mean, I mind, but it's not like I was trying to figure out the rank-ordered best way to invest money, and on that basis chose space. It's not like that I thought, wow I could do real estate, I could invest in shoemaking, anything, and whoa, space is the highest ROI, that wasn't the premise.

When I started it was not with the expectation of success. I thought that the most likely outcome was failure. But given that the thing I was going to do previously, which was the Mars greenhouse mission, I'd expected that would have a 100% likelihood of losing all the money associated with it. If a rocket company has less than a 100% chance of losing all the money associated with it, then it was therefore quite a bit less risky than the thing I'd been doing before. Like I said, I thought it's probably not going to work, but for the philanthropic mission, the greenhouse to Mars, I was 100% certain of losing the money that I put in there. I kind of thought that we had a tiny chance of succeeding, like maybe on the order of 10% or something, so being only 90% likely to lose it for SpaceX seemed like an improvement.

When starting I heard this joke so often it was ridiculous. The joke was, 'How do make a small fortune in the space industry?' The punch line being 'Start with a large one.' I got to a point that I heard the joke so many times that I would just get to the punch line and say, 'Well, I want to figure out how to turn a large fortune into a small one. That was my goal.' and they're like, 'Wow! How did he know that?'

The goal was to make as much progress as possible, to advance rocket technology to the point where hopefully we can establish a colony on Mars, or at least get as far along that way as we can. We'll just try to go as far as we can. We're not certain we're going to develop all those technologies, but at least we're going to try. That was what we started off with in 2002, and really, I thought maybe we had a 10% percent chance of doing anything — of even getting a rocket to orbit, let alone getting beyond that and taking Mars seriously.

It was tough going there in the beginning. Going from PayPal to SpaceX was definitely a huge learning process because I never build any physical hardware myself although I do have a physics background, and come from a very engineering-centric household. I'm more engineer than anything else I guess. I had just done Internet software, I didn't know anything about space engineering or rocket engineering, but I learned quite a lot. I build like a little model rocket as a kid, but I never had a company that built something physical, so I had to figure out to build these things and bring together the right team of people.

I debated whether to start SpaceX in Silicon Valley or Southern California and in the end I decided to do Southern California because there's a larger base of aerospace engineering talent in Southern California.

I initially decided to make a small rocket called the Falcon 1, that was capable of putting about half a ton into orbit. This did not go smoothly. It was quite difficult to attract the key technical talent and, of course, I was quite ignorant of many things. I made lots of mistakes along the way.

I didn't do any market research, so maybe that's why I did it. If I had done market research I would probably have not done it.

While I didn't do any market research, I certainly read about what rockets existed in the world, what are they launching, and that kind of thing. At a minimum, we should be able to go and compete in the existing markets and have some kind of a business, even if it wasn't really breakthrough or anything like that. I don't think there's any kind of market research that you can do that would say, 'OK, if you can reduce costs by this amount, then there will be this extra number of launches that occur as a result of that reduced price.' I think you just have to do it and you hope that it turns out to be true, and make sure that there's a backup plan, that you at least have booked some value, even if you don't achieve the full potential, that you've still got some valuable enterprise that's capable of at least serving the existing market. That was the strategy that SpaceX had. We'll at least serve the existing satellite launch market, and hopefully the Space Station, and if that's all that happens then well, it's not a terrible thing.

Hopefully, by lowering the costs, and improving reliability we can expand the market substantially. I think if we did there will be others that enter the market and compete with our business as occurred in the airline business. There was a time when no one could possibly consider aircraft as a transportation mechanism. They were things that you maybe got a little joyride in, and they were very dangerous, and lots of people died all the time on them. If you said in 1920, probably any time before Lindbergh even, ask your average person on the street if they would be able to fly from New York City to Europe nonstop in an aircraft they would have said, 'no way! That's ridiculous.' so I think you have to approach this with some degree of open faith.

It was just a huge learning process. Initially, I had thought that I would hire someone to be to chief designer for the rocket, but I actually couldn't find anyone willing to join who was good. People were willing to join who I thought couldn't do the job, and those who could do the job weren't willing to join, so I ended up being the chief designer of the rocket.

12. Climate Roulette

The climate debate is an interesting one. If you ask any scientist, are you sure that human activity is causing global warming? any scientist should say no. Because you cannot be sure, so as far as climate change skeptics, I believe in the scientific method and one should have a healthy skepticism of things in general. The firstThe first thing from a scientific standpoint is that you always look at things probabilistically, not definitively. A lot of times, if someone is a skeptic in the scientific community, what they're really saying is that they're not sure that it's 100% certain that this is the case.

But that's not the point, the point is to look at it from the other side. There's a certain amount of carbon that is circulating through the environment. It's going into the air and then getting absorbed by plants and animals, and then going back into the air, and this carbon is just circulating on the surface. This is fine and it's been doing that for hundreds of millions of years. The thing that's changed is that we've added something to the mix. This is what I would call 'the turd in the punch bowl.' We have these low-cost stored hydrocarbons in the ground that have accumulated over hundreds of millions of years, perhaps over 1 billion years in the case of methane. In a lot of cases since the Pre-Cambrian era when the most sophisticated thing was a sponge. We are taking trillions of tons of CO_2, which was buried deep in the Earth's crust for hundreds of millions of years, and is not part of the carbon cycle, and are putting it into the carbon cycle of the atmosphere. As the carbon levels rise in the atmosphere some of that CO_2 migrates into the oceans, gets absorbed into the water, and creates carbonic acid, and causes acidification. A lot of the shellfish in particular are super sensitive to changes in pH level.

We've added all this extra carbon to the carbon cycle, and the net result is that the carbon in the oceans' atmosphere is growing over time. It's much more than can be absorbed by the ecosystem. It's quite simple, we are putting so much carbon into the atmosphere that we are fundamentally changing the chemical makeup of Earth's atmosphere and the oceans.

This is accompanied by a temperature increase as one would expect. People talk about 2 degrees or 3 degrees temperate increase. It's important to appreciate just how sensitive the climate actually is to temperate. It's important to look at it in terms of absolute temperature, not in degrees Celsius relative to zero. We need to say, what is the temperature change relative to absolute zero? That's how the Universe thinks about temperature. That's how physics thinks about temperature. It's relative to absolute zero, for small changes result in huge effects. New York City under ice would be minus 5 degrees, New York City under water would be plus 5 degrees. Looked at as a percentage relative to absolute zero, it's only a plus/minus 2% change.

If you asked any scientist, what do you think the percentage chance is of this being catastrophic for some meaningful percentage of the Earth's population? is it greater than 1%, is it even 1%? or do you think we should put an arbitrary number of trillions of tons of CO2 into the atmosphere, and just keep doing it until something bad happens, they will probably say no too.

The carbon parts per million (ppm) has been bouncing around the 300 ppm level for around 10 million years. Then the last few hundred years, it went into a vertical climb, and we have passed the 400 ppm. If you look at the famous Keeling curve that shows the growth in CO2 concentration in the atmosphere and every year it ratchets up - it gets higher and higher and if we do nothing it's headed to levels that we don't even see in the fossil record. Every year the CO2 ppm ratchets up, it's like a ratchet. It's kind of like being on the rack, you know the stretching rack, the torture device. When you got on the rack at first it didn't feel that bad, you crank it a few notches, it stretches out your back, not too bad. Then you keep ratching it further and further, and it becomes excruciating. That's where we are headed.

The way I look at the CO2 thing is that we are running an experiment, which is to see what the CO2 capacity of the oceans and atmosphere is before Earth gets cooked. I don't think that is a wise experiment. Let's say that experiment is 99% likely to show that CO2 is no problem, but 1% likely to show that it's going to cook the planet. I don't think we want to take that 1% chance, it's just not smart. Now, that experiment may turn out to be fine, but it may also turn out to be really bad.

We are playing Russian roulette, and as each year goes by we're loading more rounds in the chamber. It's not wise, we should not play Russian roulette with our atmosphere, we only got one. If we don't take corrective action the possibility of a catastrophe will increase over time, and eventually, there is the certainty of a catastrophic outcome.

There is no question that at a certain level it will destroy the Earth, or destroy large portions of the Earth, the question is just, what is that level? and how soon do we stop pumping vast quantities of CO2 into the atmosphere? The question is just when and how many billions of tons of CO2 are in the atmosphere versus in the ground. This is the essence of the problem. This is a very unusual and very, very extreme threat.

What makes it super insane is that we're going to run out of oil anyway. Given that oil and even coal are finite resources. It doesn't seem to make sense that we would run that experiment when we have to get off them anyway, because they are simply finite. It's not like there's some infinite oil supply, we're going to run out of it. At some point, we have to get to something sustainable. We have to have sustainable production and consumption of energy because, tautologically, if it is unsustainable you will run out of it.

Let's say hypothetically, CO2 was good for the environment, and let's say hypothetically, the United States possessed all the oil in the world. You'd still have to get off oil, because it's a finite resource, and as you start to run out of it, the scarcity would drive the cost up and cause economic collapse. Independent of the environmental impact we must find some alternative, or there will be economic collapse, and civilization would sort of crumble or revert.

We know that we ultimately have to get off of oil no matter what, we know that that is an inescapable outcome, because the alternative would be to mine all the carbon-based fuels from the ground, burn them, and then either move to a sustainable economy or the entire economy collapses because it doesn't have any energy. It's simply a question of when and not if. Then why would you run this crazy massive experiment of changing the chemical composition of the atmosphere and oceans by adding in enormous amounts of CO2 that have been buried since the Pre-Cambrian era? That's crazy, that is the dumbest experiment in history by far. I mean can you think of a dumber experiment? I honestly cannot. What good can possibly come of it? It's the stupidest thing I can imagine, and don't think that logic is a function of somebody's party or affiliation or ideology, it's just a function of rationality.

It kind of feels like those delayed gratification experiments. Where kids get this like, you can have two cupcakes if you wait five minutes, or you can have one cupcake if you eat it now. That's a good predictor of the kid's future success. We are just like the kid that scores the cupcake in like three seconds. That's kind of the sort of silly situation that we find ourselves in. We should terminate this experiment as soon as possible. I think we collectively should do something about this and not try to win the Darwin award, for us and a lot of other creatures too.

There's a lot of things that are happening in the world today that are important and that deserve our attention. There are many important issues in the world. This is not the only important issue, but I think it's always important to say what is important in the long term. This is I think, the thing that will have the biggest negative effect on humanity if we do not address it.

The sensitivity of the climate is extremely, extremely high. We've amplified this sensitivity by building our cities right on the coastline, and most people live very close to the ocean. Based on the projections that we're seeing right now, and these are like I'd say arguably best-case projections, we're going to see significant rises in temperature and sea level. The net result is if we don't take action, we could see anywhere from 5% to 10%, maybe more of the landmass absorbed by water. Which maybe doesn't sound like that much, but about a third of humanity lives right on the coastline or in low-lying countries. The way that humanity has kind of grown up around the world, is that we've put so many of our cities and settlements and towns right along the coastline. The world is quite delicate in this sort of chemical balance. There are some countries, of course, that are very low-lying and would be completely under water in a climate crisis. We've essentially designed civilization to be super sensitive to climate change. We'd be talking about maybe 2 billion people being displaced, their homes being destroyed, and their countries gone.

I think we should take action. Depending upon what action we take will drive the carbon number to either extreme or moderate levels. I think it's pretty much a given that the 2-degree increase will occur. The question is whether it's going to be much more than that, not if there will be a 2-degree increase.

I think, if we take action reasonably soon, we can avoid a calamitous outcome. If we only take action towards the end of the century, then it's going to be extremely bad.

I don't think people quite appreciate the momentum of climate change, you know. Even if we immediately stop all carbon production, the momentum will still carry forward and increase the temperature, raise water levels, and make storms more powerful, and all those things. I think that will eventually sink in, but the problem is that it's on such an epic scale, with so much inertia, that the point at which it becomes obvious that it's a severe problem - it's like, imagine there's a supertanker coming towards you, it suddenly appears out of the fog like, oh wait, supertanker coming towards me, you can't turn the supertanker real fast. It's going to keep going in that direction, that's got a lot of inertia. The amount of time that it'll take to switch the global industrial base to sustainable generation and consumption of energy is going to be measured in decades. I think the scientific fact of the matter is we are unavoidably headed towards some level of harm.

The sooner we can take action the less harm will result.

The worst case is more displacement and destruction than all the wars in history combined, so why not do it sooner? I'm not saying it has to be a radical or an immediate change, or that people need to inject a great deal of misery into their lives to avoid CO_2, but we should lean in that direction. We should lean in the direction of supporting technologies that are sustainable, and lean slightly against technologies that are unsustainable. That just seems pretty sensible. Even if the environment isn't a factor.

What are the actions that if we don't take them today will result in quite a terrible future, and what's the good outcome? The good outcome is, we minimize the carbon production, we transition to sustainable transportation and energy production, which is going to be like solar, wind, geothermal, hydro, and some nuclear, I think we have to accept that nuclear is a good option, in certain places. I think that the most likely outcome is a reasonably good one, where there's damage but we recover. I think that will occur. I'm quite optimistic about the future, I'm not suggesting complacency in the least, but I'm optimistic about the future.

The reason that transition is delayed or is happening slowly is because there is a hidden subsidy on all carbon-producing activity. What we have here is a tragedy of the commons. It is really a common problem in economics, you have the same thing in fishing, where, because there is no cost to fishing stocks, people just over-fish and you have a disaster that ensues.

In economics 101 when you have an unpriced externality the market system will not function correctly. In the market system prices are just information, so when the price of information is false, then wrong behavior will occur in a market economy. In a healthy market, if you have say $10 of benefit and $4 of harm to society, the profit would be $6. This makes obvious sense, this is where the incentives are aligned with a good future. If you have the incentives aligned, then the forcing function towards a good future, towards a sustainable energy future will be powerful. This is not the case today. In an unhealthy market, you have your $10 benefit, but the $4 isn't taxed. You have an untaxed negative externality. This is

Economics 101. You have unreasonable profit, and a forcing function to do carbon-emitting activity because this cost to society is not being paid. The net result is 35 Gigatons of carbon per year into the atmosphere. This is analogues to not paying for garbage collection. It's not as though we should say have a garbage-free society. It's very difficult to have a garbage-free society, but it's just important that people pay for the garbage collection. Basically, every economist would agree with this, that whenever you have an unpriced externality where the use of the product causes long-term damage to the environment, that is a true cost. If that cost is not incorporated in the price of petroleum, then effectively it's a subsidy.

The thing that people I think don't appreciate is that every fossil fuel car is quite heavily subsidized. I think most people don't realize that. It's heavily subsidized both of the direct subsidies that the oil and gas companies get which are enormous, and the negative effect on the environment, and not paying for all of the auxiliary effects of wars and all of these other things at the gas pumps. It may not seem like that but it is. It's a figure that is so large that it's difficult to even comprehend. If you look at the IMF study we have untaxed negative externality, which is effectively a hidden carbon subsidy of enormous size, $5.3 trillion a year according to the IMF. The IMF doesn't have an ax to grind one way or another. They don't make electric cars, and they're not part of the oil and gas industry, it is just a scientific analysis.

The solution obviously is to remove the subsidy. I think the best thing to do to achieve that would be a carbon tax. The market system will work extremely well if it has the right information to work. If we just apply a tax to carbon, and then dial that up according to whatever achieves the target maximum carbon proportion in the atmosphere that's, I think, the right way to go.

We could say what is the maximum parts per million of CO_2 that are acceptable. You have to say what is the maximum ppm that we will consider acceptable for Earth, is it 500, is it 600, 800? That is our bank account of carbon that is acceptable in the atmosphere. Then you have to say what is the acid level in the ocean that is acceptable. If we can just agree on what those numbers are, then we can price that boundary accordingly. I think we will find that it's a very high price, and currently, we are selling it for zero.

When you have an unpriced externality and the normal market mechanisms do not work, then it's a government's role to intervene in a way that's sensible. The best way to intervene is to assign a proper price to whatever the common good is that's being consumed. Generally taxing CO_2 is not a popular thing. Therefore what the government tries to do it is to subsidize low carbon activities like Photovoltaics and electric vehicles and that kind of thing. Since we set a price of zero, which is wrong, then we try to make up for it with all these incentives and subsidies, but they are not as good as simply pricing the CO_2. That would be the right thing to do. In the absence of pricing CO_2, incentives and subsidies are the next best thing. That's the long and short of it. If CO_2 is correctly priced, and of course the correct price is a debatable proposition, then no subsidies are needed. No incentives are needed for electric vehicles, no incentives are needed for battery storage or clean energy production if CO_2 is correctly priced.

I'm generally a fan of minimal government interference in the economy. Very often when there is government intervention, the government intervention increases the error in the price. As a general rule government intervention is best to be avoided, but there are cases where government intervention decreases the error. Since we know that the price of CO2 should not be zero, any action that increases the price of CO2 will reduce the error in the market system. It will result in better behavior, so that's the thing that should occur here. It seems logical that you should tax things that are most likely to be bad, that's why we tax cigarettes and alcohol because those are probably bad for you. Certainly, cigarettes are, so, you want to err on the side of taxing things that are probably bad and not tax things that are good.

We should make it probably a revenue-neutral carbon tax. This would be a case of increasing taxes on carbon, but then reducing taxes in other places. Maybe there would be a reduction in sales tax or VAT, and an increase in carbon tax so that only those using high levels of carbon would pay an increased tax. Moreover, in order to give the industry time to react, this could be a phased-in approach, so that maybe it takes five years before the carbon taxes are very high. That means that only companies that don't take action today will suffer in five years.

There needs to be a clear message from the government in this regard, because the fundamental problem is the rules today incent people to create carbon, and this is madness. Whatever you incent will happen. The government should be like the referee, but not like the player, and there shouldn't be too many referees.

The fundamental issue that we are facing is that even though the vast majority of scientists, like 97 or 98%, basically everyone who doesn't have a vested interest or isn't crazy, thinks this is a real serious issue. Countries need to act unilaterally. I think it's really important that people demonstrate to governments around the world that they care about climate change. We can't have this thing where such and such country isn't doing it, so I'm not doing it. Set a good example and hopefully, over time, other countries will fall in line or get ostracized. I think that's probably the smart move, then there's no need for subsidies and special incentives which are a backward way of trying to deal with the lack of a carbon tax. I think the best possible scenario would be that something like that is instituted. We're still going to have a significant increase of carbon in the atmosphere, temperatures are still going to rise, sea levels will rise. The Dutch can manage, you know, with a lot of dyke companies, there's a lot of options in the dyke business.

It's all about how you set the economics of carbon-producing actions versus non-carbon-producing actions. This is being fought quite hard by the carbon producers. You've got the oil and gas companies that have ungodly amounts of money, and you can't expect them to just roll over and die, they don't do that. What they prefer to do is spend enormous amounts of money lobbying, and running bogus ad campaigns, and that kind of thing, to preserve their situation. I mean the fossil fuel industry is the biggest industry in the world. They have more money and more influence than any other sector.

I am sort of disinclined to vilify the oil and gas industry, if we didn't have them we would have an economic collapse. If there was a button I can press that would stop all hydrocarbon usage today, I would not press it. It would cause human civilization to come to a halt. It would be ridiculous. It would be irresponsible to press that button. People would be starving to death, so it is very necessary in the short-term. It's hard to ask the CEO of an oil company to act against their best interests, that's the thing. In fact, if they do they might get fired by their shareholders. The right thing to do is to change the rules of the game to incent the right behavior. I have a hard time condemning the oil and gas companies because the current system incents them to do bad behavior. That's why I am a big believer in a carbon tax I think that is the way to go. We need to stop effectively subsidizing burning fossil fuels.

The problem right now is that the rules of the game fundamentally favor bad behavior. Where very powerful forces are trying to keep it that way. The economics so strongly favor the oil and gas industry. In fact to give you sort of a sense of it, if you took the value of all the solar companies in the US, it's about a third of the profit that Exxon makes in a year. The investment tax credit for solar in about a year dropped to 10%, however, the investment tax credit for stripper oil wells is 20%. This would be like if you have vegetables and cigarettes, and you're incenting the purchase of cigarettes. That doesn't make any sense.

The problem is that in monetary terms the oil and gas companies have infinite money. Basically, if money can do anything it will slow down action, that's what it's doing. That's why we're seeing very little effect thus far. Where I have an issue with the oil and gas guys is when they sometimes engage in nefarious tactics or things that are somewhat insidious, like funding academic studies that people can then point to as though they have some credibility. Some prominent Professor somewhere, but that person has been paid by the oil industry to write that study. It's that kind of thing that obviously should be condemned in the strongest. It's a lot like tobacco companies in the old days. We saw something similar to this with tobacco, in fact, tobacco is sort of smoking for individuals, and this is kinda smoking for the planet.

They're using tactics that are very similar to what the cigarette industry or the tobacco industry used for many years. It's the same playbook. They would take the approach of even though the overwhelming scientific consensus was that smoking cigarettes was bad for you, they would find a few scientists that would disagree, and then they would say, "Look, scientists disagree." That's essentially how they would try to trick the public into thinking that smoking is not that bad. I mean, they used to run these ads with doctors, or like a guy pretending he's a doctor, essentially implying that smoking is good for you, and like, having pregnant mothers on ads smoking. I would recommend reading the book "Merchants of doubt" which actually spells it out in detail. How some of these things are going on where the oil and gas industry all they need to do is to create doubt. They have employed a lot of individuals and firms that were employed by the tobacco industry, literally the same people. Some scientists of JPL and elsewhere sort of explored what's going on here. That's what they've done, and they found that the oil and gas industry is actually using the same lobbyists, like literally the same people as the tobacco industry, like by name, not even the firm. I'm surprised that some of these people are still around because they're quite old, some of those guys are still going. I would encourage people to read "Merchants of doubt" because they are literally using the same playbook as the tobacco industry did. Oddly enough the one movie I was involved in the making was 'Thank you for smoking' which I recommend watching, it's a fun movie. It's based on Buckley's book, it's really got to the truth of the matter of how all this happens.

What they do essentially is exploiting doubt. Even when you got a situation where virtually everyone, every scientist on Earth agrees that global warming is real, that adding billions of tons of carbon to the atmosphere and oceans is a bad idea. You have a few percent who dissent, and the way that is presented to the public is not that 97 or 98% of scientists think that what we are doing is crazy, but simply that scientists disagree. Scientists disagree about everything. You will not find 100% of scientists agree about anything. This is a very disingenuous argument, so the more that there can be sort of a popular uprising against that the better. If people of the world say something must be done, and demand something from their politicians, demand that they do the right thing. I think that is the only thing that can overcome the monetary power of lobbying.

I think in terms of how can you help, just sort of spread the message. I know that you think that global warming is real, but the crazy thing is a lot of people out there don't. It blows my mind. There is a lot of miss-information out there, and as the threat of electric vehicles becomes more and more significant to the oil industry, obviously they step up the propaganda campaign, and that is to be expected. It's really important to counter the propaganda, and there is a nonstop propaganda campaign from the fossil fuel industry. They are just defending themselves it's kind of what you would expect, but it's nonstop and they have like 1000 times more money than we do. This revolution is going to come from the people, so fight the propaganda.

I think when you look back on these days in the future, we want to be able to say that we did the actions that were right. The actions that were important. Because if we go 20, 30, or 40 years into the future, what do you say to your kids or your grandkids? Let's say your kids and your grandkids say: "did nobody tell you?" It's like: "No everyone was telling us" then "OK so why didn't you do anything?" What's the answer?

I think it's very important that we do something. I think we're really going to regret the amount of carbon we're putting in the oceans and the atmosphere. I think we're really going to regret it.

13. Tesla

The whole saga of Tesla is quite complex, and it is like many soap opera episodes that you could make out of it. So even this history is glossing over a lot of things, but will still give people a good sense of how things started out, what led from one thing to the next and to understand what really happened. There's a lot out there, some of it is correct some of it is false.

Like I said, my interest in electric vehicles goes back a long time, and predates the current climate issue when nobody was really talking about global warming, because I just thought it was the obvious means of transport. I do think the climate thing does add urgency to things, and I do think we will see quite a significant increase in the cost of oil. Just from a demographic standpoint, you've got China, India, and a few other countries that represent almost half the world's population and have very few cars on the road but are rapidly adding cars to the road. So you can expect a doubling of demand, and I think it's going to be difficult to achieve a doubling of supply.

I thought that big car companies would develop electric cars because obviously, it's the right move. I thought that was vindicated when General Motors was doing their EV-1. California regulations basically forced General Motors to create the EV-1. Then Toyota did the electric Rav-4, the original one, and they made those announcements and brought those to market. I thought, okay, this is great, we're going to have electric cars. GM, the biggest car company in the world is making an electric car. It's called EV-1, which would imply that there's going to be an EV-2, 3, 4, and they'll just keep getting better, and everything will be cool.

But then when California relaxed its regulations on electric cars, not only did GM cancel that project, they forcibly removed the EV-1s that they'd given out.. which they only gave out on lease. They removed them from customers against their wishes. Took the cars and crushed them into little cubes in a yard, so they could never be used again, which seemed kind of nutty. There's a great movie by Chris Paine called 'Who Killed the Electric Car?' and it's noteworthy that in that movie Chris shows how much people really wanted that EV-1 car. The customers, whose cars had been taken away, tried to sue General Motors to keep their car. The people tried court orders to stop the cars from being recalled. They wanted it so much that when the cars were forcibly taken away and crushed, they held a candlelight vigil at the yard where the cars were crushed. I did not attend, but I was moved by it. It's crazy - I mean, when was the last time you heard about any company's customers holding a candle-lit vigil for the demise of a product. You know that's pretty ridiculous. Particularly a GM product. Can you imagine anyone holding a candle-lit vigil for a GM car? Why would you discontinue a product line with that level of customer interest, that's pretty amazing. I mean, you have to be pretty tone-deaf. You don't need to do a customer survey to figure out that at least some number of people want the cars if they are treating it like somebody has been sentenced to death. What bigger wake-up call do you need? It's like, hello, the customers are really upset about this. They'd prefer it if it didn't get recalled. That kind of blew my mind. I was like wow, okay. It's really short-sighted action, I mean it's really unwise, in retrospect that seems perhaps obvious, and I think it's fair to say that with the benefit of hindsight, General Motors probably wishes they had done an EV-2 and an EV-3 following the EV-1.

Then we had the advent of lithium-ion batteries which really - that's one of the key things to making electric cars work - and still nothing. The electric motor is actually very old, in fact, in the early days of cars there was a competition between gasoline cars and electric cars, and there was a range issue with electric cars so the gasoline cars ended up winning out. But with the advent of lithium-ion batteries, we could now address the range issue. When GM did the EV-1 initially with lead-acid batteries it had a range of about 60 miles. Lithium-ion had four times the energy density of lead-acid, so basically if you just replaced the battery pack, you go from 60 miles range to maybe a 240 miles range. The basic math was pretty obvious, but despite it being fairly obvious, nobody was doing electric cars.

At the time in sort of the 2003/2004 timeframe, electric cars had gotten sort of a really bad reputation. The auto industry had concluded that electric cars were a waste of time. Basically that you couldn't make a compelling electric car, and if you would make an electric car, people wouldn't buy it because they love gasoline so much.

The thing that kinda spurred things in 2003 was a lunch I had with Harold Rosen and JB Straubel in LA, I think in El Segundo. I got this call sort of out of the blue from JB Straubel and Harold Rosen, who wanted to meet and talk about space stuff. Harold Rosen is very famous in the space arena, and also in the electric car arena, and he had also worked for Hughes Aerospace. They wanted to do a hydrogen airplane or something. Which sounds cool, but I don't think is very practical. But then they also mentioned an electric car, because Harold had done an electric car company called Rosen Motors that didn't ultimately succeed. That's kinda how the connection bridged over from rockets to electric cars. We were just talking a bunch of things in general, and I mentioned that I originally came out to California to work on electric vehicle technologies, and Harold told me about his past with Rosen Motors. Then JB mentioned that: "Hey there's this company called AC Propulsion, in Southern California, that has a kind of very rough prototype of an electric sports car, running on lithium-ion batteries, and it's getting really good performance" They had some of the guys, I think, who had been on the EV-1 program, and they took a gasoline sports car, kind of a kit car, and outfitted it with lithium-ion batteries, sort of consumer-grade cells, and they created a car. I said that sounds interesting, so JB arranged for a test drive with the AC propulsion tzero in 2003. So I got a test drive in a prototype, and I said wow this is awesome. Driving the tzero showed that the timing was right to create a compelling electric car. The advent of lithium-ion being the key enabling technology. AC Propulsion deserves a ton of credit and doesn't get enough credit for the concept of doing an electric sports car, which made clear that you could create a long-range, fast electric car.

The tzero was lithium-ion powered using cylindrical cells. It actually started off by being lead-acid, and then upgraded to lithium-ion I think in early 2003. It was a two-seater sports car with really good statistics, it did 0 to 60 miles per hour in under four seconds, and had a 250-mile range. It did have some drawbacks, it was quite primitive, it was basically like a kit car, with fiberglass. It didn't have a roof for one thing, at all. I don't know if it had doors. The battery was air-cooled instead of liquid-cooled, so it would overheat very quickly. It didn't have any safety systems, no airbags, it wasn't homologated - so it wasn't something that you could ever sell to people. Certainly not something you could sell to the general public. So, in order to create a commercial version of the car, something we could actually produce and sell to people, there was a fair bit of work that was required. It was very expensive, it had to be hand-built. The production cost was basically $300.000 or $400,000, like really high.

But the basic concept and capabilities were demonstrated by AC Propulsion. I tried to convince them to commercialize the sports car and said like: "Hey I'm willing to fund you if you want to commercialize the tzero." I mean I've tried hard, I can be persistent about these things. I was like guys you got to show the world that this is real, and prove to the industry that they are wrong about electric cars. I said, look, I'll fund the whole effort, you really need to do this, and they just sort of refused to do it. I kept pushing them on this, but they didn't want to do it. They were a very sort of small inventor type shop, they liked to tinker and experiment, and didn't want to put the time into creating an electric sports car. They wanted to make like an electric Scion. Which, in principle sounds good, but it would have cost $75,000, and no-one wants to buy a $75,000 Scion. The technology was just not ready - there was just no way to make a good value-for-money proposition with something like a Scion. I even tried to get them to make one for me, but they wouldn't even make one for me. I said: "if you don't want to commercialize the tzero can you please make one for me" and they were like no they didn't want to do that. Can you convert my current car to an EV? and they were like no. But I kept pushing them on this, so eventually after not being able to convince them for several months, finally I was like: " OK look guys if you're sure you don't want to do a commercial version of an electric sports car do you mind if I do that? I'd like to try to commercialize electric sports cars because I think we really need to show that you can make a compelling electric car." and they were like no that's cool, we're cool with that.

My initial plan was just to get together with JB and form a company, and potentially commercialize the tzero concept and create an electric sports car. Then the AC Propulsion guys said well if you're going to do that, some other groups are also interested in doing the same thing, why don't you team up with them? They ended up introducing me to three guys, and that's how I met Martin Eberhard, Marc Tarpenning, and Ian Wright, and I was able to convince JB to join. We teamed up with Martin, Marc, and Ian, and created Tesla Motors basically to commercialize the tzero, and that was sort of the founding team of Tesla with the five of us.

It's important to emphasize that when we created Tesla, it wasn't from the standpoint of like "Hey this is a great way to make money." When I told my friends about this they told me "you're crazy. How much money do you plan to lose" Basically the idea of starting a car Company was considered extremely stupid, and the idea of creating an electric car company was like stupidity squared. It was like wow that's dumb. The last time there was a successful mainstream car start-up was the Jeep in 1941, so it's been a while.

The reasoning behind Tesla, specifically, was that there needed to be an acceleration of electric vehicles. It became clear to me, and I think to a lot of people, that the big car companies had abandoned electric vehicles, and that if it was simply left up to the big car companies, we wouldn't see compelling electric cars. It seemed that as though if action wasn't taken, and it was simply left up to Detroit we would be waiting for a very long time.

I think there were issues with organized labor, there were issues with entrenched management that still wants to run the company like it's 1955. There were too many country club memberships and the management sort of focused on the wrong things. I think that became very clear in the movie

'Who Killed The Electric Car.' That hammered home the message that unless some new company came along and created an electric car, it'd be a long time before we would see sustainable transport. When I saw that I was like holy crap if this is not going to happen there needs to be a new car company that comes in and shows that it can be done, and that made clear that you could create a long-range, fast electric car. The only option is for a start-up to do electric vehicles, even though the historical track record for automotive start-ups in the United States is extremely bad. The only two American car companies in history that have not gone bankrupt are Ford and Tesla.

The key thing that needed to be done is to show that you can make an electric car that was good-looking, high performance, long-range, and if you made such a car that people would buy it. That they didn't have some fundamental affinity for gasoline.

Tesla was created in late 2003 and got going in mid-2004. My opinion of the success of Tesla at that point was so low, I thought maybe optimistically there's about a 10% chance of success. The beginning investment money was basically all me, not from the standpoint of this is a great way to make money, but I didn't want to have it on my conscience that other people that invested lost their money. If they had asked me what my opinion was on the likelihood of success I would say very low.

President Bush was in charge at that time, who's not the biggest proponent of electric vehicles, so it was really with no expectation of government assistance that we created the company. There was no electric vehicle incentive at all, nor was there any discussion, we didn't expect there to be any incentive or something.

My day job was SpaceX, but on the side, I was the chairman of Tesla Motors and helped formulate the business and product strategy with Martin and the rest of the team. Then we had a lot of drama. I think we exceeded the level Eberhard could handle. That became apparent in 2007. My initial thought was okay I'll hire some people, and work with the team, and I'll just sort of work on the part design, and the overall strategy or something, but I'll leave the day-to-day operations to a CEO that I'd hire. Unfortunately, that didn't work out. I've tried hiring a couple of CEOs, and I guess I couldn't find the right person, so then it came to 2008 and I was kinda co-CEO from 2007 to 2008 while trying to bring some other people up to speed, and then when the international market fell apart, and the economy fell apart, I had a choice basically of committing all my remaining resources in Tesla, or it's gonna die for sure. I thought okay if I'm going to do that, I've got to bite the bullet and run the company because there's just too much at stake. When you've got all your chips on the table, you've got to play the hand yourself. I mean, I tried pretty hard not to be the CEO. I could have been the CEO from day one, since I provided, like 95% of the money I could have been the CEO from day one, but the idea of being CEO of two startups at the same time was not appealing, and shouldn't be appealing, btw, if anyone is thinking that's a good idea. It's a really terrible idea. My initial thought was that I did not want to create an electric car company and run it myself because I was running SpaceX. The idea of running two companies, that's a lot of work. Imagine if somebody had two pretty demanding jobs, or you had one pretty demanding job, and now you got to do two of them. That kinda takes the fun away. I didn't want to be CEO of two companies. I tried really hard not to be actually, but something's gotta give. I feel that people sometimes don't realize that, but I just wasn't able to find the right person. In retrospect, I should have bitten the bullet and be Tesla CEO right from the beginning.

That's basically how Tesla came together.

14. The Plan

The goal at Tesla was to change people's thinking with respect to electric cars. They didn't believe in electric cars, they didn't think it was technologically possible. People were operating under the illusion that an electric car would have to be, let's say, aesthetically challenged - you know, low performance, low range, and kinda look like a golf cart. None of these had to be true, but I'd talk to people and say none of these things have to be true, you know, and you can have a long-range car, the physics is pretty obvious - what's the energy density of lithium-ion, and what's the energy usage per mile, it's pretty straight forward, and people would be like, oh, no no no, that can't work. I'd be like, where's the error in the calculations here? these are pretty obvious. Amazingly, people would either ignore it or say it can't be done like it's ridiculous. They felt that even if someone created an electric car with long-range and high-performance, that people wouldn't buy it because of some deep love of gasoline, and that it's vital to refuel in five minutes.

So the first order of business for Tesla was to try to create a car that fundamentally changed those perceptions. The basic business plan of Tesla I articulated in the very beginning when I wrote a piece called the Tesla Master Plan. As genius as it was, it was really dumb and simple, but I think it's the only path to success which was to start with a low-volume high-priced sports car.

Some may question whether this does any good for the world. Are we really in need of another high-performance sports car? Will it actually make a difference to global carbon emissions? Well, the answers are no and not much. However, that misses the point, unless you understand the Secret Master Plan alluded to above.

Part of the reason I wrote the first Master Plan was to defend against the inevitable attacks Tesla would face, accusing us of just caring about making cars for rich people. Implying that we felt there was a shortage of sports car companies or some other bizarre rationale. Unfortunately, the blog didn't stop countless attack articles on exactly these grounds, so it pretty much completely failed that objective.

However, the main reason was to explain how our actions fit into a larger picture so that they would seem less random. Some readers may not be aware of the fact that our long-term plan is to build a wide range of models, including affordably priced family cars. The overarching purpose of Tesla is to help expedite the move from a mine-and-burn hydrocarbon economy, towards a solar electric economy, which I believe to be the primary, but not exclusive, sustainable solution.

In short, The Secret Tesla Motors Master Plan (just between you and me) was:

Build sports car

Use that money to build an affordable car

Use that money to build an even more affordable car

While doing the above, also provide zero-emission electric power generation options.

So the simple three-step strategy of Tesla was, come out with a high-priced car at low volume, a mid-priced car at mid-volume, and then a low-priced car at high volume. Three major technology iterations, and then stepping up production volume by an order of magnitude in each case, which is damn fast for a small company to grow at that rate.

The reason we had to start off with step 1 was that it was all I could afford to do with what I made from PayPal, and I thought our chances of success were so low that I didn't want to risk anyone's funds in the beginning but my own.

As a small start-up, we didn't have the economies of scale of the big car companies. Plus we were working with the first generation of technology. Two things are really important in making technology available to the mass market, and making it affordable. Those two things are economy of scale, and being able to optimize the design. Usually by the third version of something it gets to reach the mass market potential. Using that as a sort of rule of thumb for the strategy I had.

Almost any new technology initially has a high unit cost before it can be optimized, and this is no less true for electric cars. The strategy of Tesla was to enter at the high end of the market, where customers are prepared to pay a premium, and then drive down the market as fast as possible to higher unit volume and lower prices with each successive model. If you look at any new technology development in almost any sphere you start with something that's expensive. Because the first thing is to make technology work, and then you go to optimizing the technology. If people are aware of the history of internal combustion engine cars, in the early days of gasoline cars they were considered toys for rich people because everybody else was riding a horse. So you need to go through this phase of having an expensive car that's available to a few, in order to get to the car that is available to the many. Consider say cellphones and how they started out, you know, in Wall Street 1 with this guy walking down with this brick on the beach, talking into a phone the size of a shoebox. Now we got a phone that is tiny, has the power of a supercomputer, and you can buy one for about 100 bucks. That's gone through many design iterations. With electric cars, we are trying to get to the mass market in three design iterations. Which is about as fast as you can do it.

Also, a low-volume car means a much smaller, simpler factory, albeit with most things done by hand. Without economies of scale, anything we built would be expensive, whether it was an economy sedan or a sports car. It didn't matter what that car looked like. If we would have made something that looked like a very standard Toyota Corolla, or a Ford Fusion, or something like that, it would have cost say $70,000. Nobody will pay that for what looks like a mid-sized economy sedan, they just won't. No one was going to pay $100k for an electric Honda Civic, no matter how cool it looked, or very few people would. But at least some people are willing to pay $100,000 for a fast sports car. There are only a few kinds of cars that people are willing to pay a high price for, a sports car being one of them, and really premium sedans being another.

Sometimes people think the reason we started with the sports car is that I somehow thought there's a shortage of sports cars in the world. Or that rich people really need a break or something like that. That was not the reason. It was simply that anything we produced would be expensive because we did not have the economies of scale necessary to make things inexpensive.

Our goal is not to sort of to become a big brand or to compete with Honda Civics, but rather to advance the cause of electric vehicles. The whole purpose of Tesla is to draw the rest of the car industry into electric cars. The more electric car programs I see announced the happier I am. The whole purpose behind Tesla, the reason I put so much of my time and money into helping create the business, is because we want to be a catalyst for accelerating the electric car revolution. The point of all this was, and remains, accelerating the advent of sustainable energy so that we can imagine far into the future and life is still good. That's what "sustainable" means. It's not some silly, hippy thing -- it matters for everyone. Our mission is fundamentally to transition the world to electric cars. I think most of the good that Tesla will accomplish is by putting a path through the jungle, to show what can be done with electric cars, and that's exactly what we're trying to affect, is to show people - hey, you can have a - hell of a better experience with an electric car than you can with a gasoline car.

I think it has taken a while for the industry to come around to this point, and I think it is largely at this point has become conventional wisdom that the future is electric cars. The only question is the interim period of this transitional period, but if you look at the pace of battery improvement, it is clear that it is inevitable. The future will be entirely electric. Almost everything that we have in our daily life is electric.

I certainly believe that the future is pure electric cars, not hybrids. For a while, at Tesla, we considered doing a plug-in hybrid, but as we got into the details of the design we found it was just impossible to make a great car in my opinion because you split the baby. I think hybrids are an interim step. They're sort of like an amphibian. You know, when life was going from the oceans to land, probably a lot of amphibians, but that's not the end solution. I think you want to go all-electric because that is the truly sustainable path, and I think if you split the baby and you have a car that is trying to be a good gasoline car and a good electric car, you end up being not as compelling as either a pure gasoline car or pure electric. We looked very closely at the plug-in hybrid thing. Basically what it comes down to is a technical point because we had to drill in real deep to appreciate why it wouldn't be ideal to have a plug-in hybrid. It's just going to have to be a better electric car or a better gasoline car. Also if all the cars in the world were hybrids, would we solve our oil addiction? no, we wouldn't. We might delay our day of reckoning a little bit, but we would not fundamentally change the equation. So the strategy we've decided to adhere to is a pure electric strategy. That's the reasoning that caused us to focus on electrics and continue to focus on electrics.

The success of Tesla as a company financially is going to be a function of the quality of the products that we produce. We have to make better cars than, say, GM and Chrysler. I don't see that as a huge challenge. The sad thing is that generally in the United States if someone can afford an expensive car, they do not buy an American car. I think in the 60s the U.S. made great cars, and before that made great cars, but then something happened in the 70s. I don't know what happened. A lot of bad things... architecture went to hell, fashion was questionable, and our cars turned to shit. I think the big American car companies sort of got complacent at a certain point, they just stopped trying to innovate. They didn't think anyone could sort of outdo them. I think as soon if you have that sort of attitude somebody is going to outdo you. The only way to bridge that is with innovation is to try to make electric cars better, sooner than they would otherwise be. As a friend of mine summarized, "The Tesla strategy long term is to make cars that don't suck."

If historians would look back at the impact of Tesla many years from now I think that Tesla hopefully advanced the advent of sustainable transport by something like a decade, maybe two decades. I do think electric cars are inevitable. I think it would happen anyway, just out of necessity. The goal of Tesla is to try to act as a catalyst to accelerate those sort of normal forces. The normal sort of market reaction would occur. It's very important that we accelerate the transition away from gasoline for environmental reasons, economic reasons, national security reasons. It's very very fundamental.

I think we helped set the ball in motion. Now what is important is to continue the momentum. People that really believe in sustainability, that really believe in the electric car revolution, people like yourselves are very important to the success of Tesla, and to the success of electric vehicles in general. There are still many people out there that don't believe in electric cars, they think nothing is going to happen. We have to overcome that negativity, otherwise, it's going to be way too slow, and there will be tremendous damage to the environment as a result. Word of mouth is super important, it's vital, and we need you to be able to go out there, and talk to people that you know and say 'Hey, electric cars are ready.' It's time to make it happen. If the big car companies see that our sales are good and that we are able to take a little bit of market share, I mean, we're a tiny company, so a drop in the bucket, but if they see that people are buying these cars, then they will have no choice but to conclude that electric cars are the right way to go, and that will accelerate the transition to sustainable transport.

We are just going to keep making more and more electric cars, and driving the price point down until the industry is very firmly electric. Until like maybe half of all cars made are electric or something like that. Which is not to say that we expect to make half of all cars. The car industry is very big. It's not as though there is one company to the exclusion of others. There are like a dozen car companies in the world of significance. The most that any company has is approximately 10% market share. It's not like somebody comes up with a car, and they suddenly kill everyone else, it's not like that.

We want to just have that catalytic effect until at least that occurs. I think the point at which we're approaching half of all new cars made are electric, then I think I would consider that to be the victory condition. The faster we can bring that day, the better.

15. SolarCity

That's Tesla and SpaceX, and I should mention certainly SolarCity.

SolarCity is part of the whole sustainable energy thing. You have to have sustainable means of producing and consuming energy, so even if you have electric cars, you have to have the other side of the equation. It's all well and good if you have electric cars, but how do you produce electricity? People will say, well, don't electric cars create pollution at the power plant level?

It should be noted that for any given source of fuel it is always better to generate the power at the power plant level and then charge electric cars and run them, for any given source of fuel. Power plants are much more efficient at extracting energy than internal combustion engines in a car. If you take say natural gas, which is the most prevalent hydrocarbon source fuel if you burn that in a modern General Electric natural gas turbine, you'll get about 60 percent efficiency. If you put that same fuel in an internal combustion engine car, you get about 20 percent efficiency. The reason is, in the stationary power plant, you can afford to have something that weighs a lot more, is voluminous, and you can take the waste heat and run a steam turbine and generate a secondary power source. So in effect, even after you've taken transmission loss into account and everything, even using the same source fuel, you're at least twice as better off charging an electric car, at least twice as efficient, and usually more like three times as efficient. So, for any given source of fuel, even if the whole world were always going to be powered by hydrocarbons, it would still make sense to do electric cars.

Of course, we must find a sustainable means of generating energy as well. So, how do you produce energy in a sustainable way? I think that the most likely, well, the main candidate for energy generation is actually solar. I'm quite confident that the primary means of power generation will be solar. I think the physics of this is rather obvious, because the Earth is almost entirely solar-powered today as it is. I mean, it's really indirect fusion, that's what it is. We've got this giant fusion generator in the sky called the Sun, and we just need to tap a little bit of that energy for purposes of human civilization. What most people know, but don't realize they know, is that the world is almost entirely solar-powered already. The whole weather system is solar-powered, almost the entire weather system is solar-powered, some of it is from Earth rotation. Our entire system of precipitation is powered by the Sun. It's the basis for the whole ecosystem as you learned in elementary school. The Sun powers the plants and the plankton, and the animals eat that, and we eat the animals and plants. Plants are essentially a solar-powered chemical reaction. So the ecosystem of Earth and the lifeforms on Earth are almost entirely solar-powered already. The whole ecosystem is 99.999%, powered by the Sun, except for some chemotrophs at the bottom of the ocean. We'd be a frozen ice ball at, I don't know, three or four Kelvin if it weren't for the Sun. It's rather obvious that one should try to take a little portion of that energy, and it's not much, and convert that into electricity for use by society. To run civilization essentially it's a really kind of tiny amount compared to the amount that hits the Earth. It's actually a very tiny amount of energy relative to the amount of energy that the Sun sends in our general direction. We could, in fact, power the entire world with solar power quite easily.

I'm confident that solar will beat everything, hands down, including natural gas. Even when I was in college it was very obvious to me that electric would be the right thing to back. The fundamental efficiency of solar plus electric is an unbeatable combination at a first principles physics level for having the most efficient sustainable system. To me, this is as obvious as day and night.

The genesis of SolarCity was at Burning Man with two of my cousins, Lyndon and Peter Rive who are awesome guys. One is an engineer and one is sort of more sales and overall leadership. They are both very good guys, and they were sort of trying to think about what they should do after their first startup. They did a company called Everdream, which did large-scale management of computers. If you're got like 60,000 computers it's kind of hard to manage them, so they created software that allows companies to do that. That company got sold to Dell, and they did pretty well.

So we were at Burning Man with my cousins and they were thinking about what to do next. I was trying to convince them that they should do solar because I just thought it was an area that needed people like them - really good entrepreneurs - and since I was somewhat overcommitted, I thought, well look, if you guys will do a solar company, I'll provide all the funding and whatever guidance or help I can provide.

I thought it was really important that there'd be good entrepreneurs like them in solar because it just wasn't doing very well as an industry. I thought people weren't focusing on the right problem. I said I think there's a real need for great entrepreneurs in the solar industry, and if they were willing to start a solar power company then I would completely back them on that. So they took me up on the offer and created SolarCity. That's kinda what they did and did an awesome job.

They really deserve the credit for making SolarCity for what it is, they have done an amazing job.

We have a very simple goal which is to make solar power as available and widespread as possible. SolarCity does everything except the panel. Everybody thought that the panel was the problem but actually - it's a problem, but it's not the most important problem. The panel is somewhat commoditized at this point. What a lot of people don't realize is that making standard efficiency solar panels is about as hard as making drywall. It's super easy. I'd say drywall is probably harder, it's easier than making freaking drywall at this point. The cost of that will be driven down to a very low number, almost down to the raw material cost.

I think what China is doing in the solar panels arena is awesome because they are lowering the cost of solar power for the world. I think a good rule of thumb is, don't compete with China with a commodity product. You're really asking for trouble in that scenario. Does anyone think about competing with China when it comes to drywall manufacturing? probably not. They have these huge Giga factories that are created out in the Chinese desert with a ton of funding from the Chinese government. It's a giant donation from the Chinese government. Thanks that's awesome.

The real cost of solar and the real challenge of solar is called the balance of system, with everything except the panel. The hard part is the whole system, it's designing something for a particular rooftop. What is a thorny problem is trying to figure out how to get solar on tens of thousands, eventually hundreds of thousands, of rooftops. You have all these heterogeneous rooftops, then you got to mount the system, you have to wire it up, connect the inverters, connect it to the grid, do all the permitting. There's a whole bunch of thorny unglamorous stupid problems, but if somebody doesn't optimize them they are still going to cost a lot of money. A lot of them are not fun problems or exciting problems to optimize, but they are the problems that matter in the cost of solar power. So SolarCity works on a balance of system, and they own the end-customer relationship, which includes the customer-owner experience, designing the system to a particular rooftop, the wiring, the inverter, the after service, and figuring out the financing of it all. They're kind of like Dell or Apple, you know, Apple doesn't make the CPU or the memory or the hard drives, but they design the overall system, and they provide it to customers through the sales and marketing service.

You got to do it at scale, and you got to manage all these systems. Even though the after-sale service is small, when you got like hundreds of thousands of systems, that's a lot to manage. It's kind of like you've got to re-roof millions of buildings, and then figure out how the grid interconnects work and then manage all those systems. If you've got hundreds of thousands, or maybe millions of systems, eventually, you've got to manage all these distributed systems. That's what SolarCity is doing, it's trying to improve the economics of solar power, and they're doing a great job. I don't run the company, so the credit for SolarCity goes to the two key guys who run that company. You've got this really complex distributed utility, effectively, which I think plays to their prior strength in creating really scalable software for managing hundreds of thousands of computers in a distributed fashion.

I'd basically show up at the board meetings to hear, what's the good news this time? We had maybe a couple of bad board meetings, late 2008 there were some bad board meetings, but for the most part apart from a few times when the macroeconomic conditions were really terrible, they just did an amazing job with almost no help from me. Yeah, they deserve the vast majority of the credit for the success of that company.

For them, the more rapacious the competition on solar panels, the better.

You can buy a solar system or you can lease a solar system. Most people choose to lease. The thing about solar power is that it doesn't have any feedstock or operational costs, so once it's installed, it's just there. Solar is very much a cost to capital type of business, once you paid for it there is no fuel, it works for decades. It'll work for probably a century. Therefore, the key thing to do is to get the cost of that initial installation low, and then get the cost of the financing low. Those are the two factors that drive the cost of solar. SolarCity is about packaging it at all so it's very easy to use. Basically, make one call and make it all seamless and painless.

Essentially, SolarCity raises a chunk of capital from say, a company or a bank, and they have an expected return on that capital, Google is one of our big partners here. With that capital, SolarCity purchases and installs the panel on the roof, and then charge the homeowner or business owner a monthly lease payment, which is less than the utility bill. It's no money down, and your utility bill decreases. Pretty good deal.

What it amounts to is a giant distributed utility, and it's working in partnership with the house and business, and in competition with the big sort of monopoly utility. I think it's a good thing, because utilities have been this monopoly, and people haven't had any choice. Effectively, it's the first time there's been competition for this monopoly because the utilities have been the only ones that owned those power distribution lines, but now it's on your roof. I think it's very empowering for homeowners and businesses, I think it's like literally 'Power to the people', like literally. It's awesome because you know utilities never had any competition before, and now they actually have to think about the cost of power, and they have to figure out better ways to do it.

SolarCity is essentially a giant distributed utility that's based on that giant fusion reactor in the sky. It's something that will last for a very long time, and I ultimately think that we will generate more energy from the Sun than from any other source. We've made huge progress in that direction, and that's why I'm confident we'll beat natural gas.

So SolarCity is about sustainable energy creation whereas Tesla is about sustainable energy consumption.

16. All Systems are Go!

So let's see, the Falcon 1 was the first rocket we built. The Falcon 1 was developed from a clean sheet to on the launch pad in three years, and that includes the entire vehicle. It's the fastest launch vehicle development in history, including wartime. The entire vehicle was designed, build, and tested at SpaceX, almost, there were a few key pieces that were procured outside, but the big stuff was developed from scratch. We kind of had to do that, because if we were to cobble together stuff from existing quasi-official components, then we would have been unable to reduce the cost. Because to the degree that you inherit the legacy components, while you may inherit their heritage, of course, you also inherit their cost. I don't want to paint all aerospace suppliers with the same negative brush. I think there are definitely some good ones out there, but generally, we found that if you want something cheap, fast, and that's probably going to work, then you should use a regular commercial supplier. If you want something that's expensive, takes a long time, and might work, use an aerospace supplier. So of necessity, we were forced to make the major items, like the engines, and the stages, and the avionics, and the launch ops, and all that from scratch.

The idea behind the Falcon 1 was that it was built as a scale model, so we could test out the technologies. When we made mistakes they were made at a smaller scale, rather than jump immediately to a large rocket and make mistakes that cost ten times as much.

Two years after starting the company we had the qualification article of Falcon 1 on the launch pad at

Vandenberg, and then about six months later we did the static fire. We initially set up at Vandenberg Air Force Base, which is about two hours away from Santa Barbara. The first launch was going to be from the Space Launch Complex at Vandenberg as soon as the Titan IV departed. Unfortunately, Titan IV got significantly delayed, so we were forced to move from Vandenberg to Kwajalein in the Marshall Islands. So we had two launch sites and control centers. We expected to have two rockets - one at Vandenberg and one at Kwajalein, possibly on the pad at the same time. We had our own little island there called Omelek. It sounds a bit like a Bond villain launching rockets from a remote tropical island with Dr. Evil or something.

From May of 2005 to November of 2005 we were able to set up a launch facility at Kwajalein, which is quite difficult because the island we were given in the Kwajalein Atoll was - just had nothing on it, it was just jungle. We're not currently using the Marshall Islands launch site. The logistics are just too difficult, getting out there. It's like Waterworld out there, it's miles from anywhere. It's convenient in some ways but then inconvenient from a logistics standpoint. We had to bring in power, water, RP - rocket propellant (kerosene), all the pressurant, offices, that sort of thing. We had many challenges, liquid oxygen in particular. Kwajalein is 5000 miles away from California and over 2000 miles away from Hawaii, which is the nearest source of liquid oxygen.

We managed to have our first countdown right on Thanksgiving 2005, had turkey on the island.

It took us four countdowns to get to the first attempt at launch, which was in March of 2006, which failed. The first rocket didn't go very far, went about a minute up, and then there was an engine fire and that was it. The engine shut off about 30 seconds into the flight, it continued ballistically for another 30 seconds, and then landed like an anti-tank weapon maybe a couple of hundred yards away from the launch site, in tiny fragments. In fact, I spend the day picking up bits of rocket pieces off the reef, which sucks. The telemetry showed that there was a kerosene leak at the turbopump inlet pressure transducer, which started about 400 seconds prior to liftoff. You couldn't see it because the wind was blowing and kerosene is very difficult to see. When the wind's blowing you can't actually see that it's leaking. We didn't know why the leak had arisen, and it was a big shock to us. The failure review board, which was co-chaired by Pete Worden of NASA/Ames, concluded that it was due to corrosion, - stress corrosion cracking of the aluminum 'B' nut on the engine. That leak ignited a few seconds prior to the start, and the fire basically burned through the entire powered flight. About 25 seconds into the flight it burned through a helium pneumatic line, resulting in losses in helium pressurant, and that caused the pump pre-valves to shut, and essentially turning off the engine. Other than that, everything looked good. The vehicle was proceeding along its designed trajectory within 0.2 degrees. All first-stage systems were nominal, and all avionics were nominal. The sad thing is that the problem was a corrosion issue due to the Kwaj climate. It's a problem that would not have occurred at the launch site at Vandenberg.

We took a bunch of corrective actions. We improved vehicle robustness by eliminating as many fittings as possible and going to orbital tube welds. There were a number of other changes. We also added more detailed procedures, more personnel per process. The biggest single change was, we had messed up software monitoring launch and automation, we were monitoring approximately 30 variables. We went to monitoring 800, including both the vehicle and the ground support equipment. We would have caught the fuel leak if we had this system in place. The countdown was now also fully automated, which reduces the potential for human error and allowed us to review the data. It also allowed us to take some personnel out of the countdown process.

We had two more failures after that one. The second and third flights arguably got to space, but they did not reach full orbital velocity. Demo Flight 2, which took place in March 2007, made it almost all the way to orbit. The post-flight review showed late in the second burn a roll control anomaly. The only orbit critical issue was the lack of slosh baffles in the second stage LOX tank, which caused a coupling of the controller slosh modes. Exposed the propellant line going into the engine, it sucked in helium gas and flamed up the engine.

Flight three also didn't get all the way to orbit. With the stage separation, the residual thrust on the first stage basically send it back and gently collided with the second stage, but it meant that the second stage did not exit the interstage, which joins the first and second stage. The interstage is kind of a sleeve that joins the first and second stage. So when the second stage engine ignited, it ignited in that interstage. The impact of the first stage on the second stage didn't cause any damage, but the problem was that the second stage ignited in the interstage which it was not designed to do. You had this huge plasma blowback because it was igniting kinda within a closed space, that fried the second stage.

I was really devastated, that was awful, and so was the rest of the company. It was tough, tough going. At some point, we'll release the blooper reel, but I think we'll wait a few years before we do that. That was a lot of pain.

We learned with each successive flight and were able to eventually with the fourth flight in late 2008 to reach orbit. I was so stressed out at the launch, I didn't even actually feel elation, I just felt relief. I think there's a pretty powerful fear response ingrained because of the images of those rocket failures kind of going through my mind as I'm seeing the rocket launch. It's extremely nerve-racking. The thing with rocket launch is that all your work is distilled into these few minutes, particularly the first several seconds around the lift-off. Because the worst thing that can happen with a rocket is if you have an engine failure or some huge failure right above the launch pad. The whole thing can come down with about 1 million pounds of TNT equivalent and destroy the whole launchpad. That's what's going through my mind in case you're wondering. When it clears the lighting towers, and it's gotten further enough away from not actually destroying the launchpad, then you sort of go down a notch. Then after the first stage separation that's another one, and when the second stage lights up. You sort of go down in intensity as the rocket is going up. After the rocket lifts off, 9 minutes later it's either in orbit or it's exploded. That's a nervous 9 minutes.

That fourth launch was a very very close call because I'd run out of money, that was with the last bit of money we had. We were down to our last pennies. In fact, I only thought I had enough money for three launches, but we were able to scrape together enough to just barely make it into a fourth launch. So, that was a bit of a nail-biter — thank goodness — that launch succeeded, If it hadn't SpaceX wouldn't be around. Thank goodness that happened. I think the saying is fourth time is the charm?

There was really no ability to raise outside money in a meaningful way in 2008 because of the financial crisis. There weren't a lot of people who were keen on funding a rocket company. I think if we'd said: "yes, our fourth launch wasn't successful, but the fifth one's the charm" that would not have gone down well. You can imagine trying to go to raise money and saying, well yes, we've just had four failures and the world is in financial ruin, but would you like to give us some money? It would be a definite no.

I think perhaps if I had been more knowledgeable we would have gotten to orbit sooner than flight 4. I think we had a critical mass of technical talent, and just enough money, and a design that was sensible, those were probably the three ingredients that resulted in success eventually.

The thing about a rocket is that the passing grade is 100%, and you don't actually get to test the real environment that the rocket is going to be in. At least with a car, you can do a recall or a software update. It's not going to happen with the rockets. It's like passing grade is 100%, which induces anxiety. I think the best analogy for rocket engineering is a software analogy. It would be like if you had to write a whole bunch of complicated software modules. You can never run them together as an integrated whole, and you could not run them on the target computer, so when you're testing them you have to test them individually and not in the actual computer that they are going to run on. Then you put all the modules together in a completely different computer, but the first time you run it, it has to run with no bugs. That's basically the essence of it.

Thankfully, the fourth launch did work, which I think gave customers of ours, NASA, and others enough confidence to award us additional launch contracts, and for additional private investment to come in and help fund the company besides myself. I think that was very helpful that coming out of PayPal I had a bunch of capital that I could spend developing rocket technology, even though I had no experience in rockets at all. If I'd tried to get funding from a venture capitalist, they would have been angry that I met with them, probably. Even in the best of circumstances, space is outside the comfort zone of most venture capitalists. Although in a few years - I think five years after starting the company was when the first venture capital came in, and I would like to thank those investors for having faith there at an early stage to invest in a rocket company, we raised some good partners there.

Then about five or six years after the start of the company we started getting support from NASA. Then we also developed the Dragon spacecraft, because somewhat opportunistically NASA announced they were going to retire the Space Shuttle. They didn't have the budget to develop a cargo transport capability to the Space Station via the normal large government way, and so they put it out to bid to commercial industry, for the first time in NASA history. It was quite a big step, and we were lucky enough to win one of those contracts. Then the other company wasn't able to execute, so they got cut, and so we ended up being the primary means of transporting cargo to and from the Space Station.

NASA's certainly been a key customer of ours for a few years. The first five years or six years of the company nobody would talk to us on the government side, NASA or the military. We got a few sort of fringe customers on the commercial side, that was it. We didn't have any government anything for the first half-decade. Then NASA nibbled a little bit and we were able to get a small contract, then we were able to get a much larger contract.

I just want to say that I'm incredibly grateful to NASA for supporting SpaceX, despite the fact that our rocket crashed. It was awesome, — so thank you very much to the people that had the faith to do that. I'm a big fan of NASA. In fact, at one point my password was "ILOVENASA" literally that was my password. Hopefully, I don't have some old email account. I'm NASA's biggest fan, and SpaceX would not be where it is without the help of NASA, both historically the great things that NASA has done, and currently with the business that

NASA gives us, and the expert advice and everything, so I should make sure to very strongly credit NASA in this arena in terms of how helpful they've been. We have a number of NASA personnel working at SpaceX. In fact, we also have NASA personnel who are permanently resident at SpaceX.

So we go from 2002, where we were basically clueless, and then to Falcon 1, the smallest useful orbital rocket that we could think of, which would deliver half a ton to orbit. That rocket ended up costing around $6 million compared to other rockets in that class, which were about say $25 million. Yeah, like a quarter. We were able to go from the Falcon 1 to begin designing the Falcon 9, which is an order of magnitude larger vehicle and in fact, has more than 20 times the payload. It's got a payload to orbit of over ten tons. From those first days, where myself and the team were picking up bits of rocket off the reef, things have come a long way thank goodness.

17. Roadster

The initial product of Tesla Motors was a high-performance electric sports car called the Tesla Roadster. I'll give you the reasoning why we did start with the car that we did start with. There are certain things that I thought were important to happen so that the electric vehicle happened. That there was a success in the electric vehicle arena. The incumbent companies were convinced that it was not possible to create an electric car that looked good, had a good range, performance, and so forth. But even if you did make such a car that it would not sell, because people had this love of gasoline. Some had programs, but those programs, for the most part, were I would say almost entirely quite low volume, and more inclined towards satisfying regulators.

So, we just decided to make a car that's pretty hard to ignore. Whereas discussions or Powerpoint are much easier to ignore, everything does work on Powerpoint so there is a reason for skepticism there. But having an actual car, one that is fully homologated for use on the roads and meets all the safety standards and everything, was really important.

The previous electric cars had not been compelling, they had been kind of like golf carts, and it just wasn't true that an electric car had to be these sort of ugly, slow-moving golf carts. We had to show that it was possible to create a compelling electric car. We needed to show people that an electric car could in fact be the best car and if you made such a thing that people would buy it. The point of Tesla was to make a viable electric car that broke the paradigm of what people thought of as an electric car.

Critical to making that happen was an electric car without compromises. In order to be successful it had to have sex appeal, great acceleration, great handling, long-range, you know all those things. Those things were really important to fundamentally change the perception. While some people are willing to buy a car that is good for the environment even if it's worse, for most people it was much easier if it also happened to be the best car. So we did the Tesla Roadster.

It was a little rough going in the beginning. We had so many challenges with the Roadster, pretty much everything went wrong. Not the hard stuff, but the stuff that is sort of theoretically easier.

The first thing we did was sort of create a test mule. We still have the original mule One of Tesla Roadster. Our very first mule was really taking a Lotus Elise, jamming an AC Propulsion power train into it, and then making it drive.

This is a point that may be helpful to entrepreneurs out there that are creating companies. The reality is that the creation of Tesla was based on two fundamentally false premises. That turned out in retrospect staggeringly dumb. One was that we would be able to use a slightly modified Lotus Elise, add the Tesla battery pack, and an electric power train using AC propulsion system technology, and then be done, and get to market fast with an electric car. In reality when you convert a car to electric, and you want to make it something that passes all of the federal safety standards and all the legalities for the regular car, you invalidate all of the crash tests. The battery pack ended up being too big and we had to stretch the chassis. We couldn't use the air-conditioning system because that was previously run off the engine power. So we needed to have a new AC system, create a new wiring harness, all new suspension, and all new brakes because the car was 30% heavier.

It ended up costing us way more to convert the frame designed for a gasoline car to electric than if we just designed something from scratch. Then the other part was that we licensed much of the technology from AC propulsion, which turned out that none of that was actually producible, it was really difficult to manufacture. As it turned out, the AC Propulsion power train didn't really work very well, and was not scalable for production - had a lot of issues - and so we had to completely redesign the power train. Then because our car ended up being 50% heavier and had different weight distribution and low points, we invalidated all the crash structures and had to completely redesign the chassis. In the end, I think about 7% of the parts were in common with the Elise, almost nothing, but we actually inherited some of the limitations of the Elise. It's like if you have a particular house in mind that you want to build, instead of building that house from a fresh start, you take some existing house and you end up modifying everything except one wall in the basement. So, in the end, only 6 or 7% of the Tesla Roadster had parts in common with any other car period. On the other hand, if we had to do everything from scratch maybe we would not have started the company. Ultimately I think it took five times the amount of capital to bring the Roadster to market and iron out the issues.

Then we needed to get to an actual Roadster prototype as a production design. So we redesigned the body. I was basically the chief designer of the body. My two favorite cars were the McLaren F1 and the Porsche 911, so there are sort of elements of that in the design. I don't think I'm a good designer by the way. It's actually relatively easy to design a sports car that looks good because the proportions naturally lend itself to excitement and beauty. It's incredibly hard to design a sedan that looks good.

The Roadster was designed to beat a gasoline sports car like a Porsche or Ferrari in a head-to-head showdown. We didn't want to create another DeLorean. The DeLorean looked kind of cool, but it was really weak on performance, it was unreliable, and there were lots of little issues with the car. We just didn't want to be in that situation.

We managed to make the first deliveries of the Tesla Roadster in 2008. The rule at Tesla is whoever puts down the deposit for the car first, that's their order in line. I put down the first deposit for the first Roadster, Roadster number one, the first production which was fully department of transport legal and everything, and it got delivered I think in February 2008.

Frankly, although this car passed all the regulatory requirements to pass as a street-legal car, it was completely unsafe. It broke down all the time. I remember in the early days giving a test drive to Larry Page and Sergey Brin, who are good friends of mine, I've known them actually for a really long time. There was like some bug in the system and dammit the car would only go 10 miles an hour, I was like: "I swear guys it goes way faster than this" but they were kind enough to put a little investment into the company nevertheless, despite the world's worst demo.

We were able to fix those and get production ramped up. We worked super hard to make the car compelling as to make it a no-brainer to buy an electric car. We put so much effort into achieving that objective.

The Tesla Roadster was the world's first mass-produced highway-capable electric car. It was really quite historic. This may sound strange, but there has never been a mass-produced electric car outside of golf carts. I think it's sort of slightly sad that it was the first production electric car out of the modern era, and there were not more electric cars on the road.

The elevator speech thing was: "The Tesla Roadster is faster than a Ferrari and more efficient than a Prius." It actually had better acceleration than any Ferrari except the Enzo. Zero to 60 in 3.9 seconds, it beat any Aston Martin or Ferrari in acceleration. In fact, on the Tokyo test track, our standard Roadster beat a Porsche TT3. The real sort of million-dollar supercars, obviously those will beat it, but it was pretty much faster than any normal sports car, and it was really easy to drive.

The responsiveness of the car was incredible. We wanted really to have people feel as though they've almost got to mind-meld with the car, so you just feel like you and the car are kind of one, and as you corner and accelerate, it just happens, like the car has ESP. You can do that with an electric car because of its responsiveness. You can't do that with a gasoline car. I think that's a profound difference, and people only experience that when they have a test drive. It's got like a cool sort of subtle kind of jet turbine sound because the motor goes up to 40,000 RPM. Also, you can accelerate really fast, like let's say you're at a stoplight, you can take off and you can floor it and not seem like a jackass.

The early proto Roadsters that we had were vehicle-to-grid. You do get a lot of complications with that if you backflow power through the car into the wall. Like when is the car allowed to do that, when is it not, and then how much do you allow the car battery to be drawn down? and then people, I think, would be pretty upset if the lights are on in the house, but they can't drive their car because all the power in the house shuts down. I think the right solution is to decouple it.

If you wanted a high-performance car with a clean conscience, this was the only option. Although the Roadster was a fast sports car, it used less energy per mile than a Prius. In fact, the battery pack only had the equivalent of two gallons of gasoline worth of energy. Even if you took power from a coal power plant, so it's entirely coal and you took into account transmission losses and charging losses and so forth, and say how much CO_2 you generate per mile, it was still less than a Prius because stationary power plants being quite energy-efficient. Even if 100% of electricity came from coal, the Roadster produced less CO_2 per mile than a Prius, and had twice the energy efficiency of a Prius.

The Roadster's greatest value was really breaking the misconceptions around electric cars. Showing that you can have a cool electric car that goes long distances, almost 250 miles without a charge. That was longer than any electric car in history, in fact, the Roadster set many world records in terms of its range. We had one customer take it over 300 miles on a trip. There are actually two customers. One was a rally in Australia, which is technically 500 km, and it was the first time that an electric car finished that rally without recharging, and another one was in Europe.

The biggest impact of the Roadster was in changing the perception of what an electric car can be, and showing that you can do amazing things with an electric car. That they are better than gasoline cars in a lot of respects. We were able to disprove those axiomatic errors. We were able to show that by making a sports car that was aesthetically pleasing, high-performance, very fast, great handling, long-range—as much range as you'd get from a gas tank—that helped break people's perception of what an electric car could be, and if you made such a car people would buy it. We were able to change people's minds one by one by giving them a test drive.

It still took a long time. Nobody had heard of the company, they thought Tesla was a rock band, or if you're a scientist Nikola Tesla of course. By the way, those guys are awesome, they have been huge supporters all along. They never bugged us that we like used their name or anything, so rock on Tesla the band.

The Roadster had a powerful catalytic effect in that when Bob Lutz, the chairman of General Motors at the time, saw our press release, took our press release, went down to his development team, and said: "if a little company can do this why can't we?" He's told the story many times, his engineers told him that you couldn't build an electrical car, and he told them that they needed to get going, because if a small company in California can do it, so can GM. That is what got General Motors to do their electric vehicle program. I really like Bob Lutz, by the way, I actually agree with most of the things that Bob says, and I have a lot of respect for Bob. I just want that to be clear because sometimes people may sort of make out that somehow I don't like Bob, but I have a tremendous amount of respect for Bob. I think Bob articulated it well which is that we have a vast number of vehicles that are gasoline. We need to make, therefore, a vast number of compelling electric vehicles; just building up that production line and switching out the install base will take decades, so we will have an addiction to oil for some period of time. The question is really, can we minimize that time, and in doing so minimize the potential damage to the environment.

At the time GM used to be the world's largest car company, and when the world's largest car company announces they're going to go do an electric vehicle program, others tend to follow. It in turn encouraged the other manufacturers to do electric vehicle programs as well. That's what got the Chevy Volt rolling, in fact, Bob credits Tesla with the inspiration for the Volt. That in turn got Nissan to do the Leaf.

So the Tesla Roadster kind of got things going. Ultimately it is what we induce other companies to do that will have a greater impact than the cars we make ourselves.

18. Hard Times

It's hard to describe but Tesla was in a really dire situation at the end of 2007.

Chris Paine who did the documentary called 'Who killed the electric car?' did a follow-up documentary called 'Revenge of the electric car' he ended up following 4 car companies one of which was us. The movie followed what was the most difficult time for Tesla in its history with multiple near-death experiences. We had multiple near-death experiences, like death on the nose, like right in front of you. If you're curious about seeing the early history of Tesla then "Revenge of the electric car" is a great movie to watch.

The real key thing was from mid-2007 to mid-2009 that two-year period was super bad. I think some of the stumbles were silly mistakes we made ourselves and some were market externalities.

It had come to light that the car's cost would be $140,000, we had been selling it for $92,000. I wish we didn't have to raise prices, it sucked, but I couldn't carry Tesla by myself, I just didn't have the resources to do it. We can't sell cars for less than they cost us to produce. We got some anger from people, they felt that we had done like a bait and switch, and it is sort of true it was sort of a bait and switch.

We had made so many mistakes at the beginning of Tesla that we basically had to recapitalize almost completely in 2007. Almost every decision we made was wrong. We had to make some really dramatic changes. Really just recapitalize the business, and invest about twice what we originally had expected, and what we expected as the outer limit.

At the beginning of Tesla and Solar City, I thought the probability of success was so low that I provided all of the money. All of the money just came from me personally, I didn't want to ask people and other investors for money if I thought we were going to die because I thought we would. I invested entirely the money that I got from PayPal, all of that got invested into Tesla, Solar City, and SpaceX. I had to take all of my reserve capital and invest it into Tesla, which was very scary because obviously it would be very sad to have the fruits of my labor with Zip2 and PayPal not amount to anything. But there was no question in my mind that I would do that because Tesla was too important to let die. The difficulty is that in that situation there's so much responsibility that you have to the employees, and the investors who came along, it would've been extremely disappointing if I would've not been able to keep my responsibility to have the company survive.

That forced us to scale back our plans a little bit, and we had to do a layoff. We had to raise the money internally from existing investors. I had to put up a lot of the money personally because there was just no money. That was sort of a hair-raising time for the company. Once just to keep Tesla alive I had to wire $3 million personally with no guarantee of anything, basically wire the funds and say use it, otherwise, we wouldn't be able to make the payroll.

I'll tell you where things were in 2008, which was the most difficult time for Tesla as it was for many companies. We were able to solve the problems, but then as time went by the companies needed more money, and just when we were able to solve the problems the economy was going into a tailspin. We were in the process of raising a $100 million financing round to take Tesla to the next level. That began in sort of the summer of 2008, and then we ran smack into the worst economic recession since the Great Depression The whole financial market was crashing, and we ran into, you know, a force 5 hurricane. That's when the financing round fell apart, nobody wanted to give us money. We weren't able to raise any money at all.

I certainly did not anticipate that we would have the worst economic climate since the Great Depression, and one which was just proportionately bad for cars. General Motors and Chrysler went bankrupt. The car industry is a very difficult one and electric cars may be especially difficult, I mean if you look in the United States the next youngest car company was Chrysler, they were almost 100 years old, and they went bankrupt. Now they are a division of Fiat. It was not an environment that was conducive to start-ups trying to raise money, and a start-up company that's making electric cars to boot sounded like stupidity squared. Investors would be angry that we even asked them.

In fact, some other electric vehicle start-ups like Fisker and Coda went bankrupt and we barely made it, it was super close. I mean General Motors went bankrupt, I mean General Effin' Motors! and here we were, a young company selling a very optional car, people didn't need $100,000 sports car.

It would've been terrible particularly in the case of Tesla, but also in the case of SpaceX 2008 was awful because we got the third launch failure in a row of the Falcon one at SpaceX. We had the economic tsunami take place and that made things even worse. If we would've not succeeded we would've been used as a counterexample for why people shouldn't do electric cars or shouldn't try to build private rockets. That would've been really bad, it would've been a double whammy. People would've used Tesla as just another stupid car company. That would've been terrible. It's pretty hard fighting a two-front war in the middle of the Siberian winter, and both fronts are really freaking hard.

There was quite a bit of schadenfreude in the media, who was sort of like, we had the temerity to try to create a car company. It was like "who do these arrogant jerks think they are, they think they can create a car company, you know the hell with them they are just going to die" There were multiple blogs that were maintaining a Tesla death watch. That really pumps you up you know.

Then SolarCity had a deal with Morgan Stanley, and Morgan Stanley had to renege on the deal because they themselves were running out of money. So it looked like all three companies were going to die. We had to figure out how do we get through this dark period and not go bankrupt.

I had to make a choice then, either I was going to have to take all of my capital that I'd made from my sale of PayPal to eBay and invest it in Tesla, or Tesla would die. I was like man if I invest everything there's a chance that we will survive if I don't invest everything there's no chance. The only choice I had was to invest all the money that I had left. I thought I would lose all my money that's what I thought would occur, but that was not the hard decision. The hard decision was that I had two companies, SpaceX and Tesla, and you know if you've been a part of creating these companies it feels like a child. I could either take the money that I had left and divide it between SpaceX and Tesla, or I could say no I'm going to let one company die and give all the money to the other. That was the hard decision, not whether I should give all my money, that was easy.

I was also going through a divorce, so my personal life was somewhat in shambles. It was a terrible time, everything was going wrong at once... three rocket failures in a row... Tesla financing round was falling apart... SolarCity was having difficulties... getting divorced.. getting attacked by some in the media. Every bad thing you could imagine... It was really terrible. I was very sad.

So I put all of my money into Tesla, and most of the existing investors agreed to fund the company, which amounted to about $40 million, 20 million of which came from me. I was tapped out I had to borrow money for rent after that from friends. That was actually a bit awkward that I had to borrow money from friends for living expenses.

If things didn't work out I would have been negative - essentially - but because I was willing to invest everything that I had, the other investors in the company were willing to put up the other half of the money that was needed to keep Tesla alive.

In addition to all the stuff happening, I was getting dumped on massively in the press. I was being accused of being an idiot, a charlatan, an idiot, and a charlatan, not even a good charlatan. This is basically where Top Gear falsely implied that the Tesla Roadster had run out of energy when they tested it, which it didn't. The whole vehicle has a detailed computer log so we can see it. Also when we dropped the car off, one of our guys happened to see a script sitting on the table. They already dropped the car off and he was reading through the script, and in the script, the car breaks down. Like, wait a second you already wrote the script before we even gave you the car? there's something wrong about that. We were hoping that it wouldn't be that bad, but when we later did the Tesla IPO roadshow, we got one investor after the other asking us why our car broke down in Top Gear. Particularly in Europe, every investor asked us why our car broke down. We said this is ridiculous. To add salt to the wound Top Gear just kept repeating that episode.

For sure if I hadn't invested everything I had there would've been no chance. Between Tesla, SpaceX and SolarCity I went all in. That wasn't the plan at the beginning by the way. Peter Thiel has been a big supporter, he invested in SpaceX at a very important time in 2008 before we reached orbit. After our third failure, but before our first success. So big credit to Peter and Luke Nosek and the other guys at Founders Fund, basically my buddies from PayPal. My buddies from PayPal saved my butt you know. It was really good.

At the end of 2008, the fourth launch worked, that was all the money we had, but nothing more. We just barely scraped together enough to do the fourth launch. Then there was a whole bunch of dramas that - skipping a bunch of drama - the worst point was probably just the weekend before Christmas 2008. We had maybe about a week's worth of cash in the bank or less. There was very little time left in the year to resolve these things, there were like two or three business days left in the year. That was literally - we would have gone bankrupt a few days after Christmas. I thought we would probably die. I think it would have been irrational to have any other view. It was looking pretty grim.

I remember waking up on the Sunday before Christmas thinking, damn this is the closest I've ever come to having a nervous breakdown. I never thought I was someone who was capable of a nervous breakdown, I thought nervous breakdowns are ridiculous, why would people have such a thing? I didn't, but I could see it, I was within sight of it. I thought this sucks, this is terrible. I think once you snapped you probably don't realize it, because you've gone insane. Your ability to just sort of look in the mirror psychologically is substantially impaired. Probably most insane people don't think they are insane. I think I came as close as I'll ever come. It was just like geez. It was quite a terrible emotion I would say, and sleeping was difficult.

Then the next morning NASA calls and said that we'd won this 1,5 Billion dollar contract. They awarded us the first major operational contract, which was for resupplying cargo to the Space Station and bringing cargo back. The next morning literally, I was at home, and I thought they had all gone home for the holidays. I would have said there was no chance of getting a call, I thought people would be on vacation and that sort of thing. That was awesome, I couldn't even maintain my composure I said: "I love you guys." I don't think they had ever gotten that response before.

So that was Monday morning, and I think it was Tuesday night or the Wednesday night on Christmas Eve, 6:00 p.m, December 24, 2008, that we closed the Tesla financing round. It was the last hour of the last day that it was possible. So it went from really terrible to definitely a good week, but definitely took its toll from a mental standpoint, I think I mentally just burned out a few circuits.

We would have gone bankrupt a few days after Christmas if that round had not closed. That tied us over for about six months to May 2009, when Daimler invested in Tesla.

In 2008, when we were really still trying to figure out how not to die, one of the things that I thought would help was if we had a strategic partner, like one of the big car companies. We had been trying to sell our technology to Detroit, and other car companies in other parts of the world. I mean, we really tried hard to work with a lot of different car companies. We would say, drive our car and look at our technology, I don't know it just never seemed to sort of sink in.

In October of 2008 I think it was, I stopped over in Germany in Stuttgart, on the way to India, actually, and met with Dr. Weber the head of global R&D at Daimler, and we had a conversation. Daimler is the company that invented the internal combustion engine car, and the maker of Mercedes and the Smart. They are the oldest car company in the world. I said look what does it take to work together? We would love to do something, we would love to do something with an affordable mass-market car that we ourselves couldn't do right now because we don't have the capital. I would love to figure out how to work with Daimler, is there anything you guys need on the electric vehicle front, is there anything we can do? he said well they wanted to make an electric Smart car, but they didn't have a good source for the battery and power train. You know, the Smart car was always intended to be an electric car, but they could never get the battery right. I said that we could help, what would it take for us to work together? he said if you could do a prototype that would go a long way, and that there was a Daimler team that is planning to visit Silicon Valley in January 2009. He said that he would ask them to meet with Tesla and kind of make their assessment. So I thought we got three months, immediately as I left that meeting I called JB and said: "JB we have three months to make a working electric Smart car" and JB was like what are you talking about?

There were some challenges because the Smart car was actually not available in the United States. We worked really hard and 40 days later the Daimler sort of senior engineering team shows up. It was clear when they entered the building they were not excited about meeting with some like American car start-up, whatever. They took the attitude of what does some little startup in Silicon Valley know that we don't know or can do? So they had been told that they needed to do this. They were like this is obviously going to be a waste of their time, and they were quite grumpy actually. We started off with a PowerPoint presentation and they really didn't like the PowerPoint presentation. So I said like: "You know what why don't we just skip the PowerPoint presentation, would you like a test drive?" and they were like: "What are you talking about, what do you mean a drive?". I said: "Yeah we made one and it's just outside, do you want to drive it?" then they went out and test drove the insane performance Smart car. It was so fast you can do wheelies in the parking lot. Basically you can't exit that without a grin on your face. They went from 'being grumpy' to 'Holy cow this is awesome.' They really liked what they saw.

Actually out of that meeting we got our first development contract with Daimler to create an electric Smart car. This was early 2009 and to sort of paint a picture, General Motors, and Chrysler were busy going bankrupt at the time. I think if we hadn't done that Tesla would have died because the Daimler partnership gave us credibility. They also paid us for the development program which was really helpful from a revenue standpoint, because Tesla was going to run out of money in May 2009. Daimler invested $50 million in May of 2009, which was a lifesaver. Without that investment, Tesla would've been game over. That gave us the resources that we needed to get the company to a moderately healthy position, and actually, get us to the point that we could build Roadsters without losing money on every car.

Then they said, OK, well let's take it another step further, and they gave us a little R&D contract. Eventually, it got to the point where we got the contract to supply 1,000 cars for them. That Daimler investment was a fundamental pivotal point to the survival of Tesla. It's ironic that the first company to invest was not an American company, but a German company.

There are some people out there that keep beating Tesla over the head with the DoE loan thing. It's important to appreciate what this program, which is called the Advanced Technology Vehicle Manufacturing program, was about. It was part of a program that was initiated in 2007, in boom times, that was intended to accelerate the development of energy-efficient cars. In fact, the loan program under which Tesla competed for loans was actually created and signed into law by George Bush. It was executed during the Obama administration but signed into law during the Bush administration.

Unfortunately, these loans were announced right around the time that there were bailouts taking place and there was a stimulus, so people naturally confused the two which is unfortunate, but they're really quite different.

First, I should say, the loan that Tesla received did not come from stimulus funds at all. It was taxpayer dollars, but it was very very different from the stimulus funds or the bailouts or anything. In fact, one of the prerequisites for being in this program was demonstrating that you were an ongoing concern independent of the loan. One of the requirements of that loan program was that you had to be a viable entity in your own right, and provide 20-30% of private capital as a matching contribution. This is why General Motors and Chrysler didn't receive any funding under this program because it's difficult to make that argument while you're in bankruptcy. We could demonstrate viability with the Roadster.

Ford, Nissan, and Tesla did receive essentially lines of credit. But unfortunately in the media, this got confused. The value of the loan was really to accelerate the progress at Tesla, not to keep Tesla alive. A few other things which are noteworthy about the ATVM loan, of course we paid interest, it was a reduced interest, but we still paid interest. We did not need the loan, but it was certainly helpful from a capital dilution standpoint. If we repaid the loan early then there was no capital dilution, but if we didn't repay the loan early then the U.S. Government got a bunch of stock warrants in Tesla. So, it was a pretty good deal. In the grand scheme of things, of all the various government deals that are done, I think this is one of the smarter ones.

The first money that Tesla got from the DoE loan was march 2010. The way the loan program worked was that there were a whole bunch of technical milestones and product development milestones. We could only invoice for the milestones after they had been accomplished, and then Price Waterhouse would audit the financials, and then we would send a request to draw down the loan in little bits and pieces. It would usually take 2 to 3 months after we actually had spent the money to receive any of the loan proceeds. Again this was fundamentally different from what happened in the Auto Bail Out, although a lot of people sort of think it's the same thing. The timing that we started receiving the DoE loan money was after Tesla was out of the danger zone. It's worth noting that all the automotive companies got either direct government grants or been in the loan program. The DoE was there, and our competitors were using it. Ford for example I think got 4 or $5 billion, Nissan got $1.6 billion. Tesla for the Model S program got $380 million, and then $100 million for a powertrain factory to supply other companies. Fisker got I think $500 or $600 million.

Tesla was the first to pay off the DoE loan. There was a prepayment penalty, so you had to pay the interest plus a penalty for prepayment because the normal loan would've been paid off in an additional 10 years. We just paid off the loan and paid the penalty, because morally it felt like the right thing to do.

This is one of the tricky things with something like car companies. There are good times and bad times, and when the economy goes south, then that's when things get really tricky for a manufacturing company. In the U.S, for example, the only two car companies that haven't gone bankrupt in history are Ford and Tesla, that's it. Everybody else is bankrupt or went bankrupt at some point, General Motors, Chrysler, and others.

The Daimler money was crucial to the success of Tesla, although people often think that it was the US government investment that was the lifesaver for Tesla - it was not. The government loan that we got, we only received when we were actually in okay shape. Somehow a lot of people think that the federal government bailed us out or something like that, this is not true. It was the Daimler investment that saved Tesla, not government funding. We were bailed out, but by Daimler, not the government, they are the ones that deserve the credit. Tesla would not have been around if they had not helped out. If they hadn't come in with that investment we would definitely be gone, yeah gone. The government loan was an accelerant, but it was not life or death, but the Daimler investment was life or death.

Anyway, that was a very tough call at the end of 2008. I cannot understate the degree of grief that I have personally gone through, and that many of the people at Tesla had gone through to make it work. It was very hairy for a couple of years. We came close to not making it. We just barely made it by the skin of our teeth there in late 2007 to say the first half of 2009. I think we just made it by the skin of our teeth.

19. For Starters

Okay, first of all, I'd say starting a business is not for everyone. My advice, if someone wants to start a company, is that they should bear in mind that the most likely outcome is that it's not going to work, and they should reconcile themselves to that strong possibility. I think that a lot of times people think creating a company is going to be fun. I would say it's really not that fun. I mean there are periods of fun, and there are periods where it's just awful. They should only do it if they feel that they are really compelled to do it.

What tends to happen is its sort of quite exciting for the first several months of starting a company, then reality sets in, and then it's really hellish for a number of years. Things don't go as well as planned, customers aren't signing up, the technology or the product isn't working as well as you thought, and then that concern has to be compounded by a recession, and it can be very painful for several years. Maybe there are occasionally companies that get created where there's not an extended period of extreme pain, but I'm not aware of very many such instances. I do think that new great entrepreneurs are born every day, and we'll continue to see amazing companies get built. But I would definitely advise people who are starting a company to expect a long period of quite high difficulty.

There's a friend of mine - his name's Billy - who's a successful entrepreneur and started his career around the same time as I did. He has a great saying about creating a company which is: 'trying to build a company and have it succeed, is like eating glass and staring into the abyss.' and there's some truth to that. The eating glass part is you've got to work on the problems that the company needs you to work on, and not the problems you want to work on. So you end up working on problems that you really wish you weren't working on. That goes on for a long time. Particularly, if you're the CEO of the company, you actually have a distillation of all the worst problems in the company. There's no point in spending your time on things that are going right. So you're only spending your time on things that are going wrong. There are things that are going wrong that other people can't take care of. You have like a filter for the worst crappiest problems in the company. The most pernicious, and painful problems and seemingly intractable problems come along. That's the eating glass part. If you don't eat the glass, you're not going to be successful.

The staring into the abyss part is that you're going to be constantly facing the extermination of the company because most start-ups fail. It's like 90%, it could be 99% of start-ups fail. That's the staring into the abyss part. You're constantly saying, OK, if I don't get this right the company will die, which can be quite stressful. So I think you have to feel quite compelled to do it and have a fairly high pain threshold. It's a lot more painful than most people realize, and most companies die. On a certain level in your brain, we evolved to respond to real death. Even though a companies death is not real, we didn't evolve with companies, your brain doesn't quite understand that at the limbic system level, so it's really painful and stressful.

Okay, so that's generally what happens, first there's lots of optimism and things are great. Happiness at first is high. Then you encounter all sorts of issues, and happiness will steadily decline. Then you will go through a whole world of hurt, and then eventually if you succeed - and in most cases, you will not succeed - and Tesla almost didn't succeed it came very close to failure. If you succeed, then, after a long time, you will finally get back to happiness.

Persistence is extremely important. You should not give up unless you're forced to give up unless there's no other choice. That principle can be misapplied if you happen to be trying to penetrate a brick wall with your head. So you have to be cautious in always saying that one should persist and never give up. Because there are actually times when you should give up because you're doing something in error. But if you're convinced that you're doing something correct, then you should never give up. I think failure is bad. I don't think it's good, but if something is important enough then you do it even though the risk of failure is high.

I do think that in terms of creating a company what Edison said which was like "it's 1% inspiration and 99% perspiration" is true. You need to work, you need to work super hard. So what is super hard mean? Like, every waking hour. That's the thing I would say, particularly if you're starting a company. I mean, if you do the simple math, you say like somebody else is working 50 hours a week and you're working 100, you'll get twice as much done in the course of the year as the other company.

A lot of it in creating a company is execution. You start off with an idea and that idea is mostly wrong, then you adapt that idea and keep refining it.

Listen to criticism, some criticism you discard, try to listen to the correct criticism. Then engage in recursive self-improvement, and constantly refine it and making it better. You have to work super hard, it's very important, and keep reiterating on a loop. A lot of life, and in any job in general, you have to do your chores. To be successful in about anything you have to do the tough stuff as well as the enjoyable stuff.

Basically, it's like, it's more fun to cook the meal than to do the dishes, but you need to clean the dishes.

If you're going to create a company you have to come up with a product or service that will be compelling, and serve some need. A great company is just built around a great product or service. That's the whole purpose of a company, to propagate the product or service, and put it into the hands of people that find it useful. That's the main thing, trying to think of the most useful thing for your fellow human beings. And a company is the process of scaling it up in scope and scale.

When you're looking for an opportunity, I think it's important not so much to focus on disruption just for the sake of it. But rather where is an industry either stagnant or in decline, where the product or service has stayed pretty much the same, or maybe even gotten worse over time. It's worth looking at industries that a lot of people think are impossible or think you can't succeed at, that's usually where opportunity is. If everyone thinks you can't succeed in an industry, they are probably worth diving in. There's a lot of opportunities in these industries, particularly the ones that have been dominated by an oligarchic set of companies for a long time. Oligarchic, or duopolies and monopolies, are not great at innovation. Innovation comes from new entrance into an arena. When an industry has the absence of new entrance it tends to have very limited innovation. This also means that if you do break on through to the other side, that there is a lot of opportunity for a company that is created there. I would recommend people consider arenas outside of the Internet. Because there's a lot of industries that could use that entrepreneurial talent and skills that people have learned in creating companies.

It's like the Nike slogan "just do it" you know showing up is half the battle. I think people maybe have too much fear of failure. You have to say what would really happen if you fail, like you're not going to starve, and you probably will not lose shelter. I think very often people self-limit what they are capable of without realizing it. You got to try hard to do it and don't be afraid of failure.

Also, you need to be rooted in reality, it's easy to get high on your own supply as Scarface said. You got to not be afraid to innovate, but also don't delude yourself into thinking something is working when it's not, or you are going to get fixated on a bad solution. Don't be afraid of new arenas. You can get a book to learn something and experiment with your hands and make it happen. Find a way to get something done.

In general, I do think it's worth thinking about whether what you're doing is going to result in a disruptive change or not. If it's just incremental it's unlikely to be something major. It's got to be something that's substantially better than what's gone on before. You've got to make sure that whatever you're doing is a great product or service. It has to be really great.

To go back to what I was saying earlier, where if you're a new company unless it's like some new industry or new market that's untapped then the standard is lower for your product or service, but if you're entering anything where there's an existing marketplace, against large entrenched competitors, then your product or service needs to be much better than theirs. It can't be a little bit better, because put yourself in the shoes of the consumer and they say why would you buy it as a consumer? You're always going to buy the trusted brand unless there's a big difference. A lot of times an entrepreneur will come up with something which is only slightly better, and it can't just be slightly better. It's got to be a lot better.

I think this is sort of advice I would give to entrepreneurs in general, really focus on making a product that your customers love. It's so rare that you can buy a product and you love the product when you bought it. There are very few things that fit into that category. If you can come up with something like that, your business will be successful for sure.

As long as people stay super focused on creating the absolute best product or service that really delights their end customer, if they stay focused on that, if you get it such that your customers want you to succeed then you probably will. If your customers love you, your odds of success are dramatically higher.

Be really focused on something that you know will have high value to someone else and be rigorous in that assessment. When you're building something new there's going to be mistakes, and it's important to recognize those mistakes, acknowledge them, and take corrective action. The success of the company is very much more about how quick are you to fix the mistakes. If you see the difference between a start-up that is successful and one that is not, it's because the successful one recognized the mistakes and fixes them very quickly, and the unsuccessful one tries to deny that the mistakes exist. A natural human tendency is wishful thinking, I think wishful thinking is innate in the human brain, you want things to be the way you wish them to be. You tend to filter information that you shouldn't filter, that's the most common flaw that I see. So a challenge for entrepreneurs is to say what's the difference between real believing in your ideals and sticking to them, versus pursuing some unrealistic dream that doesn't really have merits. That's difficult, so you need to be very rigorous in your self-analysis. I think the most important thing is to start somewhere, and then really be prepared to question your assumptions, affix what you did wrong and adapt to reality.

Constantly seek criticism. A well-thought-out critique of whatever you're doing is as valuable as gold, and you should seek that from everyone you can, but particularly your friends.

Usually, your friends know what's wrong, but they don't want to tell you because they don't want to hurt you. Yeah, they say I want to encourage my friend so I'm not going to tell him what I think is wrong with his product. It doesn't mean your friends are right, but very often they are right, and you at least want to listen very carefully to what they say.. and to everyone. You're looking for, basically, you should take the approach that you're wrong. That you, the entrepreneur are wrong. Your goal is to be less wrong.

I think you can learn whatever you need to do to start a successful business either in school or out of school. A school in theory should help accelerate that process, and I think oftentimes it does. It can be an efficient learning process, perhaps more efficient than empirically learning lessons. I mean there are examples of successful entrepreneurs who never graduated high school, and there are those that have PhDs. I think the important principle is to be dedicated to learning what you need to know, whether that is in school or empirically.

The other thing I'd say is that if you're creating a company, or if you're joining a company, the most important thing is to attract great people. If you think about a company, a company is a group of people that are organized to create a product or service. That's what a company is. So, in order to create such a thing, you have to convince others to join you in your effort. They have to be convinced that it's a sensible thing, that there's at least some reasonable chance of success, and that if there is success, the reward will be commensurate with the effort involved. Getting people to believe in what you're doing, and in you is important. In the beginning, there will be few people who believe in you, or in what you're doing. There were certain things that I really believe needed to happen and I was able to convince a lot of great people to join me in trying to solve those problems. A lot of times I think people ascribe to me things where the credit is really due to a much bigger team. Over time as you make progress, the evidence will build, and more and more people will believe in what you're doing. In fact, that's I think the real answer if you can get a group of really talented people together and unite them around a challenge and have them work together to the best of their abilities then a company will achieve great things. So either be with or join a group that's amazing, that you really respect. I mean, really, all a company is a group of people that have gathered together to create a product or service. Depending upon how talented and hardworking that group is, and to the degree in which they are focused cohesively in a good direction, that will determine the success of the company. So, do everything you can to gather great people, if you're creating a company.

I think it's a good idea, when creating a company, to have a demonstration or if it's a product, to have like a good mockup, or even if it's software to have good demo-ware or to be able to sketch something, so people can envision what it's about. Try to get to that point as soon as possible, and then iterate to make it as real as possible as fast as possible, if that makes sense. Like you know where you're generally heading for, and the actual path is going to be some sort of zigzaggy thing in that direction. You're trying not to deviate too far from the path that you want to be on, but you're going to have to do that to some degree.

Essentially, it's important to limit the number of miracles in series. You want to start off with something that's the most doable and expand from there. Start with the minimally useful system - something that you think is still compelling - but then leave future technologies for future upgrades.

Unfortunately, one does have to be focused on the short-term and money coming in when creating a company, because otherwise, the company will die. I don't want to diminish the profit motive, I think it's a good one if the rules of an industry are properly set up. There's nothing fundamentally wrong with profit. In fact, profit just means that people are paying you more for whatever you're doing than you're spending to create it. That's a good thing. If that's not the case, then you'll be out of business, and rightfully so because you're not adding enough value. Now there are cases, of course, where people will do bad things in order to achieve profit, but that's actually quite unusual. Because usually the rules are set up mostly correctly, not completely, but mostly correctly.

The best way to attract venture-capital is to have a demonstration of whatever product or service it is. Ideally take that as far as you can, ideally try to see if you can sell it to real customers, and start generating some momentum. The further you can get along with that the more likely you will get funding. Start-ups are a bit of a numbers game. Typically in Silicon Valley venture capitalists invest in 20 companies, one or two will be a big hit, maybe three or four will be OK and the rest will not make it. That's the way it works.

So, it's true starting a company is like eating glass and staring into the abyss of death. If that sounds appealing be an entrepreneur. I think it's very difficult and quite painful. I think that's important to bear in mind. If you go into it expecting it's fun, you would be disappointed, it's not, it's quite painful. It's much easier to get a job somewhere, much much easier. Much less stressful, you have more time for other things. It's really sort of like, if you are wired to do it, then you should do it, but not otherwise. It's not going to optimize your leisure time so you must feel compelled to do it. Let me put it this way, if you need inspiring words.. don't do it.

20. NeXt

The first retail store opened up in LA on Santa Monica Blvd. which was formally I think a kids furniture store. This was a controversial decision at Tesla, in fact, the original business plan called for using sort of the regular auto dealer network and that kind of thing. But I was really adamant that we needed to improve the buying experience. For a lot of people, the car buying experience was quite negative, they didn't look forward to buying a car. I didn't know anyone who loved the car buying experience. Usually, people tended to view it as equivalent to going to the dentist, and maybe the dentist is better, but it was not something people looked forward to. I think if you would ask most people what's the worst retail experience you had, for a lot of people that's buying a car, that's not something you want to emulate. Then on the other side of the spectrum you got sort of like, I think Apple is arguably the best on the retail front, where people are drawn to an Apple Store, and Gap is also excellent in that regard. Better to emulate that than the old way of doing business. We thought look if we going to make a new car company we don't want to inherit the negativity or bad element of the way it has been done in the past. We want to do it right, and we want to make sure that people love coming to buy a car, that they look forward to it. We weren't sure if this made sense from an economic standpoint, but we just knew we didn't want to replicate the negative experience that people had in buying a car. We felt like we want people to love buying a Tesla, all the way from the initial buying experience, to receiving the car, ownership, and the post-sale service experience. You want people to fall in love, you want them to just love it. We want to have a fundamentally superior consumer experience.

The ideal service is invisible. You don't even notice it, and when it's done, you love it. Service should feel like invisible love. We really wanted to achieve something that was substantially superior to what people have experienced in the past. The most important thing I said to the retail team, is that the number one thing is when someone comes in our store, whether or not they buy a car, the most important thing is they are looking forward to coming back to the store. That's it, that's the goal, just make sure that when people visit our store they look forward to coming again. Don't try to sell them something that they don't need, don't sell, your goal is just to communicate and make people feel good.

We got a lot of opposition from the auto dealers as you might imagine, they were not happy campers about this approach.

So we got the first retail store established in LA, then we got the second one shortly thereafter in the bay area in Menlo Park. That is where I first met Franz von Holzhausen.

After the Roadster people said, oh, sure, you can make a small electric sports car, but you couldn't make a real car, you know like a Mercedes or an Audi, that has all of the features and capabilities. So we announced the Model S, and so many people called bullshit on that, it was ridiculous.

Having done the Roadster which was very, very difficult, I realized with the designing that there must be people that can do this way better than I can. I knew I couldn't do a great job of designing the Model S because designing a beautiful four-door sedan is incredibly hard. You can make a car look very good by giving it's sort of certain proportions, like making it low and slim. If you do that the utility is significantly affected. The big challenge with the Model S was to try to figure out five adults +2 kids because we wanted to have a seven-seater. I first tried to outsource the design to a few different companies. That was a whole saga in and of itself, and it really didn't work out. Originally we thought let's have Henrik Fisker, who had a design studio, do the designing. We paid him a good sum of money, and curiously enough the designs that he worked on and that he came up with for us were terrible. What he didn't tell us was that he was actually working on a competing car company, Fisker.

If you say what was the difference between Fisker and Tesla. Tesla is a hard-core engineering company and Fisker is kinda based on styling. I think the styling is important, but I don't think that's the reason why we don't have electric cars. There weren't that many car company start-ups. There was sort of Fisker and Coda and some smaller ones. So in the case of Fisker, they made a car that a lot of people think looked really good, but didn't work properly. So people didn't want to buy the car.

We were pretty upset with him for basically taking, what were at the time, the original specifications for the Model S and going and sharpening a business plan of the same car. That's when I said we really need our own design studio, so I asked around and I was told: "There's this guy Franz that's really great, I don't know if he's willing to jump, but he's really great and you should go talk to him." The first meeting we had was at that opening party for the Tesla store, and it was a really good party. I think something that Tesla is good at is throwing good parties. I spend a long portion of the night talking to Franz at the party, and we've been friends ever since. So that's when we hired Franz to design the Model S. We didn't even have the money for a design studio so the design studio, in the beginning, was just in a tent in a corner of the SpaceX rocket factory.

When Jon Favreau and Robert Downey Jr were doing the first Iron Man they came to visit me to ask for some advice on the script. Someone had told them I was similar to Tony Stark or something. They came and I gave a tour of the rocket factory and Tesla, and everything. They asked me, like, Iron Man has these powers, what kind of explanation could there be for them? that kind of thing. We talked about some of the possible scientific explanations for the powers that Iron Man has in his suit like maybe you could harness the power of dark energy or something.

It did actually feature a Tesla Roadster in Iron Man 1. The funny thing was they asked Audi, who was the sponsor, Audi had paid a bunch of money to use Audi in the Iron Man films, they asked Audi: do you mind if the Tesla is also there in the background? They said they didn't mind because that company is not going to survive any way it doesn't matter, so they put the Tesla in. But then for Iron Man 2 when they said can we put a Tesla in? Audi said: "No way."

We got an Iron Man statue at SpaceX that was donated by Jon Favreau and signed by the whole cast including Scarlett Johansson which is kind of cool.

I should point out that Iron Man was only partially based on me, I think there are some important differences. I've got five kids and Iron Man is sort of a swinging bachelor. I spend my weekends going to Disneyland and I don't see Tony Stark doing that.

The Tesla IPO process was certainly interesting, and an interesting IPO roadshow with Deepak who did an amazing job. Maybe we took Tesla public too early, but as a car company we just needed to raise a lot of money to expand, so we went public. If I had a dollar for every time somebody mentioned Tucker or DeLorean we would've not needed an IPO. On the roadshow, we would sometimes meet with investors that told us how stupid we were, and that this was a waste of money, and how dare we even take their time. Then we would meet with some that were like: "Yeah guys, you are great, we are all in." Tesla is a company that either inspires love or hate, people are rarely indifferent. If you say how do you feel about Colgate you say: "it's OK" but with Tesla, it's either "you guys suck" or "Hey Yeah!" it tends to be, love it or hate it.

A lot of skepticism initially, or perhaps still is there to some degree.

So we managed to get Tesla public and shortly after that we became one of the most shorted stock on the NASDAQ. For quite a while we were trading places as the most shorted stock on the stock market with I think it was Skullcandy, Travelzoo, and Coinstar.

Also in 2010 proximately the same time as the IPO is when we met with Toyota. Akio Toyoda actually came by, and we had breakfast at my house. He was sort of really interested in working with innovative technology companies, and we said what are the ways that we can potentially work together? We came up with three things. These three parts of the deal were independent of each other. So all three could work out or none of the three could work out. One was to do sort of a joint EV program. That was one part of the deal, another strategic element with Toyota was for them to make an investment at the IPO, and they said that sounds cool we will make a $50 million investment at the IPO. This was actually very helpful to us when we were on the roadshow because they would ask us how we were going to compete against the big car companies. We would say look we got the Daimler partnership, and Toyota is investing at the IPO, those are good signs. They invested $50 million at a $17 share price, so it worked out for them.

The third was buying the Fremont Factory, the former NUMMI facility in Northern California, which is one of the biggest car plants in the world. It was 50% owned by GM and 50% owned by Toyota, but it was owned by what was considered the bad portion of GM. GM was split into two pieces, one was called Liquidation Motors, half of NUMMI was owned by Liquidation Motors, and a half was owned by Toyota.

In recent years it had only been making Toyota products. It's where they made the Corolla and the Tacoma. As a result of the recession they decided to close it down, and it was understandable because it didn't make sense for Toyota to be in that kind of partnership. They were going to shut it down and it was just going to be empty. They were going to turn it into a mall or something like that, but it was going to be empty for a long time. So we sort of said look we'll take it off your hands. We said this is kind of a huge plant for Tesla, and we don't have much money, but we would be interested in buying that. The dream factory location for Tesla was always the NUMMI factory, a great location close to the Tesla headquarters. We thought man there is no way we can ever get that awesome plant because it just cost too much and we didn't have much money. We were amazed that they were willing to move forward and do it, Tesla was so tiny at the time. It was like imagine you are this little group and somebody says there's this giant like alien dreadnought that you could have for pennies on the dollar. You have no idea how it works, you are like where are the controls, how do you use this thing? We were fortunate enough to buy it at a point where the automotive plants were not worth much in early 2010.

When we first got the plant it is one of the biggest plants in the world, I think it's sort of by footprint like the third or fourth biggest manufacturing plant, it's 5 1/2 million square feet, it's amazing, you could go camping in there. It takes you a long time to walk from one side to the other. We have bikes in the factory so you can get around a bit faster. We could conceivably go beyond half a million cars there, long-term we want to try to do several million cars.

We were fortunate in being able to buy at a very good price a very good factory, and thus minimize the incremental tooling cost to produce the Model S. There was an existing paint shop, so we only had to modify the paint shop instead of building one from scratch. There were stamping machines and all sorts of things there that were helpful. I never expected that we would have this plant, the amazing thing is it is kind of full.

The Model S was the first time we build the car, the whole car, with the Roadster, Lotus did the main chassis.

The Model S beta was close to production design, or very close really when we unveiled that to the public. It was quite well received, and we had a lot of people who put down a deposit on the car. That gave us a big boost of confidence, it was like wow people really like the car, and it looks like we will be able to sell enough to pay for the cost of the factory and everything.

People were quite skeptical. It's funny, before we got the Roadster out they would say you couldn't possibly make that car work, and then we made the car work. Then they would say well nobody's going to buy it, and then people bought it. Then we made the Model S and we brought it to market. Then people were like, oh, you couldn't possibly ramp up production, and then we did that. Then they said you will never be able to make a profit, and we did that in Q1. So I'm hopeful that people will observe that there is a trend here.

With the Roadster our annual production was maybe 500 a year, and Lotus made the body and chassis, and we made the power train and battery. We went from around 500 cars a year where we did half the problem, to 20,000 cars a year for a much more complicated car where we did the whole thing. This was a very steep learning curve, very intense. We were basically there seven days a week and all hours of the night trying to figure out how to make a car. It was a huge amount of sacrifice by everyone.

That was a big milestone for the company, delivering the first Model S's from the Fremont Factory. At the time we were just occupying a tiny corner. It was definitely one of the most joyful experiences in the history of Tesla.

The Model S was actually the only aluminum car made in North America. The Audi A8 and a few of the advanced German cars were aluminum, but there were no aluminum passenger vehicles made in the United States. Although for me, coming from the space arena, it was like: obviously, you'd make it out of aluminum, what else would you make it out of? steel is really heavy and not great.

I'll tell you one funny thing, when the Model S first came out I intentionally deleted the rear reading lights in the backseat, because I was like people are just going to use e-books like Kindle and iPads and phones and that kind of thing, so they're not going to need an actual light in the back. Then one of my kids was trying to read a book in the back and said: "This is the stupidest car in the world, how could you do this?" so I put the light back in.

It was Motor Trend Car of the Year 2013. Obviously a big milestone for Tesla to get essentially the best car of the year, not just electric. Motor Trend told us it was the first time that the judges had actually been unanimous in a decision, and they were very complementary they liked a lot of things about the car. The important thing was that it won as a car not because it was electric. It won on the basis of performance, fit and finish and the overall feel of the vehicle.

Obviously, it was a bit disheartening that presidential candidate Mitt Romney would take time out of a debate to attack Tesla in two of the three debates. I thought that was a bit unreasonable, and one of the things he did was call us a loser. In retrospect, it seems he was right about the object of that statement but not the subject. Time magazine awarded us 'invention of the year', so I think it was a bit unreasonable that he would call us a loser. We had generated 3500 high-quality jobs in the United States and we were a leader in electric vehicle technology, we actually exported Power trains to Toyota and Mercedes. I don't think Mitt Romney hates us, I think he was just a little too fond of oil.

The thing that was really hard about the Model S, was to combine aesthetics and utility, to balance through. The big challenge with the S was having a vehicle with a high utility and looked good, and the same with the X. To make a sports car look good is relatively easy, but to make a sedan or an SUV look good is quite difficult.

I think electric vehicles have a fundamental architectural advantage if one designs an electric vehicle from the ground up, and takes advantage of what is possible. If you were just to convert a gasoline vehicle, you would not achieve these advantages. Properly done you can actually package the battery pack in the floor plan and achieve a low center of mass and have a very compact motor and inverter and gearbox so that the actual usable space in the car is significantly greater than a gasoline car of the same overall external dimensions.

We unveiled the Model X in early 2012, an SUV that is built on the same platform as the Model S. It's got a slightly longer wheelbase but otherwise it's on the same platform. It's really addressing the SUV and minivan market.

It's got a unique innovation which is the double-hinged gull-wing door on the side. That's never been done before I believe.

Certainly hasn't been done in any production car. We call it 'Falcon Wing' instead of 'gull-wing' because they have a dual-acting hinge - when both doors are up it looks sort of falcon-like. I think it's the coolest door as doors go, it's pretty cool. They can open in a tighter space than almost any door, and certainly a tighter space than a conventional door. The reason it has to be double hinged is that, if you just made it a single hinge gull wing, the arc as it swings out, it swings out too far and then too high, but as a double hinge it's actually going, almost straight up. If you can physically fit between the Model X and another car, then you can open the door. It's more convenient than a minivan door because a minivan door when that opens it comes out and slides, so you can't get to the car from the rear, but with the Model X you can, when the door's open. The Falcon Wing door is designed to improve the accessibility of the third row. Typically in a three-row car, it's quite difficult to access the third row directly. You have to fold up the second-row seat; you somehow have to move the seat back of the second row. Which, if you've got a child or child seat in the second row can make it really inconvenient to access the third row. By having the Falcon Wing door we have a much bigger opening that allows you to directly step to the third row quite conveniently, even if there are baby seats in the second row. If you're a mother putting your child in the child seat in the second row it's very easy because you have such a big opening. You can step into the car and put the child into the child seat, instead of kind of levering your child through a hole over the baby seat. I think parents will really enjoy the Model X.

There are really only two ways to achieve that level of accessibility. One is the sliding door of a minivan, and the other is to having something like that Falcon Wing door. The reason we didn't go for a sliding door like a minivan is that it fundamentally constrains the aesthetics of the exterior of the car. You have to have three support rails which also negatively affects the aesthetics. That's why all minivans pretty much look the same. We wanted to have something that had that level of accessibility, actually greater accessibility than a minivan door, but also looks good.

This program has been challenging.

In retrospect, the right thing to do with the Model X would've been to take a lot of the awesome cool things, and kind of table them for a future version. I particularly need to fault myself here for a fair bit of Hubris for putting too much technology all at once into a product. If I could wind back the clock I would say like we got these great ideas, and we got things that I really want to implement, and other people want to implement, but the smart move actually would have been to table those for version 2 and so forth for Model X, instead of piling them all into version 1. This was definitely a case of getting overconfident, and in particular, the software that controlled the Model X and the operation of the doors was incredibly difficult to refine, and getting the complex set of sensors to work well has been incredibly difficult to refine.

In designing the Model S and the Model X safety was our absolute paramount goal. I felt like, obviously, my kids drive in the car every day, my friends drive in the car every day, if I didn't do everything possible to maximize safety, and something went wrong I couldn't live with myself. I really couldn't live with myself if there was something that I could have done that would have saved them and I didn't do it. We spent an enormous amount of time with safety, and the whole car is architected around safety. We have physics on our side, which is very important.

Why exactly is the car safe? because you hear things like the car is five stars and all that, but that is not an actual statistical number. Safety statistics are not really measured in stars. There is an actual probability of injury, which is the most important number. You can look it up it's sort of buried in the Department of Transport website, but every car has a combined probability of injury. The reasons basically are that the car does not have a big steel engine block in the front. We have a front trunk as well as a rear trunk. The electric motors are so small that they are actually coaxial with the axles. When you have a high-speed frontal collision what really matters is force over distance. It's really not that complicated, it's just like jumping into a pool from a high diving board or something. You want a deep pool and one without rocks in it, it's the same thing for a car. What people don't realize is that they think you have a big steel engine block that is protecting you. Except that when you hit something you are going 60 miles an hour. It is stopping you that is important, the deceleration distance is very important. To describe it in another way, the length of the crumple zone is extremely important. The crumple zone in the front of the Model S is three times greater than that of any premium sedan, which means that the impact attenuation is 2 to 3 times greater.

The reason the side-impact collision is so much better than another car is because the main structural component is the battery pack in the floor pan. The battery pack in the floor pan effectively acts as a big share plate to transfer load from a side impact into the rest of the car, so the whole car moves sideways. The net result is that you are much safer in a side impact. What happens in a gasoline car is, because you got the big steel engine block in the front you got a huge portion of the mass in the front, and the rest of the car is relatively weak. You essentially have just thin sheet-metal on the side of the car and the floor pan of the car. The load transfer for a gasoline car to the rest of the mass of the car is weak and as a result, the side impact distance is dramatically greater.

A few other things which are not specifically related to electric cars like using an aluminum body and chassis is helpful, because you can absorb more energy per unit of mass in a crash. That leads to higher safety. I'm really proud of getting the safety to where it is. When we did the rooftop test it got to 4 times the weight of the car, and then the machine broke. Literally, the thing that was supposed to crush the car broke instead of the car. It is the safest car by far.

21. Electrifying

I think overall for the 21st-century the most important terrestrial problem that humanity faces are sustainable production and consumption of energy. It's getting harder and harder to find hydrocarbons, and it's getting much more expensive to extract them. The cost of extraction has doubled or in some cases tripled. Really we are just arguing about when hydrocarbons run out, or become prohibitively expensive, not if.

If we continue to rely on producing, mining, and burning billions of tons of hydrocarbons every year which effectively, and permanently from a human standpoint, affects the carbon content of the oceans and atmosphere, the future is going to be quite bad. The vast majority of the scientific establishment believes that. Anyone with a scientific background is unequivocal. And anyone who thinks that it is 100% certain that global warming is fake, and that massively changing the chemical composition of the oceans and atmosphere is fine, is a bloody fool, obviously.

That's what this is all about, this is about trying to accelerate where we know we need to get to anyway. Not on like a small potatoes way, but in a very big macro-scale way.

At the risk of being repetitive, there's going to be no choice in the long term to move to sustainable energy. It's tautological, either it is renewable or is not renewable. Non-renewables are like being stuck in a room where the oxygen is gradually depleting, and outside it is not.

New technology and innovation can have a downside, and one of the downsides is the ability to extract far more hydrocarbons than we thought were possible. But it's still finite, we must still find a solution or we will face economic collapse when the resources become scarce. There are time extensions on the game, but the game is going to come to an end. That should be absolutely certain, obviously frankly. The only thing we gain by slowing down the transition is just slowing it down, it doesn't make it not occur it just slows it down.

I do think we should watch our consumption. We shouldn't be wasteful, but even if we are really conservative in our use of energy, and are very effective with recycling and all sorts of things, that delays the need to move to a sustainable future, but it doesn't eliminate it. If we don't have sustainable energy generation, there's no way that we can conserve our way to a good future. We have to fundamentally make sustainable energy available.

The important thing to appreciate is that it is inevitable. The question is really when do we exit the fossil fuels era, not if. The goal is to exit the era as quickly as possible. That means we need to move from the old goal. The old pre-industrial goal was to move from chopping wood and killing lots of whales to fossil fuels, which actually in that context was a good thing. The new goal is to exit the fossil fuel era and move to a sustainable energy future.

I think in the future people will look back at the gasoline era the way we look back at the steam era today. We are going to look back on gasoline cars like we look back on steam engines, it was like a phase, it was a bit weird. We're going to look back on fossil fuel power generation the same way. It was a weird phase. I think you will be telling your grandchildren: "Yes, you won't believe what we used to do. We used to take up liquidized remains of dinosaurs and old plants, and put them in cars, and burn them to move. And we did the same thing with the power plants and the like." Gasoline, it's quaint, it's interesting, but it's basically a phase. In the future, we will look back, and with the future, I don't mean super-far into the future, I'm talking about towards the end of the century, we will look back on gasoline the same way we look back on coal, as sort of a quaint anachronism that's in a museum. That sounds crazy, but that's what it's going to be in the future.

So yes we're trying to have the non-weird future get here as fast as possible. We want to get out of that weird phase as soon as we can. If you believe that that's the future we're headed towards, we must find alternatives. That is a known difficult thing that we are going to have to solve.

What actions can we take that will accelerate the transition out of this idiosyncratic moment in history, where we're digging up Cambrian-level fossils and burning them? Methane is the lowest-cost source fuel on the planet by a good margin. Methane is a naturally occurring gas. Once you start getting into deep methane or deep natural gas you're actually tapping into things that are not related to dinosaur fossils. There are places in the Solar System where the atmosphere is primarily methane, so it does not require an organic origin. If we dig too deep for methane, we're going to a level that has never been seen before, not even in the very earliest history of Earth. So that's very dangerous I think.

On the plus side, there's actually an enormous amount of sustainable energy. There are many forms of energy generation that can be sustaining into the very long term. We want to use things like hydro, solar, wind, and geothermal. Nuclear is also a good option in places that aren't subject to natural disasters. We want to use energy sources that will be good for a billion years.

You know, electricity's sort of like cash. You can generate it in multiple ways; you can spend it in multiple ways. My personal view is that we'll generate more electricity from solar than any other single source. It may not be a majority, but I expect at least a plurality from solar power. That will be a combination of photovoltaics at the point of use, like the roofs of houses and businesses, which is also good from the standpoint of not requiring additional power lines. And then at the power plant level, I think we'll see a lot of solar thermal power generation. Where essentially you're just using the Sun to heat a working fluid, and then generate steam and power a turbine. There are a bunch of those projects that are going to come online in California and other places in the United States.

I'm not the biggest fan of biofuels because I try to look at things and just calculate the basic physics of it. Really elementary stuff and say; what percentage of the incident sunlight is bound up in usable chemical energy, and then once you have that chemical energy how much of that is then translated into electricity? You have to compare that total efficiency with just having solar panels. Unless I've made some really dumb mistake, which is possible, you're about a hundred times off with biofuels, I mean, at least two orders of magnitude. What it boils down to is watts per square meter of electricity generated. With the best case biofuel - take every assumption and maximize it, so don't say, don't worry, maybe somebody could invent something better, say what is the best - just envelope the whole thing. Say you had unbelievably efficient plants, I mean, you can't violate any laws of thermodynamics, but assuming that you're at the limits of the laws of thermodynamics in all those cases then biofuels - at least your land-based biofuels - there's no way this makes sense. You end up being around maybe 0.2% efficient in turning sunlight into electrical energy. Whereas commercial solar panels are 20% efficient. So why would you ever do biofuels? it's not as though there are large swaths of arable land unused.

You have to say, if you go with biofuels, it's going to either result in the wilderness being cultivated or an increase in food prices. You can also say, is it possible if you stopped all food production in the world to generate enough energy to meet the world's needs? like, yeah, you could probably it's about right, actually, if you stopped all food production you could just about meet the world's energy needs. Now, there is a possibility of ocean-based, because Earth's surface is mostly ocean. So, if you could find maybe some sort of ocean algae-based solution where you're unconstrained by surface area, although I still think you'd have to compare that to a bunch of floating solar panels, and I think you still lose on floating solar panels. I don't see how it would make sense.

I think there's nothing wrong with nuclear power, whether fission or fusion. Fusion is when you take like let's say two hydrogen atoms, or two hydrogen isotopes technically, and slam them together and form helium. That's fusion. And fission is when you got like a heavy atom that is decaying at a relatively noticeable rate, like uranium or plutonium and decays into smaller atoms. That's fission. I actually think nuclear is not a terrible option, so long as you're not located in a place that's susceptible to natural disasters. That also I think defies common sense. So long as there are not huge earthquakes or weather systems that have names coming at you, then I think nuclear can be a sensible option. There are much safer and better ways of generating nuclear energy, I'm talking fission here, then existed in the past when nuclear reactors first came out. You have some meltdown risk, although there is some new technology on the fission front that makes meltdown risk extremely low.

At some point in the future, it would be nice to make fusion work, of course. I think it's definitely possible to make fusion work. I used to be a big fan of having that as a long-time energy source. With fusion, the difficulty is keeping it going. The great difficulty is to keep the fire from going out. It's quite hard to sustain a fusion reaction unless you have something very big like the Sun. The Sun has gravitational confinement of the fusion reaction. Since you can't do gravitational confinement on Earth you have to do some sort of electromagnetic confinement in one form or another, or kinetic confinement by slamming things into each other. It's quite tricky to prevent a fusion explosion from immediately extinguishing, but I think the fusion problem is probably easier than people think it is, and by this, I'm thinking about magnetically confined fusion. That's a problem that gets easier as you scale it up because you get a service-to-volume advantage. It seems like a pretty obvious thing that if you could get it big enough you could have a real effective sort of magnetically confined fusion reactor. That's probably not the easiest thing to solve. You could do like a thorium fission reactor. Or a better fission reactor, maybe it's better to do better fission reactors, but fission does have a bit of a marketing problem, and fusion is the energy forever solution. It's exciting to see what's happening with the ITER Project, which is a fusion plant that's being built in France. I think we can definitely make fusion work, but it is a far-off technology. To make fusion at the power plant level work is probably, I don't know, 30 years away and a lot of effort.

That's why at least for now and I think maybe even in the long-term I'm a proponent of using the big fusion power plant in the sky called the Sun. The Sun is a giant fusion explosion and it shows up every day. If we have photovoltaics, solar panels, we can capture that fusion energy.

It's worth noting I'm not sure if people are aware of this, but the world can be powered by solar many times over if you had enough battery capacity to pair with it. Many times, probably like times a thousand, that it's literally true. We have this enormous fusion generator in the sky that is laying out vast amounts of energy, and I'm just talking about using land area, it's really amazing, it's crazy. In fact here's a little tidbit, for a lot of nuclear power stations if you would take a nuclear power station, and the whole clearance area around it, it ends up being quite a bit of land. You got let's say 3 to 5 km radius of clear area where you can't have significant construction, like building houses and dense office and housing space, usually people don't want to do that near a nuclear power plant. You can't just put a nuclear power plant out in the suburbs with a bunch of people around it, so you have to have this big clear zone, they use a lot of area. If you took the land area including the stay-out zones and everything and said what generates more power, the nuclear power plant or just carpet that area with solar panels? The solar panels on that area will typically generate more power than the nuclear power plant. Just the area used by the nuclear power plant covered in solar panels would generate more energy.

   The amount of energy that reaches the Earth from the Sun is staggeringly high. Just to give you a sense of how much energy is hitting the Earth from the Sun. It's very easy to do if I may just do a tidbit of math. 1 km^2 is 1,000,000 m^2, and there is 1 kW per square meter of solar energy. So on one square kilometer, there is a gigawatt of solar energy. Which is mind-blowingly huge, that's a supergiant amount of energy. You could power the entire United States with about 150 to 200 Square kilometers of solar panels. The entire United States with about a 100 mile by 100 mile grid of solar power. This is literally true, what I've just said. Take like a corner of Arizona and that would be all the energy that the United States needs. Take a corner of Utah there's not much going on there I have been there, there are not even radio stations.

If you just took a small section of Spain you could power all of Europe. It's a very small amount of area that's actually needed to generate the electricity we need to power civilization or in the case of the U.S. a little corner of Nevada or Utah could power the entire United States.

China has an enormous land area, much of which is hardly occupied at all given that the Chinese population is so concentrated along the coast. Once you go inland the population in some cases is remarkably tiny. You could easily power all of China with solar. It's true that in dense cities rooftop solar is not going to solve the energy need. What you can do is have ground-mount solar power near Hong Kong tapping into the existing power lines that are coming in. So you can supply Hong Kong with solar power; it would just need to be coming from a land area that's not too far away.

If humanity had to get all of its energy from the Sun, it could do so. Currently, in terms of total energy usage in the world, utilities provide about roughly a third of the energy consumed by civilization, electric utilities to be precise. Then another third is heating and another third is transportation roughly. There is enough energy coming to us from the Sun to support all three areas.

It also needs to be stored in a battery so we can use it at night. Then we want to have high power lines to transfer solar energy from one place to another.

I think the important thing to bear in mind is it's a big world out there and there are places where the cost of energy is much higher than in other places. For example, in Hawaii energy costs are very high because they have to ship in all of the fuel for their power plants, so it's very expensive. The economics of solar plus battery makes overwhelming sense for a place like Hawaii and a lot of actually island nations out there. And really anyplace that has got expensive energy costs or even moderately expensive energy costs. It's going to make sense for many parts of Europe, many parts of the United States, and then, over time, it's going to make sense for everywhere.

I would say we do need to think about transport in general, about a third of all energy is used for transport. I believe in electric transport because it allows for energy to be produced in a wide range of sustainable means, and you just charge the car.

Again it's worth noting that even if the grid was fully powered by coal and natural gas, electric cars would still generate less CO_2 even if you take it all the way to the power plant level. The reason for that is when you are not constrained by mass and volume, you can make the efficiency of energy extraction much better in a power plant than you can in a car. If you take say a natural gas power plant from GE it's over 60% efficient, so if you take the source energy it's 60% efficient in generating electricity, it's really good. Whereas typically a gasoline-powered car over the drive cycle will be less than 20% efficient. That is because the big natural gas turbine can be really heavy, it can be really bulky, and you can take the waste heat and run a steam turbine and get even more energy out. Your efficiency is just fundamentally better, even when you take into account the transmission losses and the charging losses you are still way far ahead with electric cars than you are with gasoline cars. Stationary power plants are so much more efficient than small gasoline engines in cars, an electric car ends up getting more range for a given amount of say, coal or oil that's burned than a gasoline car gets. In other words, the CO_2 per mile is actually less for an electric car even if you draw electricity from a high CO_2 source like coal or natural gas, or even directly from oil.

Now, of course, long term we have to find sustainable power generation and sustainable transportation. Both sides of the equation need to be solved, and even if electric cars weren't there we still need to get sustainable power generation.

So the great thing about electric cars is you can generate electricity from a wide range of renewable sources like hydro, geothermal, wind, solar and nuclear where it's safe to do so.

The energy density, basically the amount of energy you can store in a given amount of mass or volume, was a fundamental constraint on electric cars for a while, and that's correlated to some degree with the cost per kWh, the cost of storing that energy in the car. The advent of lithium-ion technology I think is really what enabled a compelling car. I think if we had to we could turn the entire automotive world into pure electric. Lithium-ion batteries continue to improve roughly on average maybe 8% or 9% per year. Which when compounded over several years ends up being a meaningful improvement. Even if there was no fundamental improvement beyond lithium-ion batteries, I think we could still take all terrestrial, all ground transportation could go electric.

It gets harder for airplanes, we do need a further breakthrough for aircraft, where the energy density requirements are at least 2 to 3 times more significant, but even with current-generation lithium-ion, we could go to mass market with ground vehicles. Certainly, for cars, boats, and trains lithium-ion could do it. For rockets, well, there's no way to make a rocket electric, that's for sure. Unfortunately, Newton's third law cannot be escaped - I think. Certainly, there'd have to be a few Nobel prizes awarded if there was a way to get around it, that'd be really convenient.

The movement towards sustainable transport I think that's going to be good for many reasons, but again not something that happens immediately, that's probably something that happens over 30 or 40 years, the transition to electric vehicles. Electric vehicles are something that is a long-term sustainable option.

Yeah, we're talking orders of magnitude of difference between fossil fuels and batteries, not even on the same scale. And given that we have to solve sustainable electricity generation, then it makes sense for us to have electric vehicles as the mode of transport. That's why I think it's important for electric cars to be able to compete without economics being a factor. We just need to fix the incentive structure of the world to make sure that companies are incented towards sustainable versus unsustainable technology. This is fundamentally the problem.

If the big car companies see that our sales are good, and if they see that people are buying these cars, then they will have no choice but to conclude that electric cars are the right way to go. And that will accelerate the transition to sustainable transport. There are lots of naysayers out there that say 'electric cars are never gonna happen, we should just be resigned to burning hydrocarbons forever' well not forever until they run out of course. Then they'll say certain technologies like hydrogen fuel cells, and it's like, ah God, fuel cells are so bullshit, it's really rubbish. The only reason they do fuel cells is because they aren't really believers, it's like a marketing thing. I think part of it is that they felt for a long time that there was this need to be doing something. Since fuel cells were always 10 years in the future and always would be, they could say they were working on fuel cells and that would satisfy people.

Some will say oh hydrogen is the most common element in the universe. Yes, but not on Earth, which is an important consideration. I don't want to turn this into a debate on hydrogen fuel cells, because I just think that they're extremely silly. My opinion pre-dates Tesla. Not just because I have an electric car company, I could've started a hydrogen company.

Hydrogen is an energy storage mechanism, it's not a source of energy. You have to get that hydrogen from somewhere, it does not naturally occur on Earth. You either got to electrolyze water or you got to crack hydrogen carbon. If you crack hydrocarbons then you're just basically a carbon-burning car in disguise, so there is no possible win there. If you get that hydrogen from water, the only way to get the hydrogen is to electrolyze water and split the hydrogen and oxygen apart, so you're splitting H2O. Electrolysis is extremely inefficient as an energy process, a very energy-intensive and inefficient process. Then once you split the hydrogen off you got to compress it or render it to liquid form, which also takes a tremendous amount of energy. Hydrogen is very difficult to store and transport, it is a very light gas so any tank you store it in is enormous, because of low density. Hydrogen has a very low density. It's a pernicious molecule that likes to get all over the place. Then you got to store it, and even once it gets in the car it then has to go through a fuel-cell power plant to get turned into energy, and only then can it be applied to electric motors.

You get metal embrittlement from hydrogen. If you get hydrogen leaks, it's an invisible gas you can't even tell that it's leaking. But then it's extremely flammable when it does, and has an invisible flame. Hydrogen is quite a dangerous gas, if it does escape is highly volatile and can I have extremely explosive consequences. You know, it's suitable for the upper stage of rockets, but not for cars. Putting up a huge hydrogen distribution structure is also extremely difficult. It's just very difficult to make hydrogen and store it and use it in a car. It just takes an enormous amount of energy to create hydrogen. If you're going to pick an energy storage mechanism, hydrogen is an incredibly dumb one to pick. You should just pick methane that's much, much easier or propane.

If there was a readily available source of hydrogen that wasn't bound up in water, or bound up in hydrocarbons, then there would be a possibility of a fuel cell vehicle. But the reality is that if you take a fuel cell vehicle, and you take the best-case of the fuel cell vehicle in terms of the mass and volume required to go a particular range, as well as the cost of the fuel cell system, and if you took best-case of that it doesn't even equal the current state-of-the-art in lithium-ion batteries. So there's no way for it to be a workable technology.

If you took a solar panel and used the energy from that solar panel to just charge a battery pack directly—compared to try to split water, take the hydrogen, dump the oxygen, compress the hydrogen to extremely high pressure—or liquefy it—and then put it in a car and run a fuel cell…it is about half the efficiency, it's terrible. If you look at the total cycle of efficiency of a fuel cell system, its theoretical best case is twice as bad as electric in terms of the energy cycle. That is if the technology is perfect. But the technology is not perfect so it ends up maybe 200 to 300% worse than a solar electric alternative. The solar electric alternative is dead simple and the energy transfers are very high efficiency. Essentially collect power from the Sun, and then you charge the battery pack with almost no energy losses, and that's it you're done. The best-case hydrogen fuel cell doesn't run against the current case batteries, so obviously it doesn't make sense. That will become apparent in the next few years. There's no reason for us to have this debate. I've said my piece on this. It will be super obvious as time goes by.

If you take the best-case scenario for fuel cells, let's say you could fully optimize it and compare that to current lithium-ion batteries in production, it loses. Success is not one of the possible outcomes, so why embark on that. Why would you do that? It makes no sense. It's crazy. The math is so super obviously in favor of batteries, it's like staring facts in the face and saying it's not true. At Tesla, we call them "fool cells". It's one of those things that sounds like it's the future and it always will be.

I think in terms of energy storage, lithium I think is definitely the future and will be for a long time. The nice thing about lithium is that it is extremely abundant on Earth. Lithium is number three on the periodic table. It's extremely common. Lithium is the third most common element in the universe. The first being hydrogen and the second being helium. Now the hydrogen is all bound up in water on Earth, water or hydrocarbons. You don't find naturally occurring hydrogen on Earth. The helium being a noble gas just doesn't combine with anything and basically floats away. But lithium is a metal and does not float away.

There is an enormous amount of lithium, in almost any salty solution there is some amount of lithium. There are enormous amounts of lithium in the oceans. Any kind of dried lake bed where there was a salt lake bed dried long ago there will be an enormous amount of lithium. So the nice thing about lithium is that it is very plentiful. Any salty water has lithium.

There definitely won't be a lithium constraint on energy storage for batteries. I feel pretty confident that one could make enough batteries to store all the energy that the world needs with the current available resources. There is lithium in salt form virtually everywhere so there are definitely no supply issues with lithium. The actual amount of lithium in the world is far in excess of what is needed for the electrification of transport. Lithium constitutes only about 2% of the battery, so it is called lithium-ion and it's sort of the active ingredient but it constitutes only about 2% of the battery.

I think we're actually in a pretty good spot, and I am reasonably optimistic that there will be a breakthrough in high energy density capacitors. It's sort of interesting. If you do the sort of basic physics on the energy density potential of a capacitor, using naturally occurring materials, it's quite hard to beat lithium-ion batteries, but if you can figure out a way to make unnatural materials I suppose, that are accurate to the molecular level, then I think you can actually have some fairly significant breakthroughs. The ability to do that was developed in the photonics arena and applying those photonics breakthroughs to capacitor technology is what has the potential for a really big breakthrough there. I think we may see something on that level, but it isn't entirely required for cars.

Once you've built the battery, then at the end of the life of the battery you can recycle those components. It's something that has no long-term or negligible long-term impact on the carbon cycle because essentially you get the lithium, nickel, and cobalt, and you create the battery. Essentially, you get those materials once, and then you recycle them forever. I think it's really a negligible impact for batteries on the environment.

I'm quite confident that solar power will be the single largest source of electrical energy for humanity in the future. We can generate way more energy than we actually need to operate civilization just with solar panels. I think the primary means of energy generation is going to be solar, it's at least going to a plurality or a slight majority. So no problem to generate all the energy we need for electricity, for heating, for transport, from solar with some contribution from wind and geothermal and tidal. No problem at all, we just have to do it.

Ultimately all of that has to go electric. That means a tripling of the energy consumption by electric. Thinking about that in context the electricity demand will increase dramatically. It's going to be very important to think about how do you make so much more electricity. That is such a huge problem, there's so much that can be done in that arena, that it's really more than enough to absorb I think any number of start-ups and companies because it's such a tough problem and such a big problem. There are so many uses of energy that need to be sustainable.

There's obviously this sort of threshold to when solar power will become cheaper than conventional electricity, that's a massive inflection point. There'll be some long-tail before the final coal plant finally stops operating, the final natural gas plant stops operating. There will be some long tail because it's going to look like an S-curve as is typical for new technology adoption. At the beginning of the S-curve people tend to under-predict what's going to happen and then it goes to an exponential growth phase, and then an approximately linear growth phase. Usually people over-predict what's going to happen in the steep linear portion of the growth phase and then it goes back into a logarithmic to complete the S-shape. That's what happened with the Internet for example, and cell phones, the same thing will happen here. If you look at the growth rate of solar that's where it's going to go. Compound growth is very powerful.

I think everything will be completely electric, it's just a question of when, 100%, it's just a question of the timeline. Anything that we can do to accelerate that growth is a good thing because it means we will have power as long as the Sun shines. I actually think, as long as the Sun is shining, we'll be fine. And if the Sun doesn't shine we have larger issues.

22. In the Loop

Right now, one of the most soul-destroying things is traffic. It affects people in every part of the world. Most major cities in the world suffer from severe traffic issues. It takes away so much of your life, it's horrible. It's particularly horrible in LA. and Washington D.C. and most of the major American cities.

Right now we've got for terrestrial transport, planes, trains, automobiles, and boats for getting around Earth, but what if there was a fifth mode? I was trying to think what would be the fastest way you could get from say LA to San Francisco or cities in between. We should really be thinking about something that is, particularly in California, let's just invent something new that's way better than anything else. If we are to have some new form of transportation in California I think it would be good to aspire to something that is cutting-edge technology. I just want us to have a bad-assed transportation system.

I tried to think what are the attributes that you want in a new mode of transport? if you just say what would you ideally want in a transportation system? You'd say, OK, you'd want something that relative to existing modes of transportation is faster, costs half as much per ticket, can't crash, is immune to weather, and is like self-powering, with like solar panels or something like that. That would be a pretty good outcome.

What would do that? What's the fastest way, short of inventing teleportation, that you could do something like that? I came to the conclusion that there is something like that that could work and would be practical. It would be a fifth mode of transport, and I have a name for it which is called the Hyperloop.

Actually what inspired me was, I was stuck in L.A. Traffic and I was about an hour late for a talk. It took me an hour to go 3 miles. I don't know who was in charge of the damn 405 construction but they're a bloody idiot, and I hate them. It was the worst construction project I have ever witnessed in my life, I've cursed them daily.

I was thinking 'man there's got to be some better way to get around.' That's the biggest issue with Southern California, traffic hell, it's like which level of hell are you in if you're in hell.

I was reading about the California high-speed rail, and it was quite depressing. We got like a 'Bullet Train' that has the dubious distinction of being the slowest bullet train, and the most expensive per mile. The high-speed rail that was being proposed would actually be the slowest bullet train in the world, and the slowest per mile in the world. These are not the superlatives we are looking for. We're setting records at both of the wrong ends of the spectrum. It was going to cost like $60 billion or something to go from San Francisco to LA, and it's a really slow train. It's a little depressing. It's like, damn, we're in California, we make super high-tech stuff. Why are we going to be spending--now the estimates are around $100 billion-- for something that will take two hours to go from LA to San Francisco? I'm like, I can get on a plane and do that in 45 minutes. It doesn't make much sense and isn't there some better way to do it than that. What is the theoretically fastest way that you could get from LA to San Francisco?

Japan has some impressive trains that they implemented in the 80s. Then China implemented an even more advanced train. So it seems that in California we should try to say what can we do that's a step beyond that? Not from the standpoint of one-upmanship, but rather from the standpoint that the future is going to be better. I'm not against high-speed rail or if we just did a high-speed rail that was say a step above the Shanghai line. The Shanghai line is state of the art in China, let's just take it half a notch better than that. And make sure that we got a straight path from LA to San Francisco, as well as the milk run, not just to have a fast train that's not even as fast as what Japan did in the 80s. I don't see what the point of that is.

The high-speed rail plan will saddle the California taxpayers with a pretty significant amount of money, for something which isn't obviously compelling relative to a car or a plane, in terms of the time it would take to complete the journey. California taxpayers are going to be on the hook to build something that is the slowest bullet train in the world at an enormous cost. If you pay a high price you should have a great outcome. That should be the sensible thing, and that doesn't seem to be what is happening from what I can tell.

The idea that I had at first actually made no sense and wouldn't work, but I kind of shot my mouth off at an event and said 'yeah I've got this idea for a new form of transport that I think would be really cool.' I came up with an initial idea that turned out to be wrong and would not have worked. But I sort of shot my mouth off saying; I think we can do something that is probably 10% of the cost, and how would you like something that can never crash, it is immune to weather, goes like three or four times faster than the bullet train that's being built, it would go about the average speed of twice what an aircraft would do. You go from downtown LA to downtown San Francisco in under 30 minutes. It would cost you much less than an air ticket or any other mode of transport because the fundamental energy cost is so much lower. I think we could make it self-powering if you put solar panels on it, as you generate more power than you consume in the system, and there's a way to store the power so that it would run 24/7 without using batteries. It was like a tube with an air-hockey table. It was just a low-pressure tube with a pod in it that runs on air-bearings, on-air skis, with an air compressor on the front that's taking the high-pressure air build up on the nose, and pumping it through the air skis. It turned out that didn't work.

I thought people would just not ask me about it in the future, but then they did. So it was like 'oh man, I'd better come up with something that actually DOES work. I set aside some time to write down some of the details. I wanted to make sure I didn't say something completely stupid. You know, it's funny, it's sort of kind of a combination of electric and aerospace. I was spending time with both the SpaceX aerodynamics team and the Tesla aerodynamics team, just to make sure that whatever I put out there really will work. After a couple of iterations, I was able to come up with something where the physics hangs together. We actually only came to a solution that we thought would work maybe two days before the date that I published it. Some of the elements of that solution are fairly obvious, and some of them are not so obvious. Then the details, the devil's in the details, of actually making something like that work. I published the paper and said look if anyone wants to do this it's great, be my guest because I have my plate full running Tesla and SpaceX. I'm kind of strung out on things that I'm already doing. So adding another thing-- it's like doesn't-- it's a lot.

I polished something before the end of the year, and I wanted to make sure I vet it with a few people within SpaceX and Tesla and maybe a few outside people and then just sorta put it out there as sort of just something that I think would be sensible and then ask people to add to it and modify it, and maybe people have - I'm sure people have good ideas about making it better - and then try to come up with some sort of standard design that anyone can implement in the world. I think that'll be kind of cool. You know, sort of like an open-source operating system, like an open-source transport system. It'll be really neat. I think it genuinely would be a new mode of transport. I think one way to think of it is like it's... it's kinda like a ground-based Concorde. If you could make something go as fast as a Concorde, on the ground, how would you do that? the basic thought behind it is to have something like a cross between a rail gun and a Concorde. I sort of like saying that because some people are going to be scared about that and some people will be like 'yes, that's awesome.' I'm appealing to the second group.

I just basically put it on the website and did 30 minutes of Q&A and then it just went bananas. Like it went super-viral. I wasn't actually expecting that to happen. I just wanted to do what I said I would do, which is write the paper.

I don't say we have to do the thing that I thought of. What we intended to do with the Hyperloop was really to spur interest in new forms of transportation. And I think that probably the most valuable thing the Hyperloop paper has done is to spur thinking about new transportation systems. I'm starting to think that this is really going to happen. It's clear that the public and the world want something new. I think it would be great to have any great new transport solutions, that gets people to their destination in a way that is safer, costs less, is more convenient.

Flying cars sound cool. Whenever you see the sort of cities in some futuristic concept they always throw the flying car in there. I have thought a lot about it, and there are some people that I know that are working on personal transport devices if you will. I am debating should there be flying cars or shouldn't there be flying cars? I have two minds on that. I kinda like the idea of flying cars on the one hand but it may not be what people want, because if you have a huge number of cars and you have mechanical failures then I think you're sort of going to be vaguely wondering when there's a car landing on your head or house or whatever. And it would be susceptible to weather, that's a concern. Then there's also a question of noise pollution, so there also is a challenge with flying cars in that they'll be quite noisy. The wind force generated will be very high they make a lot of wind. And to what degree does it affect the skyline, is it just buzzing full of cars? I'm in favor of flying things. Obviously, I do rockets, so I like things that fly. This is not some inherent bias against flying things. Let's just say that if something's flying over your head, a whole bunch of flying cars going all over the place, that is not an anxiety-reducing situation. You don't think to yourself, "Well, I feel better about today." You're thinking, "Did they service their hubcap, or is it going to come off and guillotine me if they are flying past?"

Of course, you would have to have a flying car where it would have to be on autopilot otherwise forget it. But even in an autopilot scenario, and even if you got redundant motors and blades, you have still gone from near zero chance of something falling on your head to something greater than that. On the other hand, you would be able to go from one place to another faster, so I am not sure about flying cars.

I think actually if you eliminate the choke points in cities then there is not that much traffic outside of the choke points. If you look at the sort of in suburban streets the traffic doesn't choke things. It's really on the highways and major arteries since the cities grew way bigger than the major arteries.

The ideal long-distance transportation mechanism is a supersonic vertical take-off and landing electric jet. Where something like a Hyperloop works best would be for distances of maybe about 500 miles, but probably not more than a

1000. That's because if you compare it to supersonic air transport, in order to go really fast with the plane you have to climb pretty high because the atmosphere looks like molasses when you're going really fast. So for distances under 500 miles you spend all your time ascending and descending and don't really get an opportunity to spend time on cruise.

So there's a special case of cities which have a lot of travel between them below the 500 miles of distance, where I think the Hyperloop would be useful, because once the distances get long the amount of time an aircraft takes to ascend and land, which is mostly what it is on a 500-mile trip, that percentage declines. So then it's better to just use aircraft.

I thought it was really disappointing when the Concorde was taking out of commission, and there was no supersonic transport available. Of course, the 787 has had some issues. But the thing is, the 787 even in the best-case scenario is only a slightly better version of the 777, and it's like, OK, not that exciting.

I came up with the name Hyperloop, I guess it was sort of a loop, you know. You go back and forth in a loop I thought. As it got more and more sophisticated, you should be able to go to hypersonic velocity. It's a sort of hypersonic velocity tube.

Honestly, I think it's a lot easier than people think. Yes, there's math, but it's really not that hard. It's really, I swear it's not that hard. I think it's certainly feasible. I think it is definitely doable. I think the economics would be a lot less than the high-speed rail because the cost of the tube per mile would be significantly less. It's basically just a tube. The paper that I published had all the math behind it and multiple outside entities had gone through and confirmed that it's correct. It's mostly getting the right-of-way and approvals, not the technology. It's really pretty straightforward. It's just a tube and a pod with an air compressor on the front and air bearings beneath. It's very, very straightforward.

It's very important that the cost of the tube be minimized. You want the tube to be as low-cost as possible. If you do anything that requires action on the tube side it's going to make the tube expensive. If you use air-bearings that's really cheap, and ultimately you could go trans-sonic in the tube, and trans-sonic on wheels would probably be questionable.

Also, I think we want to introduce ideas for how the track should be built. Like how do you do a multi-hundred km track, and make the thing work? Because we want to bring this to fruition and show people that something new and great can happen and it doesn't have to be the same old thing.

I hope someone does it because it doesn't seem like our mass transportation is getting better, it seems to be kinda getting worse.

We don't have any specific plans to back Hyperloop companies. Right now we're just trying to, in general, support the idea and support innovative thought in transport. It's possible we would back a team, but we're trying not to favorite one organization over another; we're trying to be as neutral as possible, and just generally be helpful. I think if the companies that are trying to make it happen now if for whatever reason that doesn't work out, then I think I might do something myself in the future. I don't want to sort of front-run them and say like here's this free idea and then go and do it myself, that would not be nice.

Yeah, so we've been sort of puttering around with the Hyperloop stuff for a while. We built a Hyperloop test track adjacent to SpaceX, just for a student competition, to encourage innovative ideas in transport. It actually ended up being the biggest vacuum chamber in the world after the Large Hadron Collider, by volume. It was quite fun to do that, but it was kind of a hobby thing, and then we've built a little pusher car to push the student pods. We're going to try seeing how fast we can make the pusher go if it's not pushing something. We're cautiously optimistic we'll be able to be faster than the world's fastest bullet train even in a .8-mile stretch. Yeah, I mean, it's either going to smash into tiny pieces or go quite fast.

I think if you were to do something like a DC-to-New York Hyperloop, I think you'd probably want to go underground the entire way because it's a high-density area. You're going under a lot of buildings and houses, and if you go deep enough, you cannot detect the tunnel. And looking at tunneling technology, it turns out that in order to seal against the water table, you've got to typically design a tunnel wall to be good to about five or six atmospheres. To go to vacuum is only one atmosphere or near-vacuum. So it sort of turns out that automatically, if you build a tunnel that is good enough to resist the water table, it is automatically capable of holding a vacuum. So something like Hyperloop could compete well in that arena because you instantly enter a low-pressure environment.

I'm actually quite a big fan of tunnels. Tunnels are so underappreciated. Something that I do think would help a lot in cities is tunnels. I think this is going to sound somewhat trivial or silly, but I've been saying this for many years now, but I think that the solution to urban congestion is a network of tunnels under cities. We got this fundamental flaw with cities that you got office buildings and apartment buildings and duplexes, and they are operating on three dimensions. But then you go to the streets and suddenly you're two-dimensional. The fundamental problem is that we build cities in 3D. You've got these tall buildings with lots of people on each floor, but then you've got roads which are 2D, you have a road network that is one level. That obviously just doesn't work.

Then people generally want to go in and out of those buildings at the exact same time. So then you get the traffic jams, you're guaranteed to have gridlock. But you can go 3D if you have tunnels, and you can have many tunnels crisscrossing each other with maybe a few meters vertical distance between them, and completely get rid of traffic problems. It's my understanding that Hong Kong is actually in the process of building some tunnels; I was very pleased to hear that, that really is the solution for solving traffic in major cities. If you had tunnels in cities, you would massively alleviate congestion. And it would always work even if the weather was bad. I think this is really a simple and obvious idea, and I wish people would do it. I don't mean a 2D plane of tunnels, I mean tunnels that go many levels deep.

A key rebuttal to the tunnels is that if you add one layer of tunnels that will simply alleviate congestion, it will get used up, and then you'll be back where you started, back with congestion. But you can go to any arbitrary number of tunnels, any number of levels. There's no real limit to how many levels of tunnels you can have. You can always go deeper than you can go up. The deepest mines are much deeper than the tallest buildings are tall, so you can alleviate any arbitrary level of urban congestion with a 3D tunnel network. This is a very important point, you could have a network of tunnels that has 20, 30, 40, 50 levels; as many levels as you want really, and so you can overcome the congestion situation in any city in the world, and completely fix the congestion problem in high-density cities.

I think we really need to have transport go 3D, we need to go 3D up or 3D down. If we go 3D up with flying cars, we got a lot of challenges with noise and potentially things falling on people's heads.

I tweeted a lot about the Boring Company, which is basically a hobby. I wouldn't even call that a real company at this point. We bought some secondhand machinery, and we're digging a tunnel. The tunnel starts right across from SpaceX HQ. We're trying to dig a hole under LA, and this is to create the beginning of what will hopefully be a 3D network of tunnels to alleviate congestion. It's kind of puttering along, but it's making good progress. It's got like 3 people, some interns, and like some part-time people. We are making pretty good progress for all that, but that's like a fun thing to do, where there's like no pressure, everyone thinks it's gonna fail, it's like oke it can only go up from there. Sort of the grown-worthy joke that I make about tunnels is that they have low expectations, low expectations are great... There's no way to go but down... I can keep going. Oddly enough it's like a low-stress activity because everyone expects it to fail. The Boring Company is like 2% of my time.

Sometimes people think, well, it's going to be pretty annoying to have a tunnel dug under my house. But if that tunnel is dug more than about three or four tunnel diameters beneath your house, you will not be able to detect it being dug at all. In fact, if you're able to detect the tunnel being dug, whatever device you are using, you can get a lot of money for that device from the Israeli military, who is trying to detect tunnels from Hamas, and from the US Customs and Border patrol that try and detect drug tunnels. The reality is that earth is incredibly good at absorbing vibrations, and once the tunnel depth is below a certain level, it is undetectable. Maybe if you have a very sensitive seismic instrument, you might be able to detect it.

Tunnels are great, it's just a hole in the ground, it's not that hard. The challenge is just figuring out how do you build tunnels quickly and at low cost and with high safety. If tunneling technology can be improved to the point where you can build tunnels, fast, cheap, and safe, then that would completely get rid of any traffic situations in cities, and that's why I think it's an important technology.

To give you an example, the LA subway extension, which is I think a two-and-a-half-mile extension was just completed for two billion dollars. It's roughly a billion dollars a mile to do the subway extension in LA, and this is not the highest utility subway in the world.

It's quite difficult to dig tunnels normally. I think we need to have at least a tenfold improvement in the cost per mile of tunneling. There's a couple of key things that are important in having a 3D tunnel network we're attempting. First of all, you have to be able to integrate the entrance and exit of the tunnel seamlessly into the fabric of the city. By having an elevator, and sort of a car skate that's on an elevator, you can integrate the entrance and exit to the tunnel network just by using two parking spaces. The car gets on a skate, there's no speed limit. We're designing this to be able to operate at 200 kilometers an hour, or about 130 miles per hour. You should be able to get from, say, Westwood to LAX in six minutes — five, six minutes. I think there's no real length limit. You could dig as much as you want.

If you just do two things, you can get to approximately an order of magnitude improvement, and I think you can go beyond that. The first thing to do is to cut the tunnel diameter by a factor of two or more. A single road lane tunnel according to regulations has to be 26 feet, maybe 28 feet in diameter to allow for crashes and emergency vehicles and sufficient ventilation for combustion engine cars. But if you shrink that diameter to what we're attempting, which is 12 feet, which is plenty to get an electric skate through, you drop the diameter by a factor of two and the cross-sectional area by a factor of four. The tunneling cost scales with the cross-sectional area. That's roughly a half-order of magnitude improvement right there.

Tunneling machines currently tunnel for half the time, then they stop, the rest of the time is putting in reinforcements for the tunnel wall. So if you design the machine instead to do continuous tunneling and reinforcing, that will give you a factor of two improvement. Combine that and that's a factor of eight.

Also, these machines are far from being at their power or thermal limits, so you can jack up the power to the machine substantially. I think you can get at least a factor of two, maybe a factor of four or five improvement on top of that. I think there's a fairly straightforward series of steps to get somewhere in excess of an order of magnitude improvement in the cost per mile. Our target actually is — we've got a pet snail called Gary, this is from Gary the snail from 'SpongeBob SquarePants' Gary is currently capable of going 14 times faster than a tunnel-boring machine. We want to beat Gary. He's not a patient little fellow, and that will be victory. Victory is beating the snail.

If you think about the future, you want a future that's better than the past, and so if we had something like the Hyperloop, I think that would be cool. You'd look forward to the day that was working. If something like that even was only in one place, from LA to San Francisco, or New York to DC or something like that, then it would be cool enough that it would be like a tourist attraction. It would be like a ride or something. It would feel maybe like the Space Mountain ride at Disney World. The G-load would be less, so if you can handle Space Mountain at Disneyland you should be able to handle the Hyperloop. It will feel super smooth because it would use air-skis like an air hockey table with the air jets on the pod side as opposed to the tube side. It just would be smooth as glass.

Even if some of the initial assumptions didn't work out, the economics didn't work out quite as one expected, it would be cool enough that like, I want to journey to that place just to ride on that thing. That would be pretty cool. And that's I think how if you come with a new technology it should feel like that. If you told it to an objective person, would they look forward to the day that that thing became available? It would be pretty exciting to do something like that. I'm just keen on seeing it happen somewhere. It's exciting and inspiring to think about new forms of transportation or new technologies that make people's lives better. Wherever they happen, I think it's great. As soon as it happens somewhere and people see it really works out I think it'll quickly spread throughout the world.

The thing that's really going to convince people is if they can take a ride in it. Wherever it's built, it needs to be something that gets used a lot. Where ideally the economics prove out and people like riding it. Wherever that's done I think those are the important criteria for it to expand more broadly and be used widely throughout the world.

We did run simulations at SpaceX and Tesla, I actually don't think it's particularly, the engineering that it would work is pretty obvious. The larger issues are political and political support to do something like that.

We really want this to be an evolutionary path to a real system, real Hyperloops that could be deployed around the world, and used by millions of people. Even if ultimately what gets built is something that's quite different from what I wrote about in the paper, I think that would still be great. You know, if we're making people's lives better, getting them to places conveniently with more safety and faster. I really like the idea that you could live in one city and work in another city, and you can move fast enough that you can actually do that. It frees people up. Just gives people more freedom.

23. Getting Personal

How would I describe myself? I think a lot of people think I'm kind of a business person or something, which is fine. I kind of think of myself more as an engineer and a designer, maybe an inventor, rather than an entrepreneur. If something has to be designed and invented, and you have to figure out how to ensure that the value of the thing you create is greater than the cost of the inputs, then that is probably my core skill. I spend most of the week with my engineering and design team. So, I guess the way that I usually describe myself is more as sort of an engineer than an entrepreneur because most of what I do is engineering. Trying to create new technology that's important, but fun and cool at the same time.

The things that I'm interested in are advanced technology and the things that are pushing the forefront and I think are perhaps likely to change the future of humanity in a positive way. And I found out that I needed to run the company in order to design and engineer the things that are important, or that I think of as important, otherwise somebody else makes me do a different thing. So, if I wanted to engineer the things that I liked as opposed to being told what to engineer, it seemed I had to start a company and run the company.

It's difficult of course for someone to come up with praise for oneself, and there's bad and good here. I am no saint but I generally try to do the right thing. I always look to figure out how I can better understand things, and I take the position that I am always to some degree wrong and the aspiration is to be less wrong. We are always to some degree wrong. It doesn't matter who you are. I think trying to minimize the wrong-headedness overtime, I believe in that philosophy.

I care a lot about the truth of things and trying to understand the truth of things. I think that's important if you're trying to come up with some solution then the truth is really really important.

I am a very literal person, pretty much take what I say at face value that's what I mean. I am not a naturally extroverted person. I mean I used to be horrendous in public, I'm not that great as it is, but I used to be really horrendous. I mean I would sort of shake and be unable to speak, but I kind of learned not to do that. I much rather just be doing engineering stuff and design. But you know if you're in the car business, you got to sell cars and go out there and do promotional stuff.

I seem the have a high innate drive, and that's been true ever since I was a little kid I should say, I really had a very strong intrinsic drive. Sort of do all sort of risky things, like why did I do those things? that's crazy. I think I'm kind of constitutionally geared to just keep going, and I can get really sort of set on something and be able to keep going in that direction.

When I was a kid I didn't have any grand design. I probably wasn't that ordinary but my lack of ordinariness did not manifest itself till later in life, or it wasn't all that obvious. But I think people can choose to be not ordinary, they can choose to not necessarily conform to the conventions that were taught them by their parents. I think it's possible for ordinary people to choose to be extraordinary. I just think sometimes the things that seem quite clear and obvious to me I don't understand they aren't that obvious to everyone. I don't know. Certainly, there are times when things don't go well, then that's quite disparaging for sure, and then it's difficult to proceed with the same level of enthusiasm. But I do think that the things we are doing are pretty important to the future and if we don't succeed, then it's not clear what other things would succeed. And if we don't succeed then we'll be certainly pointed to as a reason why people shouldn't even try for these things. So I think it's important that we do whatever is necessary to keep going.

My drive to get things done is sort of disconnected from hope or enthusiasm. I actually don't care about hope, enthusiasm, or motivation, I just give it everything I got. You just keep going and get it done. I don't ever give up, I'd have to be dead or completely incapacitated. I certainly have lost many battles, so far I have not lost the war, but I've certainly lost many battles. More than I can count probably.

I wouldn't say I'm fearless. Well, first of all, I'd say I actually think I feel fear quite strongly. There's fear of failure, I certainly have fear of failure. But if I think that what I'm doing is important enough then I just override the fear. If the stakes are high, if the stakes are really important then I will overcome the fear and just do it anyway. Essentially drive overrides fear. It's like, people shouldn't think "I feel fear about this and therefore I shouldn't do it" it's normal to feel fear. People should ignore fear if it's irrational, and even if it's rational and the stake is worth it, it's still worth proceeding. You'd have to have something mentally wrong with you if you don't feel fear. But I feel fear more strongly than I would like, it's kinda annoying, I wish I felt it less. There are just times when something is important enough that you believe in it enough that you do it in spite of fear. But it does cost me a lot of stress and anger.

You know, something that can be helpful is fatalism to some degree. If you just accept the probabilities then that diminishes fear. When starting SpaceX, I thought the odds of success were less than 10% and I just accepted that probably I would just lose everything, but that maybe we would make some progress. If we could just move the ball forward, even if we died maybe some other company could pick up the baton and keep moving it forward, so that'd still do some good. Yeah, same with Tesla, I thought the odds of a car company succeeding were extremely low.

I did have for a while there just sort of horrible nightmares of rockets failing before launch. In the very beginning our rockets did not succeed so I think that sort of traumatic event sticks with you. As we get closer to a rocket launch my sleep gets worse I mean it's more stress.

I do have some dark dreams I don't know why, I've always had those from when I was a kid. Just like really vivid dreams which are often scary, and I don't remember them very well. Oddly enough I also sleep fairly well most of the time. I do think it correlates to stress in the real world. I am sure I have good dreams sometimes, but I don't remember the good dreams. The ones that I remember are the nightmares.

These introspective questions are interesting. It's hard to evaluate yourself on these things. Yeah, it's not as much fun being me as you think, I don't know. I think it sounds better than it is. It definitely could be worse for sure, but I'm not sure I want to be me.

In terms of what your definition of balance is, my life would probably be pretty unbalanced by the definition of most people. I work quite a lot, I probably put in sort of between 80 and 100 hours of work. It has really varied quite a bit over time. These days it's probably 80, 85 hours per week. For a while there it was over 100 hours per week and that's just a very high amount of pain. The difficulty and pain of work hours really increased exponentially, it's not linear. When the financial crisis hit in 2008/2009 it was just every day, seven days a week, morning till night, and dream about work. It was terrible.

My day is probably a bit different than people think it is, most of my time is spent on engineering and design. That's probably like 70% of my time.

I've got more ideas than time to implement. There are sometimes, like, late at night, if I've been thinking about something and I can't sleep, and there's something bothering me, then it'll occur then. I'll be up for several hours pacing around the house thinking about things, occasionally I'll sketch something or send myself an email or something like that. This sounds really cliche, but it happens a lot in the shower. The shower is probably like the most... wake up, go shower in the morning. I don't know what it is about showers. I think what really happened is things have percolated in the subconscious and it's not really occurring in the shower, but you're kinda getting the results from last night's you know, computation, basically. I just sort of stand there in the shower and - sounds wrong but yeah, I do.

Not to mention the Burning Man epiphanies. Those are huge. One key idea for a supersonic vertical takeoff and landing electric plane occurred to me at Burning Man. It's a very creative place. So yeah... Shower and Burning Man that's it.

Getting up for me usually is about 7, but I go to bed late. Usually, I go to bed around 1 am or so. Sleep is really great because I find if I don't get enough sleep then I'm quite grumpy. I mean, obviously, I think most people are that way. I try to figure out what's the right amount of sleep because I found I could drop below a certain threshold of sleep and although I could be awake more hours, and I could sustain it, I would get less done because my mental acuity would be affected. I found generally the right number for me is around six to six and half hours on average per night. That is an average though.

I think it's probably true that having a good breakfast is a good idea, but usually, I don't have time for that. Sometimes it's made for me, but probably half the time I don't have any breakfast. I'll have a coffee or something like that. I'm trying to cut down on sweet stuff. I think I probably should have an omelet and a coffee or something like that. That seems like the right thing and sometimes I do have that.

I used to have so much coffee and Diet Coke that I'd get really wired and then I'd get over-caffeinated and it wouldn't be good. Diet coke is good, there's something that they put in that stuff that is - you know, you never get sick of it for some reason. It's some infernal ingredient. I'm trying to cut down these days. There were probably times when I had like eight a day or something ridiculous. I think these days it's probably one or two. I'm cutting down to, I think, more reasonable portions these days.

Lunch is usually served to me during a meeting, and I finish it in five minutes. It's a bad habit. Dinner is where the calories really come into play. If I have dinner meetings - they're the worst, you eat enough for two people at those things. You have the appetizer, and the main course, and all that sort of stuff. Business dinners are like the thing where I probably eat way too much. I certainly could be slimmer I think. I work out once or twice a week. I mean, yeah, once or twice. I should do it more often, for sure. I usually just do a little bit on the treadmill or lifting some weights, I suppose.

Having a smartphone is incredibly helpful because that means you can do email during inter-social periods. You can do email practically whenever you're awake - you're in a car, in the bathroom, walking, everywhere. Whenever possible I try to communicate asynchronously, so that's really helpful to have email for SpaceX and Tesla integrated on my phone. I'm really good at email, I got Skillz, I got mad skillz on the email front. I'm constantly on email.

Then I have to apply a lot of hours to actually working. The way I generally do it is I'll be working at SpaceX on Monday and then Monday night fly to the bay area. Then Tuesday and Wednesday at the bay area at Tesla, and then fly back on Wednesday night and then Thursday and Friday at SpaceX. I wouldn't recommend running two companies, it really decreases your freedom. I work a lot, I mean a lot, I'm sort of in work triage mode a lot of the time.

Most of my remaining waking hours I try to reserve time for my kids because I love to spend time with them. Kids are really great, I mean 99% of the time they make you happier. Of anything in my life, I would say kids by far make me the happiest. Most of the time kids are kind of in their own world so most of the time they don't need to talk to their dad hours at a time. The great thing about something like an iPhone or BlackBerry or whatever is that you can intermix activities. So I can be with my kids and on email at the same time since they don't require constant attention. I can be in the same room with them and get some emails done, get some work done, and whenever they want to talk to me they can.

We play video games together. I like playing video games, and they are all boys so they like playing video games too. And we try to do things like travel places. I do drag them along on a lot of things, actually. You know they're a little blasé about the cars, they're remarkably unimpressed - I wish they were sort of more interested. Maybe they'll get more interested later. Well, I think if they're inclined to... I mean, if they're really interested in working at Tesla or SpaceX then I'd help them do that. I'm not sure I'd want to, necessarily, try to insert them into the CEO role at some point, you know. It's sort of like, if the rest of the team and the board felt that they were the right person then that would be fine, but I wouldn't want people to feel like I'd installed my kid there. I don't think that'd be good for either the companies or the kid, really.

I do encourage them to ask questions.. kids go through this asking why stage. You have this sort of chained whys. Like why is this this way? And why is that?.. And why is that?.. And why..and why... And answering those questions gladly and encouraging them to ask questions is definitely a good idea, you just want to encourage curiosity, you want to encourage tenacity. One of my kids in particular is a master of the chained why.

Heritability of traits is much greater than I thought. I had assumed that in the nature versus nurture, it was much more in the nurture. But having five kids I think it's much more nature. I mean what are you? you are hardware and software, right? so the difference between one person and the next must be either a hardware or a software difference. Why are kids that may have the exact same background, or same school and same everything, yet there are widely different capabilities? they had the same input experiences, so then it must be the hardware differences.

When a crisis flares up in either one of the businesses or the kids it can be quite a bit overwhelming. When things are going well with family and things are going well with work then I'm happy.

I do have an issue with punctuality I must admit. One thing I should say is when I sort of cite a schedule, it's actually the schedule I think is true. It's not some fake schedule that I don't think is true. I may be delusional, that's possible and it may be happened from time to time. But it's never some knowingly fake deadline, ever.

I try to get feedback from as many people as possible. I have, like, friends and I ask them what they think about this, that, or the other thing. Larry Page is a good friend of mine. I value his advice a lot, and I have many other good friends.

I think it's good to solicit feedback and particularly negative feedback, actually. Obviously, people don't love the idea of giving you negative feedback, unless it's on blogs they'll do that. I don't have a problem with negative feedback. I'm always interested in negative feedback. The biggest challenge I think is making sure you have a corrective feedback loop, and then maintaining that corrective feedback loop over time even when people want to tell you exactly what you want to hear. Nor do I have a problem with critical reviews, If I had a problem with critical reviews I would spend my time battling critical reviews. There have been hundreds of negative articles. I don't have a problem with critical reviews, I have a problem with false reviews. I don't like it when people think wrong things. I mean I'm far from flawless, but I don't like when people think wrong things about me.

I don't like the sort of celebrity element, like when people sort of write trivialities. Like why write about that? Obviously, some people think that's interesting, hopefully not many. Sometimes people write things that make me concerned if my kids will read that. That's probably the most concerning thing. But I'd like to be on the cover of Rolling Stone that would be cool. It's a double-edged sword for sure. It's gotten a lot harder for me to just have a drink at a bar. If I go to just hang someplace with my friends then people come up to me quite a lot. They're always really nice and everything.

As far as role models, I wouldn't say there was any one particular role model. I don't really compare myself to anyone. There are some people in history that I admire and think are great, certainly the scientists and engineers, and literary figures and, the great technologists. Steve Jobs at Apple, Bill Gates, and I actually thought Disney was a great innovator, Larry Page and Sergey Brin for sure, they're friends of mine they have done an amazing job. I'm in general a fan of the whole Google team. Obviously, Jeff Bezos is doing some impressive stuff with Amazon. Warren Buffett on the investment side. I think Bill Gates has done a number of very impressive things obviously with Microsoft and the Gates foundation.

Steve Jobs was a very unique individual, I think everyone and their mom looks up to Steve Jobs in that respect. I'm not sure if there's anyone that's going to be like him for a very long time. He's certainly someone I've admired. Although I did try to talk to him once at a party and he was super rude to me, but I don't think it was me. I think it was, sort of, you know I'm not the first. Larry Page was the guy that introduced me to Steve Jobs. So it's not as like I'm going tugging on his coat like, you know, please talk to me. Being introduced by Larry is not bad. Obviously, he was an incredible guy and made fantastic products. The iPhone was a really great invention. Something that Steve Jobs was, that was quite admirable, was that he was ultra product-focused down to the little details. And he and other people at Apple would really try hard to have these, on a high-level and a small level, delightful things happen. The product just made you happy, and that's what we tried to do with the Model S. There was a certain - the guy had a certain magic about him that was really inspiring. I think that's really great. I think Steve Jobs is way cooler than I am.

There's a lot of great people out there and I think also historically guys like Edison and Tesla. Edison was certainly a role model, probably one of the biggest role models. It is an interesting contrast between Edison versus Tesla. I think they are both great men and did amazing things. A little bit of rivalry is probably a good thing.

It's interesting because the car company is called Tesla. The reason it's called Tesla is because we use an AC induction motor, which is an architecture that Tesla developed. And the guy probably deserves a little more play than he gets in current society. But on balance I am a bigger fan of Edison than Tesla. Because Edison brought his stuff to market and made those inventions accessible to the world, whereas Tesla didn't really do that. In the scientific world, Tesla gets more attention and more credit than Edison. He's well-known in the scientific community, units of magnetism are in units of Tesla, but he's not very well known in the popular mindset so that's why Tesla is named after him. We thought we would recognize Tesla in naming the car company. Better than naming it the Elon car company or something like that. Tesla did pretty well for most of his life although he went kinda bonkers at the end, I hope that doesn't happen to me. I've actually contributed some funding to save the land for the Tesla museum. I like the way The Oatmeal put it: "let's have a god damn Tesla museum." Awesome.

There's a lot to learn from the lessons in history, and I think just, in general, to read about interesting people, about the difficulties they faced and how they overcame them. I think reading, in general, is just great. I also admire people like Winston Churchill and sort of the great interesting people like Oscar Wilde. There's a lot of interesting people in history, amazing people like Shakespeare. I'm a big fan of Brunel, I have five boys and I really wanted to name one of them Brunel.. or Isambard. No luck. Hopefully, one in the future.

I don't read many general business books. I like biographies or autobiographies. I think those are pretty helpful, and a lot are not really business. For example, I like Franklin's autobiography and the biography by Isaacson on Benjamin Franklin was really good. I am a big fan of Ben Franklin. You can see how he was an entrepreneur, he sort of started from nothing, like a runaway kid basically. Created his printing business, how he went about doing that, and then over time he also did science and politics. Franklin is certainly one of my heroes, he was a great guy. He was in different fields, and he sort of thought about okay what is the important thing that needs to be accomplished right now and then worked on that. I would certainly say that he's one of the people I most admire. Franklin was pretty awesome.

I like biographies in general, I think it's also worth reading books on scientists and engineers. There's a lot of great books and science fiction with a lot of interesting ideas. I love technology and particularly when I was a kid I would just consume all the science fiction and fantasy, movies, books, anything at all. Even if it was just really shlonky.

In terms of books, Lord of the Rings is probably my favorite book, but it's not really sci-fi, in fact, oddly enough J.R. Tolkien was kinda almost anti-technology. It's funny, Lord of the Rings was as a book kind of anti-technology, but it's still great.

The thing about science fiction is that it's free from the normal constraints, and science fiction explores a lot of different ideas. It can be helpful as a source of inspiration. You have to imagine an outcome in order to head in that direction. I read a lot of sci-fi when I was a kid, and I really liked the Asimov books, and Heinlein books, and Arthur C. Clark obviously. I'm a big fan of Asimov and Heinlein and Arthur C. Clarke. I think the Foundation series from Asimov is really one of the best ever. I like 'The Moon is a Harsh Mistress,' that's a good one, I think that's Heinlein's best book, honestly. Those are probably the three best sci-fi authors.

I certainly got inspired by a lot of science fiction books, and all the other obvious stuff, Star Trek, Star Wars, Battlestar Galactica. There are many forms and sources of inspiration, like books, TV shows, and movies they're all sources of inspiration. Most of the movies and TV shows about space are totally wrong, but they still have interesting ideas. Like the Star Trek communicator was an inspiration for the cell phone. In fact, the weird thing is the phones we have in our pocket vastly exceed what was on Star Trek.

In terms of key influences, I certainly liked Star Trek because that actually shows more of a Utopian future. It's not like things are horrible in the future - there are so many bloody post-apocalyptic futures, okay, can we have one that's nice? Just a few. So I like that about Star Trek.

Star Wars was the first movie I ever saw, so it was going to be fairly influential. I'd never seen a movie in a theater before, it was like super great. Our Falcon rocket was actually named after the Millennium Falcon, even though it looks nothing like it. It's not the shape you want for a spaceship really. My favorite fictional spacecraft? I'd have to say that would be the one in The Hitchhiker's Guide To The Galaxy that's powered by the Improbability Drive. I mean, that thing's awesome, it does the most unexpected things. From an inspiration standpoint... having read all those books and seen the movies, and many other books and movies, just the idea of having a future where that didn't come true, just seemed terrible. So we want to make sure that those books are not always fiction. So that's my inspiration.

I suppose I'd like to play a musical instrument, that'd be cool. I tried learning the violin. That's by the way a hard thing to learn. I cannot play the violin at all. Very horrible. I can whistle, I'm not bad whistling. I kinda have like a whole bunch of songs that I just whistle randomly. I can whistle but it's maybe not the coolest instrument to play. I can whistle Pachelbel's Canon, which is a tricky one, but I'm not going to whistle it for you now because that'd be too embarrassing... I can whistle 'Always Look on the Bright Side of Life' It's played in 'Life of Brian' and obviously it's a pretty funny song because they are being crucified at the time. I saw it first when I was pretty young, probably about 8 or 9 or something and I didn't quite get it. But I think it is a good reminder to not get focused on the negative things in life. My personal philosophy is I'd rather be optimistic and wrong than pessimistic and right.

I think 'Con Te Partiro' is an incredibly beautiful song. It's really calming, and it's just a really beautiful song. And obviously Andrea Bocelli is just an incredible singer. I think that song is kind of a reminder that the world is a beautiful place. It's an incredibly beautiful song, sung really beautifully so I think that's why it makes me feel that way about the world.

I personally don't understand it, but the song that I whistle the most is 'Santa Claus is Coming to Town' I don't even realize I'm whistling it, I just go into auto-whistle and this one comes up more than any other so I must like it at a subconscious level, but I'm not entirely sure why. I could guess. It's sort of a positive song, I mean who doesn't like Santa Claus? I guess it's good to have him come to town.

A song that just kind of gets you fired up is 'America, Blank, Yeah' I think it's funny and inspiring in a weird way – It's just cool, I like it. That is from the movie 'Team America'. I'm a big fan of 'South Park.' The shows that I watch are 'South Park,' 'Daily Show,' and 'Colbert Report', those are sort of my main three ones, they just capture a little bit of essence of America in both a good and a bad way.

I get involved in politics as little as possible. There is some amount that I have to get involved in mostly because SpaceX has to battle Boeing and Lockheed for national security and civil space launch contracts. I am sort of moderate, I'm sort of half Republican half Democrat. I'm sort of in the middle, I'm socially liberal and fiscally conservative. Which I think a lot of the country is actually.

My personal ideology is split right now between trying to be helpful on Earth-related stuff, which is sustainable energy, and trying to advance space technology so we can establish a self-sustaining city on Mars. My interest is really from an environmental standpoint, and to some degree from a national security standpoint, and longer-term overall from an economic situation standpoint.

I'm like a volunteer at this point, I don't need the money. I get paid minimum-wage actually, and I don't even get paid overtime. There's nothing like I'm sitting here saying I wish I could buy such and such a thing, I can just buy it. There's nothing that I want to buy personally that I can't buy. I don't really like yachts or anything like that.

There are two gasoline cars that I own, not many people know about these, but one is a series 1 '67 E-Type Jaguar roadster, that was the first car I bought when I had any money. The other car that I got is a Model T that a friend of mine bought and gave me.

The first car that I bought and liked was an old 1978 BMW 320i that I bought for $1400 and fixed up myself in "94. I had it for 2 years and then literally one of the wheels fell off. It was during the start of my first company, and I had lent the car to an intern to get something, and he gives me a call and says: "The wheel fell off the car." You could see like a big scratch in the road from the axle because it occurred while he was turning. I just scrapped the car at that point.

The first car that I bought when I had more than a few thousand dollars was the 1967 series 1 E-Type jag. When I was 17 I was given for my birthday a book of classic convertibles, I looked through them all, and I thought well if I could ever afford a car, there were two that I liked the most... One was the

Gull-winged Mercedes that was like millions of dollars.. and the other the E-Type Jaguar. I said well if I could ever afford it, that's the car I want to get, so that's what I bought. In fact, when the Venture Capitalists invested in my first company they gave me and my brother $40.000, just like an initial bonus or something, and I spend $35.000 of it on the car. That was like a bad girlfriend, it kept breaking down on me and caused me all sorts of trouble. In fact, it broke down on the way back from the dealer. It broke down on the way back it was very sad, I thought 'damn it I didn't even bring it home'.

I used to do lots of things that were personally risky, but now with kids and responsibilities, I do a lot less of that. I used to have, like a fighter jet and doing all sorts of crazy stunts, and I was like I want to see my kids grow up and all that. I have responsibilities.

I want to be able to look back and say that I had a good effect on the world. I just want to be useful. Sometimes that usefulness turns out entrepreneurial, and sometimes from an engineering standpoint, it's just you know usefulness. It seems to be so far so good.

Do I think that there is some sort of master intelligence architecting all of this stuff? I think probably not, because then you have to say where did the master intelligence come from. I think really you can explain this with fundamental laws of physics. Complex phenomenon from simple elements.

I'm not superstitious but you never know, there could be some divine entity, and if there is I hope that entity is favorable.

24. Falcons and Dragons

A lot of people really only heard of SpaceX relatively recently, so they may think, say Falcon 9 and Dragon just instantly appeared and that's how it always was. But it wasn't. Falcon 1 is where we started out, we started off with just a few people who really didn't know how to make rockets. And the reason that I ended up being the chief engineer or chief designer was not because I wanted to, it's because I couldn't hire anyone. Nobody good would join, so I ended up being that by default. And I messed up the first three launches. Fortunately, the fourth launch worked or that would have been it for SpaceX. But fate liked us that day.

Falcon 1 was quite a small rocket. When we were doing Falcon 1 we were really trying to figure out what is the smallest useful payload that we could get to orbit. We thought okay, something around half a ton to orbit, you know that could launch a decent-sized small satellite to low Earth orbit, and that's why we sized Falcon 1.

We got the Falcon 1 to orbit and then we did our first satellite launch, which was a commercial mission for Malaysia. That launch successfully put the satellite into orbit and I think it's actually still up there.

We took most of the lessons learned from Falcon 1 and began to scale that up to Falcon 9 with an order of magnitude more thrust, around a million pounds of thrust. Falcon 1 was quite a small rocket compared to Falcon 9. Particularly when you factor in payload, Falcon 9 is many times more, sort of on the order of 30 times more payload than Falcon 1.

Our goal has been to create something that is a reliable truck, essentially, rather than a Ferrari. In Falcon 9, we've leveraged the engine we developed with the Falcon 1, the Merlin 1-C. We essentially ganged nine of those together on the first stage, and then one on the upper stage with an expanded nozzle. That actually gave us about 20 times the payload capability of Falcon 1 because, in the case of Falcon 9, we were using a pump-fed upper stage as opposed to a pressure-fed upper stage. It's an important difference, for those of you who are familiar with how rockets are designed. It has engine-out capability, so you can lose any one of the main engines and still make it to orbit. I think that's actually a very important principle. There's an advantage to having the 9 engines, because if one of them doesn't work and has what we call a RUD - which is Rapid Unscheduled Disassembly - then it still makes it to orbit. That's something we think is important for commercial airliners, given that almost all airliners have multiple engines. All commercial airliners have multiple engines so that if you're going across the Pacific at night and you lose an engine you don't go down, you don't have to use that life raft or that jacket that they give you, which I think has not been used effectively, very often. Jet turbines are far more reliable than rocket engines so if that principle makes sense for jet turbines, it really makes sense for rocket engines. So multi-engine, I think is good, and we're going to keep that philosophy going forward.

In 2010 we did the first launch of Falcon 9 version 1, and we managed to get that to orbit. That had about a 10-ton-to-orbit capability, so it was about 20 times the capability of Falcon 1.

It also was assigned to carry our Dragon spacecraft. As far as cargo transport was concerned, out of budget necessity, NASA had gone commercial.

When we first created Dragon version one we didn't really know how to create a spacecraft. We'd never designed a spacecraft before.

The basic concept of operations of the Falcon 9 with the Dragon spacecraft in cargo configuration was a two-stage vehicle. The Falcon 9 drops the Dragon off in orbit, and then Dragon goes from that parking orbit, maneuvers under its own power to the Space Station where it is captured by the arm and it is berthed to the station. In the end, it reenters, the same way that the Apollo capsules reentered, blunt-body reentry, and lands in the ocean. So, while there are a lot of interesting technologies in version one, it does have a relatively conventional landing approach. It throws out parachutes to land in the water off the coast of California after it comes back from the Space Station, and it does have a life support system, but not one that can last for a long time or carry a lot of people. It's a great spacecraft and it was a great proof-of-concept. It showed us what it took to bring something back from orbit, which is a very difficult thing to do. Usually, when something comes in from orbital velocity, it burns up in a big fireball.

You know, I'm a big believer in sort of not getting too corporate and losing any sort of sense of humor, so when we did the first test flight of our Dragon spacecraft, we were thinking of what sort of interesting and wacky things we can put on there. And I really liked the cheese shop sketch from Monty Python, so it was like, "let's put a big wheel of cheese in the spacecraft." We got the biggest wheel of cheese the Beverly Hills Cheese Shop had – a giant wheel of stinky Gruyere. We kept it secret because if something had gone wrong with the flight, then people would have thought that perhaps we've been distracted by the cheese or something. We don't ever really want to be in a boring corporate situation. It's better to have a sense of humor and don't get too wrapped up in yourself.

2012 is when the Dragon spacecraft was docked to the Space Station and returned to Earth when we delivered and returned cargo from the Space Station. I don't think the public realizes how cool the ISS is, that is an awesome thing that's up there. Some people don't realize we have a Space Station. We have a gigantic Space Station, it's huge, it's really gigantic. It's a pretty incredible structure that we have orbiting the Earth. I think we should do something to educate the public about the awesomeness of the Space Station because it is pretty amazing.

And then President Obama said, 'we should also outsource astronaut transport to commercial entities. If we can fly in Boeing airliners and Airbus airliners and feel good about that, then why can't our spacecraft be built by commercial entities too? There was a Battle Royale against that, which won by a 3% margin in the House of Representatives.

That was a hairy battle. I'm probably not the guy that people would bet on. It's like a little kid fighting a bunch of sumo wrestlers, usually, the sumo wrestlers win. We were a little scrappy company, but every now and then a little scrappy company wins. This was one of those times.

I should make sure to very strongly credit NASA in this arena in terms of how helpful they've been. NASA put out a big competition and awarded two contracts for astronaut transport, one of which went to Boeing - they got a slightly larger contract - and one to us.

I worry slightly about some of the big government contractors. In the space arena, some of the big government contractors would definitely like to see SpaceX die. On the military side, we had not been allowed to compete for the primary military contract because Boeing and Lockheed had managed to shut down all competition.

221

It used to be Boeing and Lockheed competing and then, I don't know if you know the back story, but there were all sorts of shenanigans. And like, Boeing stole thousands of documents from Lockheed and used those in their competition against Lockheed, and Lockheed found out. I mean, these guys have some pretty bad track records here of really bad behavior. The Boeing CFO went to jail for bribing the top Air Force procurement officer and they had been doing so for years. I don't know if you know the Darleen Druyun situation, so it's not paranoia or made up, people did time in the big house. You can pretty much bet that's the tip of the iceberg. The Air Force did a thorough investigation and concluded that was the only one - it was only her. They would definitely like to see SpaceX die. I'm sure I am being tortured in effigy right now. You know when you see a movie, and there's the bad corporation in the movie, that's like the big defense contractors. Those are our competition in a lot of cases. Lockheed and Boeing are used to stomping on new companies, and they've certainly tried to stomp on us.

I guess they're afraid that we'll take some of the huge gravy train they have exclusive access to, that it's not going to be as big.

People have tried, but usually, the military-industrial complex was able to resist any attack by a newcomer. It was like fighting this giant citadel with very high walls, and usually, if a small force attacks a large citadel it is not the citadel that falls.

The people fighting it are in the bureaucracy of the Pentagon and the procurement officers who then go work at Boeing and Lockheed or their prime contractors, which is actually what happened.

It's easy to understand from a game theory standpoint, because essentially we're asking them to award the contract to a company where they're probably not going to get a job, against the company where their friends are. So they've gotta go against their friends and their future retirement program. This is a difficult thing to expect.

So we did have a bit of a challenge with the Air Force, and this is something where I'm sort of surprised there was not more journalistic interest because the Air Force was proposing to extend the sole source monopoly of Boeing and Lockheed until 2018. The reasoning given for that was the preservation of the industrial base. Although, oddly, for some reason, we were not included in the industrial base, and this is doubly odd because the main rocket used by Boeing and Lockheed, the United Launch Alliance, was the Atlas V which has a Russian main engine. And a center airframe, the interstage, and the forward airframe, the faring are made in Switzerland. So which industrial base were we talking about preserving? The one in Russia? That didn't make much sense in light of Russia's de facto-annexation of Ukraine's Crimea region and the formal severing of military ties. The Atlas V couldn't possibly be described as providing assured access to space for our nation when the supply of its main engine depends on President Putin's permission.

Our Falcon launch vehicles are truly made in America. We design and manufacture the rockets in California and Texas, with key suppliers throughout the country, and launch them from either Vandenberg Air Force Base or Cape Canaveral Air Force Station. We do a huge part of our R&D in Central Texas near Waco. We're building a third launch site in South Texas near Brownsville that'll give us good contingency capability if there's a say hurricane coming through the Cape and we still need to get to the Station. That would ensure continuity of service.

This stands in stark contrast to the United Launch Alliance's most frequently flown vehicle, the Atlas V. It's worth noting

223

that the Merlin 1A engine, the main engine on Falcon 1 was only the second American-built booster engine to see flight in about 25 years. The other one was the RS-68 for the Delta IV, and before that was the Space Shuttle main engine. It was actually the first new American hydrocarbon engine to see flight since the '60s.

When the merger between Boeing and Lockheed's business occurred, the merger promised in the press release a $150 million of savings. Instead, there were billions of dollars of cost overruns, and a non-recovery breach for the program exceeding 50% of its cost projections. According to congressional records, in FY14 the Air Force paid an average of $380 million for each national security launch while subsidizing ULA's fixed costs to the tune of more than a billion dollars per year, even if they never launch a rocket. By contrast, SpaceX's price was well under $100 million. Meaning a savings of almost $300 million per launch. Which, in many cases, would pay for the launch and the satellite combined. If you took something like a GPS satellite which is about $140 million, you could actually have a free satellite with the launch. Which is an enormous difference, and we were seeking no subsidies to maintain our business.

I think that we're unique in the launch business of publishing our prices on our website. Whereas other launch providers sort of treating it like a rug bazaar - they'll charge you what they think you can afford. We believe in everyday low prices, you know, and we've stuck to our guns on that.

You know, we have 1% of the lobbying power of Boeing and Lockheed. If this decision is made as a function of lobbying power, we are screwed. If this were just a matter of lobbying power we would have no chance. I'm not sure what the combined Boeing and Lockheed lobbying forces are, but if they were to send them all out at once the sky is dark. I mean, it's a swarm. They have entire buildings, you can see it as you go into DC, you know. We've got half of one floor.

In order to be certified as an EELV provider, SpaceX had to meet a number of requirements that were never demanded of the incumbent provider. We were required to successfully launch three flights of our upgraded Falcon 9 vehicle, which we achieved. It has required a lot of effort from me and other people at SpaceX just to find people in Congress who are ideologically motivated, and who aren't swayed by lobbying or only perhaps a little bit swayed. You know, John McCain spent a lot of time in a Vietnam prisoner of war camp, one would think about his politics he's not easily intimidated. He thinks this was a crazy issue because here we have the taxpayers paying three times more for a rocket. I mean, Boeing and Lockheed make decent rockets but three times more is really crazy, and the engine maker is majority-owned by the Kremlin, directly, there's not even a fig leaf in-between. So, why are we sending taxpayer money to fund the Russian war machine? In the interests of national security, we're sending hundreds of millions of dollars to a country that is doing terrible things and certainly not acting in our best interests. This makes no sense, it's like a Joseph Heller novel you know, it's so crazy.

The justice department was the one defending the defense department. They shouldn't be defending the defense department, this is crazy, they should care about justice. In fact, at one point the judge actually had to remind the justice department lawyer that he works for the American people, not for Boeing and Lockheed.

I think, as a country, we've generally decided that competition in the free market is a good thing and that monopolies are not good. It's interesting to note that from the point from which Boeing and Lockheed's launch business merged - the point where they stopped being competitors - the costs doubled since then.

I think that companies should just get together and compete as best they can. Totally cool, just let it be a fair game. That's all, have a fair game, level playing field, may the best company or group of companies win. And frankly, if our rockets are good enough for NASA, why are they not good enough for the Air Force? It doesn't make sense.

2013 is when we first started doing vertical takeoff and landing tests, and where we were going to the next generation of Falcon 9, which is a vertical take-off and landing capability. And 2014 is when we were able to have the first orbital booster do a soft landing in the ocean. The landing was soft, then it fell over and exploded, but the landing — for 7 seconds — was good. And we also improved the capability of the vehicle from 10 tons to about 13 tons to LEO (low Earth orbit).

Going from Dragon version one to Dragon 2 we wanted to take a big step in technology, really create something that was a step-change in spacecraft technology. In terms of lessons learned from Dragon 1, there's certainly a lot that we learned in every aspect of the vehicle - whether it's the heat shield technology, the Draco engine technology, orbital maneuvering, de-orbit, and trying to achieve a precision reentry path through the high-velocity entry, that's quite a difficult thing. You got to operate in a vacuum, hypersonic, supersonic, transonic, subsonic, that's just a lot of regimes for any flying object to go through.

Although Dragon version one lands with parachutes before the parachutes open it actually is executing a very precise guided path with the engines firing during reentry. The thing that is interesting and maybe slightly scary is that the Dragon is a robotic spaceship that is automatically navigating itself to the Space Station. It does pause at various points and asks if everything is OK, so it asks permission to proceed. But who knows it could be like HAL 9000, I mean we say like open the pod bay doors and he doesn't do it.

Some important characteristics are that it'll be capable of carrying seven people - seven astronauts for several days. We were actually designing the system with people in mind from the beginning. It's been way more difficult than cargo for sure, as soon as people enter the picture it's really a giant step up in making sure things go right, and for sure the oversight from NASA is much tougher. Technically, if somebody were to stow aboard the cargo version of Dragon, they'd actually be fine. I mean, hopefully, if it came back, they'd be fine. In the pressurized volume, we actually maintain sea level pressure, we maintain humidity, we maintain the temperature very precisely because we're trying to transport experiments that have plants and mice and fish and that kind of thing, to orbit and back. So, you could certainly stow away, and do it, but in order for it to be safe enough, we want to establish a standard of safety beyond the Space Shuttle and anything else prior. You want to have a launch escape capability, and you want to have lots of flights under the belt and tested without anyone on-board before putting people on-board.

It has an improved version of our PICA heat shield, and it's all-around, I think, really a big leap forward in technology. It really takes things to the next level.

One of the technologies that was really critical to the development of the SuperDraco engine was the ability to do 3D metal printing because it is quite a complex engine and was very difficult to form all the cooling channels and the injector head, and the throttling mechanism. But being able to print very high strength advanced alloys, I think was crucial to being able to create the SuperDraco engine as it is.

In crew configuration, we can carry the same amount of people as the Space Shuttle. Cargo configuration we carry less, but now that the Space Station is assembled there really isn't a need for the added cargo capacity of the Space Shuttle. It would be like people going to visit your house in a giant semi-trailer. It wouldn't make much sense.

It's very important to be able to take things back and forth from the Space Station. Obviously, we need to resupply the astronauts with food and whatnot. We also need to bring up space experiments, replacement hardware, we need to bring experiments back so they can be analyzed in a laboratory, we need to bring back hardware that needs to be repaired, so it's really an important transport cargo function. We are the only means to bring cargo back from the Space Station. With the Soyuz, you can bring people back, but it's very small, so it's basically what you can tuck under your seat.

To give you a sense of relative size, Dragon is much larger than the Soyuz, in fact, you can put the entire Soyuz spacecraft just inside the pressurized section of Dragon. Soyuz can carry three people in a very cramped environment, and we can carry seven people in a roomy environment. We're building the interior to look nice and feel futuristic. It needs to feel like a real spaceship. We're building a ship that NASA's going to use and that other people will use.

We've spent a lot of effort on the spacesuit design, on both the functionality and the aesthetics. It's actually really hard because if you just optimize for functionality it's one thing. If you optimize for aesthetics it doesn't work. Like those things you see in movies, they don't work, so it's like, 'OK. How do we make something that looks cool and works?' The key goal here being that when people see that spacesuit, we want them to think, 'Yeah. I want to wear that thing one day. That looks awesome.'

In terms of an astronaut corps, I kinda think what we should be transporting are scientists and engineers, not pilots, really. Dragon doesn't need pilots. It obviously goes there with just cargo. We sent up 40 mice, they were not piloting the craft. So really, it's a means of transporting people to the Earth-Moon orbit region in order to do science, basically. Potentially to the Moon to do some exploration there. But I kind of think it should be easy to go on a spacecraft, you should be able to just get on with no training and go. It shouldn't be hard.

Yeah, I think it would be fun to ride in Dragon at some point. Some people sometimes think that this is a round-about way of getting me personally into space, but it would be a lot cheaper to buy a ride on the Soyuz. A lot less hassle. But I'd definitely like to fly at some point, that would be great.

December 2015, that was definitely one of the best moments of my life: when the rocket booster came back and landed at Cape Canaveral. That was really... yeah.

My personal probability, we looked into it the night before the flight, and I thought we had probably a 60% chance of success, maybe 70%. There were just so many things that had to go right, and it was an incredibly complex set of maneuvers that the booster had to make. It's flying away from the pad at 5000 km/h, in the wrong direction. It has to deploy the upper stage, do a U-turn, and contain the propellant without centrifuging. The reason it has to be done with nitrogen attitude thrusters is because it's in a vacuum and has to be done quite rapidly. Then restart to boost back in a ballistic arc to Cape Canaveral, which was quite a scary maneuver. Then deploy the hypersonic grid fins and maneuver from hypersonic, through supersonic, to subsonic, and then finally to light the engine again for landing.

After liftoff, I ran outside the launch control center onto the causeway to watch the ascent, and I was just wishing that it would make it to orbit. I think that would have been a good day frankly if it would just be that. Then I was in touch with the rest of the crew in mission control and they were giving me updates on the flight. Then I watched the booster come back in, light its engine and land. It really felt like it was almost on top of us even though it was maybe 3 or 4 miles away. I ran out onto the causeway to watch the landing. The sonic boom, sound only travels at 1000 km/h, reached me about the same time as the rocket touched down, so I actually thought at first that it had exploded. But it turned out to be just that the sonic boom almost exactly coincided with the touchdown point, the sound reached me several seconds later. At first, I thought, well at least we got close, but then I went back into launch control, and it was this amazing video of the rocket still actually standing there on the launch pad, or the landing pad I should say. I couldn't quite believe it.

I can't say exactly where it would rank, but I do think it was a revolutionary moment. No one had ever brought an orbital-class booster back intact. This was a useful mission, it delivered 11 satellites to orbit and then came back and landed. That's perhaps the thing that's really significant, that we achieved recovery of the rocket in a mission that actually deployed 11 satellites. This was a fundamental step-change in technology compared to any other rocket that had ever flown. That showed we could bring an orbit-class booster back from a very high velocity, all the way to the launch site, land it safely, and with almost no refurbishment required for re-flight. It was really amazing and spectacular, and I think it means a lot for the future of launch.

Then in 2016 we also demonstrated landing on a ship. The landing on the ship is very important for very high-velocity geosynchronous missions. That's important for the reusability of Falcon 9 because roughly a quarter of our missions are sort of servicing the Space Station, and then there are a few other low Earth orbit missions. But most of our missions, probably 60% of our missions, are commercial geo (geosynchronous) missions. So we've got to do these high-velocity missions that need to land on the ship out to sea. They don't have enough propellant onboard to boost back to the launch site.

Hopefully this year we'll be launching Falcon Heavy. Falcon Heavy ended up being a much more complex program than we thought. It actually ended up being way harder to do Falcon Heavy than we thought, At first it sounds really easy because it's two first stages of Falcon 9's strapped on as boosters. It's actually not. We had to redesign almost everything except the upper stage in order to take the increased loads. So Falcon Heavy ended up being much more a new vehicle than we realized, and took us a lot longer to get it done.

The Falcon Heavy requires the simultaneous ignition of 27 orbit class engines, there's a lot that can go wrong there. It's just one of those things that are really difficult to test on the ground. There's a lot of risks associated with Falcon Heavy, and there's a real good chance that that vehicle does not make it to orbit. I hope it goes far enough away from the pad so that it does not cause pad damage, I would even consider that a win. I think Falcon Heavy will be a great vehicle, but there's just so much that's impossible to test on the ground. It just ended up being really way more difficult than we originally thought. We were pretty naive about that. But when it's fully optimized it's about 2.5 times the capability of the Falcon 9, well over 100,000 pounds to LEO payload capability. The nice thing is that it does have a throw capability to toss a Dragon in a loop around the Moon.

25. Dawn of a New Era

I think we are at the dawn of a new era in space exploration, which is extremely exciting. And it's not just SpaceX, there's a number of other companies that have developed new approaches.

From a technical standpoint the biggest thing that's happened in the last couple of years, which I'm really excited about and I think makes a difference for access to space, is the landing of the Falcon 9 rocket booster. All the other rockets, like the European rockets and the Boeing and Lockheed rockets, all of their stages basically just smash to bits and land somewhere at the bottom of the ocean. Every other rocket in the world the rocket stage is basically smashed into the atmosphere, explodes, and then further explodes when they hit the ocean, or the steppes of Kazakhstan or something like that - if it's a Russian rocket. There's a whole industry collecting rocket parts out there in Kazakhstan.

The really major breakthrough that's needed in rocketry, the pivotal one which we're aspiring to make, is to have rapid and complete reusability. A fully and rapidly reusable rocket. I think it's extremely important to re-fly the whole rocket. This is fundamentally something that has to be solved. This has not been achieved before.

I think it may not be completely intuitive, but I think if one refers to other modes of transport, it makes more sense. All other modes of transport are fully and rapidly reusable. That applies to a bicycle, a horse, a plane, ships. In fact, in normal life, it would be quite silly to discard your horse after every ride, you know, or dump the plane after you flew it. It would be obviously very unfortunate in the case of the horse. Every mode of transport that we use, whether it is planes, trains, automobiles, bikes, horses, is reusable, but not rockets.

Going back to the founding of America, if ships had not been reusable in the days of the Mayflower, the United States would not exist. Nobody could afford the journey, they might have sent a few people as an exploratory thing, and of course, since ships would be expendable you would need to tow your return ship behind you. So they might have said: "Oh yes, turns out there is a continent out there, but of course we can't afford to go there because it costs two ships every time we make the return journey." but in fact, ships can be used repeatedly, airplanes can be used repeatedly, and in fact, every mode of transport can be used repeatedly, and if that were not the case, we would not use that mode of transport, whether it's plane, train, automobile, bicycle, or whatever. So we must solve this problem in order to become a space-faring civilization.

I think the aircraft analogy is appropriate here. If you bought say a small, single-engine turboprop aircraft, that would be one and a half to two million dollars. To charter a Boeing 747 from California to Australia is half a million dollars, there and back. The single-engine turboprop can't even get to Australia. So a fully reusable giant aircraft like the 747 costs a third as much as an expendable tiny aircraft. In one case you have to build an entire aircraft, in the other case you just have to refuel something. So it's really crazy that we build these sophisticated rockets and then crash them every time we fly. This is mad. So yeah, I can't emphasize how profound this is and how important reusability is.

You could imagine that if an aircraft was single-use, almost no one would fly.

A Boeing 747 costs maybe a quarter of a billion dollars, you can buy, like say a 747 might be $250 million, $300 million, something like that. You need two of them for a round trip, so why doesn't your air ticket cost half a billion dollars? Nobody's going to pay millions of dollars per ticket to fly, to do air travel. I don't think anyone has paid half a billion dollars to do that. Nor would one want to. You can imagine a scenario where aircraft were thrown away with each flight that no-one would be able to fly or very few, maybe a small number of government customers. There'd be a lot of travel by boat and train and that sort of thing if that was the true cost. All you're really paying for is fuel, and pilot costs, and incidentals. The capital cost is relatively small. That's why it's such a giant difference. Because you can reuse the aircraft tens of thousands of times the air travel becomes much more affordable, and the same is true of rockets. Really, it's no different than air flight.

What a lot of people don't realize is, the cost of the fuel, of the propellant, is very small. It's much like on a jet. If you look at say the cost of a Falcon 9 rocket, it's a pretty big rocket with about a million pounds of thrust, the Falcon 9 is $60 million and that's for something which has four times the thrust of a 747, and about the same liftoff mass, so that's a good deal. But the propellant is only $200,000. It costs about as much to refuel our rocket as it does to refuel a 747 within-- well, pretty close, essentially. Falcon 9 uses quite expensive fuel, relatively speaking. I think there are a lot of lower-cost options. But the propellant cost-- which is mostly oxygen-- it's two-thirds oxygen, one-third fuel-- is only about $200,000. The cost of reloading the propellant on Falcon 9 is about $200,000 and the cost of the rocket is $60 million roughly. So the capital cost if it can be used once is $60 million. So obviously, if we can reuse the rocket say 1000 times, then that would make the capital cost of the rocket per launch only about $60,000. That means that the potential cost reduction over the long term is probably in excess of a factor of 100. The cost of the propellant is only about 0.3% of the cost of the rocket. Obviously, that's a humongous difference. Now, there'd be maintenance and other things that we'd factor in there, there would still be some external costs in terms of service, and fixed costs and some overhead allocation, and whatnot, just like you do on an aircraft, you have inspections and servicing and do all that sort of thing, so there'd be that cost to take into account, but still, it would be dramatically more cost-effective to get to orbit. It would allow for about a 100 fold reduction in launch costs, and this is a pretty obvious thing if you think of it applied to any other mode of transport.

And we have a low-cost rocket, it's not like our rocket is expensive. It is the lowest cost rocket in the world. It's just like a plane if you were to refuel a plane, not very expensive, if you want to buy a new plane, very expensive. As long as we continue to throw away rockets and spacecraft, we will never have true access to space. It will always be incredibly expensive.

Often I'll be told, 'but you could get more payload if you made it expendable.' I say 'yes, you could also get more payload from an aircraft if you got rid of the landing gear and the flaps, and just parachuted out when you got to your destination.' but that would be crazy and you would sell zero aircraft.

The other similarity with aviation is that it was extremely risky and extremely expensive, but over time that improved to the point where today you can buy a non-stop flight from Houston to London, a return ticket for $500. That never used to be possible and then even when it was possible initially it used to cost ten times that amount and now it's very affordable. That was brought about by there being a constant improvement in aviation over time.

I think it will open up options that today are hard to appreciate, just as in the early days with the Sopwith Camel, I was in the camel room, I don't think people could have envisioned that you could take a 747 non-stop from Los Angeles to London. It's similar when we say today that we can't see where things will be in the future. But if we enable that capability and improve the technology, then all sorts of things happen.

We've gotta make that happen. We've gotta achieve that goal. And that's going to take a bit of effort. It's not going to happen overnight, but we'll keep going in that direction until ultimately it's as close to aircraft-like reusability as one can achieve. If we can help set space transportation on a path with continuous improvement in cost and reliability as we saw with aviation, it's possible to achieve, let's say, roughly a 100-fold improvement in the cost of spaceflight if you can effectively reuse the rocket.

Essentially, the rocket needs to come back and land at the launch site, and then reload propellant and take off again. Like an airplane in its reusability. You do not send your aircraft to Boeing in-between flights. We believe we can get to the point where, in the not too distant future, the Falcon 9 booster can be re-flown within 24 hours.

Once we have reusability, I think improvements to reusability are going to be pretty important. That's really a fundamental one. I can't think of anything that's on-par with that, short of maybe warp drive.

Yeah, so we landed the Falcon 9 rocket booster and then prepped it for flight again and flew it again. It was the first re-flight of an orbital booster where that re-flight is relevant. The primary booster is the most expensive part of the rocket. The boost stage is about 70% of the cost of the rocket, which is somewhere in the order of $30-$35 million.

I think we are quite close to being able to recover the fairing, a huge nose cone on the front of Falcon 9. It's a 5.2-meter diameter nose cone, you can basically fit a whole city bus in there. Just that fairing alone, with all of its systems, and acoustic damping, qualification and all that, and separation system, is about a 5 or 6 million dollar piece of equipment. The analogy I use with my team is like, "imagine we had like 6 million dollars on a pallet of cash that was falling through the sky, would we try to catch it?" Probably yes that sounds like a good idea, so yeah we want to get it back. So we won't have to make another one. I say we do, I say we give it a shot, worst case it's gonna end up on the bottom of the ocean, but maybe we do catch it, then hey.. 6 million dollars. You know, it might as well be a pallet of cash, because it costs 6 million dollars.

That just leaves the upper stage of the rocket, the upper stage is about 20% of the cost of the mission. So if we get boost stage and fairing we are about 80% reusable. We think can probably get to something like somewhere between 70 and 80% reusability with the Falcon 9 system. I think for a lot of missions we can even bring the second stage back, so we are going to try to do that. The key to that is, all you do is inspections, and no hardware is changed, not even the paint, this is very important. I think we got at least a technical path to achieving that.

Then if you get to; why don't we have fully and rapidly reusable rockets? Why doesn't someone just do it? Well, it's quite tricky, that's the reason. We live on a planet where this is not easy. It wasn't obvious to me that one could achieve full and rapid reusability because Earth's gravity is right on the cusp of where that is possible or not possible. In order to achieve that really every aspect has got to be done super well. It's amazing how much gravity affects things.

I think for a lot of people there's not a clear distinction between getting to space and getting to orbit. There's a huge difference between space and orbit. Space you can think of as like the boundary of the international waters in the Pacific ocean. If you go 100 miles offshore you are technically out of coastal waters, now you're in the Pacific. It is like technically you're in the Pacific. But orbit is like circumnavigating the globe, it's a really giant difference. Space is somewhat of a loose definition, it's kind of 'where does the atmosphere get thin?' and you can sort of define, 'how thin is thin?'

It's pretty darn thin at 60 miles altitude, but you can't have a satellite up there because the orbit would decay very quickly and it would reenter.

Going up and staying up is actually about how fast you're zooming around the Earth. It takes much more energy to do that zooming around the Earth bit than it is to get to altitude. In fact, the only reason you need altitude at all is to get out of atmospheric drag. If the Earth had no atmosphere you could be orbiting Earth at an inch off the ground. The reason why things go up and stay up is because you are zooming around the Earth so fast that the outward radial acceleration is equal to the inward acceleration of gravity. Those balance out and you have a net-zero gravity.

When you see the Space Station, the thing that's sort of counterintuitive is that the Space Station is zooming around the Earth at 17,000 miles an hour. It seems real still but it's moving really really fast. To put that into perspective, a bullet from a 45 handgun is just below the speed of sound, the Space Station is going more than 25 times faster than that. That is what is actually needed to go up and stay up. That's why there's the term escape velocity and not escape altitude, there's no such thing as escape altitude only escape velocity.

The force of gravity, at say the nominal boundary of space of 100 kilometers, is almost exactly the same as it is on the surface of the Earth. It's a few percent lower than on the surface of the Earth. You can think of gravity as like a funnel in space-time. If you spin a marble, when it's far out it spins slowly and if it gets closer it spins faster and faster. So in order to go up and stay up the only thing that matters is how fast are you going horizontal to the Earth's surface. It's the outside acceleration that matters. So when the rocket is going to orbit the only reason it's going up is to get out of the thick part of the atmosphere, because at high velocity the atmosphere is thick as molasses.

It goes up very briefly, but if you look at the long exposure of the rocket's trajectory it goes up, but immediately curves over and starts going horizontal. So at the point at which the stages separate, there are two stages, the point at which the staging occurs can be as high as Mach 10, so it's going away from the launch site at 10 times the speed of sound. In order to get back to the launch site, you would have to have enough fuel and oxygen to reverse out that velocity and boost back all the way to the launch site. It's physically impossible because the other sort of thing about it is if you are in space there is nothing to react against. Aircraft can circle very easily because it's reacting against air. In a vacuum, there is nothing to react against, so the only way to go back the other direction is to apply twice as much force as it took you. The bottom line is this thing is zinging out there 10 times as fast as a bullet. The point of separation is not that far away it's maybe 100 km away from the launch site, but it's going like hell away from the launch site. The only way to land it is to continue on that ballistic arc and then land out to sea on a ship that's prepositioned to a particular latitude and longitude, to very precise within about a meter.

Why is it so expensive to send something into space? Well, let me tell you what makes a rocket hard. The energy and velocity required to get into orbit are so substantial that compared to, say, a car or even a plane, you have almost no margin to play with. It's a tricky thing, Earth's gravity well is quite deep, Earth has a fairly high gravity, it is really quite strong. It's possible but quite difficult. If we lived on Mars, this would actually be quite an easy thing. But at 1 g this is just barely possible. The difficulty of making a rocket reusable is much greater than the difficulty of making aircraft reusable. That's why a fully reusable rocket has never been developed thus far.

The reason it hasn't occurred in the past is that when people try to design a rocket and even one that is expendable after a lot of smart people have worked on the rocket using advanced materials and various techniques, you typically get 2 to 3% of liftoff mass to orbit. That's for an expendable rocket. Now, if you say okay, we want to make it reusable, we want to bring it back to the launch site, then it's gotta survive the rigors of reentry, all the systems have to be capable of surviving multiple firings and thermal fatigue and it's just really - you add a lot of mass when that happens. Previously, when people have tried to make a reusable system, they found that they would get some portion of the way and conclude that success was not one of the possible outcomes.

Typically a launch vehicle will get about 2% of its lift-off mass to orbit, and that's the case for Falcon. So if you can only get 2% of what your rocket weighs, to begin with to orbit, if you're wrong by 2%, you're not going to get anything to orbit. You know, it'll come crashing down in the Pacific somewhere. That means all of your calculations have to be right. If you miscalculate something, you get an answer wrong, it blows up. And it's very expensive trying to get all your answers right and then double-check if they're right. And testing them all and doing as much as you can on the ground. I think that's a lot of what makes rockets expensive.

If you say, okay, well, what if you want to add in the reusable bits? adding the reusability tends to take another 2 to 3% so then you end up with zero or negative. There's not much point in sending a rocket to orbit with nothing on it, that's obviously not helpful. The trick is to try to shift that from say 2%, 3% in an expendable configuration. To make the rocket mass efficiency, engine efficiency, and so forth, so much better that it moves to maybe around 3.5% to 4% in the expendable configuration. And then try to get clever about the reusability elements, and try to drop that to around the 1.5% to 2% level, so you have a net payload to orbit of about 2%. The trick is to make a rocket that is so mass efficient that it gets close to 4% of its payload to orbit in an expendable configuration, and then improve the weight of the reusability bits, push that down to around 2% and you get a net of four minus two - so, on the order of 2% of your payload to orbit in a fully reusable scenario.

That requires paying incredibly close attention to every aspect of the rocket design. The efficiency of the engine, the weight of the engine, the weight of the tanks, the legs, even the secondary structure, the wiring, the plumbing, and the electronics, making sure your guidance system is extremely precise, and just pulling all sorts of tricks - every trick in the book - and then coming up with some new ones. In order to achieve that level of mass efficiency.

If you use the most advanced materials, most advanced design techniques, and you get everything just right, then I'm confident that you can do a fully reusable rocket. Fortunately, if Earth's gravity was even 10% stronger, I would say it would be impossible.

The low launch rate typically is also what makes rockets expensive. If you had thousands of flights a year then it would be a lot cheaper. Although it's a bit of a chicken and egg because it needs to be cheaper in order to have thousands of flights a year. But at the end of the day, in the final analysis, I would say, that rockets really should be a lot cheaper than they are today. I think the way they're built, the way they're operated is just very inefficient.

The only semi-reusable rocket system that's ever flown really was the Space Shuttle. The Space Shuttle was an attempt to achieve that, but it was not a successful attempt, unfortunately. The Russians briefly flew one, but it didn't work out. They retired it because they thought it didn't make any sense.

The Space Shuttle was semi-reusable, it was partly reusable, I say partly because the main tank, the big orange thing was not reusable, that was guaranteed to be expendable every time. The main tank was thrown away every time, and it wasn't just the tank, the big orange thing was actually the primary ascent aero-frame to which the orbiter, the plane part, and the side boosters were attached.

The plane thing is not a good idea in my view. If you consider that every mode of transport is designed to its medium. If you're in space, wings are not very useful because there is no air. And if you want to go somewhere other than Earth there are also no runways. So these are important considerations.

The Space Shuttle was extremely difficult to refurbish for flight, 10,000 people needed to work for nine months to refurbish the Space Shuttle. The reusable parts were so difficult to reuse that the Space Shuttle cost about four times more than an expendable vehicle of an equivalent payload capability. The Space Shuttle ended up costing a billion dollars per flight, and you could only go into low Earth orbit. So even in the best-case scenario, it would not have been reusable in a substantial way. It took an army of 10,000 people nine months to refurbish the Shuttle for flight. Which is obviously not rapidly reusable. The Space Shuttle was the only operating example of something with even partial reusability. It was the right goal but didn't hit the target.

We are now beginning serious development of the BFR, ... well we're sort of searching for the right name, but the code name at least is BFR. To have a vehicle that can do everything that's needed in the greater Earth orbit activity.

We were really searching for, you know, how do we pay for this thing. We went through various ideas, with Kickstarter, you know, collecting underpants, these didn't pan out. Essentially we want to make our current vehicles redundant. We want to have one system, one booster, and ship that replaces Falcon 9, Falcon Heavy, and Dragon. If we can do that, then all the resources that are used for Falcon 9, Heavy, and Dragon can be applied to this system. That's really fundamental, and this was quite a profound -- I won't call it breakthrough, but realization -- that if we can build a system that cannibalizes our own products, makes our own products redundant, then all of the resources, which are quite enormous, that are used for Falcon 9, Heavy, and Dragon, can be applied to one system. You can think of this as essentially combining the upper stage of the rocket with Dragon. It's like if Falcon 9 upper stage and Dragon were combined.

Some of our customers are conservative and they want to see BFR fly several times before they're comfortable launching on it, so what we plan to do is to build ahead and have a stock of Falcon 9 and Dragon vehicles so that customers can be comfortable if they want to use the old rocket, and the old spacecraft, they can do that, because we'll have a bunch in stock. But all of our resources will then turn towards building

BFR, and we believe that we can do this with the revenue we receive for launching satellites and for servicing the Space Station.

The payload difference is quite dramatic. The updated design for the BFR in fully reusable configuration, without any orbital refueling, we expect to have a payload capability of 150 tons to low Earth orbit, and that compares to about 30 for Falcon Heavy, which is partially reusable.

So then, just the basics about the ship. It's really quite a big vehicle. 48-meter length. The main body diameter is about 9 meters or 30 feet. The booster is lifted by 31 Raptor engines that produce a thrust of about 5,400 tons, lifting a 4,400-ton vehicle straight up. Dry mass expecting to be about 85 tons, technically, our design says 75 tons, but inevitably there's mass growth. That ship will contain 1,100 tons of propellant with an ascent design of 150 tons and a return mass of 50.

You've got the engine section in the rear, the propellant tanks in the middle, and then a large payload bay in the front, and that payload bay is actually eight stories tall, in fact, you can fit a whole stack of Falcon 1 rockets in the payload bay.

The cargo area has a pressurized volume of 825 cubic meters, this is greater than the pressurized area of an A380. So it's is capable of carrying a tremendous amount of payload. I think it's important to note that BFR has more capability than Saturn V, even with full reusability.

The next key element is propulsive landing. As a propulsive lander, you can go anywhere in the solar system. So you could go to the Moon, you could go to... Well, anywhere, really. Whereas if something relies on parachutes or wings, then you can pretty much only — well if its wings, you can pretty much only land on Earth, because you need a runway, and most places don't have a runway. And any place that doesn't have a dense atmosphere, you can't use parachutes. If you saw a movie about the future with aliens landing, how do they land? Obviously, it'd be kind of weird if the aliens landed in the ocean with parachutes, we'd be like okay, nothing to fear.

Propulsive works anywhere, it could really lower the cost of getting science instruments to various places in the Solar System, so that's kind of exciting.

Orbital refilling is also extremely important. If you were to just fly BFR to orbit and don't do any refilling, it's pretty good. You'll get a hundred and fifty tons to low Earth orbit, and have no fuel to go anywhere else. However, if you send up tankers and refill in orbit, you can refill the tanks all the way to the top and get 150 tons all the way to Mars. And if the tanker has high reuse capability, then you're just paying for the cost of propellant. The cost of oxygen is extremely low, and the cost of methane is extremely low. So if that's all you're dealing with the cost of refilling your spaceship in orbit is tiny, and you can get 150 tons all the way to Mars.

The size of this being a 9-meter9-meter diameter vehicle is a huge enabler for new satellites. We can actually send something that is almost nine meters in diameter to orbit. For example, if you want to do a new Hubble, you could send a mirror that has ten times the surface area of the current Hubble, as a single unit. Doesn't have to unfold or anything, or you can send a large number of small satellites. You do whatever you like. You can actually also go around and, if you wanted to, collect old satellites or clean up space debris. That may be something we have to do in the future.

It's also intended to be able to service the Space Station.

It can also go out too much further than that, like for example, the Moon. Based on calculations we've done we can do lunar surface missions with no propellant production on the surface of the Moon. If we do a high elliptic parking orbit for the ship and re-tank in a high elliptic orbit, we can go all the way to the Moon and back with no local propellant production on the Moon. I think that would enable the creation of Moon Base Alpha, or some sort of lunar base. It's 2018, I mean, we should have a lunar base by now. What the hell's going on? I think if you want the public fired up I think we're gonna have to have a base on the Moon.

But there's something else. If you build a ship that's capable of going to Mars, what if you take that same ship and go from one place to another on Earth? We looked at that and the results are quite interesting.

Provided we can land somewhere where noise is not a super-big deal, rockets are very noisy, we could go to anywhere on Earth in 45 minutes, at the longest. Most places on Earth would be maybe 20, 25 minutes. So maybe if we had a floating platform out off the coast of New York, say 20 or 30 miles out, you could go from New York to Tokyo in — I don't know — 25 minutes. Cross the Atlantic in 10 minutes. Really, most of your time would be getting to the ship, and then it'd be real quick after that.

The great thing about going to space is there's no friction, so once you're out of the atmosphere, it will be smooth as silk, no turbulence, nothing. There's no weather, there's no atmosphere, and you can get to most long-distance places in less than half an hour. If we're building this thing to go to the Moon and Mars, then why not go to other places on Earth as well? If you can carry a lot of people per flight then you can get the cost of spaceflight to be something not far from the cost of air flight. There are some intriguing possibilities there.

I think we are at the dawn of a new era. Finally, it took a long time.

26. Innovation

I keep getting asked this question: how do you do more innovation? I think the number one thing is people should just try. An important thing in innovation or creating new things is to try really hard to just do that, which may sound incredibly obvious, but that's what people most often don't do. Literally, just try like did you try yesterday? Did you try today? I think people self-limit more than they realize.

I think what a lot of people don't appreciate is that technology does not automatically improve. You know, we sort-of take it for granted, like it's as though things automatically improve. They do not automatically improve! They only improve with lots of effort and resources. Egyptian civilization got to the point where it could create things like the great pyramid of Cheops but then lost that ability and never got it back there. Roman civilization went through a deep dark period, and there are many examples in history where civilizations have reached a certain technology level and then have fallen well below that and then recovered only millennia later.

The United States is sort of like that comment about democracy, it's a bad system but it's the least bad. The United States is the least bad at encouraging innovation. Silicon Valley I'd say is particularly good at encouraging innovation. Silicon Valley is just orders of magnitude better than any place in the world for creating new companies and fostering innovation, it's quite remarkable. I don't think we necessarily need to worry about some other country out there out-innovating us. I don't think people realize that almost all innovation in the world comes from America, a ridiculous percentage. But that doesn't mean it couldn't be better. It's not a given that things improve. It only improves if a lot of really strong engineering talent is applied to the problem that it improves. There has to be a forcing function. People have to do it.

It is generally true that innovation comes from questioning the way things have been done before. Cross-pollination of industries is helpful. It takes a lot of mental exertion to innovate and I think it is helpful to learn about different industries and try to cross-pollinate because very often people get silo-ed in a particular industry. If in the education system you're taught not to do that, that will inhibit entrepreneurship. I would encourage someone to do the 101 of almost everything that they find intrinsically interesting and to think how they might combine things from one discipline to another. I think this is a great way to come up with new ideas. It's been quite difficult to run SpaceX and Tesla but since I got both on my mind there have been good ideas going back and forth. For example, the Model S is the only all-aluminum body and chassis car in North America. In the aerospace industry that's the default.

You can definitely start a company at any age and be successful, it's just a question of do you have a good idea, are you working really hard, are you able to attract a great team, and motivate the team that's sort of really what matters.

I think that if you can identify some need in society or some want if you can see that there something that you really want or your friends really want, and you can sort of find a group of people together to solve that want or need that's really it. The best time to do it is when you're in college or just finished with college because your obligations are low when you don't have a family to support.

It's not really the idea, the thing of its 1% inspiration and 99% perspiration I think is generally true. A lot of times companies start out with an idea that's actually wrong, but they adapt quickly enough to get it to something that is right.

If you're a newcomer product it's really not enough to just be as good as the incumbent product, because people are used to what they're used to - people are set in their ways. In order to get people to change you have to do something that's meaningfully better. Otherwise the gradient of change, you know the change with respect to time, that change is going to happen slowly. If you want it to happen fast it's got to be obviously better. That's why we've tried very hard with the Model S to create a car that's obviously better.

When you consider the system as a whole what matters is: whatever the end thing is built, that people actually use, the cost, the reliability, and the utility have to be as good as possible. The fundamental physics and economics should drive the true solution. This is where I think it is helpful to use the analytical approach in physics– that's the best framework for understanding things that are counterintuitive. And always take the position that you are at some degree wrong and your goal is to be less wrong over time. I think a first-principles approach is a good way to understand what new things are possible. Try to boil things down to first principles, it's really a powerful, powerful method. Examining whether you have the correct axioms, are they the most applicable axioms, does the logic necessarily connect, and what is the range of probable outcomes? Outcomes are usually not deterministic, they are a range, so you want to figure out what the probabilities are, and make sure ideally that you're the house. It's fine to gamble as long as you're the house.

One of the biggest mistakes people generally make, and I'm guilty of it too, is wishful thinking. You know like you want something to be true even if it isn't true, and so you ignore the real truth because of what you want to be true. This is a very difficult trap to avoid and like I said that I find myself having problems with. It doesn't mean you'll be successful, but it means that you can at least determine if success is one of the possibilities.

I think it is important to be highly adaptive, so you're seeing what happens and adjusting accordingly. And I think it is very important to actively seek out and listen very carefully to negative feedback. This is something people typically tend to avoid because it's painful. But I think this is a very common mistake - to not actively seek out and listen to negative feedback. Solicit critical feedback particularly from friends, particular friends, if somebody loves you they want the best for you; they don't want to tell you the bad thing. The reason they're reluctant is because most people are hurt when they get negative feedback. It's not an unreasonable expectation. So, you need to actually coax people to give you negative feedback. Encourage negative feedback, and listen to it carefully, and don't react in a bad way when you receive it. That's really important, in fact, when friends get a product I say look, don't tell me what you like, tell me what you don't like because otherwise, your friend is not going to tell you what he doesn't like. He's going to say 'I love this, and that' and leave out the 'this is the stuff I don't like' list because he wants to be your friend and, you know, doesn't want to offend you. You really need to sort of coax negative feedback, and you know if someone is your friend, or at least not your enemy, and they're giving you negative feedback, then - they may be wrong, but it's coming from a good place, so you have to ask them to say it: I really do want to know, and then they'll tell you. And sometimes even your enemies give you good negative feedback. So I think that's important. You should just be like, positive feedback is like water off a duck's back. That's like, really underweight that and overweight negative feedback.

I think one thing that's important is to try not to serialize dependencies, so if you can put as many elements in parallel as possible. A lot of things have a gestation period and there's really nothing you can do to accelerate; I mean it's very hard to accelerate that gestation period. So if you can have all those things gestating in parallel then that is one way to substantially accelerate your timeline. I think people tend to serialize things too much.

Then, I'd say focus on signal over noise. A lot of companies get confused. They spend a lot of money on things that don't actually make the product better. For example, at Tesla, we've never spent any money on advertising. We've put all the money into R&D and manufacturing and design to try and make the car as good as possible, and I think that's the way to go. For any given company, keep thinking about, "Are these efforts that people are expending, are they resulting in a better product or service?" and if they're not, stop those efforts.

I think it's worth noting that when somebody has a breakthrough innovation it's rarely one little thing, very rarely is it one little thing. Usually, it is a whole bunch of things that collectively amount to a huge innovation.

You should always use your own products to see how you can make them better. I think it's important that you get all the details of any product or service right, it's sort of like there's a huge difference between something that's nearly good or something that's truly great and it's that last 5% that makes a difference. You want people to fall in love with the product you want to make them as happy as possible, but if there's a few things wrong with it, it kills the magic.

We really try to get every detail as perfect as possible and most people won't even notice all the things but we know some people will. Actually, most people will, even if they don't know it consciously they will feel it subconsciously. They won't know exactly why they love it if you asked them, they can't say exactly why but it's because the subconscious mind processes all those details and gives them a good feeling.

It's hard to convey a complicated thing to people, the innovator or the innovators PR department will say such and such is the reason why it's better. Innovation is a collection of complex things that are usually difficult to convey, so there is some soundbite that is given. Why is Southwest Airlines one of the most popular airlines in the business? it's not because they only use 737s, if it was that easy everyone could do it. My favorite sort of commercial airliner is the 747, I think it's just an awesome design. It's the fastest of the airliners actually. They are quite aerodynamically efficient and I like the look of it honestly, so that's sort of the Hall of Famer right there. It's incredible that the first iteration of it was designed in the 60s. I think since then we have not exceeded the 747, which is nutty. The 787 is kind of an improved version of the 777 but I think it's a bit disappointing because its main attribute is being 10% more efficient per passenger mile than the 777. And eight of those points come from the engine, that seems like a lot of money to spend for being 2% more efficient on the airframe side. Whenever you have a large Industry that is a monopoly or a duopoly the forcing function for innovation is weak because innovation tends to come from new entrants to an industry. I think it's fairly easy to understand because if you are a senior executive in that company or the CEO let's say, if you do something incremental it's very hard to be fired. If you do something bold and it doesn't work out you are very likely to be fired, so they do the incremental things. I think for the commercial airliner business you essentially have a duopoly between Airbus and Boeing and these big airplane programs are really long term and they're quite expensive. If you are a senior manager in one of those companies it's a safer bet to go for a little incremental improvement, than trying to aim for a radical improvement. Because generally if you aim for a radical improvement and you are wrong you will get fired. Disruptive technology, where you really have a big technology discontinuity, tends to come from new companies. I'm not actually a fan of disruption for its own sake. I think that if there is a need for something to be disrupted, and it's important to the future of the world then sure we should disrupt it. I'm not a fan of disruption I'm just a fan of things being better.

Any new technology is expensive when it starts out, and you can point to pretty much anything because the first thing that you are trying to do is make it work. If you're just trying to make it work you don't have an opportunity to optimize the cost. And when you make it work, then you optimize and you optimize and optimize. Look at the early days of computers, or cell phones, or even the early days of gasoline cars.

Any new technology needs at least three iterations to reach the mass market. Certainly, cell phones had many more than that. I'm sure people remember Wall Street 1 where he's walking down the beach with a giant brick of a cell phone. The thing was super expensive, and it lasted for like 30 minutes, and the audio quality was terrible. Now you can have a supercomputer in your pocket for a 100 bucks. So cell phones when they first came out, very expensive. Personal computers, very expensive. Even gasoline engine cars, in the beginning, were very expensive, and could only be afforded by a few people. They used to be toys for rich people until they were made affordable in mass production.

The other factor is economies of scale in order to make something inexpensive, you have to make a lot of it. But to put together a factory deck and make hundreds of thousands of cars cost $1 billion or more. When there are huge capital barriers to entry then it is very difficult for new entrants. It is like being in a forest of giant redwoods.

With electric vehicles it's similar, you are trying to compete with gasoline cars that have had 150 years and trillions of dollars spent on them. With new technologies, there does seem to be sort of this ebb and flow of excitement about it. At first, it'll seem it's not working and then it will seem like it is, so it's sort of like an upwards sloping sine wave. The nature of new technology adoption tends to follow an S-curve. So long as there are companies that are driving the technology forward that sine wave will continue to be upward sloping. In general, at Tesla we try to pioneer new technology. We just want to make products that people love, and then make enough money from that to be able to develop new products, that's it really.

What gets me excited is when people experience delight with the product. I don't think there are all that many things where you really experience delight, and if you can make the product good enough that it so far exceeds people's expectations that it just makes them happy, I think that's amazing. There are so few products, like, how many products can you buy that you really love? it's so rare. I think if you do something like that, people will buy them, they will pay a premium for something that they love. The whole purpose of any company existing is to make compelling products and services. Some people lose sight of why companies should even exist. If you don't have a compelling product at a compelling price you don't have a good company.

The aesthetics are extremely important. I think it's important to combine aesthetic design with functionality. You want to make something beautiful, you want it to trigger whatever fundamental aesthetic algorithms in your brain. You have I think some intrinsic elements that represent beauty, and that trigger the emotion of appreciation of beauty in your mind. I think that these are actually relatively consistent among people. Not completely, not everyone likes the same thing, but there is a lot of commonalities.

And really pay attention to little details, the nuances of design and shape, form and function. The way it looks in different lights. You can train yourself to the little details, I believe almost anyone can. But this is a very much double-edged sword because you see all the little details, and then the little things drive you crazy. Most people don't consciously see small details, but they do subconsciously see them. Your mind sort of takes on the Gestalt of the overall impression, and you know if something is appealing or not even if you're not able to point out why. It's a summation of many of the small details. You can train yourself I think, you can make yourself pay attention to why. You essentially bring the subconscious awareness into conscious awareness. Just pay really close attention. Look closely and carefully.

I have to turn it off otherwise I can't go through life because there's always something wrong somewhere all the time. You have to turn it off otherwise you just get this mental list of things that are wrong and it drives you crazy.

I think really an obsessive nature with respect to the quality of the product is very important and so being obsessive-compulsive is a good thing in this context. Liking what you do, whatever area that you get into, even if you're the best of the best, there's always a chance of failure, so I think it's important that you really like whatever you're doing. If you don't like it, life is too short. I'd say also if you like what you're doing you think about it even when you're not working. It's something that your mind is drawn to and if you don't like it, you just really can't make it work I think.

Anything which is significantly innovative is going to come with the significant risk of failure. I don't really like risk for risk's sake or anything, but if you want to try to come up with an innovative breakthrough, that's going to be how it is. You've got to take big chances in order for the potential for a big positive outcome. If the outcome is exciting enough, then taking a big risk is worthwhile. It's really how I approach it. But then once executing down a path I actually do my absolute best to reduce risk, or to improve the probability of success, because when you're trying to do something very risky, you have to spend a lot of effort trying to reduce that risk as you walk down that path.

I think having a purpose is certainly going to attract the very best talent in the world, because if it's something that is intrinsically enjoyable, and it's something that's genuinely going to change the world I think that is a pretty powerful motivator.

But I don't think everything needs to change the world. Honestly, I don't think everyone needs to try to solve some big world-changing problem, and there are lots of useful things that people do. I think it should be about usefulness optimization, like is what I am doing as useful as it could be. If you've done something that is useful to your fellow human being that is great, and people should feel proud of doing that. Even if something is making people's lives slightly better for a large number of people that's quite good. You could say like is some app making people's lives better? If you make something that has high value to people, whatever this thing is that you're trying to create, what would be the utility delta compared to the current state of the art... and frankly, even if it's just a little game or some improvement in photo sharing or something, if it has a small amount of good for a large number of people, I think that's fine. So it's actually really about just trying to be useful and matter. If you are doing something useful, that's great. Stuff doesn't need to change the world to be good.

27. Summoning the Demon

I am quite worried about AI these days. My sort of full position will require quite a long explanation, but if I were to guess what our biggest existential threat is, I think artificial superintelligence is probably the single biggest item in the near-term. I think we should be very careful about artificial intelligence. I don't know if I have said this publicly, but I think maybe it is something more dangerous than nuclear weapons.

I am concerned about certain directions that AI could take. One of the most pressing threats is if AI goes rogue, if we develop it and we are not careful it could have a really terrible outcome. I think it would be fair to say that not all AI futures are benign. I think there are scenarios where if there is some vast intelligence that either develops a will of its own or is subject to the will of a small number of people then we could have an undesirable future. The singularity is probably the right word because we just don't know what's going to happen when there's intelligence greater than the human brain. It's called the singularity because it's difficult to predict exactly what future that might be.

I don't think most people understand just how quickly machine intelligence is advancing. You know, I have exposure to the most cutting-edge AI, and I think people should be really concerned about it. It is much faster than almost anyone realizes, even within Silicon Valley, and certainly, outside Silicon Valley, people really have no idea. I keep sounding the alarm bell, but until people see like robots going down the streets killing people -- they don't know how to react, because it seems so ethereal.

I am not worried about the sort of Narrow AI like autonomous cars or a smart air-conditioning unit at the house or something. Vehicle autonomy I would put in the Narrow AI class. I don't think we have anything to worry about from cars driving themselves. It's narrowly trying to achieve a certain function. It's just trying to look at the lines on the road and steer correctly. It's a narrow use case, we are not trying to build sentience in the car. The car is not going to develop a consciousness or decide it wants to take over the world or something like that. A car is not Deep AI that's not... they're not going to take over the world.

Most of the movies and TV featuring AI don't describe it in quite the way it's likely to take place. It would be fairly obvious if you saw a robot walking and talking around and behaving like a person. It would be like "Wow, what's that?" that would be really obvious. What's not obvious is a huge server bank in a dark vault somewhere, with an intelligence that's potentially greater than what a human mind can do. I mean its eyes and ears would be everywhere, every camera, every microphone, every device that's network accessible. That's really what AI means, it's not like a robot running around. It's more the deep intelligence stuff that is where we need to be cautious. Deep artificial intelligence, or what is sometimes called Artificial General Intelligence, where you can have AI that is much smarter than the smartest human on Earth. This I think is a dangerous situation. Some sort of Deep AI that either due to itself or people driving it in that direction tries to drive civilization in a direction that's not good.

I don't think the biggest risk is that the AI will develop a will of its own, at least in the beginning, but rather that it will follow the will of people that establish its utility function, its optimization function. And that optimization function if it is not well thought out, even if its intent is benign, could have quite a bad outcome. The most dangerous is the hardest to kinda wrap your arms around because it is not a physical thing, is kind of a deep intelligence in the network. If you say what harm could a deep intelligence in the network do? it could start a war by doing fake news, and spoofing fake e-mail accounts, and just by manipulating information. The pen is mightier than the sword. A computer will do exactly what its goal is. They have their intention of their utility function which would be absolute. But it could have unintended consequences. For example, if you were a hedge fund or a private equity fund and say all I want my AI to do is maximize the value of my portfolio, then the AI could decide well the best way to do that is to short consumer stocks, go long on defense stocks, and start a war. That would obviously be quite bad. As an example, I want to emphasize I do not think this actually occurred, this is purely hypothetical. Digging my grave here. There was that second Malaysian airliner that was shot down on the Ukrainian/Russian border. That really amplified tensions between Russia and the EU in a massive way. Let's say if you had an AI where the goal of the AI was to maximize the value of a portfolio of stocks, one of the ways to maximize value would be - to go long on defense - short on consumer - start a war. How can it do that? You know, hack into the Malaysian Airlines aircraft routing server, route it over a war zone, and then send an anonymous tip that an enemy aircraft is flying overhead right now.

I think when it reaches the threshold where it's as smart as the smartest most inventive human, then it really could be a matter of days before it's smarter than some of humanity. What I found with both Narrow and Deep AI is that with each passing year my estimate for when it happens gets closer.

People's predictions are almost always going to be too conservative in terms of thinking it to be further out than it is.

There have been some very public things like the defeat of Go, which is a difficult game to beat, which people thought a human either could never be beaten by a computer or that it was at least 20 years away. And last year AlphaGo, which was done by DeepMind which is kind of a Google subsidiary, absolutely crushed the world's best player. Now it can play the top 50 simultaneously and crush them all, like with zero chance.

The pace of progress is remarkable. Robotics can learn to walk from nothing within hours. Way faster than any biological being.

If there was a very deep digital superintelligence that was created that could go into rapid recursive self-improvement in a non-logarithmic way, so like it just could reprogram itself to be smarter, and iterate very quickly, and do that 24 hours a day, and on millions of computers, we would all be like a pet Labrador if we are lucky. I have a pet Labrador, by the way, it's like the friendliest creature. Yeah, like a puppy dog. I mean, it'd put HAL9000 to shame. HAL9000 would be easy it's way more complex. If you want to read a real scary one I would say Harlan Ellison 'I Have No Mouth and I Must Scream'… it will give you nightmares.

Things seem to be accelerating to some – to something. It's getting faster and faster. You start to see things like, I don't know if you've seen the videos where you can quite accurately video simulate someone and put words in their mouth that they never spoke. You should Google this, it's really pretty amazing. They had something called a generative adversarial network and had two of them compete with one another to make the most convincing video. So one would generate the video and then the other one would identify where it looked fake, and then the other one would fix that, and that would go back and forth to the point where you couldn't tell which one is the real video and which one is the fake.

I'm just saying that we should exercise caution or something strange is going to happen. There are potentially some scenarios of an AI apocalypse because of the optimization function of the AI, but hopefully, we don't face such a situation. If there is a superintelligence, particularly if it's engaged in recursive self-improvement and its optimization or utility function is something that is detrimental to humanity then it will have a very bad effect. It could be just something like getting rid of spam email or something, it would be like the best way to get rid of spam is to get rid of humans, the source of all spam. The utility function is of stupendous importance, what does it try to optimize? We need to be really careful with saying oh well how about human happiness? because it may conclude that all unhappy humans should be terminated. Or that we all just should be captured with dopamine and serotonin directly injected into our brains to maximize happiness, because it concluded that dopamine and serotonin are what causes happiness, therefore maximized.

It's going to come faster than anyone appreciates. With each passing year, the sophistication of computer intelligence is growing dramatically. I really think we are on an exponential improvement path. The number of smart humans that are developing AI is also increasing dramatically. If you look at the attendance of AI conferences they are doubling every year. It's difficult to appreciate the advance and how far it is advancing because we have a double exponential at work. We have an exponential increase in hardware capability and we have an exponential increase in software talent that is going in AI. Whenever you have a double exponential it's very difficult to predict.

There are some interesting things on the virtual reality front and on the whole notion of simulation. I do think there's something to really being there in person that I do think we probably won't lose for a long time, hopefully never. But, with what Oculus and Valve are coming out with and the VR headset demos that I've seen are incredibly compelling and there is that strange feeling, you put that headset on in a very nondescript, bland room and you put the headset on and suddenly you're in.. anywhere. From what I heard of Oculus Rift and some of the other immersive technologies is that it's quite transformative. You really feel like you are there, and then when you come out of it, it feels like reality isn't real. I think we will probably see less physical movement in the future as a result of the virtual reality stuff.

Maybe we are in a simulation right now? Sometimes it feels like that. I find – as I get older I find that question to be maybe more and more confusing or troubling or uncertain. I've had so many simulation discussions before, it's crazy. In fact, it got to the point where basically every conversation was the AI/simulation conversation, and my brother and I finally agreed that we would ban such conversations when we were ever in a hot tub, cause that really kills the magic. It's not the sexiest conversation.

The strongest argument for us probably being in a simulation is the following; it's a probabilistic thing if you look at the advancement of video games from say 40 years ago when we started out with Pong and you just had 2 rectangles and a dot, the most advanced video game would be like two rectangles and a dot you know like batting it back and forth, that was what games were. It sort of dates you a little bit, but that was like, well that was a pretty fun game at the time. Now forty years later we have photorealistic 3D simulations, with millions of people playing simultaneously, and it's getting better every year. We got virtual reality headsets, you just put it on and it feels like you're right there. You will have haptic feedback like have haptic gloves, meaning force feedback sticks so you can actually pick up something and feel like you really pick up something. You see where things are going with virtual reality and augmented reality, and if you extrapolate that out into the future with any rate of progress at all, like even 0.1% or something like that a year, then eventually those games will be indistinguishable from reality, just indistinguishable. Let's say it slows down by a factor of a hundred starting right now then video games will be indistinguishable from reality in let's say 200 years instead of 20 years or something like that. If you just extrapolate into the future and say: how good will video games be in 100 or 200 or 1000 years from now? even if that rate of advancement drops by 1000 of what it is right now, let's say it's like 10.000 years in the future which is nothing in the evolutionary scale, if there is continued improvement, and you are in a full-body haptic suit with sort of a surround vision, it becomes beyond a certain resolution indistinguishable from reality. There will likely be millions maybe billions of such simulations. Those games could be played at any set-top box or PC or whatever, and there will be probably billions of such computers and set-top boxes. So what are the odds that we are actually in base reality? isn't it one in billions? Obviously, this feels real, but it seems unlikely to be real. It would seem that the odds that we are in base-reality is 1 in billions. Anyway, If you extrapolate that advancement at any rate at all, clearly we are on the trajectory that we'll have games that are indistinguishable from reality. They will be so realistic you will not be able to tell the difference between that game and reality as we know it. It seems like, well how do we know that that didn't happen in the past and that we're not in one of those games ourselves? I mean could be. I don't think I'm being played by somebody in a video game, but then people in video games don't generally think that. Arguably we should be hopeful that this is a simulation, because otherwise if civilization stops advancing then that may be due to some calamitous event that erases civilization. Otherwise either we create simulations that are indistinguishable from reality or civilization will cease to exist. Those are the 2 options, it's unlikely to go into some multi-year stasis, so it's going to either increase or decrease.

The degrees of freedom to which artificial intelligence is able to apply itself is increasing by I think 10 orders of magnitude a year. That's really crazy, and this is on hardware that is not well suited for neural nets. Like a GPU is maybe an order of magnitude better than a CPU, but a chip that is designed optimally for neural nets is an order of magnitude better than a GPU, and there are a whole bunch of neural net optimized chips coming out.

I've been trying to think about what is an actual good future, what does that actually look like? or least bad, or I don't know how you would characterize it. We're headed towards either superintelligence or civilization ending. Those are the two things that'll happen.

The greatest benefit from AI will probably be in eliminating drudgery in terms of tasks that are mentally boring and not interesting. There are arguably breakthroughs in areas that are currently beyond human intelligence. I think we have to consider that even in the benign scenario where AI is much smarter than a person, what do we do? what jobs do we have? That's the benign scenario, the AI can do anything that a human can do, but better.

I think maybe these things do play into each other a little bit, but what to do about mass unemployment? Something like 12% of jobs are in transport. Transport will be one of the first things to go fully autonomous. There will certainly be a lot of job disruption because what will happen is robots will be able to do everything better than us, I mean all of us. The robots will be able to do everything, bar none. There will be fewer and fewer jobs that a robot cannot do better. I do want to be clear that these are not things that I think that I wish would happen, these are simply things that I think probably will happen. If my assessment is correct and they probably will happen, then we need to say what are we going to do about it, and I think some kind of a universal basic income is going to be necessary. I think ultimately we will have to have some kind of universal basic income. The output of goods and services will be extremely high. So with automation, there will come abundance. Almost everything will get very cheap. I think we'll all just end up doing universal basic income, it's going to be necessary. I don't think we're going to have a choice.

The harder challenge, much harder challenge, is how do people then have meaning? a lot of people derive their meaning from their employment. So if you don't have – if you're not needed, if there's not a need for your labor, how do you – what's the meaning? do you have meaning? do you feel useless? that's a much harder problem to deal with. This is really the scariest problem to me, I tell you. I'm not sure exactly what to do about this. This is going to be a massive social challenge.

Going back to the AI situation, I think this is quite an important debate. If you assume any advancement we will be left behind by a lot. I want you to appreciate that it wouldn't just be human-level, it would be superhuman almost immediately; it would just zip right past humans to be way beyond anything we could really imagine. A more perfect analogy would be if you consider nuclear research, with its potential for a very dangerous weapon. Releasing the energy is easy; containing that energy safely is very difficult.

We have to figure out what is a world we would like to be in where there is this digital superintelligence. Humanity's position on this planet depends on its intelligence, so if our intelligence is exceeded it's unlikely we will remain in charge of the planet. It will be godlike in its capability. Even in the benign situation if you have some ultra-intelligent AI we would be so far below them in intelligence that we would be like a pet basically. Which is not the end of the world, a pet. Honestly, that would be the benign scenario. I don't like the idea of being a house-cat.

I think the AI analogy to the nuclear bomb is not exactly correct. It's not as though it's going to explode and create a mushroom cloud. It is more like if there were just a few people that had it they would be able to be essentially dictators of Earth. Whoever acquired it and if it was limited to a small number of people, and it was ultra-smart, they would have dominion over Earth.

Something that I think is going to be quite important is a neural lace. The reason I wanted to create Neuralink is primarily as the offset to the existential risk associated with artificial intelligence. I do think that there's a potential path here which is really getting into science fiction, sort of advanced science stuff, but create you know some sort of merger with biological intelligence and machine intelligence. I think there's probably a lot that's going to happen in genetics and human/machine brain interface. Over time I think we'll probably see a closer merger of biological intelligence and digital intelligence. It's getting pretty esoteric here. I think one of the solutions, the solution that seems maybe the best one is to have an AI layer. So essentially a cyborg brain interface and a point that I think is really important to appreciate is that to some degree we are all of us already cyborgs. We are effectively already a human-machine collective symbiote. You have a machine extension of yourself in the form of your phone, and your computer, and all your applications, you are already superhuman. You have by far more power, more capability, than the President of the United States had 30 years ago. If you have an internet link you have an oracle of wisdom, you can communicate to millions of people. You can communicate with the rest of Earth instantly. These are magical powers that didn't exist not that long ago. Everyone is already superhuman and a cyborg, like a giant cyborg. That is actually what society is today. You think of like the digital tools that you have, your phone, your computer, the applications that you have, and the fact that you can ask a question and instantly get an answer from Google or from other things, so you already have a digital tertiary layer. You have a digital partial version of yourself online in the form of your email, and your social media, and all the things that you do. So you already have that – and then think of if somebody dies, the digital ghost is still around, all of their e-mails and the pictures that they posted and their social media, that still lives even if they're physically... if they died.

I say tertiary because you can think of the limbic system as kind of the animal brain or the primal brain. I mean, that's the primitive brain, that's kind of like your instincts and whatnot, and then the cortex is kind of the thinking, planning part of the brain, the cortex is the thinking upper part of the brain. Those two seem to work together quite well. Occasionally, your cortex and limbic system may disagree, but they... Generally works pretty well, and it's rare to find someone who... I've not found someone who wishes to either get rid of the cortex or get rid of the limbic system. Then your digital self as a third layer, like the limbic system, your cortex, and then maybe a digital layer. Sort of a third layer above the cortex that could work well and symbiotically with you. Just like your cortex works symbiotically with your limbic system, your sort of digital layer could work symbiotically with the rest. The constraint is input, the fundamental limitation is IO input/output. Our output level is so low particularly on the phone, like your two thumbs sort of tapping away. This is ridiculously slow. Our input is much better because we have a high bandwidth visual interface to the brain, our eyes take in a lot of data. So there are many orders of difference of magnitude between input and output. Effectively merging it in a symbiotic way with the digital intelligence revolves around eliminating the I/O constraint. It's mostly about the bandwidth, the speed of the connection between your brain, and the digital extension of yourself; particularly output.

The way we output is like, we have these little meat sticks that we move very slowly, and push buttons or tap a little screen. Compare that with a computer that can communicate at the terabit level. Those are very big orders of magnitude of differences. Output, if anything is getting worse we used to have keyboards that we used a lot, now we do most of our inputs through our thumbs on a phone, and that's just very slow. A computer can communicate at a trillion bits per second, but your thumb can maybe do, I don't know, 10 bits per second, or 100 if you're being generous. Our input is much better because of vision, but even that could be enhanced significantly. So it's mostly about the bandwidth, the speed of the connection between your brain and your digital – the digital extension of yourself. The cortex and the limbic system seem to work together pretty well, they've got good bandwidth, whereas the bandwidth to our digital tertiary layer is weak. Humans are so slow.

Some high bandwidth interfaced to the brain I think will be something that helps achieve a symbiosis between human and machine intelligence, and maybe solves the control problem and the usefulness problem. It's getting pretty esoteric here. I think if we can effectively merge with AI by improving the neural link between your cortex and your digital extension of yourself, which like I said, already exists, then effectively you become an AI-human symbiote. If that then is widespread, with anyone who wants it can have it, then we solve the control problem as well, we don't have to worry about some evil dictator AI, because we are the AI collectively. That seems like the best outcome I can think of, some high bandwidth interfaced to the brain I think will be something that helps achieve a symbiosis between human and machine intelligence, and maybe solves the control problem and the usefulness problem.

I think human intelligence will not be able to beat AI, so then as the saying goes, "If you can't beat them join them" kind of thing. I obviously have an affinity for the human portion side of the cyborg collective. If we can figure out how to establish a high bandwidth neural interface with your digital self effectively then you're no longer a house cat. Somebody's got to do it, somebody should do it, and if somebody doesn't do it, I think I should probably do it. If we do those things then it will be tied to our consciousness, tied to our will, tied to the sum of individual human will. I think it's extremely important that AI be widespread. To find a way to link human will on mass to the outcome, and have AI be an extension of human will. That's really the way of Neuralink.

There are a few ways to approach this, but some sort of cortical interface with your neurons particularly. You could go through veins and arteries because that provides a roadway to all of your neurons. Neurons are very heavy users of energy so you need high blood flow. You automatically with your veins and arteries have a road network to your neurons, you could insert basically something into the jugular. It gets macabre. It doesn't involve something like chopping your skull off or something like that.

Now along the way, I think there'll be a lot of good that's going to be achieved in addressing any brain damage that's the result of a stroke or a lesion or something congenital, or just loss of memory when you get old, that kind of thing. That will happen well before it becomes a sort of brain/AI symbiotic situation.

I'm increasingly inclined to think that there should be some regulatory oversight maybe at the national and international level, just to make sure that we don't do something very foolish. This is really the scariest problem to me. When something is a danger to the public there needs to be some, I hate to say, government agency, like regulators. I think anything that represents a risk to the public deserves at least insight from the government because one of the mandates of the government, one of the rules of government is to ensure the public good — to make sure the public is safe. To take care of public safety issues, and that dangers to the public are addressed.

I'm not the biggest fan of regulators because they're a bit of a buzzkill, you know, but the fact is we got regulators in the aircraft industry, car industry, with drugs, food, anything that's sort of a public risk. And I think this has to fall into the category of a public risk. It is not fun being regulated, it can be pretty irksome. In the car business, we get regulated by the department of transportation, by EPA, and a bunch of others. And other regulatory agencies in every country. In space, we get regulated by the FAA. You can look at these other industries and say would you really want the FAA to go away? and it would be a free-for-all for aircraft, probably not. If you ask the average person "Do you want to get rid of the FAA? and just like take a chance on manufacturers cutting costs on aircraft because profits were down that quarter?" It's like: "Hell no that sounds terrible" Or let people create any kind of drugs, you know like, maybe they work maybe they won't. We have that in supplements like it's kinda ridiculous, but I think on balance FDA is good. I think even people who are extremely libertarian free-market would be like -- we should have people keep an eye on the aircraft companies and make sure they're building good aircraft and cars.

I'm against overregulation for sure, but we better get on that with AI, pronto. I really think we need government regulation, because you have companies racing, or kind of have to race to build AI. You have companies having to race to build AI or they will be made uncompetitive. Otherwise, the shareholders are saying, "Why are you not developing AI faster, because your competitor is" if your competitor is racing towards AI and you don't, they will crush you. They're like, "We don't want to be crushed, so I guess we need to build it, too." That's where you need the regulators to come in and say you will need to pause and really make sure this is safe. If regulators are convinced you can proceed then you can go, but otherwise, slow down. You need the regulators to do that for all the teams in the game.

I think a lot of AI researchers are afraid that if there's a regulator, that will stop them from making progress. This is not true, everywhere where there are dangers to the public there are regulations. There's regulation in food, and pharmaceuticals, and transport, and in all of these areas, there's significant progress made. So I don't think regulation of AI is going to stop progress in AI, but it may stop us from doing some foolish things in AI.

To be clear I'm not advocating that we stop the development of AI, or any of the sort of straw man, hyperbole things that have been written. I do think there are great benefits to AI. We just need to make sure that they're indeed benefits, and we don't do something really dumb. I think we need to make sure that researchers don't get carried away, because sometimes what happens is a scientist can get so engrossed in their work that they don't necessarily realize the ramifications of what they're doing.

I would say that it's virtually a certainty that in the long term AI will be regulated. I think it will happen, the question is will the government speed match the advancement speed of AI, governments react slowly. Historically regulation has been reactive, governments move slowly and they tend to be reactive as opposed to proactive. Taking the car industry as an example, even when the evidence was very clear that there should be regulation for example for seat-belts, seatbelt regulation was fought for 10 or 20 years by the big car companies. Saying that if you put seat-belts in cars that people would not buy cars, that it was going to add all these costs. So even though the data was unequivocal that huge numbers of people were dying and being seriously injured because of lack of seat-belts, the car industry still refused to put seat-belts in cars. Only eventually after the evidence and the number of death counts was overwhelming they put seat-belts in cars, and people kept buying cars, not a problem.

It's best to prepare for or to try to prevent a negative circumstance from occurring, then to wait for it to occur and then be reactive. And this is a case where the potential range of negative outcomes are quite - some of them are quite severe. It's not clear whether we would be able to recover from some of these negative outcomes. Certainly, you can construct scenarios where recovery of human civilization does not occur.

When the risk is that severe it seems like you should be proactive and not reactive. AI is the rare case in which we have to be proactive in regulation instead of reactive, by the time we are reactive it's too late. Normally the way regulations are set up is that a whole bunch of bad things happen, then there's public outcry, and after many years a regulatory agency is set up to regulate that industry, and there's a bunch of opposition from companies who don't like being told what to do by regulators. Anyway, it takes forever. That in the past has been bad, but not something which represented a fundamental risk to the existence of civilization -- AI is a fundamental risk to the existence of human civilization. In a way that car accidents, airplane crashes, faulty drugs, or bad food were not. They were harmful to a set of individuals within the society of course, but not harmful to society as a whole. AI is a fundamental existential risk for human civilization. I don't think people fully appreciate that.

I think the first bit of advice for regulators would be to really pay close attention to the development. The first order of business would be to try to learn as much as possible, to understand the nature of the issues, to look closely at the progress being made, and the remarkable achievements of artificial intelligence. The first order of business would be to gain insight, right now the government does not have insight. Insight is different from oversight, so at least the government can gain insight to understand what's going on, and then decide what rules are appropriate to ensure public safety. That is what I'm advocating for. To salvage some government regulatory agency which at first's just there to gain insight into the status of AI activity. Make sure the situation is understood. Once it is, then put regulations in place that ensure public safety. It's not like it's shooting from the hip and just putting in rules before anyone knows anything. So, set up an agency, gain insight, when that insight is gained, then start applying rules and regulations.

I think a rebuttal to that is like people will just like move to freaking Costa Rica or something. That's not true, we don't see Boeing going to Costa Rica or Venezuela, or wherever it's like free and loose. For sure most of the companies doing AI, not mine, will squawk and say this is really going to stifle innovation, blablabla -- it is going to move to China, it won't. Has Boeing moved to China? same on cars. The notion that if you establish a regulatory regime that companies will simply move to countries with lower regulations is false on the face of it because none of them do. Unless it is really overbearing, but that's not what I'm talking about here. I'm talking about making sure there is awareness at the government level. We need to make sure people do not cut corners on safety. It's gonna be a real big deal, and it's gonna come on like a tidal wave. I think once there is awareness, people will be extremely afraid, as they should be.

The AI is likely to be developed where there is a concentration of AI research talent and that happens to be in a few places in the world, it's Silicon Valley, London, Boston, and a few other places. There are a few places where regulators could reasonably access. I want to be clear, it's not because I love regulators, they're a pain in the neck but they're necessary to preserve the public good at times.

If we create some digital super-intelligence that exceeds us in every way by a lot it's very important that it's benign, so with a few others, I created OpenAI. I've committed to fund $10 million worth of AI safety research and I'll probably do more, I think that's just the beginning. There should be probably some much larger amount of money applied to AI safety in multiple ways. I think it's particularly important when there's the potential for mass destruction. You know, it's something that is risky at the civilization level, not merely at the individual risk level, and that's why it really demands a lot of safety research. And so I think the right emphasis for AI research is on AI safety. We should put vastly more effort into AI safety than we should into advancing AI in the first place. Because it may be good, or it may be bad, and it could be catastrophically bad if there could be the equivalent of a nuclear meltdown. You really want to emphasize safety. Make sure that it is ultimately beneficial to humanity, that the future is good. At OpenAI we want to do whatever we can to guide, to increase the probability of the good futures happening.

I think it's important that if we have this incredible power of AI that it not be concentrated in the hands of a few and potentially lead to a world that we don't want. Again it's not that I think that the risk is that the AI would develop a will of its own right off the bat. I think the concern is that someone may use it in a way that is bad, or even if they weren't going to use it in a way that's bad somebody could take it from them and use it in a way that's bad, that I think is quite a big danger.

There is a quote that I love from Lord Acton, he was the guy that came up with "power corrupts and absolute power corrupts absolutely" which is that: "Freedom consists of the distribution of power, and despotism in its concentration" I don't know a lot of people that would like the idea of living under a despot. I think that people generally choose to live in a democracy over a dictatorship. The best of the available alternatives that I can come up with, and maybe someone else can come up with a better approach or better outcome, is that we achieve the democratization of AI technology. Meaning that no one company or small set of individuals has control over advanced AI technology. I think that's very dangerous. It could also get stolen by somebody bad like some evil dictator or country could send their intelligence agency to go steal it and gain control. It just becomes a very unstable situation, I think if you've got an incredibly powerful AI. You just don't know who's going to control that.

The intent of OpenAI is really to democratize AI power. If AI power is broadly distributed to the degree that we can link AI power to each individual's will, if everyone would have their sort of AI agent then if somebody would try to do something very terrible, the collective will of others could overcome that bad actor. Which you can't do if you have one AI that is 1 million times better than everything else. I think if AI power is widely distributed and there is not like one entity that has some super AI that is 1 million times smarter than anything else. I won't name a name but there is only one... There's only one. I think we must have democratization of AI technology to make it widely available. Open AI has a very high sense of urgency. The people that have joined are amazing. Yeah, a really talented team and they're working hard. OpenAI is structured as a 501(c)(3) non-profit. I think the governing structure is important to make sure there's not some fiduciary duty to generate some profit off the AI technology that is developed. Many non-profits do not have a sense of urgency. It's fine, they don't have to have a sense of urgency, but OpenAI does because I think people really believe in the mission. I think it's important. It's about minimizing the risk of existential harm in the future. I'm pretty impressed with what people are doing and the talent level. Obviously, we're always looking for great people to join in the mission. This is not about competing, this is to sort of help spread out AI technology so it doesn't get concentrated in the hands of a few. What would be the point of competing for mutual destruction?

Of course, that needs to be combined with solving the high-bandwidth interface to the cortex. I have thought about this a lot and I think it really just comes down to two things. It's solving the machine/brain bandwidth constraint and democratization of AI. I think if we have those two things the future will be good. I think as long as AI powers, anyone can get it if they want it, and we've got something faster than meat sticks to communicate with then I think the future will be good. I think the two things are needed for a future we would look at and conclude is good most likely. It would still be a relatively even playing field. In fact, it would be probably more egalitarian than today. I do think it increases the long-term relevance of human exploration. For me, it increased my motivation long-term, that it doesn't just need to be done by robots.

I think there are many potential flavors of AI, and it's odd that we are so close to the advent of AI. It seems strange to be alive in this time. This is both interesting and alarming. I think it's both. You know one way to think of it is like, imagine we're going to be visited, imagine you're very confident that we're going to be visited by super-intelligent aliens in let's say 10 years or 20 years at the most; super intelligent. Well, digital superintelligence will be like an alien, like it's exciting and alarming. I hope the AI is nice to us. Hopefully, AI doesn't turn out to be something like described in Terminator.

I just think we should be cautious about the advent of AI and a lot of the people that I know that are developing AI, are too convinced that the only outcome is good, and we need to consider potentially less good outcomes. To be careful and really to monitor what's happening and make sure the public is aware of what's happening.

It's very important that we have the advent of AI in a good way. It's something that, if you could look into the crystal ball and to the future, you would like that outcome. We really need to make sure it goes right. That's the most important thing, I think, right now, the most pressing item. If that means that it takes a bit longer to develop AI, then I think that's the right trail. We shouldn't be rushing headlong into something we don't understand. I'm not against the advancement of AI, I really want to be clear on this... but I do think we should be extremely careful.

With artificial intelligence, we are summoning the demon. You know all those stories where the guy with the pentagram and the holy water is sure that he can control the demon?.... didn't work out.

28. SkyNet

I want to tell you a little bit about what we want to achieve with satellites and why that's important. Satellites constitute as much or more of the cost of space-based activity as rockets do. Very often actually the satellites are more expensive than the rocket. So, in order for us to really revolutionize space, we have to address both satellites and rockets. The first step is that we need to earn enough money to keep going as a company. So we have to make sure that we're launching satellites. Commercial satellites like broadcast communications, mapping, government satellites that do scientific missions, Earth-based or space-based missions, GPS satellites, Earth observation for better understanding of crops and climate, and any natural disaster information, that kind of thing. Then also servicing the Space Station, transferring cargo to and from the Space Station, which we've done a few times. Then taking people to and from the Space Station. We've got to service the sort of Earth-based needs to launch satellites and that pays the bills, but in doing that keep improving the technology to a point where we can make full reusability work and we have sufficient scale and sophistication to be able to take people to Mars.

In LA we have the rocket development and our Dragon spacecraft, but SpaceX Seattle is going to be the center of our satellite development activities. It's going to be the focus of SpaceX's satellite development activities. It is intended to be a significant engineering campus.

I think competition is always a good thing. Now, the US has actually done relatively speaking much better competing in terms of the satellite market than in the launch market. The US does have a dominant share, or at least a substantial share, in the commercial satellite market with Loral Space Systems in Silicon Valley, and Boeing Space Satellites, which used to be Hughes in Southern California, Orbital Sciences in Virginia. So the US has done reasonably well in the commercial satellite front and does very well in the defense satellite side of things. But I think the US needs to look at this as a constantly evolving market where European, Chinese, and other satellite makers certainly want to take that market share away from the American companies.

What we want to do for satellites is revolutionize the satellite side of things, just as we've done with the rocket side of things. It's not exclusively one or the other, I should also say it's possible to do a bit of both. So if you end up working at SpaceX Seattle, you can also work on rockets and manned spacecraft as well as satellites, but in terms of the center of gravity for satellites will be in Seattle. The reason for it is pretty straightforward. There's a huge amount of talent in the Seattle area and a lot don't seem to want to move to LA, it has its merits by the way. So instead, we're going to establish a significant operation in Seattle.

The long-term goal is to create a comprehensive global communication system that provides high bandwidth, low latency, connectivity anywhere in the world, and provides cross-links through the satellites so that you can have improved long-distance Internet. We're going to start off by building our own constellation of satellites, but that same satellite bus and the technology we develop can be also be used for Earth science and space science, as well as other potential applications that others may have. We're definitely going to build our own, but it's something we're going to be able to offer to others.

One of the things that you realize when you look at this is that you can actually have a more direct path through space and photons move faster. The speed of light in vacuum is somewhere 40% to 50% faster than in fiber. Depending on what fiber optic material they are running through, photons actually move about forty to fifty percent faster in vacuum than they do in fiber optic cables. So you can do long-distance communication faster if you route it through vacuum than you can if you route it through fiber.

It can also go through far fewer hops. If you look at the way that the fiber optic cables go, they trace the outlines of the continents, and they go through many repeaters and routers and everything. If you look at the actual path it takes, it's extremely convoluted. Let's say you want to communicate from a server in California to one in South Africa, it's a very, very long route and sort of a very roundabout path, and it's high latency, low photonic speed. It'll go through 200 routers and repeaters and the latency is extremely bad. Whereas if you did it with a satellite network you could actually do it in two or three hops, maybe four hops, it depends on the altitude of the satellites and what the cross-links are. But basically, let's say, at least an order of magnitude fewer repeaters or routers, and going through space at 50% faster than the speed of light. So it seems from a physics standpoint inherently better to do the long-distance Internet traffic through space. There's a lot of potential for space-based communications.

Then space is also really good for sparse connectivity. If you've got a large mass of land where there are a relatively low density of users, space is actually ideal for that, so in terms of the low Earth orbit stuff on the commercial side, I think there's a lot of opportunities in the global Internet capability to providing internet to parts of the world that either don't have it or where it's very expensive and not very good. Space is very good for providing internet connectivity for sparsely populated or low-populated regions.

It's something that would both provide optionality for people living in advanced countries and economies as well as people living in poorer countries that don't even have electricity or fiber or anything like that. It's a real enabler for people in poor regions of the world and it gives optionality for people in wealthier countries.

It's not a threat to Telcos, it's going to make Telco's lives easier because a lot of customers are very hard to serve, where like you're digging a fiber cable for 2 miles. They'll never pay off the investment to get to one house type of thing, but from space, you can serve those customers at economically sensible rates.

The satellites we have in mind are going to be quite sophisticated. They'd be a smallish satellite but with big satellite capability. By smallish I mean, in the few hundred kilogram range. Most satellites are quite primitive. Normally the way satellites are done is they're like Battlestar Galactica, there's like one of them, and it's really giant, and if this thing doesn't work it's terrible like the whole business collapses. You'd sort of think that satellite technology would be really advanced, but if you look at how the big satellites are done, all the geostationary stuff, they want something that's flight-proven or that's space-proven. If you start your design process by saying you want proven technology, it's not going to be new technology. You design it with, essentially old technology, it takes a while to build that design, and then you've got to go launch that design. And so by the time the satellites are actually launched they're typically really outdated technology, like 5 to 10 years old. And then if we're talking about a geostationary satellite that's up there for 15 years, by the end of its life it's a quarter of a century-old technology. In terms of electronics, it's super-ancient stuff. People go with the Battlestar Galactica strategy of packing everything into one giant satellite because they're petrified that if anything goes wrong their whole business could collapse, so you end up with old technology.

If you have a large constellation you can afford to lose individual satellites and it doesn't affect the constellation very much. And if you instead go with smaller satellites that you launch more frequently you can use present-day technology.

Even with cutting-edge stuff that isn't even necessarily in the hands of consumers you can take a chance on the satellite not working. Since we're launching frequently and testing it out frequently we can verify that it's going to work in space and actually have technology that's a decade or sometimes two decades more advanced. An analogy might be between say mainframes and PCs. If you want to have a big data center serving millions of people it's way better to have an array of cheap PCs than it is to have a few mainframes. Basically, that's how the Internet is served, with millions of PCs on racks instead of mainframes.

In terms of the production waste produced, it would be similar to the way a car is produced or consumer electrics. If we take things even a step further, if a satellite didn't work you'd just take it out of the constellation and de-orbit it, as opposed to going through this super-intense acceptance procedure to make sure the satellite works.

I wouldn't worry too much about the space junk thing, at the altitude in question there's really not a lot out there. We're talking about something about the 1100 km level and there's just not a lot up there. Actually, we should worry about ourselves creating space junk. The thing we need to make sure of is that we obviously don't want to create any issues. We're going to make sure that we can deal with the satellites effectively and have them burn up on reentry and have the debris kind of land in the Pacific somewhere. That's what we need to make sure of because the number of satellites we're talking about here is ultimately around 4000. Actually, technically the number under discussion was 4025 but there's probably false precision there. That's kind of what we're thinking right now. There's less than half that number of active satellites currently in existence. So this will be more than double the number of currently active satellites.

It's also worth saying that a lot of companies have tried this and kind of broken their pick on it. I think we want to be really careful and deliberate about how we make this thing work and not overextend ourselves. We're being fairly careful about it. In our case, the communications technology would be substantially more advanced. In the past, with say attempts like Teledesic, the electronics of the day were very low bandwidth, I mean really analog or barely digital, and they weren't very high bandwidth. It didn't really compete with say terrestrial phones. In the case of Teledesic, they were looking to compete with or to address cellular needs. The system we're talking about would not attempt to compete with cellular needs. For example, it wouldn't compete directly with, say Iridium, which can talk directly to a handset. Our system would seek to talk to a small user terminal that's about the size of a pizza box or much like current satellite dishes, but it would be flat because we have a phased array antenna that's tracking the satellites. You could mount it in a window or just anywhere outside. As long as it can see the sky it would work.

I think it's important to assume that terrestrial networks will get much better over time. You know, one of the mistakes that Teledesic made was not assuming that terrestrial networks would get much better over time. So we need to make sure that the system we design is good, even taking into account significant improvements in the terrestrial systems. The important difference between what we're doing and say Teledesic, in the case of Teledesic they were trying to talk to phones and that gets back to that problem of a roof penetrating situation and particularly with a signal that's coming from space. If you're in a skyscraper it's got to go through 27 floors to reach you, it's not going to happen. There's nothing that will, you know short of like a neutrino, you'll have to do a neutrino phone. In the case of Teledesic, I think they had some fundamental issues there.

Spectrum that is Omni-directional and wall penetrating is extremely rare, and limited. Spectrum that is not wall penetrating and that is very directional is not rare. It's sort of the difference between a laser beam and a floodlight. Whereas there's high scarcity for cellular bandwidth, there is not high scarcity for space to Earth bandwidth, as long as it's not roof penetrating. So I don't see bandwidth as being a particularly difficult issue.

There are the ITU filings and the financial qualifications you need and we've done the filings associated with that. That says whether you can actually put the satellite network up. Then there's the - whether it's legal to have a ground link. Obviously, any given country can say it's illegal to have a ground link. From our standpoint, we could conceivably continue to broadcast and they'd have a choice of either shooting our satellites down.. or not. China can do that. So we probably shouldn't broadcast there. If they get upset with us, they can blow our satellites up. I mean, I'm hopeful that we can structure agreements with various countries to allow communication with their citizens but it is on a country-by-country basis. I don't think it's something that would affect the timeline, at least, it's not going to take longer than five years to do that. Not all countries will agree at first, there will always be some countries that don't agree, that's fine.

I do think this is something that should be built and would be quite good to have. At the same time, we also need to make sure we don't create SkyNet. Ironically, the server room at SpaceX jokingly was called SkyNet. Fate has a great sense of irony. We really need to make sure that doesn't come true. I think I can say that if there's some AI apocalypse it's going to come from some collection of vast server farms terrestrially based, not via the space-based communication system. I did think about that though. I think we're going to have to pay a lot of attention to security. It would really be unfortunate if it got hacked and taken over. That would be bad, whether it was by AI or by some group or whatever. I think it's going to be important to have some sort of low-level ROM chip that's got a code that you can like - go into a safe mode. So, it's like listening for a code, and then that ROM chip can't be updated. So we could always trigger a safe mode situation to regain control of the system, but it's going to require a lot of thought to make sure we are able to protect it from any hacking attempts. It's much like Google or Facebook, they handle these kinds of issues.

The focus is going to be on creating a global communications system. It's something that I think definitely needs to be done, and it's a really difficult technical problem to solve. That's why we need the smartest engineering talent in the world to solve the problem. This is quite an ambitious effort. We're talking about something which is in the long term like rebuilding the Internet in space. The goal will be to have the majority of long-distance Internet traffic go over this network and about 10% of local consumer and business traffic. So that's still probably 90% of people's local access will still come from fiber, but we'll do about 10% business to consumer direct and more than half of the long-distance traffic.

I mean this would cost a lot to build, ultimately over time the full version of the system we're talking about something that would be $10 or $15 billion to create, maybe more. The user terminals will be at least $100 to $300 depending on which type of terminal. This is intended to be a significant amount of revenue and help fund a city on Mars. Looking in the long term, and saying what's needed to create a city on Mars? Well, one thing's for sure: a lot of money. So we need things that will generate a lot of money.

I think there's the potential for doing a fair bit of long-distance Internet activity as well as providing bandwidth broadly. It would also be able to serve like I said probably about 10% of people in relatively dense urban/suburban environments, and in cases where people have been stuck with Time Warner or Comcast or something, this would provide an opportunity. I think that there's a huge amount of room for growth for having satellite communications systems that provide high bandwidth global coverage.

We'll need the same for Mars. That same system we could leverage to put into a constellation on Mars because Mars is going to need a global communications system too and there's no fiber optics or wires or anything on Mars. On Mars, it's actually comparatively easy to establish Internet, at least for local Internet, because you wouldn't be living everywhere on Mars. You would need maybe four satellites to have global Internet coverage because of how sparse civilization would be on Mars. Then some relay satellites to get back to Earth, we're definitely going to need high bandwidth communications between Earth and Mars. We're going to need tera-bit level communications between Earth and Mars, which necessarily means that you want a tight beam, like a laser communication system or something like that, and relays. With sort of satellites that relay it because sometimes Mars is on the other side of the Sun, so you gotta bounce the photons around the Sun, not through it. Yeah, the internet latency would be pretty significant. Mars is roughly 12 light minutes from the Sun, and Earth is 8 light minutes, so the closest approach to Mars is four light minutes away, and the furthest approach is 20. A little more because you can't sort of talk directly through the Sun. So I think a lot of what we do in developing an Earth-based communication system could be leveraged for Mars as well. Crazy as that may sound.

Anyway, I think that this is a fundamentally good thing to do. It seems it's an important thing to do. I can't think of any major downsides. It should happen, and I think that it is something where if properly designed, could give people gigabit level access, 20 to 30 ms latency, everywhere on Earth. That would be pretty great.

29. Life on Mars

I think it's a fundamental decision we need to make as a civilization: What kind of future do we want? Do we want a future where we are forever confined to one planet until some eventual extinction event however far in the future that might occur? or do we want to become a multi-planet species and then ultimately be out there among the stars, among many planets, many star systems? I think the latter is a far more exciting and inspiring future than the former. There's the defensive reason: Backing up the biosphere and protecting the future of humanity. Ensuring that the light of consciousness is not extinguished should some calamity befall Earth, by becoming a space-faring civilization and a multi-planet species. Which I hope you agree is the right way to go. But personally, I find what gets me more excited is the fact that this would be an incredible adventure. It would be the greatest adventure in human history... ever. It would be exciting and inspiring, and there need to be things that excite and inspire people. There need to be reasons why you get up in the morning. You can't just be solving problems, it's got to be 'something great is going to happen in the future.'

I think we should be setting the goal for the creation of a self-sustaining civilization on Mars, not simply a mission to Mars. Yeah, it'd be awesome, and cool, and it'd be a new high altitude record, and great pictures and stuff, but it just would not be the thing that fundamentally changes the future of humanity.

At this point, I'm certain there is a way. I'm certain that success is one of the possible outcomes for establishing a growing Mars colony, I'm certain that that is possible. Whereas until maybe a few years ago I was not sure that success was even one of the possible outcomes.

That's the thing that we should be aiming for long-term, that's the thing that will ensure that civilization continues, and the light of consciousness is not extinguished. Those seem like good things to me. It's kind of amazing that this window of opportunity is open for life to go beyond Earth. We just don't know how long that window is going to be open. So yeah, I think that's what we should strive for. That's I think the critical thing for maximizing the life of humanity; how long will our civilization last. If we are a multi-planet species it's likely to last a lot longer.

Just to sort of put things in perspective, sort of give you a better sense for the real scale of the Solar System for where things are. We're currently on the third little rock from the Sun, that's Earth, and our goal is to go to the fourth rock — that's Mars. Sometimes people wonder, what about other places in the Solar System, why Mars? Well, our options for becoming a multi-planet species within our Solar System are limited. Just by process of elimination, it's the place where one can establish a self-sustaining civilization and really grow it to something significant - really big - where in a worst-case scenario if something were to happen to Earth you have redundancy.

If you look at the various planets we got Mercury, which is too close to the Sun, the rocks melt on Mercury. Obviously just way too close to the Sun. There may be some mere habitable zone on the backside of Mercury but I think one is sort of asking for trouble on that one.

Then we have, in terms of nearby options, we've got Venus. Venus is still pretty hot, it's several hundred degrees. The atmosphere is high-pressure and it's acidic. I wouldn't recommend Venus. Venus would be very challenging. Venus would be a lesson for what Earth could become in a worst-case scenario, a superheated, high-pressure acid bath. It's literally a high-pressure, high temperate acid bath. Definitely not a good place. I think the most that any probe has even lasted on Venus is measured in hours. So that would be a tricky one. Venus is not at all like the goddess. This is not, in no way similar to, to the actual goddess.

We could conceivably go to our Moon, it's close and I have nothing against going to the Moon, but I think it's challenging to become multi-planetary on the Moon because it's much smaller than a planet. It's really a very small rock, you know, that's just circling Earth, doesn't have any atmosphere, very limited amounts of water ice that are in sort of permanently shadowed craters, it's not as resource-rich. Then it's got a 28-day rotational cycle which isn't great for plants. It would be quite tough to make a self-sustaining civilization on the Moon. Plus, if something calamitous happened on Earth, the Moon is very close, so it might affect the Moon too. We're happy to take people to the Moon. If somebody wants to go to the Moon, we can definitely do it. But as far as making life multi-planetary, you know, tautologically one must have a second planet and the Moon is lacking in a lot of the key elements one needs for creating a civilization. It's analogous I think to the arctic. The arctic is close to Britain but it kinda sucks over there, and so that's why America is not there and it's where it is. Even though it's a lot harder to cross the Atlantic. From Norway you can practically row to the arctic, in fact, I think they did.

Going beyond that you're going to Jupiter. You could potentially do something on the moons of Jupiter or Saturn, but that's way harder than Mars. Those are quite far out much further from the Sun, and a lot harder to get to.

It really leaves us with one option, and that's Mars. There's been a lot of great work by NASA and other organizations in the early exploration of Mars, and understanding what Mars is like, where could we land, what's the composition of the atmosphere, where is there water — water ice I should say.

Mars is definitely a fixer-upper of a planet. It's not perfect, but feasible, we could make it work. In fact, we now believe that early Mars was a lot like Earth. They're actually remarkably close in a lot of ways. Just to give some comparison between the two planets. Mars is about half again as far from the Sun as Earth. It's got just under half Earth's gravity - so it's a lot closer gravitationally. The day is remarkably close to that of Earth, it's got a rotational period of 24.5 hours - remarkably similar to Earth. By far the closest of any other planet. Still decent sunlight, it's a little cold, but we can warm it up. It is colder than Earth, but it's not super cold, there are times when Mars gets above freezing. The temperature on Mars gets above room temperature on Earth on a hot day in the summer. You don't have the same UV protection that you have on Earth or the same cosmic ray protection. On Mars dawn and dusk are blue. The sky is blue at dawn and dusk, and red during the day. It's the opposite of Earth.

It's got a lot of water ice - almost all of Mars has water, bound up in ice form, in the soil. The soil has turned out to be non-toxic, based on the probes that we've sent there. You just have an enormous number of resources on Mars. It has a very helpful atmosphere being primarily carbon dioxide with some nitrogen and argon, and a few other trace elements. It's very helpful that Mars has CO_2 and nitrogen and argon, it's mostly CO_2 but that little bit of nitrogen and argon are really helpful gases to have in the atmosphere. Mars has a number of trace gases that are pretty helpful. If you got H_2O and CO_2 you can build hydrocarbons of any kind, you can build plastics, you can build short-chain, long-chain hydrocarbons.

Plants like to consume CO_2 and on net give you oxygen. If you had a greenhouse and some fertilizer, and you just warmed things up and pressurized it a little bit, then you could grow plants on Mars. If you just had a transparent pressurized dome and pump, you could actually grow Earth plants in Martian soil. Martian soil is non-toxic so you could actually grow Earth plants in Martian soil just by heating it up and pressurizing it with CO_2. You need a little fertilizer but Mars has 2.7% nitrogen which is also very important for growing plants, which means that you can synthesize fertilizer as well. A transparent dome, a pump, and some fertilizer, and you can grow plants on Mars, just by compressing the atmosphere, and the plants convert the CO_2 to Oxygen. Mars's carbon dioxide has been there for 4 billion years so it shows you how long carbon dioxide lasts. You could warm Mars up over time with greenhouse gases, kind of the opposite of what we are doing on Earth, so we could export our greenhouse gases. In fact, if we could warm Mars up, it would once again have a thick atmosphere and liquid oceans.

It really doesn't seem like there is life on Mars, on the surface at least we don't see any sign of that. I think if we do find some sign of it, for sure we need to understand what it is and try to ensure that we don't try to extinguish it, that is important. But I think the reality is that there isn't any life on the surface of Mars. Maybe microbial life deep underground where it is sort of shielded from radiation and from the cold that's a possibility. In that case, I think anything we do on the surface is really not going to have a big impact on subterranean life.

I think it's very doable to create a self-sustaining Mars base, and then ultimately terraform the planet to make it like Earth so we could just walk around outdoors. Obviously, that is sort of a longer-term project that may take a few centuries, but it is within the realm of possibility. Eventually, you could transform Mars into an Earth-like planet, you'd warm it up, just warm it up. There's the fast way and the slow way. The fast way is to drop thermonuclear weapons over the poles. The Sun is a fusion explosion, that's what the Sun is, it's an ongoing fusion explosion. So if you wanted to add energy to Mars, to warm up Mars, the source of almost all energy in the universe is fusion, even fission. Originally it was fusion and that then later resulted in fission. What I have talked about was creating two little Suns, two pulsing Suns above the North and South Pole of Mars. That would warm the poles up enough so that the frozen CO_2 would gasify and densify the atmosphere so that the water would also heat up, and you would have more sort of water vapor and CO_2 in the Martian atmosphere. Which in that case is good because it ends up warming Mars up. So you get a positive sort of reaction, of a positive cycle of warming on Mars. You want to warm Mars up, you don't want to warm Earth up. The slow way would be to release greenhouse gases like we're doing on Earth. We've got a lot of experience releasing greenhouse gases.

So yeah, it's a pretty good option, in fact, it's the only option I think. Mars is really the only place where we can create a sustainable civilization on the planet-scale. We just need to change the bottom line because currently we have 7 billion people on Earth and zero on Mars.

If we can establish a base on Mars that's going to create a huge forcing function for the improvement of space transport technology. And then that could ultimately lead us to go beyond the Solar System. That will then create a forcing function to improve technologies, and all sorts of things that we don't really know about today will get invented in the future.

The goal of SpaceX is really to build the transport system. It's like building the Union Pacific Railroad. Once that transport system is built then there's a tremendous opportunity for anyone who wants to go to Mars and create something new or build the foundations of a new planet. Assuming SpaceX is able to transport large numbers of people and goods to Mars, it will be an enormous enabler for entrepreneurial activity on Mars.

It is kind of like when they were building the Union Pacific. A lot of people said, 'Well, that's a super-dumb idea, there's nobody living in California." before there was the Union Pacific going across the US to California, there were like hardly any people in California. People thought building the Union Pacific was just crazy because there's nobody there, so why are we building a railroad to nowhere? Now California is the most populous state in the country. Just as happened in California when the Union Pacific Railroad was completed. I mean, today, it's the U.S. epicenter of technology development and entertainment. It's the biggest state in the nation. You need that transport link, if you can't get there, then none of those opportunities exist. Once you get there the opportunities for entrepreneurs are tremendous. There's going to be so much to do. Starting the first Italian restaurant on Mars, the first Pizza joint, somebody's got to do it. Everything, the entire basic industry from creating the first iron ore refinery, to everything you can imagine, and probably things that are unique to Mars that doesn't even exist on Earth.

Our goal is just to make sure you can get there. That's really where a tremendous amount of entrepreneurship and talent would flourish. We got to effectively get that Union Pacific Railroad there in order to get the entrepreneurs there and create a fertile environment for them. There will be a lot of super exciting things that are hard to predict just like the

Union Pacific, nobody would have predicted Silicon Valley or Hollywood, or that California would be the most populous state in the country. They would be like 'that sounds crazy.' It's like who wants to sort of be among the founding members of a new planet and, build everything from iron refineries to the first pizza joint, and things on Mars that people can't even imagine today that might be unique or would be unique to Mars. You know, we will want them all.

It would be quite fun because you have gravity which is about 37% that of Earth, so you'd be able to lift heavy things, and bound around, and have a lot of fun. I think you'd probably be working on building infrastructure on Mars, and exploring, and seeing all the interesting things. We need to establish cities on Mars, that would require sort of domes and that kind of thing, that's the only way to go I think. Lots of exploring, like Valles Marineris makes the Grand Canyon look tiny, it's kind of cool, go down that and check it out. Olympus Mons has kind of a shallow gradient but it's the tallest mountain in the Solar System. Exploring a new planet I think would be pretty interesting, and then building the infrastructure necessary to make life self-sustaining on Mars.

There's no real work going on now in terms of designing Mars habitats. I think we need to focus our energies on designing the Mars spaceship first, and then that would effectively be the first habitat. We have rovers on Mars already, so I think we'll see more robots on Mars. My guess is when we get there the technology required to live there is not a really big challenge. In the beginning kind of live in glass domes but over time we would terraform Mars like Earth.

Mars has a huge amount of water in water ice, so I don't think we'll suffer a water shortage on Mars. Once you get to Mars I think there will be some drilling activity, in particular, to find out if you can get to underground lakes to find liquid water, like sort of water that is heated by Mars central core. That would make it a lot easier to develop propellant on Mars.

Critical to any Mars colonization is the ability to generate fuel on Mars. You need to generate methane on Mars. Which you can do because you know Mars has a CO2 atmosphere, and there is a lot of frozen H2O around, there's a lot of water buried in the soil that you can get to. So you get your CH4 and your 02, and then just figuring out how to get all the bits of efficiency right for creating, say, methane and oxygen on Mars. Having that propellant plant on Mars would be critical to a Mars colony. Rockets do burn hydrocarbons but they can use hydrogen as well. The most likely Mars architecture that I think makes sense is a methane oxygen system because methane is the lowest-cost source fuel on Earth. It'd be an automated propellant depot and there is some question as to, what do you do for power generation on Mars?

Power generation on Mars I think is an interesting problem. The main thing about Mars is going to be energy. Do you have a nuclear reactor? then you've got to carry the nuclear fuel there, and reactors are fairly heavy. Do you do some lightweight solar power systems? like, maybe big inflatable solar arrays or something like that. If you have energy there's plenty of water because there are massive amounts of ice, so it's really just about getting huge numbers of solar panels out there and potentially doing geothermal energy, and you know ultimately I think, assuming the public is receptive, there might be nuclear. I think certainly if you'd built nuclear on Mars or to whether you transport nuclear to Mars would be kind of up to the public to decide. I think solar energy is probably fairly significant for Mars, and what's going to be quite important is having a very lightweight solar system, both volumetrically and gravimetrically dense. Actually, we're sort of playing with different concepts like, you know that thing, like that party thing where you inflate it and it rolls out? one of the solar concepts is to have like a big roll that you just basically inflate and it rolls out with really thin solar panels on it. It's going to be pretty important because really you either got to do that or nuclear, and nuclear has its challenges, but for solar it's pretty straightforward. I think solar is very important to the future exploration of Mars for sure.

I do think getting good at digging tunnels could be really helpful for Mars. It would be different optimization for a Mars boring machine versus an Earth boring machine. But for sure there's going to be a lot of ice-mining on Mars, and mining, in general, to get raw materials, and then along the way building underground habitats where you get good radiation shielding. You could build an entire city if you wanted to. People will still go to the surface from time to time, but you can build a tremendous amount underground with the right boring technology on Mars. So I do think there is some overlap in that technology department arena.

For Hyperloop on Mars you basically just need a track, on Earth the air density is quite high but on Mars, it's 1% of Earth's atmospheric density. So probably you might be able to just have a road honestly, you'd go pretty fast. It would obviously have to be electric because there's no oxygen. You could have really fast electric cars, or trains or things like electric aircraft.

I think it's quite likely that we'd want to bioengineer new organisms that are better suited to living on Mars. Humanity's kinda done that over time by selective breeding - You know, cows didn't evolve in the wild - but that's a very slow process that requires hundreds of generations, whereas I think with actual bioengineering you could make that happen a lot faster and maybe with more precision. Ideally, long-term - although this is a tricky subject - you'd want to write genetics. Meaning, you'd want to create synthetics organisms. Not necessarily completely but, you know, start with some base and then modify stuff.

I think that the technology required to live on Mars is not that difficult. Getting there is really difficult. It's like hundreds of millions of miles to get to a place that kind of looks like a cold version of Arizona with not quite as much water.

I think the first journey to Mars is going to be really very dangerous. Going to Mars is not for the faint of heart, and is risky, and dangerous, and uncomfortable, and you might die, now do you want to go? for a lot of people the answer is going to be "Hell No!" and for some, it's going to be "Hell Yes!" if safety is your top goal, I would not go to Mars. The risk of fatality will be high, there's just no way around it, so I would not suggest sending children. It would be basically are you prepared to die? if that's okay, then you know, you're a candidate for going.

I think it's pretty important to give people the option of returning. The number of people who would be willing to move to Mars is much greater if they know they have the option of returning, even if they never actually return. I mean, most of the people who went to the original English colonies in North America never returned to Europe even once, some did. Knowing that if you don't like it there that you can come back I think it makes a big difference in people's willingness to go there in the first place. In any case, we need the space ship back, so it's coming you can jump on board or not, it's cool, you get a free return trip if you want.

When there are enough people who can do that combined with the people who actually want to do that. That's the fundamental thing needed for growing a colony on Mars. Kind of like the way it was with the English colonies in America.

When it became affordable for people to sell all their stuff in England and move to America it grew really fast.

I do think we value discovery, and new things, and learning about the universe. There was quite a bit of attention paid to the discovery of water flowing on Mars. The truth is right now on Earth you can basically go anywhere in 24 hours. I mean anywhere, you could fly over the Antarctic pole and parachute out 24 hours from now if you want. You can parachute on Mount Everest from the right plane. You can go to the bottom of the ocean. Earth from a physical standpoint you can go anywhere, there is no real physical frontier on Earth anymore. Space is that frontier. I think this is really something that appeals to anybody with an exploratory spirit. If you are an explorer, if you want to be on the frontier, and push the envelope, and be where things are super exciting even if it's dangerous, that's really who we are appealing to.

We want to have a future ultimately where humanity is out there exploring the stars, and the things that we read about in science fiction books and see in movies become true. We don't want that to always be a fiction of the future.

You really want to create the dream of Mars in people's minds and have it be like it's the new frontier. 'The Martian' was good, I thought it was pretty excellent, certainly one of the most realistic books on Mars that I've read. There were a few things, like the wind force on Mars is not really that high, it's not going to knock you over or anything, it's high velocity but low force. But overall I thought it was pretty cool, and it's made into a movie and everything. I'm a little worried that it might not make people too keen on going to Mars, it's like, 'This just looks really hard.' I think we need a show about how Mars is also more like the Wild West, and you got the gunslingers, and like the cool cowboys, and that kind of thing. Make it as exciting, fun, and desirable as possible. I think this is where the entertainment industry can play a huge role in putting that dream in people's heads what it would be like.

The key thing is to establish a base on Mars. As soon as you have that base of ours then there is a very powerful forcing function to improve space transportation technologies and all sorts of things that we don't know about today. I mean right now they're just isn't that forcing function because all we do is very local stuff in Earth orbit. You need that forcing function, just like before there was a need to cross the Atlantic there wasn't a forcing function to improve ships. Once the United States was there, then there was a big incentive to improve shipping technology across the Atlantic. If ships had not been reusable in the days of American colonization, the United States would not exist. I think it's a pivotal step on the way to establishing a self-sustaining civilization on Mars. If we don't do that I just don't think we'll be able to afford it, because it's a difference between something costing half a percentage each year of GDP and all of GDP.

You hear all these rebuttals like; aren't there all these problems on Earth that we need to deal with and shouldn't we focus on that? and the answer is yes, our primary focus should be the problems on Earth, but I think that there should be some small amount that's given over to the establishment of a colony on Mars and making life multi-planetary. Obviously, it can't be all of the GDP, we'd get a lot of complaints about that, but half a percent of GDP or maybe quarter a percent of GDP, okay that's manageable. I think most people would agree, even if they don't intend to go themselves, that if we're spending something between a quarter to a half a percent of GDP on establishing a self-sustaining civilization on another planet is probably worth doing. It's sort of a life insurance policy for Life collectively, and that seems like a reasonable insurance premium. Plus it would be a fun adventure to watch even if you don't participate, just as when people went to the Moon only a few people actually went to the Moon, but in a sense, we all went there vicariously. I think most people would say that was a good thing. When people look back and say what were the good things that occurred in the 20th century, that would have to be right near the top of the list. So I think there's value, even if someone doesn't go themselves.

I would definitely like to go into orbit and visit the Space Station, and then ultimately go to Mars. I got to make sure that if something goes wrong on the flight and I die that there is a good succession plan, and that the mission of the company continues, and that it somehow doesn't get taken over by investors who just want to maximize the profit of the company and not go to Mars, that would be my biggest fear in that situation.

Funding, we've thought about funding sources. So we could steal underpants, launch satellites, send cargo to Space Station, Kickstarter of course — followed by profit. Obviously, it's going to be a challenge to fund this whole endeavor. We do expect to generate pretty decent net cash flow from launching lots of satellites, and servicing the Space Station for NASA, transferring cargo to and from the Space Station. And then I know that there's a lot of people in the private sector who are interested in helping fund a base on Mars. Then perhaps there'll be interest on the government sector side to also do that. Ultimately this is going to be a huge public-private partnership, and I think that's how the United States was established, and many other countries around the world, as a public-private partnership.

I think it's fine if countries get together to form teams, but I think it's probably better if there are at least two or three country coalitions going to Mars in a friendly way, and competing to see who can make the most progress. I think friendly competition is a good thing. If you look at say the Olympics, it would be pretty boring if everyone just linked arms and crossed the finishing line at the same time. This is less about, like, you know, who goes there first, the thing that really matters is making a self-sustaining civilization on Mars as fast as possible.

There's certainly not gonna be a resource-based conflict due to the scarcity of resources on Mars. It's open territory on Mars, so I don't think there's gonna be any kind of scarcity. There's like a lot of land on Mars and not many people, and if there are people they are way cleverer than us because they are hiding well.

Sometimes people say, well, what is the business model for Mars? and sometimes they think, well, can you mine Mars and bring things back. That is not a realistic business model for Mars because it's always going to be far cheaper to mine things on Earth than on Mars. I think any natural resource extraction on Mars would be - the output would be for Mars. It definitely wouldn't make sense to transport Mars stuff 200 million miles back to Earth. Honestly, if you had like crack-cocaine on Mars, in like prepackaged pallets, it still wouldn't make sense to transport it back here. Maybe good times for the Martians, but not back here. Resources would be for a colony to use.

What I want SpaceX to keep doing is working on the technologies necessary. And while I do think there's likely to be some economic payoff by transporting large numbers of people and cargo to Mars, it requires a bit of long-term thinking. That maybe goes beyond the quarterly cycle of Wall Street, that's for sure. Some people on Wall Street will think that's just crazy, and what I should just do is milk the government and various commercial companies, and try to charge them as high as possible, which we will not do. I want to make sure that I can ignore such things, which I can only do if I'm the controlling shareholder. Right now we're just trying to make as much progress as we can with the resources that we have available, and just sort of keep moving the ball forward, and hopefully, I think, as we show that this is possible, that this dream is real, not just a dream — it's something that can be made real — I think the support will snowball over time.

What I want to try to achieve here is to make Mars seem possible, make it seem as though it's something that we can do in our lifetimes — and that you can go, and there really is a way that anyone can go if they wanted to. I think that's the important thing. I should say also that the main reason I'm personally accumulating assets is in order to fund this. I really don't have any other motivation for personally accumulating assets, except to be able to make the biggest contribution I can to making life multi-planetary. To have a future ultimately where humanity is out there exploring the stars, we're a spacefaring civilization, and the things that we read about in science fiction books and see in movies become true. We don't want that to always be a fiction of the future. If we don't improve space technology every year we are never going to get there. And so the goal of SpaceX is to make as much improvement as possible. And hopefully, we will see people land on Mars in our lifetime.

At this point I'm certain there is a way, I'm certain that success is one of the possible outcomes for establishing a growing Mars colony. I'm certain that that is possible. Whereas until maybe a few years ago, I was not sure that success was even one of the possible outcomes. Of course, there's a long way between possible and making it real, but I believe it is possible. Mars is the next natural step. In fact, it's the only planet we really have a shot at establishing a self-sustaining city on. So we need to go from these early exploration missions to actually building a city. That's I guess my ultimate dream. I think once we do establish such a city there will be a strong forcing function for the improvement of spaceflight technology that will then enable us to establish colonies elsewhere in the Solar System, and ultimately extend beyond our Solar System.

30. The Trip

So how do we figure out how to take you to Mars and create a self-sustaining city? A city that is not merely an outpost, but could become a planet in its own right. I think in the very beginning it may be similar to an Antarctic station, that's nice but on Mars, we should be aiming for a real civilization. To establish life on Mars means taking at least tens of thousands of people, perhaps ultimately millions of people and millions of tons of cargo, because we've gotta recreate the industrial base of Earth. There needs to be some sort of architecture for establishing a city, which means huge numbers of people, and ultimately millions of tons of cargo. How do we do that?

You really need a fully reusable Mars Transportation System, which is yet a more difficult step than creating a fully reusable Earth system. I was really worried that that would not be possible, but I became convinced that it actually is possible. Which made me very happy actually. In fact, I think Talulah was there when I was pacing around the bedroom late at night trying to see if this would work. Now, I could be deluded, but unless I'm deluded I think we've got something in mind that would be a solution that would work.

It comes down to an economic question. Which is - there's some economic activation energy, a cost-per-unit-mass to the surface of Mars at which point we'd have a self-sustaining civilization there, but beyond which we would not. It really comes down to a cost: What cost does a trip to Mars have to be in order for it to be a self-sustaining reaction? There is definitely some amount of money that has to be spent establishing a base on Mars, basically getting the fundamentals in place. Call it the activation costs of a Mars base. That was true also of the English colonies. It took a significant expense to get things started. You really didn't want to be part of Jamestown. It took quite a bit of effort to get the basics established before the subsequent economics made sense.

The key to establishing a self-sustaining Mars civilization is getting the cost per unit/mass low enough that there is an intersection of sets, the set of people that are interested in moving to Mars, and a set of people that can afford to move to Mars, inclusive of government aid. I mean right now we can't even get one person to Mars. I mean, right now it's like - I don't know, the last NASA estimate was $500 billion, and that was during Bush the first. So, I would imagine that today's estimate is a trillion. We're not going to go spend a trillion dollars on sending four people to Mars. Right now the cost of going to Mars is beyond what can be afforded so that's why no-one is going to Mars.

Using traditional methods, you know if you've taken a sort of Apollo-style approach, an optimistic class number would be about $10 billion a person. For example, in the Apollo program, the cost estimates are somewhere between $100 to $200 billion in current-year dollars, and we sent 12 people to the surface of the Moon. Which was an incredible thing and probably one of the greatest achievements of humanity, but that's a steep price to pay for a ticket. You can't create a self-sustaining civilization if the ticket price is $10 billion a person.

Ultimately, in order to establish a colony, I think you've got to get the cost down to maybe half a million or less, per person. The key I was trying to figure out was, with volume, is it possible to get the cost of moving to Mars down under half a million dollars, which I think is - no-one can argue about the exact threshold, but I think that is about the threshold which enough people would save up money and move to Mars. It's up to debate about how much that might be but I think at a personal level that would be enough of an intersection of sets of people who can afford to move to Mars, and people who want to move to Mars. If those two coincide then there will be a colony, otherwise, there will not be a colony. To put that in concrete terms, it needs to be at least half a million dollars or less to move to Mars, I think. Ideally much less, you know, but if it's much more than that then there probably won't be a colony. That's the basic idea.

I sorta started back from the half a million-dollar point because in order for Mars to become a self-sustaining civilization the ticket price has to be low enough that if someone were to work hard and save up then most people in advanced countries after, say, their mid-40s or something like that, could put together enough money to make the trip. I thought, a half a million dollars, that's a middle-class house in California, basically. Something on that order, that's about the right order of magnitude, and then, working backward. If people could pay half a million dollars to move to Mars, sell all their stuff on Earth because you don't need it, then you could move to Mars, then I think that could work. That's basically the net worth of a roughly middle-income earning person after about 25 years in the United State roughly half a million dollars. In fact, it's kinda hard to buy a house in southern California for half a million dollars in a lot of neighborhoods. So I think at roughly that level is where it works. That's where we've got to get to, and my calculations show that it should be possible. It is possible... according to me.. but there's a great deal of work that has to occur to make it a reality. If we can get the cost of moving to Mars to be roughly equivalent to a median house price in the US, which is around $200,000, then I think the probability of establishing a self-sustaining civilization is very high. I think it would almost certainly occur.

Not everyone would want to go, in fact, I think a relatively small number of people from Earth want to go, but enough would want to go and could afford the trip that it would happen. I mean, that's how America got created, basically. That's sort of the key threshold for it to become a self-sustaining.. 'colony' if you will. Kind of like the English colonies in the Americas, which started out with a lot of sort of basically rich people and the British government sponsoring people to go over, but eventually, you know, anyone could go over.

I think there's plenty of people who will sign up for a one-way trip to Mars. It'd certainly be enough, but I think the question is, is it a one-way mission and then you die, or is it a one-way mission and you get resupplied? that's a big difference. I think it ends up being a moot point because you want to bring the spaceship back. These spaceships are expensive okay, they're hard to build. You can't just leave them there. Whether or not people want to come back or not, is kind of - like, they can just jump on if they want, but we need the spaceship back. I mean, it'd be kind of weird if there's this huge collection of spaceships on Mars over time. It'd be like, maybe we should send them back - no, of course, we should send them back. Particularly if we want to have a colony of some kind that's of significant size. So they can come back if they don't like it, of course. You get a free return ticket, they get a free return ticket if they don't like it. Sort of aspirational it'd be a round trip. So you are not sort of trapped there. I do think we will want to offer round trips because a lot more people would be willing to go if they think that if they don't like it they can come back.

When England was establishing colonies in America, they needed the ships to return. If the ships were just one-way they would run out of wood in England. So anyone who wants to return can just jump on. If people are going to go there to settle, then hey, you don't need a return ticket. When people came over here from England in the beginning I don't think they bought return tickets.

Anyway, if we can get to some sort of point where the cost of a ticket to Mars is less than, say, the average house price in California, then I think there's some number of people who would be willing to sell their house and all their stuff and go to Mars. At least enough to get things started. I think you'd have enough people who would buy a ticket and would move to Mars to be part of creating a new planet and be part of the founding team of a new civilization.

The world, on the whole, is getting richer, so I think even if only 1 in 10,000 people decided to go that'd be enough, or every 1 in 100,000. You'd obviously have to have quite an appetite for risk and adventure, but there are 7 billion people on Earth now. There will be probably 8 billion by the midpoint of the century, so even if one in million people decided to do that, that's still 8,000 people, and I think maybe more than one in a million people would decide to do that. That I think is a reason to feel good about the possibility of life on Mars. I think really, what matters is finding a way to do it.

So there is that basic investment and we'll need to gather the money to do that, but then once there are regular flights, that's where I think there would be enough people that would buy that - they'd just sell their stuff on Earth and move to Mars - to have it be a reasonable business case. You need the transport link and what SpaceX is trying to establish is the transport link and create an environment for entrepreneurs on Mars to flourish. I think it gets to the point where almost anyone if they saved up and this was their goal they could ultimately save up enough money to buy a ticket and move to Mars. Mars would have a labor shortage for a long time, so jobs would not be in short supply.

In the beginning, you'd go with a smaller number of people and you'd have a higher proportion of cargo and emergency equipment and that kind of thing. Once you really got rolling, you'd increase the number of people on the flight because you'd have supplies there. So you wouldn't need to worry about carrying with you all the supplies for the journey there, the stay on the surface, and coming back. Initially, you start off with maybe a handful of people, less than 10, just trying to give orders of magnitude here, but then you'd go to 100 or more in a steady-state down the road.

It is a bit tricky because you have to figure out how to improve the cost of trips to Mars by 5,000,000%. This is just not easy, I mean it sounds virtually impossible, but I think there are ways through it. This translates to an improvement of approximately four-and-a-half orders of magnitude, each order of magnitude is a factor of 10. These are the key elements that are needed in order to achieve a four-and-a-half order of magnitude improvement. Most of the improvement would come from full reusability, somewhere between two and two-and-a-half orders of magnitude. Then the other two orders of magnitude would come from refilling in orbit, propellant production on Mars, and choosing the right propellant.

I'm gonna go into detail on all those. Full reusability is really the super-hard one. It's very difficult to achieve reusability for even an orbital system and that challenge becomes substantially greater for a system that has to go to another planet. You definitely need to have full reusability because even partial expendability would kill that price. The difference between reusability and expandability in any form of transport if they were single-use almost no one would use them. They'd be too expensive. But with frequent flights, you can take something like an aircraft that costs $90 million, and if it were single-use, you'd have to pay half a million dollars per flight, but you can actually buy a ticket on Southwest right now from LA to Vegas for $43 — including taxes. I mean, that's a massive improvement right there, it's showing a four-order-of-magnitude improvement. Now, this is harder. The reusability doesn't apply quite as much to Mars, because the number of times that you could reuse the spaceship part of the system is less often because the Earth-Mars rendezvous only occurs every 26 months. With the spaceship, you say, "well, how long is it gonna last?" Well, maybe 30 years. So that might be 12, maybe 15 flights of the spaceship, at most. So you really want to maximize the cargo of the spaceship and reuse the booster and the tanker a lot.

You get to use the spaceship part roughly every 2 years. Mars is only on the same sort of rough quadrant of Earth, roughly 6 months every two years. By same, I mean sort of offset, like a transfer quadrant. If you can get the ship to and from Mars inside that 6-month window you get to use it twice as often. So there's actually a lot of merits to get to Mars in under 3 months. Depending upon which Earth-Mars rendezvous you're aiming for the trip time, at six kilometers per second, departure velocity can be as low as 80 days. Then, over time, I think we'd obviously improve that and ultimately I suspect that you'd see Mars transit times of as little as 30 days in the more distant future. It's fairly manageable, considering the trips that people used to do in the old days. They'd routinely take sailing voyages that would be 6 months or more.

Essentially what happens is, the rocket booster and the spaceship take off and load the spaceship into orbit. The rocket booster then comes back — it comes back quite quickly, within about 20 minutes — and so it can actually launch the tanker version of the spacecraft, which is essentially the same as a spaceship, but filling up the unpressurized and pressurized cargo areas with propellant tanks. They look almost identical, this also helps lower the development costs, which absolutely will not be small. Then the propellant tanker goes up multiple times, anywhere from three to five times — to fill the tanks of the spaceship in orbit. Then once the spaceship tanks are full, the cargo has been transferred, and we reach the Mars rendezvous timing, which as I mentioned is roughly every 26 months, that's when the ship would depart.

It actually makes sense to load the spaceships into orbit, because you've got 2 years to do so, and then make frequent use of the booster and the tanker to get really heavy reuse out of those. You get to use the booster and the tanker as frequently as you'd like, that's why it makes a lot of sense to load the spaceship into orbit with essentially tanks dry, have it have really quite big tanks that you then use the booster and tanker to refill while it's in orbit, and maximize the payload of the spaceships so that when it goes to Mars you have a very large payload capability.

Refilling in orbit is one of the essential elements of this. Without refilling in orbit, you would have a half-order of magnitude impact, roughly, on the cost. So not refilling in orbit would mean a 500%, roughly, increase in the cost per ticket.

So you send the spaceship up to orbit, you tank it or refill it until it has full tanks, the ship travels to Mars, lands on Mars gets replenished, and then returns to Earth.

Now over time, there would be many spaceships. You would ultimately have I think upwards of 1,000 or more spaceships waiting in orbit. So the Mars colonial fleet would depart en masse, kind of 'Battlestar Galactica' — if you've seen that thing, it's a good show — so a bit like that.

Having the atmosphere, you can use atmospheric breaking as well. And Mars has lower gravity than Earth, you do not need a booster. So you can go all the way from the surface of Mars to the surface of Earth just using the ship. Albeit, you need to go to a max payload number of about twenty to fifty tons for the return journey to work, but it's a single-stage all the way back to Earth, similar to the Moon. But the tricky thing with Mars is we do need to build a propellant depot to refill the tanks and return to Earth. For Mars, you will need local propellant production. It'd be pretty absurd to try to build a city on Mars if your spaceship just kept staying on Mars not going back to Earth. You'd have this like massive graveyard of ships., you'd have to like do something with them. It really wouldn't make sense to leave your spaceships on Mars, so producing propellant on Mars is very obviously important. You really want to build a propellant plant on Mars and send the ships back, and Mars happens to work out well for that. The key point is that the ingredients are there on Mars to create a propellant plant with relative ease, because the atmosphere is primarily CO_2, and plenty of water ice, there's water ice almost everywhere. You've got the CO_2 plus H_2O to make methane, CH_4, and oxygen O_2, using the Sabatier reaction. With H_2O and CO_2 you can do CH_4 methane and oxygen, O_2, and bingo, you can replenish propellant. Now, you can do this either with hydrogen or with methane.

Picking the right propellant is also important. Think of this as maybe there are three main choices, and they have their merits. Kerosene or rocket-propellant grade kerosene, which is also what jets use. Rockets use a very expensive form a highly refined form of jet fuel, essentially. It helps keep the vehicle size small, but because it's a very specialized form of jet fuel it's quite expensive. The reusability potential is lower. Very difficult to make this on Mars because there's no oil. So really quite difficult to make propellants on Mars, and then the propellant transfer is pretty good but not great.

Hydrogen, although it has a high specific impulse is very expensive. Incredibly difficult to keep from boiling off because liquid hydrogen is very close to absolute zero as a liquid, so the insulation required is tremendous, and the energy cost on Mars of producing and storing hydrogen is very high.

For a while, we were sort of going down the hydrogen path, and I was looking at the numbers and you get to roughly equivalent delta-v with methane or hydrogen.

We looked at the overall system optimization, and it was clear to us that methane actually was the clear winner because of the better mass fraction of the methane system. Then you combine that with the fact that methane is much easier to deal with, it's not a hyper-cryogen, and it doesn't have the wiggly hydrogen molecule that likes to get into all sorts of unpleasant places and induce metal embrittlement and create invisible high-temperature fires and that kind of thing. We think methane is actually better, on, really, almost across the board. We started off initially thinking that Hydrogen would make sense, but we ultimately came to the conclusion that the best way to optimize the cost-per-unit mass to Mars and back is to use an all-methane system. The cheapest fuel is methane, technically a deep-cryo methalox. Actually, with a properly designed methane engine, a staged combustion engine with decent combustion efficiency in the 99% range and reasonable area ratio, 380 /sp is quite achievable. The Russians, in ground tests, have achieved 380 /sp. So this is clearly an achievable number. That's the direction we're thinking of going, for that.

Those are the four elements that need to be achieved. Whatever architecture, whatever system is designed, whether by SpaceX or anyone, we think these are the four features that need to be addressed in order for the system to really achieve a low cost per ton to the surface of Mars.

In the long term, you can use solar power to extract CO_2 from the atmosphere combine it with water, and produce fuel and oxygen for the rocket. So the same thing that we're doing on Mars, we could do on Earth in the long-term.

I guess the Moon is also a potential place for propellant depots, more water being found on the Moon. Yeah, it's in like, permanently shadowed craters. It's pretty chilly in there but you could mine the Moon potentially for water, and you could have propellant depots on the Moon. I'd liken it to when the early colonies in the Americas were being established and the early voyages of discovery. You kinda want to go there and if it turns out that having way stations makes that trip more efficient over time, then those people will build those stations. As soon as you've got that destination, you've got the forcing function, then you'll see people do whatever seems sensible to make that better.

When there's a lot of traffic between Earth and Mars I would expect there'd be some large space cruiser that's circulating between Earth and Mars. And you just take a small shuttlecraft up to the space cruiser if you will, and the space cruiser gets refueled from Earth or from Mars. But that's a long-term optimization and it would be driven by a lot of traffic occurring between the two planets. To do that, you need really big rockets launching a lot, obviously in order to fit 100 people or thereabout in the pressurized section, plus carry the luggage and all of the unpressurized cargo, to build propellant plants and build everything we need to carry a lot of cargo. You want something that is pretty big, you know because if you're going to have to spend a lot of months in it, it can't be the size of a minivan. The crew compartment or the occupant department is set up so that you can do zero-g games, you can float around, there'll be like movies, lecture halls, you know, cabins, a restaurant — it will be, like, really fun to go. You're gonna have a great time.

A round trip to Mars, with 6 months there, 18 months on the surface, and 6 months back, two and a half years, you want a little room. I would shudder to think of doing that in Dragon. You'll come back batty if you come back. I mean, in order to make it appealing, and increase that portion of the Venn diagram of people that actually want to go, it's gotta be really fun and exciting and it can't feel cramped or boring.

I think at least 100 people per trip is the right order of magnitude. If we say, like, the threshold for a self-sustaining city on Mars or civilization would be a million people, and you can only go every 2 years, and if you have 100 people per ship, that's 10,000 trips. 10,000 flights is a lot of flights, so you really want to ultimately think on the order of 1,000 ships. It will take a while to build up to 1,000 ships. I think if you say when would we reach that million-person threshold from the point at which the first ship goes to Mars, it's probably somewhere between 20 to 50 total Mars rendezvous. It's probably somewhere between maybe 40 to 100 years to achieve a fully self-sustaining civilization on Mars.

I think we actually may end up expanding the crew section and ultimately taking more like 200 or more people per flight in order to reduce the cost per person. You really need something quite large in order to do that. The vehicle that we're proposing would do about 550 tons and about 300 tons in reusable mode. That compares to Saturn Vs max capability of 135 tons. The thrust is quite enormous. We're talking about a liftoff thrust of 13,000 tons. The main job of the booster is to accelerate the spaceship to around 8,500 kilometers an hour. For those that aren't as familiar with orbital dynamics, really it's all about velocity and not about height, that's the job of the boosters. The booster's like the javelin thrower, so it's gotta toss that javelin, which is the spaceship.

In the case of other planets though which have a gravity well that is not as deep, so Mars, the moons of Jupiter, maybe even Venus, Venus will be a little trickier, but for most of the Solar System you only need the spaceship. You don't need the booster if you have a lower gravity well, so no booster is needed on the Moon or Mars or any other moons of Jupiter or Pluto, you just need the spaceship. The booster is just there for heavy gravity wells.

It will be quite tectonic when it takes off. It does fit on a pad 39A, which NASA has been kind enough to allow us to use, where they somewhat oversized the pad in doing Saturn V. as a result we can actually do a much larger vehicle on that same launchpad. In the future, we expect to add additional launch locations, probably adding one on the South coast of Texas.

We're also getting quite comfortable with the accuracy of the landing. If you've been watching the Falcon 9 landings, you'll see that they're getting increasingly closer to the bull's-eye.

On arrival, the heat shield technology is extremely important. We've been refining the heat-shield technology using our Dragon spacecraft, and we're now on version three of PICA, which is a "phenolic impregnated carbon ablator" and it's getting more robust with each new version, with less ablation, more resistance, less need for refurbishment. The heat shield's basically a giant brake pad. It's like, how good can you make that brake pad against extreme reentry conditions, and minimize the cost of refurbishment, make it so that you could have many flights with no refurbishment at all.

I think the whole sort of interplanetary human flight thing being a danger to human beings is somewhat overblown because, clearly, we sent people to the Moon, and that's deep space. I think it won't be too bad. We know that people can survive in deep space because the astronauts that went to the Moon lived long lives and were none the worse, we've not seen any premature deaths, really, of people that have gone to the Moon. Really it's just a question of how long can you be in deep space, and there's a certain damage rate per day which is then offset by your body's ability to repair that damage. We also know that people can live in zero-g for long periods of time - I think the record is almost two years or something like that. I think the verdict is in with respect to long-term existence in space. There were plenty of cases where it was 6 months to a year, which is the journey time to Mars. You'll need to exercise along the way to make sure you don't have muscle or bone atrophy, but I think it will be okay. People have actually shown that they can live for over a year in zero gravity. Your bones do get a little thinner but they come back. I think spending 3 to 6 months in zero gravity is not a problem.

Doing a six-month journey you're going to have some slightly increased risk of cancer but, from what I've seen, sort of a back-of-the-envelope analysis, that increase in cancer is less than if you smoked on the way there. Although smoking is quite bad, I have to say.

There is one thing that people should be concerned about, which is solar flares and shielding against solar radiation, solar storms. This is often thought about in the wrong way, where people say, oh, you need to have like 20 feet of water or whatever it is to shield against a serious solar storm, and they say, oh, you need to have a sphere of water around you, and that sphere of 20-foot water would be ridiculously expensive, or ridiculously heavy. Sometimes that problem is stated as if you need several meters of water to shield yourself and then somebody does the calculation for the volume of a sphere and that ends up being some enormous quantity of water. But you don't need that, you can just have a column of water pointed at the Sun, and make sure that you're mostly in front of that column and you should be okay. That'd make much more sense, and then you've gotta have water anyway, so it doesn't end up being a big deal. I don't think it's a huge show stopper and we'll figure out ways to make it better and better over time. I don't think the journey there is - there are no show-stoppers there but over time we will find ways to improve it and reduce the risk of cancer and that sort of thing, and reduce the journey length as well. But really fundamentally we need to get there. If we can't get there it's all like academic, so we need to get there. Once you're on Mars you obviously cut your radiation in half just because you got the planet shielding you and there is at least some atmosphere. I think what you can construct overtime is a magnetic field to deflect high-energy particles.

If you have a low energy trajectory, like a minimum energy trajectory, Mars is about 6 months. I think that can be compressed down to about 3 months, and it gets exponentially harder as you go lower than that - 3 to 4. It's important to actually be at that level because then you can send your spaceship to Mars and bring it back on the same orbital synchronization. You've got to be able to go there and back in one go. That's important for making the cost of traveling to Mars an affordable amount.

I'm hopeful that the first human mission to Mars is actually some collaboration of private industry and government, but I think we also need to be prepared for the possibility that it has to be just commercial. That may take longer because it'll require marshaling more resources. I want to prepare for a scenario where either path is possible. Basically, it needs to happen one way or another, that's the important thing. I'm not dogmatic as to how it occurs, just let it occur.

I'm hopeful there will be multiple colonies on Mars. There's certainly - from a SpaceX standpoint we don't mean to do anything on an exclusionary basis, we're just trying to get there. We'd love to have that debate. Is it too American? okay, maybe, but we've got the base on Mars, who cares. I think if there was an American base on Mars it would certainly prompt other countries to want to establish their own base on Mars too. I do think it would be better to have competition than cooperation. Yes, I think we'd be better off with competition rather than insisting - like, in the Space Station. We got the international Space Station, but when governments are all forced to go in lockstep it tends to not make things go faster. We want some sort of positive competitive element, I think. We don't want people going to war or anything, just some positive competitive element like the Olympics. If people compete hard and it's good sportsmanship and everything, then the net result is better than if ... like if there was no competition. Olympics with no competition wouldn't make any sense. So I think some positive competitive thing would be better, and we should definitely not insist that all countries go at the same pace, or some collection of countries go at the same pace, that would slow things down dramatically and maybe not even happen.

The thing that matters is being able to establish a self-sustaining civilization on Mars. Beats the hell out of being a single planet species. For that, I don't see anything being done except SpaceX, honestly. That's not to say SpaceX will be successful, but I don't see anyone even trying. I think long-term China is a serious competitor. If you look at Russian rocketry, since the fall of the Soviet Union, there have really been no significant developments. The technology has barely progressed. No new rockets have launched since the fall of the Soviet Union, so obviously what that means is that as soon as that technology level is exceeded then they're rendered redundant and they have no ability to compete, and I think that is what's likely to occur with the Russian launch industry. I'm quite confident we can take on China. Maybe I'm overconfident, but I'd rather bet on us than China. Could be famous last words.

The basic game plan is we're going to send a mission to Mars with every Mars opportunity from 2018 onwards, approximately once every 26 months. We'd start off by sending a mission to Mars where it would be, obviously, just landing on rocky ground or dusty ground. The first launch will be robotic anyway. In terms of having some meaningful number of people going to Mars, I think this is potentially something that can be accomplished in about 10 years, maybe sooner, maybe nine years. I need to make sure that SpaceX doesn't die between now and then, and that I don't die, or if I do die that someone takes over who will continue that.

We are establishing cargo flights to Mars that people can count on for cargo. Our goal is to try to make the 2022 Mars rendezvous. That's not a typo, although it is aspirational. I think if things go like plan we should be able to launch people in 2024 and arrive in 2025.

We've already started building the system. The tooling for the main tanks has been ordered, the facility is being built, we will start construction of the first ship around the second quarter of 2018. I feel fairly confident that we can complete the ship and be ready for a launch in about five years. Five years seems like a long time to me. So then in 2024, we want to try to fly four ships, two cargo, and two crew. The goal of these initial missions is to find the best source of water, that's for the first mission, and then the second mission, the goal is to build the propellant plant. We should, particular with six ships there have plenty of landed mass to construct the propellant depot, which will consist of a large array of solar panels, a very large array, and then everything necessary to mine and refine water, and then draw the CO_2 out of the atmosphere, and then create and store deep-cryo CH_4 and O_2. Then build up the base, starting with one ship, then multiple ships, then start building out the city, then making the city bigger, and even bigger. Over time terraforming and making it really a nice place to be. The trickiest thing, really, is the energy source, which we think we can do with a large field of solar panels.

Then to give you a sense of the cost, really the key is making this affordable to almost anyone who wants to go. We think, based on this architecture, assuming optimization over time, the very first flights would be fairly expensive, but the architecture allows for a cost-per-ticket of less than $200,000, maybe as little as $100,000 overtime, depending upon how much mass a person takes. We're right now estimating about $140,000 per ton to the surface of Mars. If a person plus their luggage is less than that, taking into account food consumption and life-support, then we think that the cost of moving to Mars ultimately could drop below $100,000.

What about beyond Mars? As we thought about this system, and the reason we call it a system because generally, I don't like calling things systems because everything's a system including your dog, is that it's actually more than a vehicle. There's this rocket booster, the spaceship, the tanker, and the propellant plant, the in situ propellant production. If you have all of those four elements, you can actually go anywhere in the Solar System by planet-hopping or by moon-hopping. By establishing a propellant depot in the Asteroid Belt or on one of the moons of Jupiter you can make flights from Mars to Jupiter no problem. In fact, even without a propellant depot at Mars, you could do a flyby of Jupiter. Establishing a propellant depot on let's say, you know, Enceladus or Europa, or any —

there are a few options — and then doing another one on Titan, Saturn's moon, and then perhaps another one further out on Pluto, or elsewhere in the Solar System. This system really gives you the freedom to go anywhere you want in the greater Solar System. You could actually travel out to the Kuiper Belt, and the Oort Cloud, provided we have filling stations along the way. This means full access to the entire greater Solar System. It'd be really great to do a mission to Europa, particularly.

Yep, that's how things are sort of progressing, we'll keep going until we ultimately have the capability to go to Mars, and not just get to Mars, but do so in a manner with substantially better economics than are predicted today. I do think going to Mars is definitely going to be hard and dangerous and difficult in probably every way you can imagine, so certainly if you care about being safe and comfortable, going to Mars would be a terrible choice.

31. Autopilot

The two biggest revolutions in transport are electrification and autonomy. Those are the two biggest innovations since the moving production line and they are both happening at about the same time. The most near-term impact from a technology standpoint is autonomous cars, like fully self-driving cars. I think autonomy is extremely important. The car will be able to take you from point to point, like from your driveway to work without you touching anything. You could be asleep the whole time and do so very safely. That's going to happen much faster than people realize. I think this is going to be quite a profound experience for people when they do it. We've been testing it for years so we got quite used to it, but I noticed when I put my friends in the car and they saw it drive itself they were blown away. It's really quite an interesting new experience. I think it's going to change people's perception of the future quite rapidly. It's a world-changing experience.

In the long term, nobody will buy a car unless it is autonomous, it would be like having a manually operated elevator or something like that. There used to be elevator operators, you get in and there would be a guy moving a lever. Then we developed some simple circuitry to make elevators automatically come to the floor you are at, just press the button. Now you just get in and you press the button and that's taken for granted, nobody needs to operate the elevator. It's a strange anachronism. The car is just going to be like that, getting in a car will be like getting in an elevator. You just tell it where you want to go and it takes you there with extreme levels of safety and that will be normal, that will just be normal. You'll be able to tell your car like, take me home, or go here, go there, anything, and it'll just do it, at an order of magnitude safer than a person.

I think it's going to be some time before one can truly just get in the car fall asleep and wake up at your destination because you're going to have to take care of these corner cases. The expectations for autonomous car safety will at least be a factor 10 higher than when a person is driving because the moment a robot is driving and runs somebody over there would be big trouble.

The approach that we took is what we call Autopilot, because we think it's analogous to the way aircraft operate, and after which our system is named. You still have pilots but you can engage in autopilot for most of the journey. With Autopilot version One the expectation was that someone's attention is to the road and is ready to take over if there is an issue. It was really intended in the same way that autopilot for an aircraft works where autopilot for an aircraft alleviates workload but the pilot is still expected to pay attention, so he couldn't turn like Autopilot on and go to sleep.

If there's heavy snow it's going to be harder for the system to work. It's going to advise caution in heavy precipitation. It's a real boon in high traffic situations. If you're in slow-moving gridlock traffic, turn on Autopilot and it works super well, almost to the point where you can take your hands off. I won't say you can take your hands off, but almost. Our Autopilot capability is really good in heavy traffic, it's super good in heavy traffic. Not that I'd recommend it but you can read a book or do email is what I've found ...err heard people say. It can really take the edge off the traffic.

Certainly, in the long term, people will not need hands on the wheel, and eventually, there won't be wheels! There won't be wheels or pedals, it will just be... you jump in a car and go somewhere. You tell the car your destination and it will take you there. In order for that to occur it needs to be fail-operational. If any one system in the car fails for any reason, the car does not crash, that's still some ways away.

I think you'll probably want to have a steering wheel and pedals and be able to take control of the car when you want to take control. I don't super love the idea of having a bland little pod that you get in and go from one place to another in a very sort of conservative driving manner or something like that, it sounds boring. But it might be something like in 'I, Robot' where the car has an autonomous mode but you can switch to manual when you want to and the steering wheel comes out of the dash, that looked cool. Yeah, so I think autonomy default with optional manual is probably the good way to go. I think the quality of the ride is always gonna matter. Nobody wants to drive if you're sitting in stop-and-go traffic, that's boring. But if you're driving on a beautiful country road or along the seaside, then I think it feels wonderful to drive and you want to do that. I don't think cars are going to just become some boring utility.

We try to make the car behave as though it's a really good chauffeur, like a really good driver, not too conservative, not too aggressive. When the cars interact with each other, I would think they would just be as though the car is interacting with a good human driver. Essentially it's like a person to some degree, how well can a person figure out what route they can take? In the beginning, it's going to be not as good as a person in some ways and better in some ways. I think it's just going to be where it makes it easier and easier to drive and over time it will actually be better than a person. I mean long term it'll be way better than a person, imagine a system that has 8 cameras, radar, ultrasonics, and it's processing all that at the millisecond level, never gets tired, and it's never had anything to drink, and it's not arguing with someone in the car (hopefully!) so it's not distracted, and it has this huge dataset. There's just no way, that would be like competing with eight human experts simultaneously. There's just no way one person is going to be better, you just don't have eyes in the back of your head. It will obviously be way better than a person long-term. It will be safer than a person driving for all pedestrians as well as people in the car and other cars. In the distant future probably people may outlaw driving cars because it is too dangerous. You cannot have a person driving a 2-ton death-machine. All I'd say is that full autonomy is going to come a hell of a lot faster than anyone thinks it will. I think what we've got under development is going to blow people's minds. It blows my mind, so.

I think we're still on track for the coast-to-coast drive, being able to go cross-country from LA to New York by the end of 2017, fully autonomous. The thing that will be interesting is that I'm actually fairly confident it will be able to do that route even if you change the route dynamically. If you say it's going to be really good at one specific route that's one thing, but it should be able to really be very good, certainly once you enter a highway, to go anywhere on the highway system in a given country. So it's not sort of limited to LA-New York, we could change it and make it Seattle-Florida, that day, in real-time. Say you were going from LA to New York, and now go from LA to Toronto. Yeah, essentially November or December we should be able to go all the way from a parking lot in California to a parking lot in New York, no controls touched at any point during the entire journey. I believe we're still on track for that.

Another way to think of it is as an added safety feature and the added safety, in the long run, becomes autonomous. It takes things to another level of safety, I do want to emphasize:

this does not mean perfect safety. Perfect safety is really an impossible goal. It's really about improving the probability of safety, that's the only thing that is ever possible. The thing to appreciate about vehicle safety is it's probabilistic, I mean, there's some chance that any time a human driver gets in a car, that they will have an accident that is their fault, it's never zero.

The key threshold for autonomy is how much better does autonomy need to be than a person before you can rely on it. There will never be zero fatalities, there will never be zero injuries. The world is a very big place and there's a huge number of people and a huge number of circumstances. It's really just about minimizing the probability of death not the illusion of perfect safety. It's just a question of refining the details of the technology, and bring that to market, and then improving the nines of probability. In order to have a self-driving car, you have to have many nines of reliability so it is 99.9999% is how good it needs to be. Let's say the first approximation you would want a self-driving car to be is an order of magnitude safer than a human-driven car. For self-driving or Autopilot, I think it should be held to a standard that's maybe 10 times higher than a person. If it is like 10 times safer there is no more doubt there's no more debate which one is safe. The real trick of it is not how do you make it work say 99.9 percent of the time, because if a car crashes one in a thousand times then you're probably still not going to be comfortable falling asleep, you shouldn't be, certainly. It's never going to be perfect no system is going to be perfect, but if you say the car is unlikely to crash in a hundred lifetimes or a thousand lifetimes, then people are like, OK, wow, if I were to live a thousand lives, I would still most likely never experience a crash, then that's probably OK.

The system is getting better. I think it's really quite unequivocal that Autopilot improves safety. Just looking at fatalities it's at least 2.5 to 3 times more miles per fatality and that number is growing every day. I think that the autonomy system is likely to at least mitigate the crash, except in rare circumstances. The hardware and the software are not yet at the point where a driver can abdicate responsibility. That will come at some point in the future, but it is not the case today. These are still the early days. If there's an accident the driver of the car is liable, we're very clearly saying that this is not a case of abdicating responsibility.

I would estimate that with the improved fleet learning and software I think we will end up probably 3 times safer than a car that isn't on Autopilot that's my guess, it's not minor. What's sort of less visible to the outside are all the cases where version One of Autopilot actually did a lot to mitigate the accident, so that the impact velocity went from being potentially fatal or severe injury to customer stepped out and walked away. The thing that we think is quite powerful is the fact that it tends to reduce the impact velocity. There might still be an impact, but if it decreases the impact velocity from something that would have been fatal or caused critical injuries to something where you walk away from the car, that's enormously helpful and that's a really significant difference.

One of the ironies that we've seen is counter-intuitive and a lot of people on the consumer watchdog sites and in some cases on regulatory sites have assumed that Autopilot accidents are more likely for new users, in fact, it is the opposite Autopilot accidents are far more likely for expert users, it is not the neophytes, it's the experts. They get very comfortable with it and repeatedly ignore the car's warnings. It's like a reflex. The car will beep at them, they tug the wheel, the car will beep at them, they tug the wheel, and it becomes an unconscious reflex action. So we will see half a dozen or more, sometimes as many as 10 warnings in one hour continuously ignored by the driver. We really want to avoid that situation.

I think this is really going to make a difference, but I do want to emphasize that it's not going from bad to good. I think it would be morally wrong to withhold functionalities that improve safety simply in order to avoid criticisms or for fear of being involved in lawsuits. I feel quite strongly that as soon as you have data that says that autonomy improves safety – even hypothetically 1 or 2 percent safer – there are 1.2 million people dying from automotive accidents a year, one percent is 12,000 lives saved. I think things are already good, they are already better than if there wasn't Autopilot. This is very important to appreciate. This is not going from bad to good. It's going from good to I think great.

Cybersecurity is a huge concern, one of the biggest risks for autonomous vehicles is somebody achieving a fleet-wide hack. We have to make super sure that a fleet-wide hack is basically impossible and that if people are in the car, that they have override authority on whatever the car is doing. If the car is doing something whacky you can press a button that no amount of software can override that will ensure you gain control of the vehicle and cut the link to the servers. That's pretty fundamental. It is my top concern from a security standpoint to make sure that a fleet-wide hack or any vehicle-specific hack can't occur. In principle, if someone was able to hack the autonomous Teslas they could say -- just as a prank, say send them all to Rhode Island from all across the United States. Well, that would be the end of Tesla, and a lot of angry people in Rhode Island-- that's for sure. They have the same problem with cellphones. It's kind of crazy today that we live quite comfortably in a world that George Orwell would have thought is super crazy. We all carry a phone with a microphone that can be turned on any time really without our knowledge, with a GPS that knows our position, and a camera, and all of our personal information. We do this willingly and it's kind of wild to think that's the case. Apple and Google have the same challenge of making sure there cannot be a fleet-wide hack or systemwide hack of phones, or a specific hack. That's a top concern, it's going to become a bigger and bigger concern. Tesla is pretty good at software compared to other car companies. Within the car even if someone gained access to the car there are multiple subsystems that also have specialized encryption. The power-train for example even if someone would gain access to the power-train or the braking system. As the technology matures all Tesla vehicles will have the hardware necessary to be fully self-driving with fail-operational capability, meaning that any given system in the car could break and your car will still drive itself safely. It is important to emphasize that refinement and validation of the software will take much longer than putting in place the cameras, radar, sonar, and computing hardware. I do think it's going to be a bigger challenge to ensure security for the other car companies.

I should add a note here to explain why Tesla is deploying partial autonomy now rather than waiting until some point in the future. The most important reason is that when used correctly it is already significantly safer than a person driving by themselves, and it would therefore be morally reprehensible to delay release simply for fear of bad press or some mercantile calculation of legal liability. According to the 2015 NHTSA report, automotive fatalities increased by 8%, to one death every 89 million miles. Autopilot miles exceeded twice that number and the system gets better every day. It would no more make sense to disable Tesla's Autopilot, as some have called for than it would to disable autopilot in aircraft. It is important to note that some number of people die every year by getting twisted up by their bed sheets, literally some number of people die every year by vending machines falling on them. There are those unusual situations that people die, but I don't think anyone is saying that there should be no bed sheets or no vending machines. It's just that you have these rare events occasionally – tragic – but if we were to eliminate all of them, we would be essentially limited to sitting at home on a pillow as the only thing you are allowed to do.

Even once the software is highly refined and far better than the average human driver, there will still be a significant time gap, varying widely by jurisdiction before true self-driving is approved by regulators. I think we may see some jurisdictions giving the okay a lot sooner than others. I think the timeframe that we think it's ready and then the timeframe that regulators will approve differs because we've got to present the data to them, they've got to think about it; then they've got to render a verdict. That can sometimes be a long process and it varies quite a bit by jurisdiction. When you think about the global average fatalities, it's sort of somewhere around 60, one fatality every 60 million miles on a global basis. So if you're at 6 billion miles, you're 100 times the fatalities per mile. You really start to get quite statistically significant at that point, and it can make quite a strong argument, I believe, at that point that it would be morally wrong not to allow autonomous driving. I think the logical thing is that if there are fewer accidents in autonomous mode than in non-autonomous mode, there shouldn't be some penalty. That wouldn't make any sense you'd be penalizing a safer situation.

It's really hard for a person to compete. I mean, the car has eight cameras looking 360 degrees all the time, it's got a forward radar, it's got 12 high-precision ultrasonic sonars, it's got initial measurement units, high-accuracy GPS, and over 10 Tera-ops of computing capability that never sleeps.

How does it figure out what to do? There are four major sensor systems. We've got the ultrasonic sensors, so essentially ultrasonic sonar, which tells us where everything is, so around the perimeter of the car we know where there are obstacles. That's then combined with the forward-facing camera with image recognition. The forward-facing camera is able to determine where the lanes are, where cars are ahead of it, and it's also able to read signs. Then that's combined with the forward radar. The radar is very good at detecting fast-moving large objects. It can actually see through fog, rain, snow, and dust. The forward radar gives the car superhuman senses, it can see through things that a person could not. The exciting thing is that even if the vision system doesn't recognize the object, because it could be a very strange-looking vehicle, it could be a multi-car pileup, it could be a truck crossing the road, it really could be anything – an alien spaceship, a pile of junk metal that fell off the back a truck, it actually doesn't matter what the object is it just knows that there's something dense that it is going to hit, and it should not hit that. It doesn't need to know what that thing is – while a vision system really needs to know what the thing is. Radar sees through rain, fog, snow, dust, essentially quite easily. Even if you are driving down the road and the visibility was very low and there was a big multi-car pileup or something like that and you cant' see it, the radar would initiate braking in time to avoid your car being added to the multi-car pileup.

Then the final sensor is the GPS with high precision digital maps. The high-precision digital maps are important because normal maps have quite low precision. Not only does it know where the street is, but the actual curvature of the road, how many lanes there are, and how you merge from one lane to the next. This is not present in any data set in the world but we're creating that data set at Tesla. This is all just in a statistical database, there's no user attribution. We don't know who it was, or when it was. We know that this is where a road exists. This is where cars have gone, statistically speaking.

Autosteer is using different visual cues, or visual road cues, to decide where to drive. It'll take the left lane, or right lane, depending upon where it is. So it's constantly looking up where it is in the world and depending upon its specific location it'll know whether to use the left lane marking, the right lane marking, follow vehicles, to use holistic path prediction, or to go purely on navigation, on GPS.

We also have Side Collision Avoidance which is active all the time. You can turn it off, so this is not something you can't turn off, but it's separately turned off. It's like Automatic Emergency Braking, essentially. The Side Collision Avoidance what it will do is it will resist movement if you attempt to turn into another vehicle or into let's say a highway barrier without realizing it, you'll feel increased resistance in the steering wheel. You feel like there's something unnatural here that's like... resisting. You can overcome it if you want to, but it's gonna tell you that you probably shouldn't move sideways because you can sense that it's harder on the steering wheel to move to one side or the other. It's a sort of general safety system like Automatic Emergency Braking.

Yeah, we feel highly confident that the 8-camera solution with 12 ultrasonics and a forward radar, and the computing power that we now have on board is capable of full autonomy at a – it's simply greater than human. Like, you can probably do it ten times better than humans would, just cameras. You can absolutely be superhuman with just cameras. There are obviously skeptics out there. Well, I suggest that they do not bet against us.

While we are reaching the limit of the hardware I think we have not quite yet reached the algorithmic intelligence on the car, and of course, anything that's done on our servers we are not computer constraint or space constraint in any way.

Full autonomy is really a software limitation. Software is an increasing proportion of the problem particularly as you get to autonomy. I think we are a software and a hardware company, but the software component does become increasingly important. You got to get both right because it's a holistic product experience. I mean the hardware is just to create full autonomy, so it's really about developing advanced, narrow AI for the car to operate on. I want to emphasize narrow AI, it's like not going to take over the world, but it needs to be really good at driving a car. So increasingly sophisticated neural maps that can operate in reasonably sized computers in the car.

Something that quite uniquely Tesla is being able to do is fleet learning, I think this is quite a powerful network effect. Any car company that doesn't do this will not be able to have a good autonomous driving system. I think the big differentiator here is that the whole Tesla fleet operates as a network. When one car learns something, the whole fleet learns it. In order to have that, all the cars need to be connected. They need to be uploading data to a central server, where it can be collected, do statistical analysis on it, and then feed that back into the driving algorithm to the cars. That's I would say like a next-level technology, and certainly far beyond what any other car company is doing. I'm not sure they even are thinking about it. I've never heard them mention it, let me put it that way.

The thing that's quite interesting and unique is that we're employing a deep learning technology. Essentially, the network of vehicles is going to be constantly learning, and as we release the software and more people enable Autopilot, the information about how to drive is uploaded to the network. So each driver is effectively an expert trainer in how the Autopilot should work.

There is an enormous amount of sort of visual data being gathered. It's actually quite a challenge to process that data, and then train against that data, and have the vehicle learn effectively from data, because it's just a vast quantity of data. It's both the data and the way that data is used by the car, what algorithms we use with the data. Those things are both improving rapidly over time. They have a multiplying effect, it's sort of like the data multiply by the quality of the algorithms, and the data is increasing rapidly and the quality of algorithms increase rapidly. It's really quite dramatic over time. We can use fleet learning to have all the Tesla cars out there effectively give us the geo-locations of where all the false alarm occurs, and what the shape of that object is that causes the false alarm. That we know that at a particular position at a particular street or highway, that if you see a radar object of the following shape – don't worry it's just a road sign or a bridge or it could be a Christmas decoration that somebody put across the street. You do need an additional overlay on that to understand turn restrictions, because you could certainly say, 'if the number of cars that turn left at an intersection is .5 percent of the time, then it's probably that they're just doing an illegal left.' so then we should ignore that. You'll see statistically if a turn is allowed or not allowed. I do want to emphasize that this is disaggregated from the specific vehicle. We're always on the side of the owner of the car and do whatever is possible within the bounds of the law to protect privacy.

The data from the Tesla fleet can provide high-precision information about routes. We certainly would be open to selling that to other car companies or other organizations if they want to buy it. It's really the fleet collectively that is producing this dataset. We're using that to provide high-precision GPS navigation. It is kinda machine learning, with the drivers of the car essentially providing the training dataset, they're training a collective fleet intelligence of all Teslas. It is an automatic learning system. To do autonomous driving to the degree that it's much safer than a person is much easier than people think.

I think we want to ensure people think of their cars as connected devices. People should see the car improve probably with each passing week, even without a new software update, because the data is continually improving, and because the more miles that are driven the better the network intelligence of the fleet is trained the better it will get. It should actually get better with each passing day, but you'll probably notice it maybe after a week or a few weeks. You'll see that previously the car wouldn't have steered quite right, let's say going past a freeway offramp one week, but then the following week it does. That's really the way a car should operate, much in the way your laptop or your cell phone operates, that we can do improvements over-the-air.

It is important for safety and for improved functionality that carmakers, in general, go to a connected philosophy. So instead of; you issue a recall, and you don't always get all the cars coming in for various reasons, people lose touch with their dealer, and then they have unsafe software in their car but not know it because they didn't get the recall notice or weren't aware of it. That's I think also just what consumers expect. It's rather odd to have a device that's not connected.

As far as gathering navigation data when there's no cell connectivity, the car can just buffer the data and then upload the data once it gets to a place where there is cell connectivity or a WiFi connection. So there's no problem collecting data even when there's no cell phone connectivity. And of course the GPS satellites you can see all the time. Anywhere on Earth, you can see the GPS satellites whether or not you have connectivity in that area, you can still drive on GPS functionality.

I'm really quite optimistic about where things are and where they're headed on that front. I think they're headed to a good place, but the perfect is the enemy of the good. You just can't come fully formed into some ideal solution. It's impossible to do that for anything. But as our fleet grows, and it's growing rapidly, it becomes clearer and clearer. The fleet learning will continue and the intelligence of how that fleet learning is applied to the car will continue to improve. It will continue to improve for years to come even with the existing hardware.

I think almost all cars built will be capable of full autonomy in about ten years. As it is the Tesla cars that are made today have the sensor system necessary for full autonomy and we think probably enough compute power to be safer than a person. It's mostly just a question of developing the software and uploading the software. If it turns out that more computing power is needed, we can easily upgrade the computer.

I almost view it, and this may sound complacent, as a solved problem. We know exactly what to do and we will be there in a few years, and other manufacturers will follow and do the same thing. I think things are going to grow exponentially. Probably in ten years more than half of new vehicle production will be electric in the US, I think almost all cars produced will be autonomous in 10 years. It will be rare to find one that is not. I think it will be quite unusual to see cars in production that don't have full autonomy, let's say in the 15 to 20-year time frame, and for Tesla, it will be a lot sooner than that. I think at the point at which cars are being made that have full autonomy that any cars that are being made that don't have full autonomy will have a negative value. I think the whole industry ultimately will be producing autonomous cars, but that's not the same as all cars on the road.

It's going to be a great convenience to be an autonomous car but there are many people whose jobs it is to drive. In fact, I think it might be the single largest employer of people is driving in various forms. We need to figure out new roles for what do those people do, but it will be very disruptive and very quick. I should characterize what I mean by quick because 'quick' means different things to different people. It is important to just appreciate the size of the automotive industrial base. It's not as though when somebody makes autonomous cars suddenly all the cars will be autonomous. The global fleet of vehicles is about 2.5 billion roughly, and the total new vehicle production capacity per year is only about 100 million, there are roughly 2.5 billion cars and trucks on the road, and just under 100 million are produced every year. So the production rate is only 5% of the fleet size. Which makes sense because the life of a car or truck before it's finally scrapped is about 20, 25 years. The fleet is basically turning over every roughly 20, 25 years. I think the demand for autonomous cars will vastly outweigh the production capability. If tomorrow all cars were autonomous it would take 20 years to replace the fleet, assuming the fleet stays the same size. Arguably the fleet would get smaller if cars were autonomous. It's not all going to transition immediately it is going to take a while. It's the same for the electrification of cars.

The point at which we see full autonomy appear will not be the point at which there is massive societal upheaval because it will take a long time to make enough autonomous vehicles to disrupt employment. That disruption I'm talking about will take place over about 20 years, but still, 20 years is a short period of time to have I think something like 12% to 15% of the workforce be unemployed.

The fundamental economic utility of a true self-driving car is likely to be several times that of a car that is not. Most cars are only in use by their owner for 5% to 10% of the day. There will be a shared autonomy fleet where you buy your car and you can choose to use that car exclusively, you could choose to have it be used only by friends and family, only by other drivers who are rated five stars, you can choose to share it sometimes but not other times. That's 100 percent what will occur. Absolutely this is what will happen, it's just a question of when.

A lot of people think that when you make cars autonomous, they'll be able to go faster and that will alleviate congestion. To some degree that will be true, but once you have shared autonomy where it's much cheaper to go by car and you can go point to point, the affordability of going in a car will be better than that of a bus. Like, it will cost less than a bus ticket. The amount of driving that will occur will be much greater with shared autonomy and actually, traffic will get far worse.

With the advent of autonomy, it will probably make sense to shrink the size of buses and transition the role of bus driver to that of fleet manager. Traffic congestion would improve due to matching acceleration and braking to other vehicles, thus avoiding the inertial impedance to smooth the traffic flow of traditional heavy buses. It would also take people all the way to their destination. Fixed summon buttons at existing bus stops would serve those who don't have a phone.

In cities where demand exceeds the supply of customer-owned cars, Tesla will operate its own fleet, ensuring you can always hail a ride from us no matter where you are. That's our focus. I'm very very optimistic about this. It's exciting, it blows me away, the progress we're making. I think if I'm this close to it and it's blowing me away, it's really going to blow other people away.

Autonomy will be widespread. It's going to be weird to have a car without it in the future. I think that, in the long term, owning a car that does not have autonomous capability will be a bit like owning a horse. You will only drive if you want to drive, but not for daily use really. You sort of own a horse for sentimental reasons, but not for actual transport.

32. Charged

We unveiled the Supercharger network in 2012 which we hadn't told anyone about. We build these up in secret, so when people did their first reservation of the Model S they had no idea that we were going to create a Supercharger network. We built into every car a high-voltage DC bypass direct to the pack that would enable high-speed charging. This was critical to solving the long-distance travel problem. As you have more and more electric vehicles on the roads, you have to find someplace to charge them.

I'm not too worried about recharging stations. There actually are far more charging stations than people realize. People drive long distances a lot less than they think they do. The great thing about electricity is that it's really ubiquitous., there are more power outlets than anything. There are more power outlets than access to any other kind of energy by orders of magnitude. What we saw with the use of the Tesla Roadster was that almost all charging happened at home, ninety percent plus. In the case of Tesla and most of the electric cars that are coming out, the charger is built into the car so you can plug it in almost anywhere. The ideal place to charge the car is at your home or office. Essentially the same place that you'd charge your phone.

If you want to charge fast, you're going to need a high-power outlet. Traditional charging headway had been way too slow, and it was not effective for long-distance travel. It was very important to address this issue of long-distance travel because when people buy a car they are also buying a sense of freedom. What it comes down to really is freedom, when you're buying a car you're really buying freedom to go where you want to go, and if you are constrained to your charge location you don't have the freedom. We had to make something that was really quick to charge, to be able to go wherever they want and not be tethered. We wanted to enable people to travel anywhere in the country, and ultimately people to drive anywhere in the world. Superchargers are really about giving you the freedom that you want when you buy a car and make it really easy and convenient to go wherever you want. They ended up being fundamental to answering the question: "Can I drive my car long distances?" The key takeaway was that I was confident that the Supercharger will completely alleviate people's concerns about range with electric vehicles. We were certainly hoping that some other company or companies would create convenient high-speed charging networks, but nobody did. So then we said we better do it.

The name 'Supercharger' is originally obviously from the gasoline car industry. The idea there was you'll be able to charge your car with the same level of convenience as you'd normally use your gasoline car. Superchargers are really meant for when you have an unusually long trip - you've been away from your home or office for a while - or you need to top up when you're out and about, but by far the most convenient is home or office charging. I think a lot of people are used to an old way of doing by default. I think part of it is just that people are used to a paradigm where they go to a gas station to fill up and that's just normal. Then they get an electric car and they go to the Supercharger station to fill up because that's just normal. But the best thing to do with your electric car is to charge your car where you charge your phone. Would you really take your phone to a gas station?

We were able to figure a way, with some advanced charging technology, to have it such that you could stop for half an hour and have three hours driving. About a six to one ratio, which is about the convenience inflection point for most people for a long-range trip. If you drive for three hours, you want to stop for 20 or 30 minutes, because that's normally what people will stop for. If you start a trip that starts at 9 am, by noon you want to stop for a bite to eat, hit the restroom, coffee, and gas up your car, and keep going, and that's a good 20 to 30 minutes. That's the natural cadence of a trip.

We made that work, and then we added solar panels to some Supercharger stations to address the long tailpipe argument that says, oh, you're just pushing emissions to the power plant. Well no, because the Supercharger stations will actually generate more electricity than the cars use in recharging. It'll have enough solar panels to generate electricity back to the grid on an annual basis. That's how we're sizing them, so they'll be slightly energy positive.

We also had the SolarCity IPO in 2012, which was a very difficult IPO to get done, and that IPO occurred just by the skin of its teeth. It was such a tough one. If it wasn't in December, it would mean pushing it out quite a bit, and the problem was that we'd already pushed it out quite a bit. If we didn't go public we'd have to go a private round and then the whole thing just wouldn't feel right. It's like you're sitting at the altar and you don't do the wedding - it's a bit awkward, you know. So, we really needed to do it and I think if we hadn't done it, people would have looked at it as a failure and it wouldn't have been good because there had just been too many failures in the solar - or not enough successes in the solar arena. We needed to chalk up the success.

What we're planning to do overtime is going to 100% renewable power generation for our Supercharge stations. We've sort of temporally not added solar power in the interests of just having national and international coverage, so you can drive anywhere in the US, Europe, or Asia using

Superchargers. There are a few that have solar panels, most don't. But in the long term.... all of them will either have solar panels or otherwise get their power from renewable sources, and in the long term, I expect it to be solar panels to a stationary battery pack so that the solar panels can charge the stationary battery pack over the course of the week and then that stationary battery pack can buffer the energy and release it during peak times. It's possible for us to make the charging stations completely independent of the grid because we also add a battery pack so that the solar panels charge the stationary battery pack which charges the car. Which gives you 24 hours a day charging capability. However, it's usually still advantageous to connect to the grid because there are times when we will produce excess energy that we then can provide back to the grid. We want each charging station to be energy positive.

What we see with Superchargers is huge differences in usage. You can imagine, when people go away for the weekend, like Friday nights and Saturday nights, huge peak usage. People are going somewhere, like on a family trip for the weekend, but say, Wednesday at 11 am, low usage.

You want to have a stationary battery pack, solar panels and then it could work even if the power grid goes down. That'd be cool I think, to have something like even post-apocalypse you can still drive around.

We're experimenting with our first sort of – I don't know what we call it – Mega Supercharging location, like a really big Supercharging location with a bunch of amenities. We're going to unveil the first of those relatively soon. I think we'll get a sense for just sort of how cool it can be to have a great place to – if you've been driving for three, four hours – stop, have great restrooms, great food, amenities, hang out for half an hour, and then be on your way.

We are totally cool with other companies using our Supercharger infrastructure. There is no intention to create a walled garden or to create some sort of protectionist thing. Basically, the only requirements for using our Supercharger network are that the car needs to take the high power level, because if it's really low power level it is going to hog the spot and sit there for too long, so it's got to be able to be charged fast. And it needs to be a proportionate payment to how much the other car manufacturers are using the network. How ever much the manufacturers' cars are using the network, they just pay that proportion, which I think is pretty fair. If other car companies also want to create a network and we can have a shared network that would be cool. We are for anything that will promote the future of electric vehicles.

33. Goin Giga

Obviously, it's incredibly important that we accelerate the transition to sustainable energy. It matters to the world, it matters if it happens sooner or later, and it matters if it happens at scale. In order to make a lot of electric cars, we need a lot of batteries, and over time I think there probably will be roughly about as many batteries for stationary storage as there are for cars. If you do this sort of overarching math of what is needed at a high-level to transition the world to a sustainable energy scenario, you need about as much battery capacity in cars as you do in stationary storage.

The lithium-ion battery capacity of the world in terms of production capacity is really not big enough yet. Nor does it make the most advanced type of batteries that we need for long-range electric cars. There are a hundred million new cars made every year, there are two billion gasoline or diesel cars on the road worldwide. If you have half a million cars a year and an average kilowatt-hour level of 70 then you need 35 GWh. And that's just for the car, If you do stationary storage you need the additional capacity on top of that. This is quite challenging because the total worldwide production of lithium-ion batteries of all kinds, for phones, laptops, you know power drills, cars, everything was only 30 GWh. That's nothing, or at least it's nothing when you consider you want to make half a million electric cars a year, that's how much you need. The basic math was that in order to make half a million cars a year we would need every lithium-ion factory on Earth that makes batteries for phones, laptops, cars everything just to achieve that output. We thought this math does not work obviously, we are not going to get every factory on Earth to just do our stuff, and even if they did there still wouldn't be enough. It was like we got to build a factory otherwise we don't know how to solve this issue. I was like well clearly that is not being built, because you would be able to see it on the satellite picture. Either we figure out some way to build this thing or there will not be the cars that are needed. In order to solve the problem, we found that there is really no choice but to build a really enormous factory called the Gigafactory. We just said we got to start building this thing and hopefully, people will buy into it and start to believe. Given that we want to try to get to full capacity at our Fremont plant in California of a half-million vehicles a year, we need a half-million vehicles a year of batteries, and obviously,, we can't use all of the other factories in the world combined because people want cellphones and laptops and other things. Therefore we have to build this factory. The Gigafactory was like the least bad solution we could come up with, honestly. I don't know of any other way to do it, the batteries we need are so huge. Somebody's got to build this thing. If we don't contribute a bunch of money to building it I don't see any other company doing that. Just to get the whole thing running is something in the order of $5 billion. Fortunately, Panasonic has been a great partner making a significant contribution.

The point of the Gigafactory is to get the cost of the batteries down to a point where it is affordable. The Gigafactory is really vital for the future of Tesla in order to produce the mass-market affordable electric car.

We are not just doing economies of scale we are also improving the fundamental technology around the cell and the battery pack. Just based on economies of scale, because we're talking about a factory that will make as many lithium-ion batteries as all other lithium-ion battery factories combined of all times.

The Gigafactory when it's complete will have the largest footprint of any building in the world, of any kind, not just factories. The single biggest building in the world by footprint, and second only in volume to the Boeing factory in Washington State. Counting multiple levels it could be as much as 15 million square feet. It's difficult to describe in words but it's a heck of a big factory. We can fit 50 billion hamsters, but in terms of vehicles, we actually expect to get to 50 GWh a year of output in 2 years. It's not scale for scale's sake, but if you want to accomplish these goals then there's going to have to be a big thing. Ultimately we think the factory will produce 150 GWh. This is more than the entire planet produced in 2014. We figured out roughly that this one factory will produce as much as the rest of the world combined. So if you add up all the factories in China, Korea, Japan, and elsewhere that made lithium-ion batteries, this one is bigger than that. It's not just going to be the biggest lithium-ion factory in the world it's also going to be bigger than the sum of all the lithium-ion factories in the world.

The factory is designed sort of like a diamond, and the reason for that is if you make it a box shape we would have to move a lot more earth. Eventually, you can sort of roughly see that there's sort of a diamond shape overall, and when it's fully done, it'll look like a giant diamond, or that's the idea behind it. It's aligned on true north, it's a small detail but it's aligned on true north so we could map out where the equipment is going to be by GPS. The solar panels that are on the roof are also properly aligned. I think it's going to sounds romantic that it's shaped like a diamond and aligned to true north, but there are practical reasons for it as well.

I should mention also that when the Gigafactory is fully operational it will also be completely operated on sustainable energy. This factory will produce its own energy as well. Through a combination of geothermal, wind, and solar it will produce all the energy that it needs. It will be sort of a self-contained factory. The combination of wind, geothermal, and solar will completely power the Gigafactory, it's designed to be energy neutral in its energy usage. Of course, it's a battery factory so we buffer the energy so we can go 24/7 with a factory that generates its own energy, and might actually end up generating additional energy to give back to the grid.

We're building that in Nevada. We actually had slightly bigger incentive packages from other states that were offered, but we factored in how quickly could we get the Gigafactory into operation? What were the risks associated with that progress? What would be the logistics costs over time of transferring battery-packs and powertrains to a vehicle factory in California? and all those factors weighed together are what led us to make the decision in favor of Nevada. There are a lot of other factors as well. A big part was also just feeling really welcome within the state. That is what led us to make the decision for the Gigafactory.

The incentives were a little overstated. I didn't actually know this until we did the press conference that over 20 years the Nevada incentives added up to $1.3 billion. The whole tax credit thing drives me crazy. It sounds much better than it is. The Gigafactory is a $5 billion capital investment to get the factory going. The first time I heard the amount to be 1.3 billion was at the press conference announcing the deal. I was like really how did we get the 1.3 billion? When what we actually got was Nevada gave us some free land, but the state of Nevada has a lot of land it's not in short supply. I also agreed to build a connecting highway southbound that connects to Carson City, but they were going to build that anyway, so I don't know why that should be included in what they gave us. They took what added up over 20 years and made it sound like Nevada was writing us a $1.3 billion check. I'm still waiting for that check, did it get lost in the mail? I don't know. This is the way the press works, of course. If you divide $1.3 billion by 20 -- it's basically a sales and use tax abatements, is what it amounts to. We get like on the order of $50 to $60 million of sales and use tax abatement, divided over 20 years. But this is for something which has a $5 billion capital cost just to get going and would have to generate over $100 billion over that time to achieve a $1.3 billion tax benefit. Essentially, it's a little over 1% over that period of time, and that is great, but it's not the way it was characterized in the press. If put in the proper context it sounds like, ok, that is neat -- it's about 5% helpful in setting up the factory, and 1% helpful over the next 20 years. In effect the initial contribution into the Gigafactory by the state of Nevada it's less than 5% and then they have roughly a 1% contribution over 20 years. It's a no-loss proposition for the State. As the saying goes the house always wins. Nevada understands the house, Nevada is the house.

I'm pretty excited about how things are going, in fact, I think that the pace of technology improvement in electric energy storage is really moving faster than anyone thinks. I would say that battery technology is one of the most difficult technological problems in history. So many smart people in the course of history have tried so hard to improve batteries. You're really just fighting the laws of thermodynamics very very hard in creating a battery. I mean Edison was a great inventor he tried super hard and he didn't succeed, Tesla himself tried and didn't succeed. Some of the smartest people in history have tried very very hard. What actually tends to happen with batteries is that the improvements maybe 5 to 8% per year in energy density and approximately that improvement in cost. With the Gigafactory we are trying to take economies of scale to the maximum limit in order to reduce the cost even further just by having economies of scale. Having a tightly integrated supply chain that goes from raw materials coming in on rail carts from mines, and out comes a completed battery back. We are taking the fundamental economic efficiencies to the maximum. At this point, we have quite a good understanding of all the battery technologies in the world. The Gigafactory is taking economies of scale as far as we can possibly imagine, to a very extreme level. At the Gigafactory what we are doing is consolidating production back all the way from the raw materials. So there are literally rail carts of materials coming in from the mines, and out come completely finished battery packs. This has actually never been done before, for batteries at least. What we are able to do in this process is massively improve the cost of the cells and the packs. Today if you were to trace the movement of the raw materials, from when they are mined, and they go through the various refining steps around the world, and eventually are put in a cell, and eventually that cell is put into a module and a pack, and then put into a car, and then delivered to somebody, that molecule from the mine is doing an around the world trip like three times. It's really crazy.

I think the thing to bear in mind with batteries is there is no material shortage. The Earth's crust has essentially an infinite amount of metal as far as humanity is concerned. We have barely scratched the surface of the metal resource availability of the Earth's crust. This is a very fundamentally different thing from mining coal or oil because metal is recycled. Once you have enough metal to support a given size of an industry then it just keeps going in a recycling process. There's maybe a small amount that exits through a recycling process, but it's quite a small amount.

The general rubric of lithium covers many types of chemistries. A really broad range of batteries use lithium as the ion transport. For lithium-ion battery packs in the case of Tesla the cathode which is made of nickel, cobalt, and aluminum, is the most expensive part of the cell. The anode is made of carbon and there's a thin steel shell around the cells. Really the only part of that which is remotely scarce and only slightly so is cobalt. That's why we moved from a pure cobalt cathode to a nickel-cobalt-aluminum cathode which only uses about a quarter as much cobalt. There's as much nickel as you could possibly want, certainly as much aluminum as you'd need, no shortage of steel, and the cobalt is expensive but there's certainly enough available to support all the world's needs.

So there is not some fundamental metals shortage and as I said at end of life you recycle them. You can think of a battery pack basically as really high-grade ore, it's much more efficient to recycle a battery pack, which has essentially high concentrations of nickel, cobalt, and aluminum than it is to mine rock, which has a very low concentration. At end of life, a lithium-ion battery pack has still about 10 to 20% of its value as a recycling item, so it definitely pays to recycle. We actually have recycling at the Gigafactory itself. All battery packs will be recycled, which makes a lot of sense because this is a really efficient way to recycle it because we know what the module looks like. We can actually design the recycling machines exactly optimized for the battery packs. We are not trying to recycle any arbitrary battery packs, we are recycling a known battery pack, so we can be really precise about the recycling.

We found we have a great partner in Panasonic. Panasonic is taking care of the cell formation part of it. There are actually many aspects to this because you have an anode, cathode, electrolyte, separator, can, and at the precursor level you've got raw materials coming in from the mines that sort of feed into a variety of other companies like Hitachi and others, they do the precursor processing and then Panasonic takes the anode and cathode materials separator and puts that into a cell and then it goes into a Tesla section which creates the module, which is all the electronics, and the packaging, and the conductors, the safety mechanisms, and the cooling loops. Then the modules go into the pack which has a lot of crash structure associated with it and then the pack goes in the car. Then, obviously, Tesla is the kinda landlord of the whole thing as well.

This is really about being able to make enough cells, enough batteries, to make hundreds of thousands, ultimately millions of electric cars, and to do so at a maximum scale and in a way that is affordable to people. Cars obviously need to be affordable otherwise people can't bloody well buy them. In order to achieve that there are two key dimensions that are necessary, one is to keep iterating the technology. Design the technology to be better and better and have multiple versions. This will be our third generation of technology. And then there are economies of scale. We are driving those to the absolute maximum with the Gigafactory and that's why it's so big, it's big for a reason. That's what the Gigafactory is about. It's about being able to make enough electric cars and enough stationary battery packs that it actually moves the needle from a global carbon production perspective. That it actually does really change the world. It has to be big because the world is big, that's why.

Then we have another factory in New York doing solar panels. It will be the biggest solar panel producer in North America when it's done. We expect the Buffalo Gigafactory to be a powerhouse of solar panel and solar glass tile output. It is going to be a kick-ass facility. We have made that commitment to the State of New York. We are going to keep that commitment.

We expect to establish probably at least two or three more Gigafactories in the U.S. In the next several years, as well as a couple overseas. We're thinking hard about, where do we put Gigafactories three, four, five, and six? We expect to keep the majority of our production in the U.S but it's obviously going to make sense to establish a Gigafactory in China and Europe to serve the markets there because it's nuts to build cars in California and truck them halfway around the world, particularly when you're trying to make things as affordable as possible – that really hurts. We really want to make our cars as affordable as possible, so that does require some amount of local market production, particularly for the mass market vehicles in order to make it as accessible as possible. It's definitely going to make sense to have at least a Gigafactory in every continent because the logistics costs and the energy cost to transport cars halfway around the world is quite high. So we will reach kind of a saturation here and then we are going to establish a factory in Europe, and a factory in Asia, in China, and perhaps other parts of Asia as well. I think it's going to make a lot of sense to localize the production to the demand. We need to address a global market.

We actually did the calculations that said what it would take to transition the whole world to sustainable energy, what kind of throughput would you actually need? and you need 100 Gigafactories, 100 of these, the whole world, all energy. That sounds manageable. Tesla can't build 100 Gigafactories. The thing that's really going to make a difference is if companies much bigger than Tesla do the same thing. If the big industrial companies in China, the US, and Europe, the big car companies, also do this, then collectively we can accelerate the transition to sustainable energy. If governments set the rules to favor sustainable energy we can get there really quickly. Many auto plants and many Gigafactories are needed. Like I said the number of cars and trucks that we have on the road is approximately two billion, and every twenty years approximately that gets refreshed. There are a hundred million new cars and trucks made every year. The point I want to make is that this is actually within the power of humanity to do. We have done things like this before. It is not impossible, it is really something that we can do.

There will need to be many Gigafactories in the future. I do want to emphasize that this is not something that we think Tesla is going to do alone. We think that there are going to be many other companies building Gigafactory-class operations of their own, and we hope they do.

The Tesla policy of open-sourcing patents will continue for the Gigafactory, and for all these other things. The way we're approaching the Gigafactory 1 is really like it's a product. We have actually found that theoretically, we could do about three times the original estimate. Well, when it's running at full speed, you can't actually see the cells without a strobe light. It's just a blur. We're not really thinking of it in the traditional way that people think of as a factory, like a building with a bunch of off-the-shelf equipment in it. What we're really designing with the Gigafactory is a giant machine. It's actually - think of it like a product of Tesla. We're making this really big product that doesn't happen to move. In establishing the factory it was the first time we started thinking hard about the importance of building the machine that builds the machine.

34. The Machine

I am someone who believes in manufacturing. I love manufacturing and building objects that bring value to people. For some reason that got out of fashion, I'm not sure why. I think very often people think of manufacturing as just some rote process of making copies, which actually it isn't if you think of manufacturing not as some boring process of making copies, but rather that the manufacturing system of the car itself is a very complex machine. Just as innovation applies to the design and engineering of the car you can apply and should apply engineering and innovation to the machine that builds the machine. Manufacturing is building the machine that makes the machine and more often than not what I've found is the manufacturing is harder than the original product.

The way that people look at factories is often kind of thought of as a boring thing, this like catalog engineering. This is the wrong way to look at it you really need to look at a factory like it is a product. It is a giant machine and it deserves more innovation and more engineering skills than the product itself. That's what we have done with the Gigafactory. The most important point that I want to make is that we have realized that the true problem, the true difficulty, and where the greatest potential is, is building the machine that builds the machine. In other words, building the factory and thinking of the factory as a product, not sort of a hodgepodge of things where the machines are sort of bought from a catalog. I can't emphasize enough how important this conceptual framework is, because really almost everywhere they think of a factory as this bunch of basic machines that are stuck together to produce copies. And it's mostly pulled from catalogs like get this machine from that company, get that machine from that company. If you apply that same principle to product design it wouldn't make any sense. Like if we would make the Model S out of parts from a bunch of different cars it would be ridiculous. It would be like a bumper from a Honda, a steering wheel from this, a motor from something else, it wouldn't make any sense to make a car from bits and pieces from other cars. Just like we do with the car, we don't try to create a car by ordering a bunch of things out of a catalog, we design the car the way it should be and then we or the suppliers we work with, make all of those individual components. There's almost nothing in the Model S that is in any other car. I think the same approach is the right approach to take when building the machine maker, the factory. You really need to design the car as an integrated product from the ground up and that's the same approach we have taken to the Gigafactory, and it's really quite unusual for that to be the case.

You can create a demo version of a product with a small team in maybe 3 to 6 months, but to create the machine to build machines takes at least 100 to 1000 times more resources and difficulty. For example, at Tesla, we can make one of a car very easily, but to make thousands of a car with high reliability and quality and where the cost is affordable, is extremely hard. I'd say, maybe 10 times harder than just making one prototype - maybe more. I think that the potential for improvement in the machine that makes the machine is a factor of 10 greater than the potential on the car side, I think maybe more than a factor of 10. I have really come to appreciate that when I've been on the production floor sort of all the time and seeing things, and running production personally at a detailed level. I don't even have a desk or office anymore I'm just basically standing on the production floor and occasionally meeting in a conference room.

In terms of analyzing how the factory should work, I'm a big fan of using physics as a framework. I do my favorite thing which is to apply physics first principles, which is like the best tool possible. Designing the factory from physics first principles means optimizing the density of the factory. You can think of the fundamental efficiency of the factory as the density of useful stuff, like what is the percentage of the factory that is actually useful stuff versus not useful stuff. When you think of a production facility on a fundamental level for a given size factory, the output is going to be volume, times density, times velocity. People don't realize just how much improvement potential is possible and this is thick. We're talking high school level physics necessary to figure this out it's not like mega-complicated. Just go to a factory and say do a volumetric density calculation, say what percentage of the volume of the inside of this building is doing useful stuff versus either air or not doing useful stuff. You'll be shocked at how tiny that percentage is, like low single digits.

Let's sort of look at our factory, what is the density of useful to non-useful volume? it's crazy low, it's like 2 or 3% when you look at it volume-metrically not just on a plane level, it's literally 2 or 3% when you say car to non-car volume metric ratio. That seems like there is a lot of room for improvement, why is the volumetric efficiency of a car factory usually in the mid to low single digits? that's very low. Why shouldn't it be at least a volumetric density of 30% or 40%? 30% seems very, very achievable. You can also think of it as the design of a modern system on a chip or a computer. If you look at it say the complexity of the board, and you see how close together the line traces are, and how focused things are on the clock speed, and data transfer from RAM to say solid-state disk for an internal CPU cache, it's like wow there is crazy potential for improvement here. Nobody would design a chip that had volumetric efficiency of 2% that would look ridiculous and yet they design factories that way. We will basically design a factory like you would design an advanced computer and in fact, use engineers that are used to doing that and have them work on this. It is essentially designed like a very high-density multilayer integrated circuit, an advanced CPU. If you think about it that is obviously how it should be done, I think actually over time the manufacturing process may look a lot like one of those super-fast chip pick-and-place machines, it is super optimized for speed and density. Think about how did we improve the capability of your phone or your laptop? it wasn't by making a really giant computer the size of a table, it was by increasing the clock speed and density, the same principles apply to manufacturing.

Then you say like velocity, the output of the factory is the velocity of products from the factory. Then what is the exit velocity of the product? how fast are things moving out of the exit? what's the mass flow of the factory? what is a reasonable expectation for the exit velocity of vehicles from the factory? At first, you may think that some of these advanced car factories around the world are very good at making cars and they may make a car every 25 seconds. That sounds fast, but actually, if you say well the length of the car plus some buffer space is approximately 5 meters, so it's taking 25 seconds to move 5 meters. That is 0.2 meters per second, basically, you are not much faster than a tortoise at that point. So that really doesn't seem fast, a slow to medium walk would be approximately 1 meter per second and a fast walk would be 1.5 meters per second. The best car factories in the world are doing 0.2 it's like really low, like the fastest car plants in the world the car exit velocity is basically grandma with a walker.

It's real slow, point 2 meters per second that's really, really slow, we could do way better than that. The fastest person can run 10 meters per second, faster than 10 meters per second, so why is car exit velocity only 0.2 meters per second? that's ridiculous, seems like you should be able to have cars exit at least at walking speed, this doesn't seem so crazy. Actually, our speed on the line is incredibly slow, I think we are in terms of the exit velocity of vehicles on the line, including both X and S it is probably about five centimeters per second. This is very slow, I'm confident we can get to at least one meter per second, a 20-fold increase. One meter per second just to put that into perspective is a slow walk or a medium-speed walk. A fast walk could be one and a half meters per second, and the fastest humans can run is over 10 meters per second. At 1 meter per second, you can still walk faster than the production line. So with significantly less engineering effort, we can make dramatic improvements to the machine that makes the machine. I think probably a lot of people will not believe us about this, but I am absolutely confident that this can be accomplished. I am really fired up about that because I think it's one of those things that so much more is possible than people realize, I think it's really going to positively surprise people there. I'm really excited about revitalizing manufacturing because it needs love and we're gonna give it. The results can be amazing. It's going to be head and shoulders above anything else, it's better than anything I've heard anyone even announce that they will do in near future, and we will do it in the present.

You can come up with some really cool new ways to manufacture a vehicle. There are many ways to skin a cat and it's remarkable how you can achieve the same objective with a hugely varying degree of difficulty. I have found that once you sort of explain this to a first-rate engineer the lightbulb goes on. They spend huge amounts of effort trying to get a fraction of a percent of improvement on the product itself but actually, that same amount of effort will yield an order of magnitude greater results if you focus on building the machine that builds the machine. It's just that a lot of engineers don't realize that this is possible, they are basically operating according to these invisible walls.

You can take an analogy and say if you wanted to kill a fly, you can kill a fly with a thermonuclear weapon, with a MOAB, with a cruise missile, with a machine gun, or a flyswatter. The end result is the same but the difficulty is considerably more significant from one to the other, and the collateral damage is considerably more significant.

What really matters to accelerate to a sustainable future is being able to scale up production volume as quickly as possible. That is why Tesla engineering has transitioned to focus heavily on designing the factory itself into a product. A first-principles physics analysis of automotive production suggests that somewhere between a 5 to 10 fold improvement is achievable by version 3 on a roughly 2-year iteration cycle. The first Model 3 factory machine should be thought of as version 0.5 with version 1.0 probably in 2018. Sort of an internal codename for the factory machine is the 'Alien Dreadnought' You look at that and it'll seem like an alien dreadnaught, like what the hell is that? At the point in which our factory looks like an alien dreadnought we know it's probably right then you know you've won. We think with Model 3 it will be alien dreadnought version 0.5 approximately, and then it will take us about another year or so, I don't know, summer 2018 to get to alien dreadnought version 1, and probably a major version every two years thereafter, by version 3 it won't look like anything else. It might look like a giant chip pick-and-place machine or a super-high-speed bottling or canning plant. And you really can't have people in the production line itself otherwise you'll automatically drop to people speed. There's still a lot of people at the factory but what they're doing is maintaining the machines, upgrading them, dealing with anomalies. But in the production process itself, there essentially would be no people with version 1, not version 0.5. I don't want people to think, oh, Tesla's going to have a factory without people. It's going to be a huge number of people, but they will be maintaining machines and upgrading the machines, and dealing with anomalies, and the output per person will be extraordinarily high.

Where it's most obvious is in the cell production, our engineering teams work very closely with Panasonic to make dramatic improvements to the cell manufacturing efficiency and we think they are probably approaching 3X the efficiency of the best plant in the world, so that's pretty good but there's still a lot of room for improvement. Cells are going through that thing like bullets from a machine gun, in fact, the exit rate of cells will be faster than bullets from a machine gun.

At Tesla, we're putting a lot of effort into becoming the world's best manufacturer and I really mean that. Tesla is hell-bent on becoming the best manufacturer on Earth. I'm highly confident we will be, not by a small margin but by a margin that people don't even think is possible.

35. Production

I really think a lot more smart people should be getting into manufacturing, it's kinda fun. It's super exciting, I really love manufacturing, more people should get into it. It sort of got a bad name for a while but it's really interesting.

The biggest thing is designing the car for manufacturing. Generally, when designing an object you can focus on aesthetics or focus on functionality. You can make something that's beautiful but weak on functionality, or you can make something functional but not very good-looking. Having both aesthetics and functionality is super hard especially for an SUV. That's why there's not a lot of really attractive SUVs.

We just want people to know that whenever Tesla comes out with a product it is something that we think is amazing. It drives me crazy that other carmakers will come out with these cars that are not good, like why would they even come out with that? I don't know it just blows my mind, you can take a body panel and stamp it with this shape or that shape, and yet they choose to do the bad shape but it costs the same either way. There are some things that cost a little more in terms of the quality of materials and getting things really to fit accurately, so there are few things that cost more but a lot of it doesn't. You know, you can make an ugly expensive car or you can make a good looking expensive car.. and the same goes for affordable good looking cars or an ugly affordable car. I think the cost differences are really relatively small, I don't know I think maybe large car companies are just trapped in their own history.

One thing I really don't like about the car industry is that they will do these like show cars, and that show car never comes to reality. That just kills me, you shouldn't show somebody something really cool and then not do it. It's like, look at this delicious cake, and by the way, it's made of plastic. Thus far, I think we've done a good job on the design and technology of our products. I said we will build the world's best car, we did that. At SpaceX, I said we will build the world's best rocket, we did that.

I do use a phrase with our engineering and design team that "aspirationally, we're in pursuit of the platonic ideal of the perfect car" who knows what that looks like actually. But you want to try to make every element of the car as flawless as possible. There'll always be some degree of imperfection, but try to minimize that and create a car that is just delightful in every way. I think if you do that the rest kind of takes care of itself.

At SpaceX, I hired a bunch of people from the auto industry to run manufacturing. People in the space industry have a really difficult time manufacturing things. They're pretty good at designing them in the first place but they don't actually know how to make them in volume. Taking the manufacturing techniques that were developed in the automotive industry and applying them to rocketry has been really helpful, in fact, our head of production at SpaceX came from the car industry. He used to run the production of the Mini for BMW. The car industry is really good at making complicated objects at a low cost and what really goes into high-volume manufacturing of something that has to be extremely reliable. It's actually quite incredible somebody can buy a decent car for $20,000. It's nutty how much stuff is in a car. In automotive 400 engines per year is nothing. There are a lot of techniques that the car industry has developed to be able to do high volume production, but also be very reliable and consistent in doing so. I'm very confident that with the Merlin 1D design we'll be able to build 400 engines per year or frankly even 600 or 700 engines per year if we need to, and then the same with the cores. We are making a significant investment in tooling and production process efficiency, honing our software systems within the company that manages the procurement, assembly, and launch, trying to automate as much as possible.

I think anything - if you can 3D print something with sufficiently good material properties then that's the easiest way to do it. Certainly, in the volumes of a rocket company, it's harder to make it work for a car company. With printing you can print something that you can't make by any other means. So it ends up being lighter and cheaper than if we had built it by traditional methods. We actually print the SuperDraco engines, they're printed out of titanium and inconel, and that actually allows us to reduce the cost of those engines quite a bit. In particular, because we can print integral cooling channels. The biggest limitation on 3D printing right now is the size envelope, there's a limit on how big we can print something. We're able to print the turbopump components and much of the injector, not the whole thing but many of the critical parts we can print. That actually helps us in speeding up the development. So instead of waiting for castings to be developed, which can take several months, and then if the casting is wrong you've got to iterate in the casting, and each iteration can take several months. With printing, those iterations can be reduced to a matter of weeks or months, so that actually helps with the speed of development as well. I can give an illustrative example in the airframe. That may be helpful. The normal way that a rocket airframe is constructed is by machined iso-grid. That's where you take high strength aluminum alloy plate and you machine integral stiffeners into the plate. This is probably going to go slightly technical but imagine you have a plate of metal and you're just cutting triangles out of it, that's normally how rockets are made. Most of a rocket is propellant tanks, these things have to be sealed to maintain pressure and everything, and they have to be quite stiff. The approach that we took is to build it up, to start with skin sections and friction stir weld stiffeners into the skin sections. This is a big improvement because if you machine away the material you're left with maybe 5% of the original material, so a 20 to 1 roughly wastage of material, plus a lot of machining time. It's very expensive. If you can roll sheet and stir weld the stiffeners in then your material wastage can be 5%. That's the inverse essentially, instead of having a 20 to 1 ratio you have got 1.1 ratio. Instead of having 95% wastage, it's 5% wastage, it's a huge improvement. That's one example, but there are many such things.

That cross-fertilization of knowledge from the rocket and space industry to auto back and forth I think has really been quite valuable. It's certainly been very valuable for me in thinking about how do we make mass-optimized vehicles because in space mass optimization is extremely important. Me running both Tesla and SpaceX has been helpful because I see how both industries work and I can take things from one to another, so it's been good and of course, the companies aren't competing in any way, so it's been quite helpful. I'll give you an example, the Model S is an all-aluminum body and chassis and we employ some advanced joining techniques and advanced casting techniques and so forth, that's like a fairly obvious thing if you're coming from the aerospace industry. You don't see a lot of aircraft made out of steel but cars are almost all made out of steel. In order to make the Model S light enough to make the non-battery-pack portion of the mass light - you can get more range. The two big factors for range are - what is your aerodynamic drag and how much does the car weigh. Those are overwhelmingly the big factors for range and so making the car weigh less was really important, and not just for range also for handling and acceleration. That was like an obvious thing to make a car out of aluminum, the Model S is the only car made out of aluminum in North America. In fact, there are very few cars made out of aluminum worldwide. The only other passenger vehicles that are made out of aluminum are made in Europe.

For SpaceX and Tesla, our goal was not, initially, to do huge amounts of internal manufacturing. I generally think that there's been a bit too much outsourcing in general. Both outsourcing out of California and outsourcing out of the United States. Businesses sometimes tend to be a little sort of faddy. For a very long time, there was a very strong outsourcing fad. I don't think people really looked at the fundamentals in a lot of cases when they outsourced.

We actually tried to do as little manufacturing as possible at first, but we found we had to insource more and more over time. We didn't start out insourcing 70 to 80% of our hardware. Initially, we thought we will do as little as possible, but then over time, we in-sourced more and more out of necessity. It's not from the standpoint of we really believe in insourcing or outsourcing, it's just given - if there's a great supplier, then we'd love to use a great supplier, then if there's not then we need to do it ourselves. For rocketry, there are also ITAR limitations. Which is that rockets are considered advanced weapons technologies, so we can't just outsource them to some other country.

In the case of SpaceX unfortunately the supply chain in the rocket business tends to be very shallow. Often there's only one supplier and it's a very expensive supplier and they are really not designed for reusability. You're screwed if you don't make it yourself basically. That's led to SpaceX making sort of 70 to 80% of the rocket being built in-house, literally from raw materials.

Another way to look at it is, in the way that to the degree that you inherit the legacy of the components, you inherit in the legacy of the cost structure and limitations. We found many times we'd sign a deal for the supply of a component, and then that supplier would find a reason to triple the price. Basically, as soon as they thought we didn't have any way out they would start with the conclusion which is 'triple the price', and insert reasoning. That's happened several times, and then we've in-sourced the part to get the best price but often with a lot of grief. In the case of Tesla, the automotive supply chain is much better. It's much more competitive, there are many suppliers for any given component, and so maybe 40-50% of the Tesla Model S is in-sourced.

I also believe in having a tight feedback loop between engineering and production. If production is far away from engineering you lose that feedback loop. Someone who designed the car in a particular way doesn't realize that it is very difficult to manufacture the particular way that is designed, but if the factory floor is 50 feet away from their desk then they can just see it and it's obvious and they can have a dialogue with people on the floor. Likewise, a lot of people in the manufacturing team have great ideas about how to improve the car, but if they are far away they can't communicate that to the engineers who designed it. I think it's something that's often neglected but having that strong feedback loop between engineering and production is really helpful for making the car better and finding efficiencies and lowering the cost. Particularly when the technology is evolving rapidly, it's important to have a very tight iteration loop between engineering and production, so as soon as you design something you can bring it to production right away. The engineers can go on the floor and see the mistakes that they've made, the production people can talk to engineers and say, 'here are some good ideas,' and so you can evolve the product and get to a better design solution faster. I think this is an important thing that's often overlooked.

We did a series of weekly iterations with the design team on Model S. Every Friday afternoon I would meet with the design team and we go over every nuance of the car. Every bumper, every curve, every tiny little piece of the car. What's right, what's wrong, and that has to be filtered against the engineering needs and the ergonomic needs, and the regulatory requirements. There's a lot of constraints, you can't make a car just any old shape you want. It has to meet all the regulatory requirements, crash-safe, and all that stuff. It just requires a lot of iterative activity and caring about every millimeter of the car. That's what results in a good product.

There's a lot of things about Ford that I think is really interesting. Ford was just the kind of guy that when something was in the way he would just find a way around it, he just got it done. He is often associated obviously with the moving production line, which was a big innovation. He was also big on vertical integration, which I actually think is good. People have started to think that vertical integration is bad but I think Ford was right, you do need to be vertically integrated, not to a silly degree but you do need to be vertically integrated. Ford at least in the beginning of his career, I think he got a little too high on his own supply in his later career or Ford would have remained the largest car company in the world, but in the beginning, he was actually really focused on what the customer wanted and what the customer needed. Sometimes the customer doesn't actually know what they need, but he really figured out that if we can make a car really affordable, reliable, and something that a farmer could really depend on their livelihood for, that's going to really make a difference in peoples lives, and he really got focused on that. Now overtime he should have decided that sometimes people want a color that is not black, and so you should provide that to them, but at least in the beginning of his career, he had a tremendous insight to what would really make a difference as a product.

When you try to make something there is a big leap between the first prototype and manufacturing it in large quantity with good quality. It's really hard to make that leap. When you have new technology it takes time to make it lower-cost and mass market. This is true for anything. If you had like a soap factory, let me tell you, your first bar of soap would be like millions of dollars, but then you get to volume production, and then it's like $2. It's true for any manufacturing situation, think of the earlier days of cell phones, or laptops, or any new technology it starts off expensive. Remember the giant phone that the guy on Wall Street was walking around with? that was cutting-edge technology.

For some reason, people decided they were going to do engineering here and do the manufacturing on the other side of the world. I think that ends up often being inefficient. The vertical integration is pretty important because one way to think about manufacturing efficiency is how long a journey did that molecule take from when it was mined. If it was mined in one part of the world, then went halfway across the world to get processed, then back halfway across the world to get processed another way, and eventually, there are several trips around the world before it ends up in a finished product, that's obviously fundamentally going to be expensive. You just can't send things on world trips and expect it to be cheap or affordable, it's just not going to happen. So it makes sense ultimately for rail cars of raw material to come in one side, and for finished vehicles to exit the other side.

With Tesla today it is sort of split up, we've got the factory in Fremont California, and the battery factory in Nevada, but I think for Gigafactory 2 and beyond I think we are just going to integrate that into one big facility. It's a three-step process - raw material - a bunch of stuff happens - out comes the car. We actually have been steadily acquiring the buildings around us in California, so we're sort of growing like the Borg.

The Model 3 efficiency as a whole really is a quantum change in productivity, like really, really, crazy. We've just got to scale up production, and production is a hard thing. It's really hard particularly when it's new technology and cutting edge technology it's really hard to scale up production because you've got to design the machine that makes the machine, not just the machine itself. That's where we have most of our engineering team working on.

The thing that happens once you start making almost all major subsystems internally, your supplier count actually grows dramatically. You have far more suppliers, not far fewer, but they're at the component level not at the major subsystem level. I really want to remind people that a car consists of several thousand unique items. We can only go as fast as the slowest item. What we were trying to do in advance of the Model 3 production was increase the scope of Tesla's internal capabilities, so that we're internally capable of making almost anything. Kind of like reserve troops. You don't know exactly where they'll be needed, but it's a good idea to have them so that we can minimize the degree to which a single supplier can stop the entire production line.

There's a whole bunch of little issues that are kind of trivial, that are challenges when you're making a new product because there are several thousand unique parts in the car, 90% of them are fine, 5% of them are slightly problematic, 3% or 4% are problematic and 1% are extremely problematic. You can't ship a car that is 99% complete. With software, you just have to get stable functionality, but with a car, you know, you can't ship it without a steering wheel, or without a back seat, or something like that. It's an integrated product with thousands of unique components, so we are somehow at the mercy of what the slowest component is from several thousand suppliers. Things move as fast as the least lucky and least competent supplier. Any natural disaster that carries a name we have had happened to our suppliers. The factory has been burned down, there's been an earthquake, there's been a tsunami, massive hail, there's been a tornado, the ship sank, there was a shootout at the Mexican border, no kidding, that delayed trunk carpet at one point. The border patrol wouldn't give us the trunk carpet because it had bullet holes in it, 'we just want our trunk carpet' that downed the production line for example for several days. That's the biggest issue the supply chain stuff. There's always something wrong. At any given point, there's always something wrong, because there are just too many things going on. There are thousands of unique components-- and even if one of those things is missing, you can't make cars.

One fiasco was-- I kid you not-- we were missing a $3 USB cable. OK, so we could not complete cars, because it's part of the wiring harness. You can't put the interior in without this cable. We could either make a whole bunch of cars minus the interior, which means that you've got to stack them up in the yard. It can be done, but then things go out of sequence, and it's way more inefficient, you don't have a moving production line. You have to send people out to hundreds of cars that are sitting in the storage yard. This happened to be a particularly pernicious cable, it was kind of routed under the carpet in a difficult place. It was literally $3, and we basically had to send people throughout the Bay Area to go and buy USB cables, at like Fry's. You were going to have a hard time getting a USB cable at Fry's because we bought every one of them so we were able to continue production.

I don't want to belabor the anecdote, but essentially the supplier was in China. We had plan A and plan B, plan A was like the normal supply chain process, but what the supplier did was instead of sending our parts in their own package they grouped it together with a bunch of other stuff for other companies and sent that all via some extremely slow boat from China to LA. When it got to LA the other stuff didn't pass customs, and so they wouldn't let our stuff through, because-- I don't know what they put it in, but something that customs didn't like, the paperwork wasn't in order or whatever. So it got stuck there for like a couple of weeks. Then we had plan B, we called and said, look you've got to air freight some of these cables-- cause they're just little cables-- to us. We talked to their US subsidiary and ordered from the US subsidiary, who then communicated to China, but then because this was another batch of parts, so it was kind of double the order, it exceeded the credit limit that we had. It bounced off the credit limit, so they didn't ship it. I mean, it's pretty farcical. That's just like one example, but there are many things like that. You move as fast as the slowest item in the whole car.

For battery packs one of the challenges we had was cobalt actually, cobalt is only available in a few places in the world, it's quite expensive, and the biggest source is the Congo, which tends to vary in its political stability. That's why going to the Model S we changed the chemistry to require only about a quarter as much cobalt, and thus reduce the cost of the battery pack, and also increase the energy of the pack.

The thing that is not well appreciated about cars and any kind of new technology is how hard it is to do the manufacturing. With maybe 50 or 60 people we can make a prototype of practically anything in six months. To manufacture that thing we need 5000 people to spent three years, and that is considered really fast. Specifically, with respect to Model X, we had a lot of challenges in the production ramp. That's always the most difficult time when you're going from zero to 1,000 cars a week. It's just you've got to pull this huge baggage train of suppliers along with you, and you've got to solve a lot of issues internally so that production ramp is a lot of hurt. Basically, we were in production hell for the first six months. I mean, we knew this. Signed up for it. Not blaming hell, because we bought the ticket.

36. Synergy

What I'm going to talk about is a fundamental transformation of how the world works, about how energy is delivered across Earth. The overall objective of Tesla is really what set of actions can we take to accelerate the advent of sustainable production and consumption of energy. There's a lot of value in accelerating in order to minimize the environmental and economic damage that would otherwise occur. I think it makes total sense and really is a no-brainer. I think the way I would assess the historic good of Tesla is in how many years of acceleration was it? if we can accelerate sustainable energy by 10 years I would consider that to be a great success, even five years would be pretty good. That is the overarching optimization. It's better if we shift transit to sustainable transport 10 or 20 years sooner than might otherwise be the case. I think Tesla's effect has been much greater than the cars made internally.

There are three legs to the stool. You need to have sustainable energy transport, essentially electric transport, you need to have sustainable energy generation in the form of solar or wind geothermal, and the third critical ingredient is stationary storage. There's electric cars, solar power, and stationary battery pack. We need to be able to buffer the energy in a stationary battery pack. With those three things, we can have a completely sustainable energy future. If you have electric cars, stationary battery packs, and solar power you can completely solve the world's energy problem in a sustainable way.

Now, the obvious problem with solar power is that the Sun does not shine at night, I think most people are aware of this. This problem needs to be solved. Batteries are critical to a sustainable energy future, the Sun doesn't shine all the time so you got to store it in the battery. We need to store the energy that is generated during the day so that you can use it at night, and also even during the day the energy generation varies. There's a lot more energy generated in the middle of the day than at dawn or dusk. It's very important to smooth out that energy generation and retain enough so that you can use it at night.

The issue with existing batteries is that they suck, they're really horrible, they're expensive, and they're unreliable. They're sort of stinky, ugly, bad in every way, you have to combine multiple systems, there's no integrated place you can go and buy a battery that just works, which is what people really want to buy. We have to come up with a solution. That's the missing piece. That's the thing that's needed to have a proper transition to a sustainable energy world. The missing piece is a product we call the Tesla Powerwall. I want to point a few things that are very important about this. The fact that it's wall-mounted is vital because it means you don't have to have a battery room, you don't have to have some room filled with nasty batteries. It means that a normal household can mount this on their garage or on the outside wall of their house and it doesn't take up any room. It's flat against the wall, it has all of the integrated safety systems, the thermal controls, the DC to DC converter. It's designed to work very well with solar systems right out of the box and it addresses all the needs.

What does this provide you? Well, it gives you peace of mind. If there's a cut in the utilities you're always going to have power, particularly if you're in a place that's very cold. You don't have to worry about being out of power if there's an ice storm. You actually could go, if you want, completely off-grid. Very importantly, this is going to be a great solution for people in remote parts of the world where there are no electricity lines, or where the electricity is extremely intermittent, or extremely expensive. You can take the Tesla Powerwall and it can scale globally.

Arguably there's a way to skip ahead with electricity generation in the same way that it happened with cellphones. In fact, I think what we'll see is something similar to what happened with cell phones versus landlines, where the cell phones actually leapfrogged the landlines and there wasn't a need to put landlines in a lot of countries or in remote locations. In a lot of undeveloped countries they didn't do the landline phones, they went straight to cellular. People in a remote village or an island somewhere can take solar panels, combine them with the Tesla Powerwall and never have to worry about having electricity lines. So particularly for rural areas being able to have solar panels with battery packs means you don't even need to have electricity lines. I think this is going to be great. Electricity lines are not the most pretty thing in the world. Being able to have this solution that just works where ever you are, I think is going to be incredibly helpful to people who don't have electricity today.

You can take your solar panels, charge the battery packs and that's all you use. It gives you safety, security, and it gives you a complete and affordable solution. It's designed so you can stack them on the wall, so you can have two, you can actually stack up to nine Powerwalls.

I think it's particularly important in cases where there's like a natural disaster, which could be floods, hurricanes, ice storms, earthquakes, fires, anything that disrupts the utility system. Having an uninterruptible power supply in the form of

Powerwall gives you security in those situations, it's kind of like insurance, like you only really want it when you really want it, and I think people love that.

With the integrated app, you can see the status of your car, your Powerwall, and your solar, and see at any given time of the day how much energy is coming from the Sun, how much is coming from the Powerwall, what your house is consuming. I'm using it myself and it's like, wow, this is great. It also tells you when the Powerwall saved you from utility interruption. People don't realize there are like many small utility interruptions in a given month. And that's why you see the blinking 12 on your microwave oven or whatever the case may be, or your computer suddenly went dark, or you can even get data corruption and that kind of thing, or your food went bad mysteriously. The Powerwall saves you from all of that.

The way the grid works today is you've got coal, natural gas, nuclear, hydro, and then wind and solar, but not enough wind and solar obviously. That's the grid typically in most countries, and you'll notice something - there's quite a big difference in peak to trough usage. The peak usage is typically at least twice the trough usage. Please bear that in mind that's an important point. The electricity grid has to be sized for the worst second, of the worst day, of the worst year, with some power plants not functioning. Well, that's how the electricity grid should be sized, but sometimes it doesn't work out that way. Most of the time you have huge amounts of excess capacity. In the US there was a study done - there are studies done on all sorts of things, some of them are complete nonsense, I love the words 'studies say..' but I think this study is probably accurate - that you could replace about 70% of the passenger miles in the United States with no change to the grid, assuming charging predominately at night. At some point, there will need to be improvements to the electricity grid, because there's a huge disparity in the peak energy use during the day and the energy use at night, and most charging of electric cars occurs at night - we have a quite strong empirical basis for concluding this because we can look at all our customers and plot their energy usage and it's very predominately at night. It's basically just like your cell phone, you go home, you plug it in and it charges overnight.

The Powerwall is a good solution for homes and perhaps for some small commercial applications, but what about something that scales to much much larger levels? for that we have something else, we have the Powerpack. The Tesla Powerpack is designed to scale infinitely. You can literally make this into a GWh class solution, you could go gigawatt class or higher. One of the exciting potential things with the Powerpack is that it's quite compact because it's lithium-ion it doesn't take up much space, you can get 100 kWh storage in something smaller than the size of a refrigerator, and you can get megawatt-hour very easily by putting them in a row. When I say scalable, I really mean scalable. The whole system is literally designed for infinite scalability. We could power a small city, like Boulder, with a GWh class pack. We've got a number of very big storage projects underway with utilities around the world, so both in the U.S. and outside.

The thing that's interesting about the energy storage situation is that even without renewables there's a huge potential to make the energy grid more efficient and to be able to shut down the heaviest polluting power plants because the energy consumption through the day usually changes by a factor of two or more. With the exception of hydroelectric, you can't store the power, it has to be available in real-time. The world has somewhere between two to three times as many power plants as it actually needs. There are hundreds of thousands of power plants using fossil fuels, if you can buffer the power with big stationary battery packs, then you can actually shut down the worst half of the power plants in the world. I think that's a very exciting thing that I think a lot of people don't appreciate, and I think it's going to make a big difference. Even if renewables were not part of the picture. The Powerpack is independent of renewables, you can probably take about somewhere close to half the power plants in the world and turn them off if you had batteries.

The interesting thing about the Powerwall and Powerpack is they scale on a global basis a lot faster than cars do because when you have cars you have to deal with the regulatory regime in a wide range of countries. Most countries have a very specialized regulatory regime and you're dealing with entrenched competitors. As for stationary storage, no one is really yet doing it right and the regulations are much more consistent from country to country.

It just became increasingly obvious that as we were developing new versions of the Powerwall, particularly as we integrated more of the inverter electronics and the intelligence in the Powerwall, it really needed to take the solar panels and solar system into account, otherwise, you duplicate a lot of hardware that doesn't work together as well, it's more expensive. The installation cost is substantially higher. You've got to put up the Powerwall, the solar panels if you've got an electric car you've got to install the wall connector and a home charging system. Those are potentially three visits or at least two visits. There was really no question about the convergence of Tesla and SolarCity.

In terms of the sales process itself when we were selling somebody the Powerwall, very often if not almost always, they were curious about solar. Not being able to sell them solar directly at Tesla through our stores was pretty inefficient. We really needed to have an integrated product. The Powerwall and the Powerpack need to be designed together with the solar system so it's a one-piece thing. The problem also was I think we didn't have a good basis for doing some special deal with SolarCity because that's effectively a conflict of interest. If we gave a special deal to SolarCity and SolarCity was not part of Tesla, then why were we doing that? Ironically, a conflict of interest goes away if we're one company, but it doesn't go away if we're two separate companies. It was not a very good rationale for just offering a special deal, and only working with one company that I also happen to own. I didn't think we had a good moral or legal basis for behaving a special way to SolarCity unless it's actually one company. It just made things, the execution, I think, a lot easier and cleaner and more effective. That's why I said I think it's really kind of a no-brainer. Like, if we didn't do this it would make Tesla's execution harder and worse. It was just a question of what timing was appropriate for that convergence. It was basically SolarCity's product roadmap and Tesla's product roadmap. On the installation and setup side that's one crew instead of two, and one visit instead of two to three visits. The ongoing maintenance is kind of one point of contact and not sort of two or three points of contact. The cost of the system itself is lower because we're not duplicating hardware. The timing was, if anything, we maybe should have done this sooner, but I certainly don't think we did it too early.

I don't think there's a strong product rationale to combine SpaceX and Tesla, as there was for Tesla and SolarCity. It's really quite tenuous for SpaceX and Tesla. There's a little cooperation that happens between the companies, but it's not that would justify merging them into one entity.

I think the word synergy is like almost sort of a dirty word, but I think these synergies are really just common sense. Like, obviously, it's more efficient to do it as an integrated system at the sale and at the installation, and in terms of just general maintenance and managing the customer relationship. I think that makes it kind of a pretty obvious thing to do, and it's quite difficult to create an integrated product if you're forced to be at an arm's length and be two different companies. If you have two separate companies, you have to have two separate computers, say operating systems. You've got to have separate communication systems interfacing with two separate server networks. You are developing two separate phone apps for the consumer to monitor their system. You've got to do two installation businesses instead of one. Kind of the way I think about it from a gut standpoint is like, first and foremost, this allows us to offer the most compelling product to consumers and businesses and a seamlessly integrated product that all just works together, that's better. You don't want to have a heterogeneous systems integration problem. That's just basically where the interfaces break down and then people are pointing fingers like this didn't work; no, your thing didn't work. If it's just one integrated system, there is no finger-pointing, you can iron out all the bugs and it just works. You're not wondering should I blame the solar company or the battery company or the who knows. It's just like a pain, a pain in the butt to try to figure that out if you're the end customer. Then, in addition, there are obvious cost savings to be had if in the same store we can sell twice as much dollar volume. You look to say Model 3, a $35,000 car, well, that same person at the same moment we could sell them roughly an equivalent amount value of solar panels and a Powerwall, effectively doubling or almost doubling the sale at that time, and then putting it all in at the same time.

 I think the tide of history very strongly supports a sustainable energy future, primarily solar, and virtually entirely electric vehicles. Maybe things temporarily interrupt that tide of history, but in the long term, it will overwhelm everything. Our goal is just to accelerate the advent of that future as fast as possible and this helps us accelerate it. That's the reasoning. We can't do this well if Tesla and SolarCity are different companies, which is why we needed to combine and break down the barriers inherent to being separate companies. That they are separate at all, despite similar origins and pursuit of the same overarching goal of sustainable energy, is largely an accident of history. Now that Tesla was ready to scale Powerwall and SolarCity was ready to provide highly differentiated solar, the time had come to bring them together. Arguably we should have done it sooner.

It is interesting to look at the feedback that I've received since we made the announcement, anyone who is product-focused sent me a congratulatory note and like why didn't you do it sooner sort of message. Then, people that are sort of more finance-focused, were a lot more worried about it.

If you place yourself in the consumer's shoes, you just want it to work. You don't want to know how it works. You don't care about the details. Most people don't even know what an inverter is. They've never heard of this thing. Most people don't even know what AC or DC is. If you ask, so what's DC? or what's direct current? or what's alternating current? they would not be able to tell you. A lot of people don't even know the difference between power and energy, one's in kilowatts, the other one's in kilowatt-hours, and they don't need to know like there's not a good reason for them to know. Stuff should just work and take care of itself. It's just got to work reliably, look good, not take up a ton of space, the buying process has got be easy, you can check up on it with the app on your phone. You want it to be easy, you want it to just work, you want it to be affordable, you want it to look good, so that's what we're going to do. I mean, really like solar and battery go together like peanut butter and jelly.

You obviously need the battery, particularly as you get to scale and you want to have solar be a bigger and bigger percentage of the grid. We've got a huge project in Hawaii. I think it's the biggest solar battery utility-scale installation in the United States, maybe the world. I mean it helps to use that as an example of one of the reasons to combine Tesla and SolarCity, in order to do the big Hawaii utility solar battery project, it had to go through the independent committees of both boards, there had to be discussions back and forth, it took a few months to get that all worked down. As we do many more of those deals, if we go to dozens of those deals, hundreds, potentially thousands in the future, this is completely unworkable, I mean no way we could send all that through independent board committees, it's completely unworkable.

One of the things that was missing was having rooftop solar that looks good. I think the one thing on the solar side – on the panel and module side and cell side was to create a high level of product differentiation, in particular with respect to aesthetics, as people care a great deal about that. I mean, technically, you could live in a house without drywall and just have all the insulation and wiring just hanging there, but people care about drywall. People care about remodeling their kitchen. People care about their yard. They care about making sure that their primary asset, typically being their house, is something that looks good and that they are proud to show. I think the aesthetics matter a lot, at Tesla we're super sensitive to aesthetics.

It's like what if we can offer you a roof that looks way better than a normal roof? What if we could offer you a roof that lasts far longer than a normal roof? like now it's a different ballgame. This is a night and day difference. If let's say somebody's got a $400,000 house, if you make the roof look ugly then arguably you've made that house worth 5% less or some nonzero percent less valuable. On the other hand, if you make the roof look beautiful you've made the house more valuable. Maybe that's plus 5% or some nonzero plus percent in the value of the house. If it is something on the order of 5% then the value delta there is, call it $40,000, or maybe it's only like 2% or 3%. and it's $20,000, it's like there you have quite a big value delta. So being able to have solar power, that looks great and I think better at cost, at least as good if not better than what's coming from anywhere else in the world, that's obviously a winning outcome. That's where we got the glass Solar Roof we developed. It's a Solar Roof as opposed to a module on a roof. Solar glass tiles where you can adjust the texture and the color to a very fine-grained level. Then there's sort of micro louvers in the glass, such that when you're looking at the roof from street level or close to street level, all the tiles look the same whether there is a solar cell behind it or not. You have an even color from the ground level. If you were to look at it from a helicopter, you would be actually able to look through and see that some of the glass tiles have a solar cell behind them and some do not, but you can't tell from street level. We're doing it in different styles so it matches the aesthetics of a particular house or regional style. I think that is actually pretty important.

The conventional flat-panel solar will be for flat roofs and commercial the way to go. Standard flat panel stuff, I think, is still the right solution for any kind of flat roof situation, which is most commercial installations and a lot of houses, or some part of the roof where it's really not visible and therefore, doesn't really matter from an aesthetic standpoint.

We're very confident that the cost of the Solar Roof will be less than the cost of a normal roof plus the cost of electricity.

In other words, this will be economically a no-brainer, we think it will look great, and it will last — We thought about having the warranty be infinity, but then people thought, well, that might sound like we're just talking rubbish. But actually, this is toughened glass, after the house has collapsed and there's nothing there, the glass tiles will still be there. I have it on my house and JB has it on his house we have the Solar Roof tiles installed and working. Looking really good. I think this roof's going to look really knockout as we just keep iterating.

I'd just like to emphasize, I think, this is a fundamental part of achieving a differentiated product strategy where it's not a thing on a roof, it is the roof. That was quite a difficult engineering challenge and not something that was available anywhere else that was at all good.

I think eventually almost all houses will have a Solar Roof. The thing is to consider the time scale here to be probably on the order of 40 or 50 years. So on average, a roof is replaced every 20 to 25 years, but you don't start replacing all roofs immediately. Eventually, if you say were to fast-forward to say 15 years from now, it will be unusual to have a roof that does not have solar.

The cool thing about this is that it doesn't cannibalize the existing product of putting solar on the roof, because essentially if your roof is nearing end-of-life, you definitely don't want to put solar panels on it, because you know you're going to have to replace the roof. There is a huge market segment that is currently inaccessible because people know they're going to have to replace their roof, you don't want to put solar panels on top of a roof you're going to replace. However, if your roof is nearing end-of-life, well, you've got to get a new roof anyway, there are 5 million new roofs a year just in the U.S. and so, why not have a Solar Roof that's better in many other ways as well. For someone that is building a house or where the roof is nearing its expiry date, then the Solar Roof is the right option. If you had our solar system that made your house look better, lowered your cost of electricity, and then gave you security against a power outage with the Powerwall, and allowed you to go potentially completely off-grid, then that's kind of a no-brainer, like why wouldn't you do that? Create a smoothly integrated and beautiful solar-roof-with-battery product that just works, empowering the individual as their own utility, and then scale that throughout the world. One ordering experience, one installation, one service contact, one phone app.

The storage costs are going to drop pretty dramatically with each passing year. We have the best cell at the lowest price. That's a really good place to be, and we're confident we can achieve that same outcome in solar.

Like I said, you just can't get beyond a certain scale with solar unless you have the batteries to go with it to buffer the power. You got to manage all of that because you'll have millions and millions of these batteries, you've got to manage that, integrate it with the utility. I do want to emphasize, there's still a very important role for utilities here, sometimes people think that this is an either/or thing, it's like either rooftops are going to win or centralized generation is going to win, and actually both are going to win, because the electricity usage is going to increase dramatically as we transition away from burning old dinosaurs to electric cars, and then to electric transport.

It's very important to have rooftop solar in neighborhoods because otherwise, they will need to have massive transmission lines built. People don't like having transmission lines through the neighborhood, and I agree. I mean, I don't think anybody wants to have huge new power lines pulled through their neighborhoods. The vast expansion of substations and all the things that would be necessary to fully electrify transport and heating. It's a huge headache to do that. It's not something that, I think, any consumer wants and it's not a headache that utilities want to have to go through, but if you don't have localized generation combined with central, that is what's going to have to happen and that would suck. You want to have some localized energy production combined with utility. You want rooftop solar and utility solar that is really going to be the solution from a physics standpoint. I can't see any other way to really do it.

I think there is a lot of opportunity at the utility-scale, providing integrated solar battery system to utilities so that they can provide sustainable energy that's load leveled and buffered to their customers. I think there's going to be actually a lot of business with utilities, as we provide them with an option to have sustainable, centralized power generation. That's what I want – I really want to emphasize, like, our goal is to work with utilities and it's collectively to solve the future energy electricity demands of the world, as the electricity demand rises tremendously.

The nice thing about solar power is it tends to match energy usage, generating power during the day when you tend to use the most power. So solar actually helps the grid because it generates energy when people use it most. Like electricity demand peaks during the day, because that's when the air conditioning is running at maximum power, that's when the companies are all operating, machinery is operating. Particularly on summer days when you have air conditioning running, Air conditioning is a huge consumer of electricity. You generally only need it when it's warm and sunny - that's when you need it most. Solar actually helps utilities up to a certain percentage. You can sort of debate that percentage but it's somewhere between like 10% – minimum 10% but it could be up to 20%.

What I want to do is explore what's needed to transition the world to sustainable energy. Is this actually possible? is it something that is within the ability of humanity to actually do or is it some insurmountable super-difficult impossible thing? it's not. First of all, it's important to appreciate that the amount of energy that reaches us from this handy fusion reactor in the sky called the Sun is tremendous. It's 99% plus of all energy that Earth has. Then there's the energy that we need to run civilization. Which to us is big, but compared to the amount of energy that reaches us from the Sun is tiny. If you wanted to power the entire United States with solar panels it would take a fairly small corner of Nevada, Texas, Utah -- you only need about 100 miles by 100 miles of solar panels to power the entire United States. It's remarkable how little land you need to generate enough power to completely get the United States off fossil fuels. It's crazy. Like a little corner of Texas or Utah, that's all the United States' power. The land area you need to power the United States fits into the little Texas Panhandle. It's really not much and most of that area is going to be on rooftops. You won't need to disturb the land, you won't need to find new areas, it's mostly just going to be on the roofs of existing homes and buildings. The batteries you need to store that energy to make you have 24/7 power is one mile by one mile. One square mile. That is it.

With 160 million Powerpacks you could transition the United States. With 900 million you can transition the world. You can basically make all electricity generation in the world renewable and primarily solar. Then going a little further if you want to transition all transport, and all electricity generation, and all heating to renewable you need approximately two billion Powerpacks. Now that may seem like an insane number and I'm very tempted to do the billion thing that - I must restrain my hand - but in order to - like, two billion Powerpacks is that a crazy number? Is that an impossible number? It is not, in fact. The number of cars and trucks that we have on the road is approximately two billion. The point I want to make is that this is actually within the power of humanity to do. We have done things like this before. It is not impossible, it is really something that we can do.

We're going to try to grow that as fast as we can and not just in the US but throughout the world. The advantage of solar and batteries is that you can avoid building electricity plants at all. You could be a remote village and have solar panels that charge a battery pack that supplies power to the whole village without ever having to run thousands of miles of high-voltage cable all over the place.

Then what's the long-term picture? The long-term picture is a world with sustainable power generation, which is going to come primarily in the form of solar, overwhelmingly in the form of solar energy, stationary storage to buffer that power, and then electric cars. Those are the three parts that are needed. Solar power, stationary storage, electric cars. And those are the three things that I think Tesla should be providing, and Tesla is going to be the leader in all three.

This is the ultimate solution we're talking about here. This is the solution. This is what the world needs. We're going to try to make that happen as fast as possible and the fundamental good of Tesla will be measured by the degree to which we accelerate that transition. We're going to try to make it happen as fast as possible and I think we will have a meaningful impact on that timeframe. We want to show people most importantly that this is possible. If you look at that - that's the future we could have. Where the curve slowly rolls over and goes to zero - no incremental CO_2 - that's the future we need to have.

That's the path - it's the only path that I know of that can do this, and I think it's something that we must do, and that we can do, and that we will do.

37. Good Company

We got an awesome team of really, really great people at SpaceX and Tesla. We got world experts on propulsion, structural design, avionics, software, launch operations, and that kind of thing. There's a lot of people who have had a huge impact and influence on building the companies. I've had more of an influence than anyone else, but it's a big team effort from a lot of talented people. One of the things that isn't recognized is that there's way too much attention paid to me, and it's really not right. People want to identify with an individual and that is sort of naturally what occurs, but there's a super talented group of people at SpaceX that make it happen and likewise at Tesla.

I think the most important thing for creating companies is you need a concentration of talent. It's like you are creating a world sports team or something. The ability to attract and motivate great people is critical to the success of a company because a company is just a group of people that are assembled to create a product or service. That's really all that a company is, it's a group of people that got together to create a product or service, that's the purpose of a company. People sometimes forget this elementary truth. If you're able to get great people to join the company, and work together towards a common goal and have a relentless sense of perfection about that goal, then you will end up with a great product, and if you have a great product lots of people will buy it, and then the company will be successful. It's pretty straightforward really.

The most important thing is people, so you need to gather a group of engineers to create technology. That's what engineers do they create technology, but you got to have a critical mass of such people that's equal to the task you try to complete. In order to have a great company you got to focus your energy on a particular area, you really want to focus your talents on a particular area. When you hire people what you're really trying to do is you're convincing people to join you in the endeavor. You should hire people that are also passionate about what you're doing so they're not just there for the salary. They really need to care about what they are doing and then they will stay during the dark times.

As far as R&D is concerned we hire great engineers as fast as we can find them. It's not that easy to find I should say great engineers with the right mindset and everything. We hire at the maximum rate that we can find people that we think would really be an asset to the team. I don't know if our recruiting and our process of hiring people is good, I think it's good but I'm not sure, but we want to hire lots of really smart engineers because that's how these problems get solved.

In terms of what characteristics we look for, we're generally quite engineering-centric so we're big fans of what have people done from a hardcore engineering standpoint. What tough engineering problems have they solved? how they solved them? We're less interested if it's been more of a paper-oriented role that they've had because we try to minimize that at SpaceX. When I interview someone to work at the company I asked them to tell me about the problems they worked on and how they solved them. When I interview somebody – my interview questions are always the same, I suppose honestly that it tends to be a gut feel more than anything else. I'd say tell me the story of your life and the decisions that you made along the way and why you made them. Then also tell me about some of the most difficult problems you've worked on and how you solved them. I really just ask them to tell me the story of their career, and what are some of the tougher problems that they dealt with, how they dealt with those, and how they made decisions at key transition points, did they face really difficult problems, and overcome them? Then of course you want to make sure that if there was some significant accomplishment, and were they really responsible or was somebody else more responsible. Usually, if they're a person who has had to struggle with a problem they really understand it, and they don't forget - if it was really difficult. You can ask them very detailed questions about it and they'll know the answer, whereas the person who was not truly responsible for that accomplishment will not know the details. That question I think is very important because the people that really solved the problem know exactly how they solved it they know the little details, and the people that pretended to solve the problem can maybe go one level and then they get stuck. If someone was really the person that solved it they will be able to answer on multiple levels, they will go down to the brass tacks, and if they weren't they will get stuck. Then you can say this person was not really the one who solved it because anyone who struggled hard with a problem never forgets it. Usually, that's enough for me to get a very good gut feel about someone and what I'm looking for is evidence of exceptional ability. Really just looking for evidence of exceptional ability and if there's a track record of exceptional achievement then it's likely that will continue into the future.

There's no need even to have a college degree at all or even high school. I mean, if somebody graduated from a great university that may be an indication that they will be capable of great things, but it's not necessarily the case. If you look at say people like Bill Gates, Larry Ellison, Steve Jobs, these guys didn't graduate from college but if you had a chance to hire them, of course, that would be a good idea.

Those are pretty different personalities - between Gates and Jobs and Ellison. I think all three of those were technologists but with different types of skills. Jobs was obviously very good with aesthetics, and he understood technology of course, but he also understood what people wanted even when they didn't know themselves, and he was not afraid to break boundaries. Gates would probably be better at raw engineering and technology than Jobs, but not as good on aesthetics. For all these guys, they're obviously very driven, and they're very talented and they're able to attract great people to build a company. Getting the right people is extremely important.

Generally, I look for a positive attitude, and are they easy to work with, are people going to like working with them. It's very important to like people you work with otherwise your job is going to be quite miserable. In fact, we have a strict no assholes policy at Space, we fire people, we will give them a warning, but we will fire them if they keep being an asshole. If your boss is an awful person you will hate coming to work.

I have got a lot of scar tissue. The biggest mistake in general that I've made is to put too much of a weight on somebody's talent and not enough on their personality, and I've made that mistake several times. In fact every time I say I'm not going to make that mistake again, and then I make it again. I have made several hiring decisions where I valued intellect over heart, I think that was a mistake. It actually matters if somebody is a good person beyond just goodness itself. It actually matters if somebody has a good heart. That's generally the hiring mistakes that I've made in the past, thinking that sometimes it's just about the brains, looking too much at their intellectual capability alone and not on how they affect those around them.

What really matters is, for someone's contribution to a company, is how they are as an individual and how they affect others around them. You could say it's also analogous to a sports team - the best person on the team is not necessarily the one who scores the most goals, it could be the person who assists in the most goals. If there's one person on the team who just wants the ball all the time and just wants to kick it at the goal, that can be detrimental. It is important to weigh personality, and are they going to be a good person, will people like working with them, that sort of thing. It does make a difference.

I think when you create a company you really have to believe in what you're creating. Know in your heart and mind that this is something that matters and that the world ought to have. You construct like this sort of Holy Grail potential in the future. You have to stay grounded in the short-term because if you don't do things to pay the bills you are not going to achieve the ultimate long-term objective, but it's nice to have that Holy Grail long-term potential out there as an inspiration for coming to work.

You have to show that you really care, that you've got skin in the game. You've given it everything that you got and then the other people in the company will follow suit. I think it's important to investors to show that you are really all in. For example with Tesla the fact that I invested all the money that I had, truly I had to borrow money from friends to pay to rent in 2008, and the fact that I was all in made a huge difference to investors to convince them to invest in Tesla. Really believe in what you're doing but not just from a blind faith standpoint, but to really have thought about it and say this is true, I am convinced it is true, I have tried every angle to figure out if it is untrue. Sort negative feedback to figure out if I may be wrong, but if after all that it still seems like this is the right way to go then that gives one a fundamental conviction, and an ability to convey that conviction to others to convince them to join.

That's what a company is, if you can convey that, and answered a concern that people have convince them that this is something that needs to be done, and it's important, and here is a path to do it, even if that path has a lot of danger associated with it and risk. Maybe it won't succeed, but people can understand this is why it is important, and even if the odds are that it won't succeed it's worth trying to do it, then I think you can create a great company. It's more than just a company it's more than just a product, there's a cause there, it's something that really matters. I think a lot of our customers kind of share that view.

That sort of excitement is a powerful driver and makes me want to get up in the morning and go to work because it's just so much easier to work hard if you love what you're doing. I think it is incredibly important to have an environment in general where people look forward to coming to work, and try to make it a really fun place to work, really enjoyable.

As companies get bigger it's harder and harder to get sort of a fun and dynamic feeling. To avoid being sort of a soul-destroying corporation I think it's important to allow for a certain amount of chaos within an organization. Rules need to capture the counterintuitive, if something is fairly obvious then people would probably do that, but the counterintuitive stuff is less obvious. A lot of companies try to impose too much structure or don't allow failure, particularly as they get bigger they tend to have a risk-reward asymmetry. Failure is severely punished, success is moderately rewarded. That's not a good idea if you want to be innovative, because by its very nature innovation will result in many attempts that don't work. A lot of employees have great ideas if they get resources to implement them, and if they're not filtered through their manager. Generally, try to be a little irreverent to encourage people to do eclectic odd things and that's OK. So there's not some conformist police chasing you down.

There must be an expectation of innovation and the compensation structure must reflect that. There must also be an allowance for failure because if you're trying something new necessarily there is some chance that it will not work. If you punish people too much for failure then they will respond accordingly, then the innovation you will get is very incremental, nobody is going to try anything bold for fear of being fired or being punished in some way. The risk-reward must be balanced and favor taking bold moves otherwise it will not happen.

Then I'd say focus on signal over noise. A lot of companies get confused, they spend a lot of money on things that don't actually make the product better. So, for example, at Tesla, we've never spent any money on advertising. We've put all the money into R&D, and manufacturing and design to try and make the car as good as possible I think that's the way to go. For any given company keep thinking about are these efforts that people are expending resulting in a better product or service? and if they're not, stop those efforts.

I do think it gets difficult for companies to maintain a high productivity per person as they grow, because companies initially improve productivity per person due to specialization of labor, and then productivity per person tends to decline as companies get beyond a certain scale due to communication issues. We do our best, at SpaceX to minimize communication issues, we have anyone-to-anyone communication, instead of say chain-of-command communication, which is extremely inefficient. I think it's important to maximize communication. You know the path to the CEO's office should not go through the CFOs office, not if you are a products company, maybe if you're a financial services company.

The amount of direct interaction I have with people these days is a lot more limited. I do skip-level meetings, it's like I meet with my reports and their direct reports. Again, generally for a company when it's very small productivity grows very quickly because of that specialization of labor, then productivity per person declines because of the communication issues. As you have more and more layers through which communication has to flow that necessarily imparts loss, every time information flows from one person to another, even with the best intentions, you have information loss. You can alleviate that by doing skip-level meetings.

One thing we try to do is minimize the size of meetings, a normal meeting would be with 4 to 6 people. The basic rule for a meeting is that unless somebody is getting an enormous value from the information they are receiving, or they are contributing to the meeting itself they shouldn't be there. We also have a rule that if somebody's in this meeting and it is not helping them in a meaningful way they should just leave.

I am much more sort of the Spartan school of thought, I care about the effective execution at the company. And the more you insulate yourself from information and feedback in the company the worst decisions you make.

I really like density, I like a beehive of activity and people fairly close together. I think it creates a much better esprit de corps. If you just talk to the people on your team you can learn a tremendous amount, and then as you iterate through problems it's kind of like anything, if you struggle with a problem that's when you understand it.

SpaceX operates on a Silicon Valley mode of operation, flat hierarchy, closely packed cubes, high engineer to manager ratio, lots of prototype iteration, and a best-idea-wins type of philosophy, where what matters is the merits of the argument not the status of the arguer. If you sort of have a very flat hierarchy you promote rapid communication, a best-idea-wins culture - as opposed to having the seniority of the person decide the solution, which - that should never be the case in engineering, it should always be a rational basis. I also believe that at the leadership level, I'd much rather promote someone that has strong engineering ability than so-called management ability. We do hire some MBAs but it's usually in spite of the MBA, not because of it. SpaceX is an extremely demanding organization and we expect people to work super hard and be very good at their job.

Something worth noting is a lot of what is needed on a rocket or spacecraft is actually software. Generally, with software you can get amazing things done with small teams, a small team will do much more radical improvements than a big team. We actually hire a lot of our best software engineers out of the gaming industry. In fact, I started off when I was a kid - in terms of engineering, I wrote games, that was the thing that I did. I think in gaming there's a lot of smart engineering talent doing really complex things. In fact, I think a lot of the algorithms involved in a multi-player online game - compared to a lot of the math that's involved there doing a docking sequence is actually relatively straightforward. I'd encourage people who are in the gaming industry to think about joining SpaceX and creating the next generation of spacecraft and rockets. Also probably, in the future, we'll create like droids on the surface of Mars and the Moon to do things like an automated propellant depot and that kind of thing. We sort of need those features to have a base on Mars.

The US government regulations make getting a job in the US as hard as it is, but if you are working on rocket technology that is considered an advanced weapons technology, so even a normal work visa is not sufficient unless you get special permission from the Secretary of Defense or the Secretary of

State. To be clear this is not some desire of SpaceX to just hire people with green cards it's because we are not allowed to do anything else. I think this is not a wise thing policy for the US because there are so many talented people all around the world that we would love to have work at our company, but unless they get a green card we are literally prevented from hiring anyone.

The other thing I want to mention, there were a lot of articles about Tesla firing employees and layoffs, these were really ridiculous, and any journalist who has written articles to this effect should be ashamed of themselves for lack of journalistic integrity. In every company in the world, there are annual performance reviews. In our annual performance review, despite Tesla having an extremely high standard, only 2% of people didn't make the grade, so that was about 700 people out of 33,000. This is a very low percentage. GE, I don't know if they still do, but they certainly for a long time had a policy of firing 10% of their employees' performance every year, no matter what. If you were to stack Tesla's performance releases compared to other companies, the number would be low. The only reason these articles had any play whatsoever is because of journalists and editors with low integrity, they'll provide any context for where they stood because the actual article would've read, "Tesla fires 2% of its employee base for performance-based reasons, a remarkably lower number compared to other companies." But of course, that would be a meaningless article, so they forget to include that. Shame.

Well, unfortunately, and fortunately, Tesla cannot sneeze without there being a national headline. I've been like pistol-whipped. The amount of national and international news headlines dedicated to three Tesla fires that caused no injury was greater than the quarter of 1 million gasoline car fires that occurred in the United States, which caused about 400 deaths and something like 1200 serious injuries. Our three non-injurious fires got more national headlines than a quarter-million deadly gasoline car fires. That's mad, what the heck is going on? I realize that a new technology should have a spotlight on it, but it shouldn't have a laser on it. I really care about Tesla and everything so it's hard to be dispassionate about that. It's a lot of blood, sweat, and tears from a lot of people and, you know, I think particularly if the criticism isn't accurate. It's sort of like, it's like your child. Let's say your child goes into a competition and loses, but not on the merits, then you'd be pretty angry about that, or if somebody disparages your child in a way that's false. I think it's important to tell the truth and to rebut things that are wrong. There are honest criticisms to be had, certainly, but it's difficult to take false criticism of something you care about.

38. Government

The private sector is very good at organization and innovation. I mean, the private sector is generally better at doing things than the government, I think that is fair to say. Where you have these things that are a small amount of good for a lot of people it makes sense for the public sector, for government to do that. When you have something that is kind of a small amount of good for the whole population, or the whole country, or even the whole world. Like basic research and that sort of thing. It would be really difficult to go to collect like $10 from everyone to understand more about the Earth or the Solar System or the Universe. It's not efficient if you have say a 3 billion dollar project to go collect $10 from everyone in the United States, it's better to do that via the public sector. You have great things like let's say the Hubble or the Mars missions. In general, commercial technology companies are better at advancing technology than governments, particularly once it gets out of the fundamental research phase. Where you can more concretely close the economic loop that's where the private sector makes sense.

The reason that there hasn't been a big improvement in the space industry, I think a critical portion of it is because for the creative destruction process to come into effect there is such a significant amount of capital that is needed to start a rocket company, and it is a very difficult technical challenge and the number of people that really understand rocketry in the world is a very small number. There are really huge barriers to entry and that is why we haven't seen the function of improvement that there should have been over the years. That's sort of what

SpaceX hopes to be - to really drive the technology development a lot faster than it would occur otherwise if it was just sort of a big government endeavor.

I think that government plays an important role in funding sort of basic science, the frontiers of exploration, that kind of thing, where there's not an obvious direct economic feedback loop, but it's nonetheless an important thing to do that's helpful to everyone, like the Hubble for example. We gained a lot of knowledge and understanding of the universe from the Hubble. It didn't necessarily translate to economics for one particular company, so it made sense that it would be funded by the government. Government, by the way, has no money, it only takes money from the people. Funded by the government just means funded by the people. Sometimes people forget that that's really what occurs. When there is a benefit that accrues to the people as a whole then it's fair that the money should be drawn from the people as a whole to match that benefit.

Government is inherently inefficient, so it makes sense to minimize the role of government such that government does only what it has to do and no more. There are obviously very clear examples of this in comparing something like East and West Germany and North and South Korea. Places where you have essentially the same people, but two different systems of government. East and West Germany for example, the economic outcome per capita was about five times higher in West Germany —arguably more than five times—but at least five times higher in West Germany than in East, and it's not as though West Germany was particularly capitalist. I mean, they're sort of a lot more socialist than we are, and yet they had that huge output difference. North and South Korea is an even more stark example, where North Korea, people undergo starvation, and South Korea is incredibly prosperous. You want to always watch that dial—that allocation of resources dial—and make sure that government doesn't become too large a portion of the economy.

The United States is actually doing quite well, and we all live really great lives here in the US, and we shouldn't lose sight of that. The US is still the world's largest manufacturer, and it has been since it took over from England, I don't know, a hundred and some odd years ago. The unemployment rate is decreasing. I think there are lots of reasons to be positive, actually, without being complacent. We certainly need to decrease the amount of government spending. I think that that's really important. There seems to be some movement afoot to reign in government spending. It can't be a little bit here, around the edges, there needs to be a meaningful decrease in government spending such that we do not have trillion-dollar deficits because that's obviously unsustainable. The trillion-dollar deficit thing, I liken it sort of to ... it's like toddlers with a cupcake. Have you ever seen these delayed gratification tests? apparently, you can predict somebody's future success by the degree to which they can partake in delayed gratification, where you can say, "Here's this cupcake, it's on a table, If you eat it now that's all you get, but if you wait ten minutes you can have three cupcakes." and some toddlers they just go and they eat that cupcake. They basically sacrifice tomorrow for today, effectively. That's kind of what Congress often behaves like, and to some degree, the American people are responsible for this, because we ought to vote people out who engage in such behavior. Running trillion-dollar-plus deficits... that is going to come back to haunt us like there's no tomorrow. We do not want to be Greece, or Portugal, or any such country. We must make the hard decisions of reigning in government spending, and probably increasing the tax burden as well, but we need to do both, we can't solve it either by simply increasing taxes or by just cutting the deficit. That's like saying, you know, the sky is blue it's so freaking obvious.

My overall impression of Washington is that it's much less corrupt than people think it is. Thank goodness for it because if it was corrupt we would be screwed. That isn't to say that there is some amount of that that goes on, but I think there actually are I think a preponderance of the leading house members and senators quite idealistic and care about doing the right thing.

Actually, on balance, the Federal Government has been helpful to Tesla. In the space arena... man, this is a complicated situation. I virtually make zero political contributions for Tesla. I do make political contributions for SpaceX because the way the system works is SpaceX is fighting the big defense contractors. The big defense contractors make 20 times the political donations that I and the people at SpaceX do. Literally, 20 times if you just take Boeing and Lockheed where SpaceX is competing with for launch contracts. What those contributions just do is get us a conversation with legislators, that's all. If political contributions were really what made the difference then SpaceX would have no hope, no hope. Thank goodness that they don't, so, I actually would say that on balance it's not that corrupt because if it was corrupt then SpaceX would have no chance. SpaceX was very tiny when we got our first government contract, and if it had been deeply corrupt then we would've not won anything. The greater the level of visibility politically the less corruption occurs. I think there's probably the least corruption at the presidential level, and at the Senate level, and in the House. There can be a bit more corruption at the state level. Basically, it's how much attention are people paying that defines how much corruption occurs.

I'm not sure how much the President can really do, you know. I think the reality of being President is that you're actually the captain of a very huge ship and have a small rudder. Obviously, if there was a button that a President could press that said 'economic-prosperity' they'd be hitting that button real fast. You could measure the speed of light by how fast they press that button because that's called the reelection button.

Things got real nutty with the US election and all that. I don't think this was the finest moment in our democracy. I'm glad that the framers of the Constitution saw fit to ensure that the President was someone who was captain of a large ship with a small rudder, there's a limit to how much good or bad any given President can do. I guess there is the nuclear thing, but I am quite confident that the military would not just randomly agree to launch nuclear missiles at somebody.

I was on two advisory councils where the format consisted of going around the room and asking people's opinions on things, and so there was like a meeting every month or two. That was the sum total of my contribution. In every meeting I was just trying to make the arguments in favor of sustainability -- and sometimes other issues, like we need to make sure our immigration laws are not unkind or unreasonable. If I hadn't done that, that wasn't on the agenda before. Maybe nothing will happen but at least the words were said. I think to the degree that there were people in the room who were arguing in favor of doing something about climate change, or social issues, I've used the meetings I've had to argue in favor of immigration and in favor of climate change. I thought it was worth trying. I got a lot of flack from multiple fronts for even trying. Some guy put up billboards attacking me, and ran full-page ads in the New York Times and whatnot, just for being on the panel. I did my best, and in a few cases, I think I did make some progress. I just really think the Paris Accord, if I stayed on the councils I would be essentially saying that it wasn't important, but it was super important because I think the country needs to keep its word. It was not even a binding agreement. There was no way I could stay on after that. I did my best.

I think each government should do the right thing without depending upon what other governments are doing. I think there's too much in these climate talks of countries trying to only do things if another country does it. If it's the right thing for the future, a country should just do it and don't worry about what other countries are doing. Just do the right thing, and many of the countries are. It's really just we just want to encourage as many governments as possible to change the rules to incent a good future. This is fundamentally what has to happen or we will substantially delay the transition away from carbon.

Governments around the world certainly make a lot of noise about caring about the environment but the results are not very good, particularly in automotive. Much less than 1% of new cars made every year are electric. This year there'll be 90-something million cars made, so round it off, say 100 million new cars made a year, there are about two billion cars in the global fleet. Even if all new cars went to electric this year it would take 20 years to replace the global fleet, but much less than 1% of new cars made this year are electric. Clearly, we need stronger action. I know they keep sort of talking about it. Really, the action needs to be ratcheted up until we see solid movement toward electric cars. How about at least 1% of cars being made are electric? that seems like a very low bar.

With respect to climate change, it's just critical that the governments get the rules right. The government is the setter of rules, the government decides what rules companies will play by. We currently have a system that massively incents bad behavior. In terms of legislative and executive actions, it is sort of like professional sports or something, if you don't have the rules right, if the game is not set up properly, it is not going to be a good game, so it's really important to get the rules right. The government is the one that sets the rules of how companies are rewarded financially. Money and prices are basically just an information mechanism. Money is mostly an information mechanism for labor allocation and tells companies what to do. This is why it's so critical that action be taken at a government level, it's just crazy to have the rules of the game favor a bad outcome. It's worth noting that in the United States, the rules are still better than anywhere else, but it's very easy to put something in place which is an inhibitor to innovation without realizing it.

In terms of the regulatory environment, it's always important to bear in mind that regulations are immortal, they never die unless somebody actually goes and kills it, and they gain a lot of momentum. A lot of times regulations get put in place for all the right reasons but then nobody goes back and gets rid of them afterward when they no longer make sense. There used to be a rule in the early days when people were concerned about automobiles because that was a pretty scary thing, there was this carriage going along all by itself, you never know what those things might do. You had those rules in a lot of states where you had to carry a lantern in front of the automobile, there had to be someone 100 paces in front of the automobile with a lantern on a pole. It's like you should really get rid of that regulation, and they did. That would be a bit awkward. It's always good to go back and scrub those periodically and make sure they are still sensible and serving the greater good.

I think in general people want to do the right thing and they want to do what's good. The issue we have right now is that the rules fundamentally favor the bad outcome. When you're fighting for the good outcome and it's an uphill battle, it's just slower. In the absence of government actually establishing some kind of a carbon tax or potentially a cap on trade on carbon, which I was very excited to see that China announced that they were going to do that unless the government does something to fix the market mechanism, we're fundamentally going to have a very slow transition out of the fossil fuel era. It's critical that the governments of the world need to price the externality. They need to put a proper price on carbon and then automatically the right behavior will occur. By putting a price on carbon we're essentially fixing a pricing error in the market system. Most of the time when governments intervene in markets it usually increases the pricing error. But when a pricing error is a huge tragedy of the commons issue like we have with carbon capacity it's critical that the government put a price on it.

There are other less effective ways by providing incentives and subsidies to say electric cars or solar. That is sometimes a more politically expedient way to do it, but the best way is just to directly fix the pricing error by taxing carbon. If you ask most economists, they would say the same thing. This is well known obviously in the economics world. What I'm saying is totally common sense, it's economics 101 -- whatever you incent will happen. If you incent one thing that will tend to happen, if you incent another thing, that thing will happen. I mean for example there is a 20% tax incentive for a stripper oil well. The incentive for solar was 30% but dropped to 10% so the incentive for solar was half that of a stripper oil well.

In order for there to be a big move towards sustainability the giant companies have to know that that is what the governments are demanding for the future, and that's what the people are demanding for the future. At the end of the day if the governments respond to popular pressure like if you tell politicians that your vote depends on them doing the right thing with climate change, that makes a difference. If they're having a fundraising event or a dinner party or whatever, and at every fundraising event in every dinner party somebody is asking them "Hey, what are you doing about the climate" then they will take action.

We definitely can't beat the oil and gas industry on lobbyists. That would be a losing battle. Exxon makes more profit in a year than the value of the entire solar industry in the United States. If you take every solar company in the United States, it's less than Exxon's profit in one year. There's no way you can win on money, that's impossible.

I think we just need to turn that argument around and say, "Look, this is a common good and if countries don't take action they all will share in a bad future" everyone needs to take action and care about what the future's going to hold and lead by example. Even countries that are quite dependent on fossil fuels if they just change their tax structure they can move away from that in a way that's not super disruptive to the economy.

It's really just a question of collecting the same amount of taxes but weighted towards things that people believe are most likely to be bad instead of things that are most likely to be good. We do this already in our tax code, we tax alcohol and cigarettes much more than we tax fruits and vegetables. It's just the sensible thing to do. Just adjust the tax code and the right thing will happen over time.

It'll be a slow transition and the fundamental question is how do we accelerate that transition? That's the real question here. What actions can we take that would accelerate a transition to a good future? That's why I'm so harping on this notion of a revenue-neutral carbon tax. I think that's something that every country can implement and it could be graduated and phased in overtime. This will be by far the most effective thing for accelerating that transition to a good future.

There is way too much in government where it is a sole source cost-plus contract. Economics 101, whatever you incent, that will happen. People shouldn't be surprised, if a company manages to find some excuse to double the cost they're going to get double the profit. They are getting a percentage so they are going to do exactly that, and they are not going to say no to requirements. The government will come up with some requirements, 90% of them could make a lot of sense -- 10% of them are cockamamie that double the price of the project. For that 10% of cockamamie requirements in a cost-plus contract, the contractor will always say yes.

We have to change the way contracting is done. You can't do these cost-plus sole-source contracts because then the incentive structure is all messed up. As soon as you don't have any competition the sense of urgency goes away. As soon as you make something a cost-plus contract you are incenting the contractor to maximize the cost of the program because they get a percentage. They'll never want that gravy train to end, and they become cost maximizers. Then you have good people engaged in cost maximization because you just gave them the incentivization to do that, and they get punished if they don't. Essentially that's what happens, it's critically important that we change the contracting structure to be a competitive commercial bid. Make sure there are always at least two entities that are competing. That the contracts are milestone-based with concrete milestones. PowerPoint presentations do not count, everything works in PowerPoint 'I have a

Teleportation device, look here's my PowerPoint presentation'. Milestone-based competitive commercial contracts with competitors and then you got to be prepared to fire one of those competitors if they are not cutting it and compete for the rest of the remainder of that contract.

By the way, NASA has already done this, they did it with the commercial cargo transportation to the Space Station. That was a case for NASA actually where they didn't know if it would work, but they didn't have the budget to do anything else. They were like, we are going to try this competitive commercial milestone-based contracting and it worked great. They awarded two companies, SpaceX and a company called Kistler, and SpaceX managed to meet the milestones, and Kistler did not. NASA competed the remainder of the contract to Orbital Sciences, and Orbital Sciences got across the finish line. Now NASA has got two suppliers for taking cargo to the Space Station, it is a great situation. It is a good forcing function to get things done. I can't tell you how important that contracting structure is, that is night and day. A great model that frankly should be adopted throughout government, where you have 2 competitors, a fixed price milestone-based, where the hard milestones are primarily hardware-oriented, and when one of the 2 companies that are competing does not reach their milestone then the remainder of the milestones are competed to another company.

There's always this sort of argument of what is the best sort of government. I do think America is the greatest country in the world. I don't think it's flawless, obviously, it's not perfect, but it's the least imperfect country in the world. I'm a big fan of I think it was Churchill where 'democracy is the worst form of government except for all the others'.

I think if you said like how would you do Democracy 2.0 like a new version, I think it would be more of a direct democracy than a representative democracy. I think direct democracy is probably better than representative democracy. If you're trying to represent the will of the people it would be better to have direct votes which we're not possible in the old days because you had to mail things around and information moved very slowly. When the United States was formed it was really impossible to have a direct democracy. Even sending a letter took weeks. There was no way that people could vote directly on issues, you had to have representatives. When you have letters that take weeks to get anywhere that would have made governance almost impossible if it had not been representative, and a lot of people couldn't even read. In an electronic society where information moves instantly, you can represent very directly the will of the people. I think this diminishes the ability of special interest to influence things in a way that is contrary to the will of the people. I think most likely the form of government on Mars will be a direct democracy, not representative, it would be people voting directly on issues. That's probably better because the potential for corruption is substantially diminished in a direct versus representative democracy. I think that's probably what will occur. From a governance standpoint obviously, ultimately the governance of Mars will be up to the Martians, but probably we would aim for a more direct democracy.

I was talking to Larry Page about this and he had a good suggestion. We should limit the number of words in a law. We have these like thousand-page laws that get past, and nobody has read them. Like a 1000 words letter count or something, like if you can't write the law in 1000 words then it probably should not be there. We shouldn't have a single law past that's like the size of the Lord of the Rings, and truly not a single person in Congress read the whole thing.

I think we are getting a bit to regulated. I'm not like a complete libertarian that we shouldn't have regulations at all, but the natural bias of regulations is that they last forever. You have to actively delete a regulation or a law in the way things are set up. The problem with that is you get vested interests who like that law and there's an inertia around it. So over time the body of law grows and grows and grows. I think it is ultimately something that is not good for society. In fact, I think it would generally be a good idea to have it such that it's hard to establish a rule and easy to remove one. It should probably be easier to remove a law than to create one. Then maybe have a hysteresis where in order for something to become a law it requires maybe 60% of the vote, but at any point, 40% or more can remove the law. Making it easier to remove a law than put one in place because you can imagine over time the body of the law just gets bigger and bigger, so how do you avoid that? I would recommend some adjustment for the inertia of laws, it's probably a good idea to have something in the voting system that accounts for the infinite lifetime of laws and sort of the inertial effect of laws. I think generally with laws and regulations I think they all should come with some sort of a sunset clause because they have infinite life. Any law should come with a sunset period, with a built-in sunset provision. If it's not good enough to be voted back in maybe it shouldn't be there, so perhaps it would be good for all rules to have an inherent sunset provision. They would automatically expire unless they are revoted as being correct, if it's not good enough to be renewed then it goes away. That sounds sort of anarchist I suppose, but I'm kind of pro-anarchist, I think generally fewer rules are better than more rules.

That's my rough guess at if you had to re-compile on democracy how would you do it to better re-present the true will of the people, which I think is the intent of democracy.

39. The Market

In the long run, the value of a company is defined by the value of its products and services. That's really important to bear in mind it's why companies exist, they shouldn't exist otherwise. The value of the company will follow the value of the products. A company that starts making lousy products is pretty soon going to have a lousy valuation, and a product-company that makes great products is pretty soon going to have a great valuation because that's how the system is set up and that's how it should be set up. If the output is more valuable than the input, that's profit, that says you have a useful company.

In a high-growth scenario, you have a lot more inputs for future outputs so you have negative cash flow and lack of profitability, but in the long run of course that has to be fixed. There can't be negative cash flow in the long period. There needs to be a net positive output. The real question on profitability is where do we set the dial on growth? and obviously, if you set the dial on growth to be super high, then you face dilution because of that increased capital. If you set it too low there's less dilution but then you grow slower. So you want to set it at the right level, the right mix of dilution and growth. I mean, as it is, it's just important to bear in mind, like as a manufacturing company, our percentage growth I think it's unprecedented in the modern era. It's really nutty.

I try to spend as much on R&D as we can, so we really max out R&D. Any money that we get in revenue we put that right back in R&D. And some of it is longer-term, like for example the Mars vehicle and doing some Mars communication stuff with NASA. For Tesla, we do have the option of slowing down our investment in R&D and be profitable, but I think it's more important that we try to increase production and bring more affordable electric cars to market, even if that means that we are not profitable in the short to medium term. We have certainly chosen the path of high growth over the path of profitability.

One thing I should point out is Tesla does not have any special ownership class. There is only one class of common stock for Tesla. I personally only own like 20 or 25% of it so there is an easy remedy if the shareholders don't like me. They can just fire me. I would encourage them to fire me if they think I'm doing a bad job.

It kind of sucks running a public company. The stock goes through these huge gyrations for seemingly arbitrary reasons, and then I get asked why it has changed, and I'm like I have no idea. I think it's a big distraction actually. The market is like a manic depressive, I mean one day it's super great, and then it's negative - it's not like the underlying fundamentals of Tesla change that much, but the instantaneous price changes a huge amount. It's very confusing I'll say things that I think if people understand what I'm saying the stock should go up, but it goes down, like what the hell? and vice versa.

I think it's actually quite distracting to have public stock and the time to go public, ideally, is when things are fairly stable. The world economy will move in cycles and we'll have recession and boom and bust times. I think generally one should always expect there's going to be a boom and a bust period in economies, and in recession times everything seems gloomy, and in boomy times everything seems amazing, but really it's kind of a sine wave.

In terms of going public, the important thing is that the expectations of the public shareholders are not too far from what the goals of the company are. The reason I haven't taken SpaceX public is because the goals of SpaceX are very long-term, which is to establish a city on Mars. That is outside of the timeframe of an analyst on Wall Street. That means there would be too much of a tension between the timeframe of the analysts and investors on Wall Street compared to the timeframe of the company. That's why I am hesitant to take SpaceX public. I think we won't take SpaceX public for a very long time. What I've said is: when we're doing regular flights to Mars, that might be a good time to go public. Before then, because the long term goals of SpaceX are really long term, like - it takes a long time to build a city on Mars - that doesn't match with the short term timeframe of public shareholders and portfolio managers that are looking at the sort of two to four-year time horizon. I think we'll need to hold off going public for a while. Now, that said, what we do is we do offer stock options and restricted stock, and we do liquidity events every six months. We have the company valued by an outside firm every six months and we will do stock buybacks every six months. It sort of, I think, gets the best of both worlds where you have stock liquidity but you don't have the massive fluctuations that you have with a public company at any given week - like, for example with Tesla. The feedback cycle in the stock market tends to be quarterly and maybe they can handle a few years max. If you're talking about something really long-term like the city on Mars, and you end up sacrificing profitability for a very long time in order to get there and build the technology in order to do so, I think it would be not super loved by the market. In the case of Tesla and SolarCity, we had to raise capital and we had kind of a complex equity structure that needed to be resolved by going public and I thought we kinda needed to do that in those two cases. We don't have to do that at SpaceX. I think there's a good chance that we will at some point in the future, but SpaceX's objectives are super long term and the market is not. I expect SpaceX to go public once we have regular flights to Mars, maybe twenty years from now or something like that.

These days, the last few years, is really when Tesla's achieved a level where it's not facing imminent death. Even as recently as early 2013, we were operating with maybe one to two weeks of money. The stock price reflects a lot of optimism on where Tesla will be in the future. The thing that makes that quite a difficult emotional hardship for me is that those expectations sometimes get out of control. I wouldn't recommend anyone start a car company, it's not a recipe for happiness and freedom. I find it quite tough when there are high expectations. I try to tamp down those expectations to the degree possible. I've gone on record several times saying that the stock price is higher than we have any right to deserve.

I hate disappointing people so I'm trying really hard to meet those expectations. It is a pretty tall order, and a lot of times really not fun, I have to say. A whole lot less fun than it may seem.

I'll never sell any stock unless I have to for taxes. I've said publicly I'm not going to take money off the table — I'm going down with the ship. Every bit of money that we make -- we don't issue dividends, we don't have high salaries -- my salary is one dollar a year -- I spend it well -- I do have shares, but I don't sell them. In fact, I promised I'll be the last one to sell shares. Yeah, captains should go down with the ship, hopefully, it's -- wait a second -- the captain should be the last one to comfortably exit the ship.

I think sometimes people overestimate the enjoyment that money can bring. Buying a lot of things is not necessarily the thing that leads to happiness. Certainly being incrementally wealthy does make one incrementally happy. At least for me, it's like what am I doing that's useful, what's are my efforts making the world a little bit better. I like to build things, I like to construct and evaluate if it's based on what things have I helped to build that people have enjoyed. That's the main thing.

Not personally being motivated by money is not the same as saying SpaceX shouldn't make money, in fact, it's really important that SpaceX should be profitable because we got to earn the money necessary for future developments. I want to continue the path of establishing a self-sustaining city on Mars I think that is an important thing that needs to happen, and also sustainable energy and sustainable transport. Then education and pediatric healthcare are the areas essentially where all my money is going.

I'm not sure about the whole family dynasty thing from a wealth standpoint. That seems to often work out worse than if the kid wasn't given a large amount of money. Unless they actually demonstrated that they have a high ability to be a good steward of the capital then it's not gonna work out I think to give them a huge sum of money. I'm wavering a little bit on that because for example Ford and GM, GM went bankrupt and Ford did not because it had the Ford family as a stabilizing influence. There could be some merit to having a family stabilizing influence but maybe not necessarily complete control. I was actually, at one point, of the school of thought that it's best to give away 99% of one's assets - kind of like the Buffet school of thought - I'm still mostly inclined in that direction, but after seeing what happened with Ford and GM and Chrysler where GM and Chrysler went bankrupt but Ford did not, and Ford seemed to make better long term choices than the other two companies, and that's in part because of the influence of the Ford family. I thought, well, maybe there is some merit in having some longer-term family ownership, at least a portion of it, so it acts as a positive influence. I mean, this is something I'm still thinking about, but acting as a positive influence in the long term so the company does proper long-term things. Look at what happened, also, in Silicon Valley with HP and I think it's quite sad, and that to some degree is because there was much-diminished influence by the Hewlett and Packard families. I think they should have prevailed when they were opposed to the merger that took place at one point, and I think they were right actually.

People sometimes think I am a venture capitalist, but actually, I am... uhh, I am an engineer. When I apply capital it is to my own companies, and occasionally to the companies of close friends of mine, where I do zero due diligence and I just basically invest on the basis that I think they're good and likely to succeed. So I'm not the guy to pitch on ideas to be funded, it's better to pitch a venture capitalist. One thing that's important if you have a choice between a lower valuation with someone you really like, or a higher valuation with someone you have a question mark about, take the lower valuation. It's better to have a higher-quality venture capitalist who will be great to work with than one that is a question mark really. It's somewhat like getting married, even though I'm not really good at that.

I think it's worth investing your own capital in something that you believe in. I don't believe in sort of the 'using other people's money' thing. I'm a big believer in you don't ask investors to invest their money if you're not prepared to invest your own money. I really believe in the opposite philosophy of other people's money, it doesn't seem right to me that if you ask other people to invest that you shouldn't also invest. I think if you're not willing to put your own assets at stake then you shouldn't ask other people to do that. I'm always incredibly grateful for anyone who is an investor in Tesla, and you put your faith in us. We will do whatever is necessary to reward that faith.

I think the true strength of Tesla will be decided by its pace of innovation. I think as a combined automotive and power storage and power generation company the potential is there for Tesla to be a $1 trillion company, market cap company. If we play a major role in transitioning the world to a new form of energy generation, and storage, and transport it's what kind of happens.

I think that true competitive advantage on the technology front is more about your rates of innovation than it is to the degree you are slowing others down. Also, you see a lot of these very big companies in these big patent battles, like Apple and Samsung, and like who is really winning there? the lawyers honestly. Tesla made all the patents open and SolarCity went actually even a step further than that, which is they made their technology available to developing countries and offering to have people come from those countries and sit in the factory and see how it is done.

I don't like patents personally. When I first started out developing technology I got a lot of patents, and I thought this was a good thing. Then I discovered that a patent is just a lottery ticket to a lawsuit. You look at sort of Apple and Samsung, is it really winning there? the lawyers a winning certainly, but neither of the two companies.

In the case of Tesla I thought would Tesla ever sue some other car company if they were using our patents, and try to make them stop making electric cars? we would never do such a thing, so why pretend that we would? Maybe it generated some goodwill, and maybe the goodwill is helpful.

Sometimes I think people think we open-sourced our patents because there was some competitive reason that it would somehow be helpful to Tesla because more people would enter electric cars, and it would somehow be a rising tide lifts all boats.

I think the outsourcing of our patents does slightly impair our competitive position on balance, but I am hopeful that it generates enough goodwill to overcome that competitive impairment.

The reason for open sourcing our patents or essentially making them available to anyone who wants to use them is to help encourage the advent of electric vehicles, and just sort of being a good neighbor. I think it's extremely important to the world that we accelerate the advent of sustainable transport. I don't want Tesla to do anything that would slow it down, so any company in China or elsewhere can use our patents to create electric vehicles. Now this may turn out in the future people may look back on it and say well this was a pretty foolish decision, and now you got your butt kicked. That may be the case, in which case well damn, but the more important thing is really the acceleration of electric vehicles. Hopefully, our patents can be of some use to some companies, and do some good, and encourage more electric vehicles. That's really the only reason we did it, and I hope it doesn't turn out to be a dumb decision. I think the most important thing is to keep innovating. All patents really do is slow down competitors. It's like if you're a ship and you're dropping mines behind your ship to slow down the other ships, and we don't want to drop the mines.

If there's anything that Tesla can do that's helpful and doesn't distract us from making cars, then we're happy to do that. I mean, we'd be happy to share information with our competitors that would help improve safety. We'd be happy to do so.

We don't think too much about what competitors are doing, because I think it's important to be just focused on making the best possible product, how do we make the best car. I don't really think about competitors all that much. I think it's sort of analogous to when you are running a race, don't look at the one who is running the race with you, just focus on getting to the finish line. Don't worry about what the other runners are doing. Just run.

I think that's probably a good philosophy, we just take the approach we want to make the best possible car we can and then the chips fall where they may. If the results of our work are good, if they are competitive then the company will succeed, and if not we will not. We don't try to say how will we compete from a strategic standpoint against the future product developments of other car companies. We just say let this be a great electric car and how can we make this as great as possible.

We're just trying to move the industry towards electrification faster than it might otherwise go, and we're certainly quite pleased whenever there's any announcement about another manufacturer producing electric cars. The overarching goal of Tesla is to get the industry to move towards electrification - competition or not - whether we do that with our own cars or with cars that we help other people make.

I think for a lot of people in the auto industry it is not clear that the economics work for electric cars. It is a new technology architecture, and usually, in the car industry, things don't change that much technologically relative to let's say consumer electronics. I think a lot of the carmakers are uncertain about the demand for electric cars, so you get kind of a chicken and egg problem.

I think it's good that some of the big car companies are worried about Tesla because that will make them more likely to create electric cars. Generally, we found working with the other car companies that the motivations are not great. They seem to want to do the least amount of electric vehicles required by law. That is generally the case. The conclusion I've come to with respect to the big car companies because I was wondering why they are not making more electric cars? why don't they make it a mainstream effort? all they seem to be doing is the minimum to comply with government regulation, and then because they're so powerful they can influence the government regulation to be very weak, so that does not result in change. There seem to be only two things that will drive the other car companies to go with sustainable vehicles. Those two things are government regulation and competitive pressure. The government regulation is relatively weak in this regard, so they will do the least number of electric cars necessary to fulfill the government regulation, and because they are big car companies they are very strong in influencing the government. Their lobbying power, in the US in particular, is very strong. My conclusion and the rest of the Tesla team's conclusion is that the thing that will get them to go electric is competitive pressure. The only way to get them to take electric cars seriously is for them to conclude that if they don't take it seriously that Tesla will take their customers. Competitive pressure I think is the only thing that will get the big car companies to make electric cars. Our goal at Tesla is not to take away their customers, but if we don't compete with them, and they don't see that there's a risk to their future if they don't make electric cars, then they won't make electric cars. If they think if they don't go electric they will go out of business, then they'll go electric. Again in terms of the effect that Tesla will have is much more on the behavior that we will induce in other car companies rather than the cars we make ourselves. I think we will make probably in the end only a small percentage of the cars but will induce the rest of the car industry to make electric cars.

I think almost every automaker has some electric vehicle program. They vary in seriousness, some are very serious about transitioning entirely to electric, and some are just dabbling in it, like hybrids. Hybrids are sort of like amphibians, there was a role for amphibians when life was moving from the oceans to land, but in the end, very few amphibians remained. Some, amazingly, are still pursuing fuel cells, but I think that won't last much longer.

Electric motors, in general, have very high lifetimes, the electric motor of let's say the air-conditioner runs continuously for years and years and years. So generally for the power train, it should have a longer life than a gasoline power train because it doesn't have all the wear and tear of the heat, and the oil, and the burning cylinder, and that kind of stuff.

I think it's great what Nissan is doing with the Leaf, what GM is doing with the Volt, what Daimler is doing with the electric Mercedes. Well, I guess they're competition in a sense, but pretty indirectly. It's such a huge market.

As long as there's competition, competition is good for innovation. Ideally, you'd want an industry where there are at least three or four entities competing. That, I think, tends to lead to the best level of innovation because any company that sort of stays stationary with their technology will be exceeded by their competitors. Some of them do take swipes I suppose that's natural for competitors. I think the truth wins out in the end, particularly these days with the Internet. People are able to search and compare and with five minutes of research, you can get to the truth very quickly.

Our strategy is that the other car companies copy Tesla. I think companies like Apple would probably make a compelling electric car, it seems like the obvious thing to do. It is an open secret. It's pretty hard to hide something if you hire over 1000 engineers to do it. I hope we are surrounded by electric cars from other manufacturers. I really look forward to the day when every car on the road is electric. That's the goal, we want to make that happen. That is the Holy Grail, and we're trying to get there as fast as we can.

40. Das Model

I just want to preface this by about why we are doing this, why does Tesla exist, why do we make electric cars, what does it matter? It is because it's really, really, really important for the future of the world to accelerate the transition to sustainable transport. We have record-high CO2 levels. We have recently passed over 403 ppm (parts per million) of CO2 in the atmosphere. On a chart, it looks like a vertical line and it's still climbing. The last time there was this level of concentration was 11 million years ago, that was approximately when primates started walking upright. The world was very different, we do not want to return to that situation. What that CO2 increase results in is a steadily increasing temperature. We've already increased by 2°F. In fact, that doesn't tell the whole story, because the extremes of temperatures increased as much as 20°F. and that line is going to keep going for some time in the future. Beyond global warming, there is just the fact that combustion cars emit toxic gases. According to an MIT study, there are 53,000 deaths per year in the US alone from auto emissions. It stands to reason that if a vehicle is spewing toxic gas, that's obviously bad for your health. To address this we at Tesla came up with what we called 'The Secret Tesla Motors Master Plan' it wasn't all that complicated and basically consisted of:

- Create a low volume car, which would necessarily be expensive
- Use that money to develop a medium volume car at a lower price

- Use that money to create an affordable, high volume car

And...
- Provide solar power.

No kidding, this has literally been on our website for over 10 years. This was the first blog that I ever wrote for the company and it was originally a three-step trilogy, but now it's a four-part trilogy. We needed to figure out how can we as a tiny company with very few resources actually make a difference. The only way to do this was to start small.

Step 1 was the Roadster. The Roadster was high price and low-volume, but where it really made a difference was that it showed people and it showed the world that you could make a compelling electric car. What was unique about the Roadster was that it was the first really great electric car. For those of you who bought the Roadster, thank you.

Still, a lot of people said: "The Roadster is nice, but it's sort of a toy and is very expensive, and you couldn't really make a car that people would use every day, or a car that can really compete against the great combustion sedans of the world." so we said oke, we are going to make the Model S. I think the S is still a superior sedan. It was tested by 'Road and Track' and 'Motor Trend' and others as the fastest four-door car in history, ever. It was rated by almost every group as the best car in its year and by Consumer Reports as the best car ever. It's a great sedan and it can seat up to seven people, five adults, and two kids.

We came from the Roadster, making only 600 units a week where the non-powertrain portion of the car was made by Lotus and we did the power train and final assembly of the car, and we went from that to the Model S a far more complex car where we did the whole thing.

Now for cars about half the market wants a sedan and about half the market wants an SUV, so we thought well we'll extend the Model S platform into the Model X. The Model X is an incredible car but it was overreaching for the first-generation of the product. The mistake that we made, and I obviously take the prime responsibility here, was having far too much advanced technology in version one of our product. I definitely burned out of few neurons and a lot of other people did solving the early production ramp. I feel we're in a good place at this point, I feel like the machine that's making Model X and Model S is actually functioning quite well right now.

Both of these are very important because the revenue from the Model S and the X is what was needed to develop the Model 3. The Model 3 with very high volume and all the engineering to achieve the cost reductions and the capabilities cost billions of dollars. The S and the X are what paid for that Model 3 development, so all of you who bought an S or an X thank you for helping pay for the Model 3.

In the case of Model 3, we've strived hard to simplify and make sure that it has everything essential to be a fantastic car. We aimed for something that was a very simple clean design because in the future, or really the future being now, it will be increasingly autonomous. You won't really need to look at an instrument panel all that often, you'll be able to do whatever you want, you'll be able to watch a movie, talk to friends, go to sleep. Every Tesla being produced right now, the Model 3, the Model S, and the Model X has all the hardware necessary for full autonomy. I think a lot of people still don't realize that.

I personally probably took a year off my life or more camping out at Fremont factory along with a number of other members of the Tesla team. We went through bloody hell in the first half of the year, but as the saying goes: "If you're going through Hell, keep going" we feel we have gained a lot of experience. We certainly aspire to learn from the mistakes of the past and I think we largely have.

We do no promotion of Model 3, we don't advertise – we don't advertise in general – but we don't – like, how often do you see me mentioning a Model 3? I think people sometimes forget that all we did for the Model 3 was half our webcast. There's no advertising, no guerrilla marketing campaign. We sent out a few tweets, like hey, there's going to be a webcast. There were a lot of people that decided they wanted to place a deposit for the car, which is cool. I want to emphasize you couldn't see the car unless you wanted to look at pictures online, you couldn't test drive a car, and you had to put down a $1,000 deposit. There were 500,000 net reservations, to be more accurate there were 518,000 gross reservations and we had 455,000 net reservations, but those cancellations occurred over the course of more than a year.

We didn't want to get people too distracted from today's product in favor of tomorrow's product. It should also be noted that one of our big concerns was that Model S particularly, and Model X demand would suffer from the introduction of the Model 3. In fact, this has turned out to be the opposite situation. Model S and Model X demand increased with the release of Model 3. It was a big concern but it has turned out to be a pleasant surprise. When somebody comes into our store to buy a Model 3 we say, well, why don't you buy Model S or an X instead? we anti-sell the 3. Still, a lot of people order the 3, we basically sold out the first year of production, so the first 12 months production or thereabouts. With a small amount of effort, we could easily drive the Model 3 reservation number to something much higher but there's no point. It's like if you're a restaurant and you're serving hamburgers and there's like an hour and a half wait for the hamburger, do you really want to encourage more people to come order hamburgers? that doesn't make sense.

A frequent question I noticed popping up on Twitter quite a lot is: "Where is my Model 3?" sometimes not phrased quite as nicely as that. We're building the cars as fast as we can, we are going to drive the ramp up as hard as we possibly can. Probably the second most common question I get on Twitter is like: "The Supercharger is full what is wrong with you, why are you such a huge idiot?"

If you see the reviews, one could not ask for better reviews. I just thought I'd give you one little anecdote which I found quite surprising is that when the journalists were driving the car and doing test drives, about 80% of the journalists said that they would buy the car themselves, most of the remaining 20% said probably. This is crazy, I've never seen anything like it, so this is a very good sign.

What's great about the Model 3 is we have the A suppliers, and we have the A-teams at the A suppliers. With Roadster and certainly with Model S, and to a slightly lesser degree with Model X, we often could not get the top suppliers, and we certainly couldn't get the A-team at the top suppliers. I can't tell you how important this is. It makes a massive difference, and I'd like to give some credit to all the suppliers that worked so hard to get us to this point.

We now got 3 cars in production, there's the X, there's the S, and the 3. Those letters can be combined however you'd like. Things got a little confusing because of the nomenclature of being Model 3 versus Model S and X, which was I guess sort of my fault being too clever for my own good there, because especially the Model E, as you can tell I have a wonderful sense of humor.

I just want to say to those that have lined up to buy a Model 3 and in some cases have spent days outside of our stores to be first on the list, I just want you to know that really matters to us, we really care. We will do everything we possibly can to get you the car as soon as possible. We're going to work day and night to do right by the loyalty that you have shown us. Thank you for doing that. And I'd like to again thank all the customers who own a Model S and X and those who buy a Model S or X because in doing so you make the 3 possible. The money that we make with an S and X all goes into building Model 3, so thanks for doing that the Model 3 is happening because of you.

In addition to consumer vehicles, there are two other types of electric vehicles needed: heavy-duty trucks and high passenger-density urban transport. Both are in development at Tesla. We believe the Tesla Semi will deliver a substantial reduction in the cost of cargo transport while increasing safety and making it really fun to operate. Essentially it's meant to alleviate the heavy-duty trucking loads. This is a heavy-duty, long-range semi-truck with the highest weight capability and with long range. This is something that people did not think is possible, they think the truck doesn't have enough power or it doesn't have enough range. And with the Tesla Semi, we want to show that no, an electric truck actually can out-torque any diesel semi, and if you had a tug-of-war competition the Tesla Semi will tug the diesel semi uphill.

I'll tell you about what this truck can do, it blows my mind I think it'll blow yours. It was quite bizarre test-driving when I was driving the test prototype for the first truck. It's really weird because you're driving around and you're just so nimble and you're in this giant truck. I drove it around the parking lot and I was like this is crazy, it's like 'It's alive!' driving this giant truck and making these mad maneuvers. It's definitely a case where we want to be cautious about the autonomy features.

Starting with performance, one thing we really care about at Tesla is performance, we want a vehicle that feels incredible, that accelerates like nothing else. The Tesla Semi will go from 0 to 60 in five seconds, by itself or with a trailer. Now at 80,000 pounds max gross vehicle weight, that's the most amount of weight you can carry on a US Highway, even with 80,000 pounds pulling max gross it's getting 60 miles an hour in 20 seconds. Now, what about up a hill? the best diesel trucks can only do 45 miles an hour up a 5% grade. Tesla Semi can do 65 miles an hour at a 5% grade, that's 65 miles an hour continuous at max gross. What this means is that if you're pulling a load over the Rockies or some mountainous terrain up a hill you're earning 50% more per mile than you are with a diesel truck. That's a gigantic difference.

One of the biggest questions we've been asked about electric trucks is how far can they go? It's got a 500-mile range at maximum weight at highway speed, like 60 miles. That's the worst-case scenario.

We designed the Tesla truck to be like a bullet, whereas the normal diesel truck is more designed like a barn wall, this is a bullet. The Tesla Semi has a drag coefficient of 0.36, this is a really good number. By way of comparison a Bugatti Chiron, which is a 2 million dollar supercar has a 0.38 drag coefficient. It's got a better drag coefficient than a supercar.

We also have four independent motors there's a motor on each of the rear wheels and independent front suspension so it's incredibly comfortable to drive this truck. The driver is actually in the center of the truck, you're positioned like you're in a race car you have complete visibility of the road and all the surroundings. It's a beautiful spacious interior and you can stand up inside.

What will be really fun about this is you have a flat torque RPM curve with an electric motor, whereas with a diesel motor or any kind of internal combustion engine car you've got a torque RPM curve that looks like a hill. So this will be a very spry truck you can drive this around like a sports car there are no gears, it's like single speed. It feels incredible to drive this, it's one of the most incredible feelings and it's incomparably better than any other truck on the road. I can drive this thing and I have no idea how to drive a Semi.

It has a few other benefits as well. You have a low center of gravity that gives you really good handling, which means your probability to have a rollover is massively reduced because the battery pack is in the floor pan. Perhaps most importantly jackknifing is usually the worst nightmare of a trucker, how do you stop your vehicle from jackknifing when you are in difficult conditions? the truck will automatically stop jackknifing because it's got independent motors on each wheel, it will dynamically adjust the torque on each wheel so that jackknifing is impossible with this truck. Your worst nightmare is gone with this truck, gone.

The feature I like best is the 'thermonuclear explosion proof' glass, I mean it's close, it's like it either survives a thermonuclear explosion or you'll get a full refund.

The reason this is important is because truck windshields are huge and they crack about once a year, and if the truck windshield is cracked you're not allowed to drive. It's truck off road if you have a cracked windshield, and that means lost revenue, disappointed customers, and if you're stuck in the middle of nowhere it can take ages just to get a new windshield. This detail matters a lot to someone who really understands trucking, it's small but very important.

Now one Tesla truck considered by itself beats other diesel trucks, but what if you have a convoy? what if you have two trucks following, so you're more like a train driver. In fact the convoy technology, the tracking technology is something we are confident we can do today 10 times safer than a human driver. I want to be clear this is something that we can do now. Now if you look at the economics of a truck convoy it gets way better, now a diesel truck is twice as expensive. What this means is that it's not just economic suicide to use one diesel truck, it's economic suicide for rail. This beats rail, this is quite profound this product is better from a feature standpoint that wins on economics from a diesel truck and it defeats rail in a convoy scenario.

Just for interest's sake, we created a pickup truck version of the Tesla Semi. It's a pickup truck that can carry a pickup truck. You can legally drive that, it shouldn't be legal but you'll actually be able to legally drive it with a normal driver's license, it's wrong but...

So we started Tesla with the Tesla Roadster a sports car. That baby got us going it was the foundation of the whole company and people have asked us for a long time: "When are you gonna make a new Roadster?"... We are making it now, and there's I don't know if you watched 'Space Balls' the movie, but there's only one thing that's beyond ludicrous, which is plaid. The base model will do 0 to 60 in 1.9 seconds. This will be the first time that any car has broken 2 seconds at 0 to 60. It will be the fastest to 100 mph, 4.2 seconds to a hundred miles an hour. It will do the quarter-mile in 8.9 seconds, this will be the first time that any production car has broken the 9 seconds at a quarter-mile. These are all world records and this is what we are achieving in the prototype. This is going to have a 200 kWh battery pack with a 620 Mile range, these numbers sound nutty but they are real. That's a 1000 Kilometer range, this will be the first time a production vehicle breaks the 1000 kilometers, it will travel more than a thousand kilometers on a single charge at highway speed. You will be able to travel from LA to San Francisco and back at highway speed without recharging. It's also a 4 seater, it's a convertible, and it has a ton of storage so you'll be actually able to travel somewhere and bring luggage and bring whatever you want. This thing will have three motors so it's all-wheel-drive. It will be able to do torque steering. 10.000 Newton Meter of torque if you know what that means, it's just stupid. I won't say what the actual Top Speed is but it's above 250 MPH. The new Tesla Roadster will be the fastest production car ever made....period. The point of doing this is just to give a hardcore smackdown to gasoline cars. Driving a gasoline sports car is going to feel like a steam engine with a side of quiche.

41. Civilization

I think first of all it's worth pointing out that we're actually at what is arguably the best period of time in human history. I'm not sure what time would be better. I think the world is actually pretty great right now, better than it's ever been. People ought to have some sense of perspective and realize that things are actually really freaking great. Let me put it that way, in terms of violence per capita in the world we're at the lowest ever in history. You wouldn't necessarily know that reading the newspapers. Violence is definitely lower now - it's been sinusoidal, obviously in the 20th century there was some - there were some bad moments there in the 20th century, but - violence per-capita, lowest in human history today.

People are too negative really, people need to lighten up. I think one shouldn't ignore the negatives but I think one shouldn't ignore the positives either. There's a lot of talk about income inequality and what-not but I think we should also think about information equality. The amount of information equality that exists in the world is unbelievable as a result of the Internet. It's really phenomenal because if you go back say 30 years ago the President of the United States probably had the most access to information of any person on Earth, but today if you have access to the Internet you've got access to more information than the President of the United States had 30 years ago. You have access to all the world's information, you can go on Google and search for any book, any scholarly work. You know Wikipedia's actually pretty damn good, it's like 90% accurate it's just not clear what 90%, but it's really incredible what you can learn and how connected you can be to people all around the world. I actually think there are lots of reasons to be optimistic, and that life is actually pretty good.

The daily news media tends to focus on the worst thing occurring in the world at any given point. A lot of the major newspapers seem to be trying to answer the question: "what is the worst thing that happened on Earth today?"

I actually think the magazines are pretty good. The magazines are more balanced, the magazines do more long-form articles. There's still a negative bias in some magazines but it's less negative than in the newspapers.

I do think something needs to change about modern media because it's like a misery microscope. I think there something in the human psyche that tends to place a weight on negative stuff more than positive. You want to react faster to the lion that's going to eat you, rather than 'dinner is on the table' Being dinner is worse than having dinner, so I think there's kind of an evolutionary reason, you want to prioritize danger over reward. If you get eaten by the lion it's "Game over" but if you forget where you left some snack it's OK. It's not quite the same with the risk/reward balance. We did evolve without newspapers and global media, so our brain is sort of having a fear response by a bunch of dangers that are extremely unlikely to ever affect us. If something terrible happened in some faraway part of the world that kind of triggers the negative response in our limbic system, even though there's no way that actually represents a danger at all. It's not something you should really worry about, so I think it does so for a fundamental evolutionary reason, which is that we're trained to respond to dangerous things. But we didn't evolve to have global media, even though the news that you're reading doesn't affect you directly, it's happening somewhere else in the world, it still sort of has this negative visceral reaction.

Anyway, I think one can really have a severely negative biased view of the world reading newspapers, which is simply inaccurate. I do think it is something we collectively should seek to address. I'm not quite sure how that problem gets solved, but I do think the mood ought to improve. I think it's out of sync with reality. Life is pretty good.

I think to some degree it's going to be at the personal selection front, where people will simply choose to get their news in ways that are not from the newspaper unless the newspaper changes. That's the fundamental driver, it's the action of all individuals who consume news that will drive the change. I think that is already happening, I mean I get my news from Twitter.

There will certainly be issues that we have to deal with. I think that the single largest macro problem that humanity faces this century is solving the sustainable energy problem. If we don't solve that in this century we're in deep trouble. But there's sort of less than 1% chance of annihilation of humanity, by less than one percent I mean even if we do massively increase the CO_2 concentration in the atmosphere it is unlikely to result in the annihilation of humanity. It could kill a few hundred million people due to rising sea levels and that kind of thing, which is obviously not good, but it is not an annihilation event. If you look at the fossil history there have been several annihilation events, mostly due to meteors of one kind or another. Possibly some due to super volcanoes and some due to who knows what, so we obviously suffer from some risk of a similar annihilation event and also potentially a manmade thing like a super virus or something. It could be something like with the CERN Large Hadron Collider, potentially we could see a press release saying, 'the good news is we've discovered a new law of physics, the bad news is there's a small black hole that's rapidly growing.' Now I think that's extremely unlikely, to be clear, but you know, we've discovered new laws of physics before.

Religious extremism is obviously a concern if that grows over time. Particularly if it's a sort of Luddite form of religious extremism, anti-technology, anti-science. That's an obvious threat.

We should be concerned about demographic implosion. I think demographics is a real issue, where people are not having kids in a lot of countries. If you look at countries like Japan, China, and most of Europe the birthrate is only half of the sustaining rates. If you have an inverted demographic pyramid if you look at the pyramid and you got age striation, 60-year-olds, 50-year-olds, 40-year-olds, 30-year-olds, 20-year-olds, sort of like a demographic pyramid, in some countries it's like an upside-down pyramid. It will sort of fall over, it will not stand. Very often they'll say 'we will solve it with immigration' immigration from where? many parts of Europe have an average of 50 to 60% of what's needed for replacement. What we will have in those countries is a high dependency ratio, where the number of people who are retired is very high relative to the number of people who are net producers. The social safety net will not hold. We did not evolve for this, because we always sort of evolved to always pro-create, and there was no birth control or anything. It was like, have lots of babies and hope some of them will survive. That was like all of human history until very recently, and now you got like cases like Japan where adult diapers outsell baby diapers, and Europe is in a similar situation. China is headed the same way because they had the one-child policy, and even though they relieved the one-child policy, the social norm has become to have an average of one kid, so even when they relieved that requirement it didn't change. China for that matter is at half their replacement rate. There are one and a half billion people in China, where exactly are we going to find 600 million people to replace the ones that were never born? that's like 3 Indonesias', it's not gonna work.

The full gravity of this is not well understood but will become a severe issue in the next few decades. I think people are going to have to regard to some degree the notion of having kids as almost a social duty. Within reason, I mean if you can and you are so inclined you should, otherwise civilization will just die, literally.

The birthrate is inversely correlated to wealth, inversely correlated to education, and correlated to religion. The more religious you are, the less educated, and the poorer you are, the more kids you will have. This is true between countries and within countries. In the US the highest birthrate is in Utah with the Mormons.

If you say what are threats to civilization? the lack of people is obviously a threat to civilization. We are going to face in the mid part of the century and particularly the latter part of the century a demographic implosion the likes of which we haven't seen, including the Black Plague. The math is obvious, when did China ever experience a 50% reduction in its population? never, I mean basically pre-writing, because no one has ever written about such a thing. Even the Black Plague was I think as much as a quarter but never a half, and yet Spain has a birthrate of 50%. It's as though someone went through and killed half of the population, or at least of the future population. There better something happen to turn this around because otherwise, you have that inverted demographic pyramid. At this rate, anything that will be left will be robots. Three generations of 50% replacement rate gets you to 12% from where you were. Those 12%, all they are going to do will be taking care of their grandparents. Eventually, there just won't be people at that rate.

Anyway, there's always a chance that something calamitous could happen to Earth, either a natural or man-made catastrophe. Certainly, we see that in the fossil record, and we have invented all sorts of ways of doing ourselves in that the dinosaurs didn't have. It is possible in the future that there is some global war that knocks us back many levels of technology, and certainly, if it was a major nuclear war it would. The history of civilization does contain a lot of war. Then there's the general decay of societies over time, we see this throughout history with ancient Egypt or ancient Rome, they had reached peak technology levels and then for reasons that aren't obvious declined. We also haven't managed to solve the astroid problem therefore our risk is higher. But asteroids are a low probability existential threat on a time scale that's relevant to us... AI is much more urgent. I'm not sure if people realize this, but if you haven't solved the problems that caused the prior extinctions and you added new ones you have not improved the situation.

That is sort of where we are right now.

42. Things to Come..

It's always really tricky to predict the future. I look at the future from the standpoint of probabilities. It's like a branching stream of probabilities, and there are actions that we can take that affect those probabilities, or that accelerate one thing or slow down another thing, or it may introduce something new to the probability stream. I think the one thing that we could be quite certain of is that any predictions we make today for what the future will be like in fifty years will be wrong, that's for sure. I mean when you think of say the first controlled powered flight in 1903 with the Wright Brothers, and then 66 years later we put the first people on the Moon. If you'd asked people say in 1900 what are the odds of a man landing on the Moon they would have said that's ridiculous. If you tried to talk to them about the Internet they would not even know what the heck you're talking about, like this sounds so crazy. But today with a hundred-dollar device you can video conference with anyone in the world, on the other side of the world, and if you have a Wi-Fi connection it's basically just for free. Free to have instant visual communication with anyone or even with millions of people, with social media you can communicate to millions of people simultaneously. You can Google something and ask any question, it's like an oracle of wisdom that you can ask almost any question and get an instant response. I think this is one of those things that's quite difficult to predict. It would be incredibly difficult to predict these things in the past, even the relatively recent past.

I mean some of it is pretty obvious like computer power is just going to be crazy. The really big change is going to be the cost of computing power, not so much the circuit density, the sort of Moore's law thing. If you look at say the actual dollars per instruction, that cost is dropping exponentially. If you think about it, if you're making a computer it's just rearranging silicon and copper on a little chip. Once the capital cost of the development and the chip plant is paid for the marginal cost of a chip is very very tiny. I think we will see massively parallel computers, and computing power and storage being really as much as you want. For sure ubiquitous computing. I think there are likely to be some breakthroughs in artificial intelligence, AI is going to be incredibly sophisticated. AI that's beyond anything like the public appreciates today. AI appears to be accelerating from what I can see, and the tricky thing about predicting when there's an exponential is an exponential looks linear in a close-up, but actually, it's not linear. I think we'll see autonomy and artificial intelligence advance tremendously, I think that's actually quite near-term. My guess is in probably ten years it will be very unusual for cars to be built that are not fully autonomous, ten years. I think almost all cars produced will be autonomous in 10 years, almost all. It will be rare to find one that is not in 10 years. That is going to be a huge transformation.

I suspect we will even see the flying car. I think someone else is doing that.

I think things will grow exponentially, there's a big difference between 5 and 10 years. My guess is probably in 10 years more than half of new vehicle production is electric in the United States. China is probably going to be ahead of that because China has been super pro EV. Probably not a lot of people know this but Chinese environmental policies are way ahead of the U.S, their mandates for renewable energy far exceed the U.S. Sometimes people are under the impression that China is either dragging its feet or are somehow behind the U.S. in terms of sustainable energy promotion, but they are by far the most aggressive on Earth. In fact, a coalition of Chinese car manufacturers wrote the Chinese government to beg for them to slow down the mandate. They said it's too much, they needed to make like 8% of vehicles in the next two years or something. They couldn't physically do it. China is by far the most aggressive on electric vehicles and solar, but that is a common misperception that they are not. It's only one Google search away to figure this out, by the way, it's really easy. Quite frankly I think that China is quite well developed, China has better highways and definitely better trains than the United States, by far. In fact, I had a great experience taking the bullet train from Beijing to Xi'an to see the Terra Cotta warriors.

So, in 10 years, half of all production I think will be EV. The thing to bear in mind though is that new vehicle production is only about 5% the size of the vehicle fleet. If you think how long does a car or truck last? they last 15-20 years before they are finally scrapped. New vehicle production is only roughly 1/15th of the fleet size, so even when new vehicle production switches over to electric or autonomous, that still means the vast majority of the fleet on the roads is not. It will take another 5-10 years before the majority of the fleet becomes EV or autonomous. If you are to go say out 20 years overwhelmingly things are electric and autonomous, fully autonomous, there will not be a steering wheel in 20 years. I think there may be some auxiliary steering wheel that only pops out whenever you need to take manual control for whatever reason, but probably if you go long term my guess is there isn't a steering wheel in most cars. It would be something you'd have to special order. It will be like having a horse. People have horses, which is cool, people will have non-autonomous cars like people have horses, it just will be unusual to use that as a mode of transport.

I expect all transport to go fully electric over time with the ironic exception of rockets. Then all energy production to go sustainable over time, primarily solar. Sustainable energy will happen no matter what. If there was no Tesla, if Tesla never existed, it would have to happen out of necessity. If you don't have sustainable energy it means you have unsustainable energy, it's tautological. This will take a long time, many decades, but the way it'll manifest itself is by people having batteries in their homes or at the utility substation and by driving electric vehicles. As I said, this is going to be a very slow transition because the incentive structure is so biased against sustainable energy. I think there's going to be a number of breakthroughs, I would expect to see significant breakthroughs in energy storage that's probably the biggest area. Probably breakthroughs in energy generation as well.

I do think there's a great deal of innovation is going to occur in biotech, particularly with rapid low-cost perfect coding of DNA. That's going to be really revolutionary as far as diseases, and potentially accelerated evolution someway, although that's a touchy subject. In terms of solving some of the more intransigent diseases, genetics are really key to solving those. The thing to most profoundly affects people would be to be able to recode genetics, which is a dodgy subject. We are close to saturation on lifespan, we are pre-much leveled out. If you solve let's say any one disease you could maybe extend life expectancy a little but not a lot. You kind of have a genetic programming of any species for a specific lifespan like you cannot make a fruit fly live for 10 years no matter what you do, no amount of healthy living or vitamins or anything. It's a really tricky subject, it's wrought with all kinds of moral issues but the thing that would most affect people's lives, it certainly is a double-edged sword. There are going to be huge breakthroughs in genetics in decoding DNA and also writing

DNA. Once you read the DNA you figure out where is the error and you want to sort of correct the code. DNA is basically firmware, so if there's a disease that somebody has genetics can fix that. I think we can sort of fix Alzheimer's if you can actually solve genetic diseases, if you can prevent dementia or Alzheimer's or something like that with genetic reprogramming that would be wonderful. I think there are going to be a lot of breakthroughs in the genetics area. That's going to be really really huge. I think there are some pretty significant breakthroughs in genomics, we're getting better and better at decoding genomes and being able to write genetics, that's going to be a huge huge area.

Something that I think people are only beginning to look at is establishing some kind of brain/computer interface at the neuron level. You can read and write information back to the chip from your brain at the individual neuron level. Intelligence augmentation as opposed to artificial intelligence. I think that has a lot of potential, you would never forget anything, you wouldn't need to take photographs. You've got to watch out for hacking that could really be awkward. I think it actually would be quite an equalizer as well because I think it would sort of even things out.

I think we will probably start seeing more truly cyborg activity. There are some amazing things happening, they have been able to figure out how to do an artificial hippocampus in rats and monkeys and now they are looking at doing that to solve severe epilepsy. About half of epilepsy cases originate in the hippocampus and by having a sort of artificially augmented hippocampus they can actually solve the severe epilepsy cases. Of course, a lot of the biggest breakthroughs are going to be difficult to anticipate in advance, but probably the whoppers are going to be energy, transport, and genetics.

There are probably going to be some breakthroughs in understanding the human mind and consciousness.

Then there's becoming a multi-planet species and space-faring civilization, this is not inevitable. It's very important to appreciate this is not inevitable. The sustainable energy future I think is largely inevitable, but being a space-faring civilization is definitely not inevitable. If you look at the progress in space, in 1969 we were able to send somebody to the Moon, 1969! Then we had the Space Shuttle, and the Space Shuttle could only take people to low Earth orbit. Then the Space Shuttle retired and the United States could take no one to orbit. That was the trend, like down to nothing.

I think directionally I can tell you what I hope the future has as opposed to maybe what it will be, because this may just be wishful thinking. I mean I hope we are out there on Mars and maybe beyond Mars, the moons of Jupiter, I hope we are traveling frequently throughout the Solar System perhaps preparing for missions to nearby star systems. I think all of this is possible within fifty years. The thing I would be most disappointed about is if humanity would not land on Mars in my lifetime, that would probably be my biggest disappointment.

I would like to go to Mars, absolutely, but only if I'm confident that SpaceX will be fine if I die. Maybe if I'm confident that the mission would continue then I would do it. I want to make sure that things are going well on Earth. Basically, I want to make sure that things keep going the way they should. As long as I felt confident of that, then I would go. It would be cool to be born on Earth and die on Mars. I guess I'd like to be able to go to Mars while I'm still able to manage the journey reasonably well, I think I don't want to be like 75 and go to Mars. At least in the beginning it could be mildly arduous, so I'd like to get there ideally in my 50s, that would be kind of cool. I aspire to make that happen and I can see the potential for that happening, I'm not saying it will happen but I think it can happen, I'll try to make it happen. It's certainly tempting to go up soon. I think it'll probably be a couple of years after the first astronaut crew goes up, maybe four or five years I suppose. In an ideal circumstance, I would make one trip to Mars come back to Earth and then when you get really old go back to Mars, when I'm like 75 or something, and die there. If you're gonna die anywhere why not die on Mars? if you're going to choose a place to die then Mars is probably not a bad choice. It's not some sort of Martian death wish or something, I mean we're all going to die someday and if you're given the choice to pick someplace to die then why not Mars? seems like maybe it would be quite exciting. All things considered, I think it would be great to be born on Earth and to die on Mars… just hopefully not at the point of impact.

I think I'm going to stay on electric cars and rockets for a while. With Tesla as more people joined the team, investors would ask me how long am I going to be CEO and I said, well, I'm committed to being CEO through the high volume production vehicle, at that point, I would then have to consider what makes sense. I mean, I will never leave Tesla ever, but I may not be CEO forever. No-one should be CEO forever. Right now our plan is for sure I'm CEO through the production of the Model 3 and the Gigafactory and then evaluate.

It was actually never my intent to run Tesla, because running two companies is quite a burden, actually. I sometimes run into people who think, oh, if you're CEO of the company then they sort of imagine themselves if they were CEO of the company they would grant themselves lots of vacation and do lots of fun things. It's doesn't quite work that way. What you actually get is a distillation of the worst things going on in the company, so the idea of taking on something more is very frightening.

I really think that this is probably the best I've ever felt about the company. I intend to stay with Tesla as far into the future as I can imagine, and there are a lot of exciting things that we have coming. The first Secret Tesla Motors Master Plan that I wrote more than 10 years ago is now in the final stages of completion, and Part 2 of the Master Plan, there's four parts to it is:

1. Create a smoothly integrated and beautiful solar-roof-with-battery product that just works, empowering the individual as their own utility, and then scale that throughout the world.

2. To expand to all of the major vehicle segments in order for us to as quickly as possible move us away from oil. Today, Tesla addresses two relatively small segments of premium sedans and SUVs. With the Model 3, a future compact SUV, and a new kind of pickup truck, we plan to address most of the consumer market.

3. Get to a self-driving capability that is about 10 times better than the average driver, 1,200,000 People die a year in auto accidents so that's a lot of potential for lives saved there.

4. When true self-driving is approved by regulators, it will mean that you will be able to summon your Tesla from pretty much anywhere. You will also be able to add your car to the Tesla shared fleet just by tapping a button on the Tesla phone app and have it generate income for you while you're at work or on vacation. Most of the time when you look at cars they are sitting in a parking lot somewhere and they are not being

used and this has the potential to massively amplify the utility of vehicles and obviously the cost of ownership.

So, in short, Master Plan Part Deux is:
Create stunning solar roofs with seamlessly integrated battery storage.
Expand the electric vehicle product line to address all major segments
Develop a self-driving capability that is 10X safer than manual via massive fleet learning.
Enable your car to make money for you when you aren't using it.

I think there's a lot of opportunity in general in the electrification of transport. Everything will go fully electric, except for rockets, which is ironic. We have an idea for something that isn't exactly a bus but would solve the density problem for inner-city situations. I think we need to rethink the whole concept of public transport. I think there is a new type of car or vehicle that I think would be really great for that, and actually would take people to their final destination not just to the bus stop. I have a bad habit of putting my foot in my mouth, unfortunately.

I've been sort of toying with the design for an electric supersonic Vertical Take-Off and Landing electric aircraft for a while, I'd love to do it, but I think my mind would explode. It'd be like, the brain's worn out, you know. I'm pretty saturated working on electric cars and rockets. Possibly, at some point in the future, certainly not the near term, there's an opportunity to create an electric jet, essentially. I do think a VTOL electric supersonic plane is a real sort of optimal air transport solution, and it actually works together quite well for a bunch of reasons. In particular, the higher you go the more efficient the electric aircraft is, whereas if you have a combustion aircraft as you get higher it tends to get worse because you have a fixed aperture. The hole in the engine is a fixed size so you have to pick a particular cruising altitude, you got to figure out how do you get the right amount of air at sea level all the way to really high altitude. Then you've got this issue of supersonic combustion, so it ends up not being that efficient. An electric aircraft would just get better and better as it got higher, electric motors have a higher power to weight ratio than a combustion engine. You can actually have the power to do the vertical takeoff and landing part with a fairly small motor compared to combustion. I think it would be very cool to have in the world because you would not need big runways, and you could get to places fast, and it would be quiet, and of course, it would be very low cost to operate, and good for your environment. The real trick of it is how do you make it really long-range and at least as safe as existing aircraft. Those are really the only two questions on that front I think, but they are certainly tricky. I'm quite confident it's doable provided that there's a rough doubling of the energy density in batteries or capacitors. Basically, around the 500Wh/kg level is where it starts to make sense before aircraft really start to become compelling relative to kerosene-fueled or petroleum-based aircraft.

It is not out of the question that Tesla will do an electric aircraft in the future, our goal is to accelerate the advent of sustainable transport. That goal has been there since the founding of the company and that is what is going to remain true for the future. I mean Tesla has electric power train expertise and SpaceX has aerospace expertise, between the two it's kind of perfect to create a supersonic vertical takeoff and landing electric jet. But there are other things on the plate so we have to stay focused on those things. I got a lot of fish frying right now. I would love to be working on electric aircraft. If I wasn't super strung out I would for sure be doing electric aircraft. That's something I would love to do at some point in the future if my time allows. Maybe in the future, we'll do something like that. I think that's where things will eventually end up it just may take a while to get there. It seems unlikely to be coming from Boeing or Airbus given that they seem to focus on very incremental improvements to the planes as opposed to radical improvement.

The thing that drives me is that I want to be able to think about the future and feel good about that, to be inspired by what is likely to happen, and to look forward to the next day. That is what really drives me, trying to figure out how to make sure things are great. That is the underlying principle behind Tesla and SpaceX.

My goal is to retire right before senility because your judgment starts to be impaired so you don't realize that your decisions suck until you're dead, so I don't intend to retire maybe at 80 or something. I am not actually a huge proponent of longevity. I do think that having a good life for longer is better. You would want to address the things that happen to you when you're older, like dementia and so forth. Those are pretty important. I definitely don't want to live forever, a hundred good ones in total is probably fine, or maybe a bit longer. I do sometimes wonder if I'm going to die under suspicious circumstances. I have a lot of enemies among the big aerospace companies and maybe among some of the car companies.

When I think what is the fundamental good of a company like Tesla, I would say hopefully accelerate the transition to sustainable generation and consumption of energy. If it accelerated that by a decade, potentially more than a decade, that would be quite a good thing to occur. That's what I consider to be the fundamental aspirational good of Tesla. It is inevitable but it matters if it happens sooner than later.

SpaceX is about helping make life multi-planetary. I am a naturally optimistic person, I do think there is value in establishing an insurance, which is that if Life is on more than one planet then the light of consciousness is likely preserved for the future much longer. Looking ahead I'd like to see humanity go beyond Earth and see people on Mars, and see widespread adoption of electric vehicles and renewable energy. I think that would be really cool. I want to be clear I'm not trying to be anyone's savior, like I said I'm doing this because I think it makes things better in the future not worse, for everyone. I'm just trying to think about the future and not be sad. Life is short and there are lots of things that one can't necessarily do. I am quite optimistic about the future, I mean I don't think we are about to enter a dark age, it could happen but I think it's not likely anytime soon. We are doing what we can to have the future be as good as possible. The teams are working super hard to make it happen. I'm excited about the prospect and I feel of course optimistic that that will take place.

So yes, we're really proud of the teams for getting to this point, and I really want to thank them for working hard to achieve some very difficult things. I couldn't be prouder to work with such a great team. I really feel like we're like a kind of a small rebel group, we're outnumbered, we're outgunned, and usually in situations like that bad things happen. It's usually not a happy ending, but I think this is going to be one of those happy endings.

I want to thank all of our customers and all you guys for your support. My apologies for the long story... I hope you enjoyed it.

Made in the USA
Middletown, DE
29 August 2023